Japanese American Relocation in World War II

In this revisionist history of the US government's relocation of Japanese American citizens during World War II, Roger W. Lotchin challenges the prevailing notion that racism was the cause of the creation of relocation centers. After unpacking the origins and meanings of American attitudes toward the Japanese Americans, Lotchin then shows that Japanese relocation was a consequence of nationalism rather than racism. Lotchin also explores the conditions in the relocation centers and the experiences of those who lived there, with discussions on health, religion, recreation, economics, consumerism, and theater. He honors those affected by uncovering the complexity of how and why their relocation happened and makes it clear that most Japanese Americans never went to a relocation center. Written by a specialist in US home front studies, this book will be required reading for scholars and students of the American home front during World War II, Japanese relocation, and the history of Japanese immigrants in America.

Roger W. Lotchin is Emeritus Professor in the Department of History at the University of North Carolina, Chapel Hill, where he taught for almost fifty years. He is a specialist in US home front studies and war and urban society and the author of numerous books and articles, including *Fortress California, 1910–1961: From Warfare to Welfare* (1992), *The Bad City in the Good War: San Francisco, Los Angeles, Oakland, and San Diego* (2003), and *San Francisco, 1846–1856: From Hamlet to City* (1974).

Japanese American Relocation in World War II

A Reconsideration

ROGER W. LOTCHIN
University of North Carolina, Chapel Hill

CAMBRIDGE
UNIVERSITY PRESS

University Printing House, Cambridge CB2 8BS, United Kingdom

One Liberty Plaza, 20th Floor, New York, NY 10006, USA

477 Williamstown Road, Port Melbourne, VIC 3207, Australia

314–321, 3rd Floor, Plot 3, Splendor Forum, Jasola District Centre,
New Delhi – 110025, India

79 Anson Road, #06–04/06, Singapore 079906

Cambridge University Press is part of the University of Cambridge.

It furthers the University's mission by disseminating knowledge in the pursuit of
education, learning, and research at the highest international levels of excellence.

www.cambridge.org
Information on this title: www.cambridge.org/9781108419291
DOI: 10.1017/9781108297592

First published 2018

Printed in the United States of America by Sheridan Books, Inc.

A catalogue record for this publication is available from the British Library.

ISBN 978-1-108-41929-1 Hardback
ISBN 978-1-108-41039-7 Paperback

*This book is dedicated to our three Asian American grandchildren,
Michael, Matthew, and McKenna Lotchin, who will carry forward
the immigrant experience of their mother, Sarah Kristine Peters
Lotchin, and their great-grandfather, Theodore Lotchin, people
from opposite ends of the Earth who fled to America by plane and
ship to escape from war, persecution, and discrimination.
And to Hatsuye Egami and Dorothy Cragen, mother and teacher,
two of the unsung heroines of World War II.*

Contents

Figures

Preface

Perhaps every author owes it to his readers to explain why he has written his book. For some of my books and articles this might be difficult, but the motivation for this one is clear-cut. I published *The Bad City in the Good War: San Francisco, Los Angeles, Oakland, and San Diego* in 2003 with Indiana University Press. In it, I included chapters on various groups, including the Japanese Americans and their unfortunate relocation experiences.[1] Soon after 2003, I was asked by Professor Robert Cherny to give a talk on Japanese relocation at the Pacific Coast Branch of the American Historical Association meeting in Honolulu. Since it was an interesting challenge and because only a hidebound mainlander who was "bereft of his senses," as the Ancient Greeks would have said, would turn down a trip to Hawaii, I accepted.

That assignment led me into a closer reading of Japanese American history in general and of relocation studies in particular. At the outset of the great civil rights movement of the latter half of the twentieth century, the subject of relocation produced an enormous literature of books, articles, dissertations, and book reviews. It is a literally stupendous oeuvre. But the principal contentions of this literature – that racism inspired relocation and that the Japanese American relocation facilities functioned as "concentration camps" – struck me as overstatements that merited reconsideration. Indeed, the literature seemed so weighted that I

---

[1] I carefully considered whether the use of the term "unfortunate" to characterize the Nikkei experience was too mild, but eventually decided that it was not because of the vastly more calamitous experience of other twentieth-century victims, not least the victims of the World War II holocaust.

came to agree with Professor John Stephan, the noted student of the Japanese Americans in the United States, Hawaii, and Asia, who labeled the relocation "literature as an orthodoxy, an interpretation enforced by the federal government, the media, and academe."[2]

But before addressing this issue, several explanations are in order. One is that only a minority of Japanese Americans ever went into either assembly centers or relocation centers or internment[3] camps run by the Justice Department. Of these, only 112,000 (33.3 percent) were sent to WRA centers. Another 157,000–160,000 lived in Hawaii; 25,000 resided in other parts of the continental United States; 16,000 went to Justice Department internment camps; and 40,000 spent the war in the Imperial Japanese domains. Finally, 8,000 voluntarily left the prohibited zone and 1,000 repatriated themselves to Japan.[4] Five of these groups never went to centers.

Second, perhaps alone among American immigrants, the Japanese employed specific designations for each generation. The term "Issei" refers to immigrants or first-generation Americans; the term "Nisei" refers to second-generation citizens; "Kibei" were those members of the second generation who were sent to Japan to be educated or raised (often as dual citizens); and "Sansei" was the third generation, a tiny minority in 1941. "Nikkei" were the entire group.

Finally, since the term "racism" figures so prominently in the Japanese American story of historians, a word about that term is in order. I have used a twofold standard to define racism. Racism is a term variously defined, but at its core refers to antagonism based on a belief in the biological inferiority of the "other." In other words, as one historian put it, "classing and differentiating a segment of the population negatively on the basis of their race, impossible to overcome by anything the individuals can do to alter that status, is commonly considered racist."[5]

---

[2] Email of John J. Stephan to Roger Lotchin, July 18, 2012.

[3] Western Defense Command and Fourth Army (General John DeWitt), *Final Report Japanese Evacuation from the West Coast 1942* (Washington, DC: US Government Printing Office, 1943), pp. 79–83ff.

[4] Statistics on the Nikkei experience do not always tally. For example, the total number evacuated varies from 107,000 to 130,000. The former would appear too low and the latter too high. I have accepted the figures of Professor John Stephan, an expert on the Hawaiian-Japanese and those who migrated or went back to Japan. See J. J. Stephan, "Review of Nikkei Amerikajin no Taiheiyo senso," *Journal of American History* (1998), 1142–3, and Stephan's reader's report on this book. The figure of 112,000 was employed by the WRA itself. I have also relied on figures presented in De Witt, *Final*, 216.

[5] Merry Ovnick, comment on reader's report for "A Research Report: Imperial Japanese, Japanese Americans, and the Reach of American Racism." *Southern California Quarterly*, Vol. 97: No. 4 (Winter 2014).

For the particulars of racism – that is, its metaphorical shorthand – I have borrowed the definitions and terms from John W. Dower's *War without Mercy: Race and Power in the Pacific War*. In it, he uses a number of markers to signify racism, including the frequent terminology of racism that posits the "other" as subhuman, "little men," serpents, reptilian creatures, lice, vermin, animals, monkeys, etc., and pictures the Japanese as a "Yellow Peril."[6] I realize that this is only one definition of racial worldviews, but to me the idea is not in need of redefinition. Superiority and inferiority stand at the heart of the concept, and Dower's litany of the allegorical characteristics of the racist is sufficiently widely accepted to justify using it as a model. So when I speak of racism, these are the standards that I am using. Others may prefer another standard, but this is mine. To argue endlessly about this meaning of racism or other words such as "racialized" is to lose sight of the ultimate goal of reinterpreting the relocation story.

The racial hypothesis both surprised and puzzled me because of the many Asians involved in World War II, most of them were US allies – Chinese, Koreans, Burmese, Indians, and Melanesians. The Japanese were the only significant body of people of another race – that is, Asians – who willingly fought against the United States. Moreover, as I have found over my career, in the world since the French Revolution, including the mid and late twentieth century and early twenty-first century that I have lived through, it seemed clear to me that the most brutal political episodes of genocide, rebellion, war, and civil war happened between peoples of the same race, whatever they might have been called. In the twentieth century that would include both world wars, the Mexican Revolution, the Russian Revolution and purges, the Spanish Civil War, the 1960s Nigerian Civil War, the World War II Eastern Front, the Maoist upheavals in China, the Cambodian genocide, the Armenian massacres, the Balkan mayhem of either the pre- or post-World War I era, of the post-World War II period, and of the 1990s, and the Rwandan genocide of the same decade. These were always catastrophic tragedies within races, not between them. The brutal American treatment of African-Americans and Indians was an anomaly, though its Civil War was not.

In fact, history would almost turn the argument of race as a fundamental explanation of extreme political behavior on its head. Something else usually was fundamental. Yet the literature on relocation follows that

---

[6] J. W. Dower, *War without Mercy: Race and Power in the Pacific War* (New York, NY: Pantheon Books, 1986), pp. 3–180–190.

standard line on race and racism and ignores many other matters, especially nationalism and nationality.

It seemed to me that this literature was in need of another overview on racism and the real government bumbling and supposed concentration camps that emanated from it. Recent overviews, like Greg Robinson's studies of Roosevelt's decision-making, are firmly in the orthodox mold.[7] So in my mind, the need for a new and larger viewpoint coincided. Thus, I decided to write a different kind of book. With it, I hope to open a re-examination of the orthodoxy by offering an alternative hypothesis about the role of racism in the story.

Nationalism in the form of great power rivalry caused the Imperial Japanese–US collision. Since so many historians have understood relocation through a parent, uncle, brother, or friend, I feel the need and freedom to confess my own connection to the world wars. My own father hailed from the tragic Balkans. He fled as a seventeen-year-old boy to North America to avoid the tragedy of World War I. I think of the world wars through his Balkan experience – not of race, but of nationalism, which World War I augmented. I also always think of another boy, Gavrilo Princip, whose assassination of the Archduke and Duchess triggered a Balkan war that became a world war.

Interpretively, I wish to provide improvements to two problems with the current literature. The first is that the literature does not supply a concise, interpretive explanation of relocation and the second is that it largely disregards the context of the war. The canon blames racism, concentration camps, Roosevelt's identity, and so forth for relocation, but seldom stitches those matters together in an interpretive statement. So I would propose that relocation occurred because the Imperial Japanese assault on Pearl Harbor triggered a backlash against Americans of Japanese ancestry and the backlash produced the removal of that group from the West Coast. There were many attendant complexities, but war, especially Pearl Harbor, and not racism did the essential damage.

A final word on sources may be in order. My work has relied heavily on primary sources and especially on the prewar press and the center newspapers. Since the relocation center newspapers had limited budgets and facilities, they depended heavily on each other. Many materials from one place came from stories or quotes from another. Often neglected by the orthodox historians of relocation, these journals are gold mines of

---

[7] G. Robinson, *A Tragedy of Democracy: Japanese Confinement in North America* (New York, NY: Columbia University Press, 2009).

information. The latter may have been "influenced" by the WRA admin-istrators, but they were by no means censored. Aside from politics, these papers, written by lucid young editors and columnists like Larry Tajiri,[8] carried wonderful and diverse information about every aspect of center life, from art to theater, work, sports and recreation, economics, visita-tion, geographic mobility, religion, and leave policy. I have not found a better source.

I have also relied heavily on oral history, such as that of the Fullerton Collection, which is equally revealing. Oral history has both its strong and weak points. I did not find the oral literature to be any more problematical than any other sources, such as the mainline commercial newspapers, politicians' memoirs, or government hearings. In any case, the orthodox side of this argument has relied as heavily on oral history in support of the canon as I have against it. It must be approached from the same critical perspective as other historical sources.

Finally, the authors of this relocation oeuvre are honest and good people and I do not mean to impugn their scholarship – I just do not agree with them. Nonetheless, as the footnotes reveal, I have consulted this scholarship extensively, but I have also added a broader context.

In writing this book, I have created more debts than I can possibly repay. My secretaries, Joy Jones, Diana Chase, Pamela Fesmire, and Renée McIntire, have done everything possible to keep the show on the road. They were aided by Christine Gang, who contributed much crucial typing. Violet Anderson, Burwell Ware, Cameron Bowe, and James Hines repeat-edly restored my word processor to sanity when it seemed that only violence would counter its many indignities. Rob Noel guided me grace-fully through the last stages of publication. Liz Gray served as my invalu-able in-house editor. Professor John J. Stephan made valuable suggestions, which helped me understand better the relocation canon. Ken Masugi provided inspiration by opposing the extreme version of relocation his-tory propagated by the redress movement. I found creative interpretive encouragement from historians Brian Hayashi, Gary Okihiro, Echiiro Azuma, Robert Shaffer, Masuda Hajimu, and Lon Kurishige. The late Zane Miller employed his matchless and wide-ranging experience as both a heavily published historical scholar and an empathetic editor to inform my manuscript in many ways. Ralph Levering was especially helpful at getting my ideas across and into print. I am also indebted to the readers of

---

[8] G. Okihiro, *Storied Lives: Japanese American Students in World War II* (Seattle, WA: University of Washington Press, 1999), p. 137.

the *Journal of the Historical Society* and assistant editor Scott Hovey for giving a close reading to a version of my basic ideas that appeared in article form in that journal. Editor Robert van Maier and the readers of *Global War Studies* did the same for an article in that journal. Merry Ovnick helped me sharpen my ideas for wider circulation of my research in the *Southern California Quarterly*.

I benefited greatly from other friends and readers, including Burk Huey, Ian Crowe, and Will Schultz, who afforded me friendly but trenchant and constructive advice. The staff at the National Archives was its usual helpful self. Geoffery Stark and his staff, Megan Massanelli, Jordan Johnson, and Kathryn Dunn, at the Special Collections of the University of Arkansas afforded me many shortcuts into their wonderful materials of the Rohwer and Jerome centers in Eastern Arkansas and also into the many records of the central office of the War Relocation Authority in Washington in their possession. My department chairman, Professor Lloyd Kramer, found monies to help fund our trip to the Fayetteville campus tucked into the beautiful, rolling Boston Mountains. I am also indebted to Larry Malley, Director of the University of Arkansas Press, and his wife Maggie, who constructively scolded me for an entire evening over good food and indifferent jazz about my heterodox interpretation of relocation.

Interlibrary Loan at the University of North Carolina (UNC) obtained many materials that we did not have at UNC, though we do have a formidable amount. Mike van Fossen, Amanda Henley, Robert Dalton, Tommy Dixon, and Beth Rowe gave unstintingly of their time and energy to identify and open these numerous relocation materials at UNC, especially the US Government documents and the invaluable center newspapers. They are extraordinarily skilled professionals.

I also benefited from the comments of diverse professional audiences, especially the noontime seminar of the UNC History Department, the Joint UNC–Duke–NC State Triangle Institute for Security Studies seminar, and a session at the biennial meeting of the Historical Society.

As always, my greatest debt is to my wife, Phyllis Morris Lotchin, who took time from her own literary pursuits to serve as my research assistant and to apply her unmatched skills as a grammarian and literary stylist to several versions of the manuscript. She refuses the formal title, but she should be considered a coauthor of this book.

Introduction

Relocation – A Racial Obsession

Asian-American Studies must move beyond the bounds of racism as its organizing principle to interventionist practices that defy those conventions of race.

Gary Okihiro, *Storied Lives: Japanese American Students in World War II*

The Japanese Empire and the American Republic seemed on a collision course from almost the beginning of Japanese immigration to the United States. The Japanese began coming to the United States in conspicuous numbers from the 1880s, at about the same time as the New Immigrants of Europe did. But the presence of Asians in the American West stretched back to the California Gold Rush. Many Chinese came to what they called "the Golden Hill" to search for its precious metal, then eventually stayed on to build its railroads, to man garment shops,[1] and eventually to help grace the tables of San Francisco with the finest cuisine west of the Mississippi River.

Yet the presence of peoples of Asian origin was never uncontested. With the advent of economic hard times in the 1870s, the onset of competition from eastern products due to the completion of the Central Pacific Railroad, and the rise of the Irish-led labor movement, their presence was increasingly resented. Demands for exclusion or restriction led to informal bans on their immigration to America in 1882 and 1892 and their formal exclusion by congressional legislation in 1902. But that still left railroads to build, immense farms and ranches to tend, and the homes of the railroad, Comstock, shipping, real estate, and other millionaires to look after.

---

[1] This early Chinese immigration was almost entirely male.

FIG. 1. High school recess period, Manzanar Relocation Center, California. The figures in this book are intended to offset the typical gloomy picture of relocation. Every center functioned as a small town. This figure is an overview of the barracks and mountains. Photograph by Ansel Adams. Courtesy Library of Congress Prints & Photographs Division, LC-DIG-ppprs-00338.

That economic development demanded hands to replace the Chinese ones, including those of native white Americans,[2] Filipinos, and Japanese Americans, to do the agricultural work. The Japanese became a noticeable presence from the 1890s onward. Luckily for them, their own background in agriculture helped them become valued manual laborers. But they did not intend to remain so for long and soon graduated to small-time proprietors. And as the great landholders came to value Japanese services, they began to collaborate with them economically. First, the Japanese worked for others as sharecroppers, foremen, or laborers, but soon worked for themselves, developing niche crops like strawberries and vegetables. They sold these as market gardeners to an exploding urban California market, especially to Los Angeles, the

---

[2] For American and immigrant labor as farm workers, see M. Dubofsky, *We Shall Be All: A History of the Industrial Workers of the World* (Urbana, IL: University of Illinois Press, 1988).

"impossible city."[3] The Japanese would undoubtedly have come into conflict with the other American farmers, laborers, and nationalists sooner or later, but international relations rudely jolted them into it.

This story has been told often and well, so only the highlights will be touched on here. The first serious episode grew out of the insistence of San Francisco anti-Japanese militants that Japanese students be taught in segregated schools rather than with other Americans. This raised a furor in Japan to match that in San Francisco and required the intervention of President Theodore Roosevelt to settle the matter. He persuaded the San Francisco school board to revoke the segregated schools order, and in return the Japanese Government promised to regulate carefully further migration from that country to the United States. But that "gentleman's agreement" did not bind other anti-Japanese militants in the rest of California, who in 1913 persuaded the State Legislature to pass a land law that prohibited aliens who were ineligible for citizenship from owning land. Since, by congressional legislation of 1790 and 1870, only white, black, or African aliens were eligible for citizenship, the measure essentially banned Japanese and Chinese aliens from owning land.

Recent scholarship has shown that diplomatic disagreements between Washington and Tokyo roiled relationships between the two nations and the two nationalities in the United States during the subsequent Wilson administration of 1913–1921. The California legislature stirred them up again in 1920 by passing another land law prohibition aimed at the Japanese, and then the status of the Japanese got tangled up with the general legislation to regulate American immigration. As a part of that process, in 1924, Congress banned all Japanese and other Asian immigration to the United States. That action created additional uproar in Japan and an outcry against the legislation by the friends of the Nikkei in America.

The argument that the 1913 and 1920 laws were either discriminatory, racist, or even anti-Japanese is fraught with peril. The laws of Imperial Japan contained the exact same supposed discriminations, forbidding alien land ownership, alien citizenship, and, for a time, immigration to that country as well. The American laws treated the Japanese exactly as Japanese law treated Americans. In addition, naturalization legislation in

---

[3] For the Japanese in agriculture, see J. Modell, *The Economics and Politics of Racial Accommodation: The Japanese of Los Angeles, 1900–1942* (Urbana, IL: University of Illinois Press, 1977).

1940 granted citizenship rights to Native Americans from North and South America.

Thus, when World War II occurred, aliens who were white, black, brown, and red could become US citizens. Only Asians of the five racial groups could not. So if four out of the five racial groups could be naturalized, the explanation for that provision was not racial. Most racial groups were eligible. Whatever the original opposition to Asians might have been, it seems to me to have been based on social class, economics, and, ultimately, nationalism by World War II.

Still, in the most important and ironic sense, the 1924 legislation did the second generation a favor. The law did prohibit immigration from Japan, but that meant the Issei, ineligible for citizenship, would steadily diminish in number and the Nisei citizens group would continue to grow. The law lessened the power of the issue as the Issei passed away. The anti-Japanese lobby had less ammunition with which to inflame the public with each passing year. And the law did contribute to the rising power of the Nisei within the Japanese American community. It is no accident that the Japanese American Citizens League, the political representative of the second generation, was founded in 1928, shortly after the landmark restriction legislation, nor that some former supporters of exclusion, like the American Legion, began to work with the Nisei thereafter.[4]

Nonetheless, the Japanese, like other immigrant groups, organized to protect themselves from the anti-Japanese actions of others. However, unlike many other nationality groups, who took the next step to organize in the United States for Cuban, Irish, Polish, or Albanian independence, Israeli nationhood, or the Mexican revolution, the Japanese did not use America as a base to alter old-world political realities. But one way or another, they kept up their ties to their motherland.

The Japanese Americans were precocious organizers and they created in America a dense network of clubs, associations, temples, chambers of commerce, language schools, and prefectural associations, almost one on top of another. Through them, they cemented their ties to each other, to America, and to their fatherland. None of this organizing would have put them in danger had it not been for the behavior of that country. Almost alone among American immigrant homelands, that of the American-Japanese laid claim to continental American territory. That set them apart from the other immigrants' fatherlands – China, for example – and at the same time put the Issei and Nisei on a collision course with

---

[4] See Chapters 2 and 3.

their new homeland. By the luck of the draw, Imperial Japan and republican America came of age economically, militarily, and mentally at the turn of the 1800s. Each was flexing its muscles, collecting colonies, and exercising its vocal cords jingoistically. In addition, they came of age as competitors for power and influence in Asia. Each created mini-empires there and elsewhere; in the case of the United States, in the Virgin Islands, Puerto Rico, Hawaii, the Philippines, and Samoa; and in the case of the Japanese, in Korea, Formosa, and eventually Manchuria.

These were relatively modest empires by the standards of the time. The Europeans, especially the British, French, Germans, and Dutch, had fortunately grabbed up most of the militarily weak territories of the world before the Americans and Japanese could fall out over them. But the Japanese made the mistake of doing so anyway, lusting for the modest empire the Americans had acquired before the Americans got over their unpretentious case of imperialism. Japanese workers flooded onto the Philippine island of Mindanâo and Japanese capital followed where laborers had led, buying up large quantities of land. They did enough of both to come soon to regard Mindanâo as a "pre-war colony."[5] And by the same token, they also hankered after the US-controlled territory of Hawaii, one of their war aims when World War II broke out.[6] Those goals were damaging enough to Japanese–American relations, but some Japanese went so far as to make similar claims on the territorial United States.

Japanese American historian Eiichiro Azuma explains that prewar Japanese governments and elites thought of the Issei in California as colonists, representing the expansion of Imperial Japan. To my knowledge, Americans never laid such claims to the territory of the Japanese Home Islands as places to colonize, but these Japanese claims carried the maximum potential for later misunderstanding. A new "colonial discourse on emigration" grew up in the 1890s in which "the main theme ... revolved around the control of a foreign land through mass migration." And elites left no doubt as to which foreign land would be involved when they discussed the American West as a "new Japan," a "second Japan," a "new home," and "an imperial beginning," and Japanese migration as "extending national power."[7]

[5] L. Horner, "Japanese Military Administration in Malaya and the Philippines," unpublished PhD dissertation, University of Arizona (1973), pp. 38–41.
[6] J. J. Stephan, *Hawaii under the Rising Sun: Japan's Plans for Conquest after Pearl Harbor* (Honolulu, HI: University of Hawaii Press, 1984), pp. 55–88, 135–66.
[7] E. Azuma, *Between Two Empires: Race, History, and Transnationalism in Japanese America* (New York, NY: Oxford University Press, 2005), pp. 22, 25.

Azuma also describes one of the Nikkei organizations, the Japanese Association of America, as a "virtual arm of the Japanese Government,"[8] which was a part of "Tokyo's policy of extraterritorial nation-building."[9] As Azuma also notes, the Empire began to walk back such comments in the 1930s, but the words were already out there. And nationalists have long memories, as witnessed in the Balkans and a host of other places in the nineteenth, twentieth, and twenty-first centuries.[10] When World War II broke out, these unfortunate Japanese words were what many American elites remembered. They were no more likely to forget them than the Japanese were prepared to disregard the words of the anti-Japanese Caucasians[11] of the late nineteenth and early twentieth centuries. Politics, whether domestic or international, is about perceptions as much as about realities, and no savvy persons would have given the opposition such opportune talking points.

But before these obviously heedless comments of the fatherland elites could do them harm, the Japanese Americans were making steady progress in the West, advancing toward economic security and developing toward political and social acceptance. They were well on the way to both[12] when World War II intervened on December 7, 1941. At first, the other Americans defended the Japanese Americans and insisted that they should not be blamed for the actions of the mother country. But with the publication of the *Roberts Report* on January 25, 1942, which revealed the full extent of the American military failure at Pearl Harbor, the tide turned against them.

The Japanese Americans came to be seen as a defense liability – not just a minority liked by some and disliked by others, but a national security threat. Fifth columns were very much in the news before the war, especially in Norway in 1940. And disloyal nationality groups, like the Austrian and Sudeten Germans, were the essential levers that Hitler used to pressure Austria, Czechoslovakia, and Poland in the run-up to war. The American Government feared that an Imperial attack on the United

---

[8] Ibid., 42. Professor Azuma's perceptive and thoughtful book is full of these discussions of Imperial Japanese and overseas Japanese associations.

[9] Ibid., 47.

[10] Balkan nationalism, often considered its quintessential variety, is treated sensitively in M. Glenny, *The Balkans: Nationalism, War, and the Great Powers, 1804–1999* (New York, NY: Penguin Books, 2001), pp. xxi–xxviff.

[11] I have employed this term "Caucasian" as equivalent to the term "white" because the Nikkei themselves used it. See B. J. Grapes, *Japanese American Internment Camps* (San Diego, CA: Greenhaven Press, Inc., 2001), p. 143.

[12] See Chapters 2 and 3.

States was possible and that if and when it came it would be aided by a significant number of Japanese Americans. In brief, they feared another Pearl Harbor aided by another fifth column. Whether the Japanese would have used Japanese Americans in this way is not known, but many US officials thought that they would do so.

That conviction led the Franklin Roosevelt administration to take the unprecedented step of moving all of the Japanese Americans, citizens and aliens alike, away from a defense zone along the Pacific Coast that included all of California, western Washington, western Oregon, and southern Arizona.

From there, the government relocated/evacuated them first to assembly centers near their homes and then to ten centers in seven western states plus Arkansas. Since this story is more than a little confusing, a clear timeline is in order. The two restricted zone orders of January 29 and March 2, 1942 (those banished by EO9066) specified first that some Issei then all Nikkei must leave the coast. At first, they were expected to do so voluntarily, but when the Army recognized that not all Nikkei would have the means or be able to leave voluntarily, the military set up *reception centers* to house, feed, "and otherwise care for" such people. Simultaneously, to speed up the evacuating of the banned zones, the Army created *assembly centers*, which eventually housed some 89,000. Yet voluntary leaving was not working out, since the 8,000 and others who tried it were running into "local opposition." The Army quickly realized that loosing 100,000 more Nikkei into the face of this local opposition would be dangerous to them. A conference of western governors seemed to confirm this danger with firm opposition and some wild statements about lynchings. So when voluntary evacuation failed, the government committed to building *relocation centers* for all the Nikkei, to be under the authority of a newly created War Relocation Authority (WRA).[13]

From the beginning, defenders of the Nikkei claimed that the relocation centers were really "concentration camps" and that that the government's motivation for placing them there was racial rather than national security.

Despite the near consensus on the matter, that charge has never been proven. The relocation centers were nothing like any historical concentration camps or any of the ones proposed at the time, and the main motivation for relocation was national security and not racism. But the

---

[13] This timeline comes from "Supplementary Statement by Mr. D. S. Myer [restricted] to the Senate sub-committee on Military Affairs."

FIG. 2. Mother and child evacuees of Japanese ancestry on train en route from Los Angeles to the relocation center at Manzanar, California. The train trip was often comfortable, as in this picture. Central Photographic File of the War Relocation Authority, 1942–45. Record Group 210: Records of the War Relocation Authority, 1941–89. Courtesy US National Archives and Records Administration.

motivation for creating the centers was complex from the outset, including military, political, economic, emotional, and racial factors stressed by Milton Eisenhower, first director of the WRA, to which we must add government policy, religion, and the role of individuals. If one must choose the most important, nationalism was the principal one.

Racism is a more important twenty-first century concern to historians; nationalism was to the 1940s governments. In arguing this point, I have sought to encourage a "civil and considered discussion" of the relocation episode.[14]

[14] "Reader's Report" by Z. L. Miller, December 19, 2012.

PART I

THE REACH OF AMERICAN RACISM?

I

Racism and Anti-Racism[1]

Long before it began, the Nikkei benefited markedly from the Pacific War. The extensive defense boom, which commenced by at least as early as the naval legislation of 1938, was definitely Nikkei-friendly. In Hawaii in mid-1941, *Pacific Citizen* correspondent Stanley Shimabukuro reported that the "Nisei in Hawaii are receiving the 'lion's share' in the highly paid defense works."[2] The Navy still distrusted them, but the Nisei were breaking down employment barriers. They were on the West Coast too, though some still missed out on the defense employment explosion by not applying for work in the defense sector. Although it would benefit mainlanders only until relocation, the arms buildup did not exclude the Nikkei. On the coast, the Japanese food growers' and purveyors' market share rose rapidly due to extraordinary wartime urban population growth. The war boom was not just an anomaly, as Japanese Americans had made steady economic progress for years before the war as well.

The ghetto economy, however restrictive it might have been, was enough to employ almost all of the Nikkei and to provide them with a foothold in the wider economic world. The Japanese Americans were justly proud of the fact that very few of them were on welfare.[3] Historians have pointed out that the Nikkei found it very difficult to get jobs in the mainstream economy. Still, the second-generation Nisei were quite young, with an average age of nineteen when the war broke out. Since many were

[1] *Christian Century* (Chicago, IL: Christian Century Press, 1942), April 18, 1942, 453.
[2] *Pacific Citizen*, July 1941, 2, 11.
[3] Commission on Wartime Relocation and Internment of Civilians, *Report of the Commission on Wartime Relocation and Internment of Civilians* (Washington, DC: United States Government Printing Office, 1082), 44. Hereafter CWRIC.

still in school at that point, it was not as if there was a huge overabundance of unemployed Nisei who could not find employment in the American mainstream economy.

As a further offset, the Nisei were able to gain employment with Imperial Japanese firms. The Kibei, educated in Japan, were in an ideal position to benefit: "Since they have a good reading as well as speaking knowledge of the Japanese language, they were the ones who often found employment in Japanese exporting and importing firms in American cities."[4] Although not all of these were employees of Imperial Japanese firms, one historian expert on the history of the American Kibei within the Japanese Empire estimated that some 40,000 (out of a total of 332,000) Nikkei "spent the war years in various parts of the Japanese Empire."[5]

Moreover, as a further counterweight to the rigid job market, Japanese American firms had developed extensive ties with many kinds of mainstream companies. This indicates that the Nisei generally were making breakthroughs in the prewar years, becoming the first Japanese American university professors, law enforcement officials, civil servants, winning jockeys at the California State Fair, and so forth.

Attorney General Earl Warren, whose job it was to enforce the laws, understood that by 1942 the famous anti-Japanese land laws were not being obeyed and that the Nikkei had found ways around them.[6] As Roger Daniels and Sandra Taylor have noted as well, the alien land laws of 1913 and 1920 were not enforceable.[7] The many resultant lawsuits triggered by these acts went against the anti-Nikkei because "the California courts acted impartially," said Daniels.[8] The Nikkei were well aware of the result. "The agricultural aspect is, despite the various legislative

---

[4] House of Representatives, Select Committee Investigating National Defense Migration, Pursuant to H. Res. 113, Seventy-Seventh Congress, Second Session, *Hearings, Seattle & Portland*, pt. 30 (Washington, DC: US Government Printing Office, 1942), 11558; Hereafter *Tolan Hearings*. S. Kurashige, *The Shifting Grounds of Race: Black and Japanese Americans in the Making of Multiethnic Los Angeles* (Princeton, NJ: Princeton University Press, 2008), 118.

[5] J. J. Stephan, review of Noriko Shimada, *Nikkei Amerikajin no Taiheiyo senso* [Japanese Americans during the Pacific War] (Tokyo: Liber, 1995).

[6] E. Warren, *Conversations with Earl Warren* (Berkeley, CA: Regional Oral History Project, 1971–2), 258–9.

[7] S. C. Taylor, *Jewel of the Desert: Japanese American Internment at Topaz* (Berkeley, CA: University of California Press, 1993), 22, 29.

[8] R. Daniels, *The Politics of Prejudice: The Anti-Japanese Movement in California and the Struggle for Japanese Exclusion* (Berkeley, CA: University of California Press, 1962), 88.

restrictions placed on it, a steadily progressing one," said the first edition of what became the *Pacific Citizen* newspaper in late 1929.[9]

Therefore, Issei farmers were able to acquire land through renting or purchasing in the names of their children. Although this subject is not usually included in discussions of the alien land laws, the Imperial Japanese had their own version of these laws, as Warren reported: "On the other hand, Japanese citizenship was not open to Americans nor were our citizens free to buy land in Japan."[10]

Even in the turbulent Progressive Era, the Nikkei had maintained good relations with big businesses. This good fortune generated ties, mostly in agriculture, and included American banks, seed companies, fertilizer companies, implement dealers, land owners, retailers, shippers, and others. These Nikkei-friendly firms lent money, rented land, or sold machinery on credit to the Nikkei for their crops, claiming a return when they were sold. By as early as 1937, some, like the Roberts Stores (Three Star Stores), helped to sell these crops. In southern California, they engaged in joint ventures with the Nikkei, which allowed them to operate their own markets within the Roberts Stores.[11] In the northwest, they profited from a lack of competition, since their vegetable and fruit niche crop production was one in which "our white population has not to any great extent engaged," said one observer.[12]

The characterization by one historian of the "semi-colonial conditions of Japanese farmers in the West" is not consistent with these joint ventures.[13] In 1929, Nikkei farmers owned 57,028 acres and, upon evacuation, they owned 230,248 acres.[14] This figure does not cover the acreage they rented, only what they owned. The Nikkei agricultural producers

---

[9] *Nikkei Shimin*, October 15, 1929, 2.

[10] E. Warren, *The Memoirs of Earl Warren* (Garden City, NY: Doubleday & Company, Inc., 1977), 149.

[11] *New World Sun*, November 27, 1937, 1. Hereafter *Sun*.

[12] *Tolan Hearings, Portland and Seattle*, pt. 30, 11558.

[13] Azuma, *Between*, 114. This argument is not consistent with the many assertions of good fortune and good prospects by the Nisei, nor with the fact that the Nikkei were easily able to evade the alien land law prohibitions on land ownership and leasing, nor with the fact that historians almost universally hold that relocation deprived the Nikkei of great wealth. Semi-colonial farmers usually do not accumulate great wealth. Carey McWilliams, one of Nikkei's foremost defenders, said these property losses were "enormous" and estimated total West Coast Nikkei losses at $200,000,000. C. McWilliams, *Prejudice: Japanese-Americans: Symbol of Racial Intolerance* (New York, NY: Archon Books, 1971, reprint of 1944 original), 136–41.

[14] Azuma, *Between*, 63; DeWitt, *Final Report*, 140.

were in fact often large enough to employ other minorities – Filipinos, Mexicans, and whites (often Okies).

If this was a "ghetto economy," it nonetheless provided city jobs, "many specialized trades in retailing, clerk[ing], unskilled labor, cleaning and laundry establishments, hotels, restaurants, domestic service, bath houses, and barber shops, and a comparatively small number engaged in the professions."[15] These trades indicated a thriving and balanced urban and rural economy that kept most of the Nikkei employed. Many of these trades were crossover ones, catering to Caucasian as well as Japanese American clienteles.

A very Nikkei-friendly expert witness, Lucy Adams of the War Relocation Authority (WRA), confirmed that Nikkei success went well beyond land:

In spite of hostility, of suspicion and discrimination, they [the Nikkei] succeeded in an astonishing degree in establishing themselves in the economy of the area, in improving their condition and in climbing the economic ladder. In spite of alien land laws they did succeed in *owning and controlling a very large portion of good land* [emphasis added]. In spite of discrimination which closed some professions they did manage to enter others and in some fields they had almost a monopoly of employment and markets.[16]

Other ties, especially on the Los Angeles waterfront, where the Nikkei had powerful political and economic allies, complemented these. For example, in a 1938 dispute over fishing boat ownership, the San Pedro Chamber of Commerce and Van Camp Sea Food lawyer,[17] Montgomery Phister, argued that Treasury Department seizure of Issei boats "would cripple the San Pedro canning industry."[18] As Jacobus tenBroek explained, the business animus against the Japanese Americans came from small concerns. Big businesses supported them, as did even the Los Angeles Chamber of Commerce, the supposed bête noir of relocation, in some cases.[19]

[15] *Tolan Hearings, Portland and Seattle*, pt. 30, 11558–9.
[16] L. Adams, "Looking Ahead," 2, Griswold Papers, loc. 733, Series 3, Box 2, Folder 2, Special Collections, University of Arkansas. Hereafter Adams, "Looking."
[17] San Pedro was a formerly independent town annexed by Los Angeles that then became a part of Los Angeles harbor.
[18] *Sun*, January 7, 1938, 1. It is well known that the controversy over fishing rights was a perennial anti-Nikkei attempt to hamper their right to fish out of California ports. Thus the point is not footnoted.
[19] J. tenBroek, et al. *Prejudice, War and the Constitution* (Berkeley, CA: University of California Press, 1968 edition), 57–62, 66–7. For the Okinawans, see B. Kobashigawa, *History of the Okinawans in North America* (Berkeley, CA: University of California and the Okinawan Club of America, 1988), 331.

It is important to remember that, though individually they were small, each of these city businesses, except that of unskilled labor, was a device for capital accumulation and therefore further economic growth.[20] These trades indicated a thriving economy that kept most of the Nikkei employed.

One of the most noteworthy breakthroughs was a long-standing and high-profile one. Hollywood had employed Nikkei actors and actresses since almost its beginning. Sometimes their roles were stereotypical and sometimes they were not. Thomas Ince, Cecil B. DeMille, John Huston, Frank Capra, and others cast Nikkei actors and actresses, sometimes in starring roles. By the time of Pearl Harbor and the subsequent relocation, Americans of Japanese ancestry (AJA) had quite a number of their own stars, like Sessuye Hayakawa, Toshia Mori, and Tetsu Komai, and held jobs as technical advisors and art directors. In contrast, African-American progress in this field was delayed until the 1940s.[21] The *Pacific Citizen* explained the AJA contrasting good fortune by its ending: "Chinese and Korean actors in Hollywood are in clover these days, with the forced departure of Japanese screen talent."[22]

When relocation occurred, it was found that gifted Nikkei doctors were already practicing medicine in major hospitals from Seattle to Los Angeles and were professors in major universities by as early as 1932. These included the University of California; Stanford University; San Francisco State University; the University of California, Los Angeles; and the California Institute of Technology.[23] That there were not more such highly qualified individuals might be explained by the fact that in 1937 the average Nisei age was only fifteen, and their average age was only nineteen when the war commenced.[24] They were also beginning to assume

---

[20] Many businesses demonstrated this. Not the least of them was coal merchant Alexander Malcomson of Detroit, Henry Ford's first financier. To give only one more example, the Mutual Insurance Company of Durham, North Carolina, the largest African-American insurance company in the United States, was founded by several barbers. See W. B. Weare, *Black Business in the New South: A Social History of the North Carolina Mutual Insurance Company* (Durham, NC: Duke University Press, 1993).

[21] For the struggle of African-Americans to get onto the screen in non-discriminatory roles, see T. Doherty, *Hollywood, American Culture, and World War II* (New York, NY: Columbia University Press, 1993), 205–27; B. F. Dick, *The Star-Spangled Screen: The American World War II Film* (Lexington, KY: University of Kentucky Press, 1985; 1995 paperback edition), 188–210.

[22] *Pacific Citizen*, June 25, 1942, 5.

[23] *Pacific Citizen*, November 1932, 6; July 1937, 1–2; K. Silber, "Wood Blocks and Water Colors," *National Parks Magazine* (Summer 2013), 33–40.

[24] *Pacific Citizen*, March 1937, 1–2.

important research functions within the universities.[25] In California, the Nikkei were admitted to University of California programs in pharmacy, dentistry, and nursing by as early as late 1937.[26] It is not known whether these professionals and quasi-professionals served Caucasians, but at the very least these qualifications allowed the Nikkei to keep some of their own money in AJA hands.

Large numbers attended western universities and they also attended enough high schools to prepare them to compete there. For example, in early 1938, Jack Murata, a 1927 graduate of Yuba City Union High School, was the co-leader of a team that presented research to the US Geological Society showing that the oceans were twice as old as was hitherto assumed.[27] All of this meant that Japanese American youngsters attended integrated, not segregated schools. For example, by the summer of 1940, Nikkei attended at least eight Los Angeles Area high schools, two in San Diego, four in Placer County – Stockton High School, Galileo, Lowell, and Commerce – as well as girls' high schools in San Francisco.[28] As one Christian minister put it: "They send their children to our schools."[29]

Almost as astonishingly in view of the many charges of racism against West Coast Americans, by the spring of 1940, the public schools were introducing Japanese language courses into their curricula. These included three LA–area high schools,[30] Area high schools, San Fernando, Roosevelt, and the Pasadena school system, which included a junior college component.[31] Although they had their own amateur leagues, the Nisei were welcome in more integrated sports as well. They excelled especially in track and field and swimming and participated on interscholastic all-star teams like the "All San Joaquin Valley track team," led by California sprint champion Ben Doi of Fresno High School.[32]

In 1941, a team of Japanese Americans, Hispanics, and one or two so-called Anglos[33] won the national Amateur Athletic

[25] *Rafu Shimpo*, June 14, 1940, 1.   [26] *Sun*, November 25, 1937, 2.
[27] *Sun*, February 6, 1938, 1.
[28] *Rafu Shimpo*, May 28, 1940, 1; June 8, 1940, 1; *Sun*, September 7, 1941, 1; September 26, 1941, 1.
[29] *Tolan Hearings, San Francisco*, pt. 29, 11208.
[30] I have abbreviated LA here and later in order to save space.
[31] *Rafu Shimpo*, March 28, 1940; *Tolan Hearings, San Francisco*, pt. 29, 11208.
[32] *Rafu Shimpo*, June 2, 1940, 11.
[33] I employed the term "so-called Anglo" because this is an artificial category that does not exist in reality. There is no such group. It is not a Census category, a racial group, an ethnic group, a religious group, nor any other identifiable group. It is a catchall term for

Union[34] swimming championship for the third year in a row.[35] The American Caucasians prevailed in the women's events in part because record-holder Fujiko Katsutani was ill and could not compete.[36] Before the men embarked for their native Hawaii, the same team won the tenth annual La Jolla "rough water swim" in that San Diego district. A large crowd of 10,000 watched this typically imaginative California event from the "north-shore cliff line" overlooking the Pacific. As the *Nichi Bei* put it, "Billy Smith Jr., and seven of his brown-skinned pals from the Alexander House community association of Hawaii swamped the field."[37]

Billy Smith Jr. swamped the rest of the field there and thereafter at Ohio State University, setting eight world records, while his Hawaiian teammate set several others.[38] This was evidence of their athletic prowess and of their acceptance in interracial sports meets. More importantly, this was evidence of racial sports integration almost a decade (1937) before Jackie Robinson stepped to the plate for a Brooklyn Dodgers farm team.[39]

Those entering government work swam in much smoother waters. By as early as 1937, the Nikkei were beginning to see the civil service as an important career opportunity because it provided job security and advancement according to merit, examinations, and seniority.[40] The civil service opened wider still in 1941 because defense jobs were luring away government employees. Some Nisei mistakenly complained about being shut out of defense jobs (they were not), but others shrewdly realized that government work offered more stable employment than defense boom-and-bust jobs.[41] By mid-1942, 300 civil servants worked for the City of Sacramento alone, and by the time war broke out, there were enough Nikkei employed by the City of Los Angeles to alarm Mayor Bowron.[42]

---

people in the West who are not Indians, Hispanics, Asians, black, and so forth. It is a noncategory defined by who they are not.

[34] The Amateur Athletic Union was a more important sponsor of sports events in the 1940s than it is today, when much of sports competition is sponsored by colleges and universities.

[35] *Nichi Bei*, August 22, 1941, 1.   [36] Ibid., August 19, 1941, 2.

[37] Ibid., August 20, 1941, 2; *Sports Section*, August 24, 1941, 2.

[38] Okihiro, *Storied*, 94.

[39] For Jackie Robinson and the integration of baseball, see N. J. Sullivan, *The Dodgers Move West* (New York, NY: Oxford University Press, 1987), 14–77; see also Kobashigawa, *Okinawans*, 337.

[40] *Sun*, December 4, 1937, 1; February 2, 1938, 1.   [41] Ibid., September 20, 1941, 1.

[42] *Pacific Citizen*, June 18, 1942, 2.

As noted above, a significant number also worked for Imperial Japanese firms either in the United States or abroad. In addition, the first-generation Issei were giving way in the ghetto economy as the second-generation Nisei came into control of parts of the fishing fleet and the agricultural businesses. Their success generated hostility from non-Japanese competitors in the flower business and the Los Angeles Produce Dealers Association, but that did not stem their advance.[43]

The Nikkei were on the move elsewhere as well. By one account, two-thirds of the hotels in Seattle were owned by AJA. Their advancement in these urban pursuits was in businesses primarily patronized by whites. Of course, this meant the transfer of wealth from the white to the Japanese American community. As one highly qualified and redoubtable admirer, John Embree, explained, even Issei with divided loyalties about the war "realized that their children's future lay in America and America had given them [their children] a chance to rise in the world such as they would never have had in Japan."[44] A report of the equally friendly WRA asserted that "probably no other group of immigrants, confronted with so many obstacles at the outset, has equaled the progress of the Japanese in adapting themselves to the wide scope of American industry and commerce."[45]

Thus, one is entitled to wonder how much damage the Nikkei difficulty in gaining employment in the mainstream economy caused. There was very little unemployment amongst Japanese Americans in 1940–41[46] compared with that amongst Caucasians, being at 9.9 percent and 14.6 percent, respectively.[47]

The Nikkei had developed spiritual bonds to complement their economic ones. Although many remained Buddhist and that faith thrived, many others affiliated with either Catholic groups like the Maryknoll parish in LA or numerous Protestant ones.[48] Affiliation with both the YMCA and YWCA allowed access to their recreational facilities, as did admittance to area swimming pools and golf clubs.[49] Participation in the Epworth League added Baptist allies.[50] The connections between the

---

[43] Catholic Interracial Council, *Report of December 16, 1945*, 438.

[44] J. F. Embree, "Dealing with Japanese Americans," 7, Griswold Papers, MC 733, Series 3, Box 3, Folder 2, Special Collections, University of Arkansas. Hereafter Embree, "Dealing."

[45] War Relocation Authority, "Myths and Facts about the Japanese Americans," 19, Griswold Papers. Hereafter WRA, "Myths and Facts."

[46] CWRIC, 43.   [47] See http://bls.gov/opub/cps/annag1.2010.pdf.

[48] *Rafu Shimpo*, June 7, 1940, 1. The subject of religion is treated at length in Chapter 20.

[49] Ibid. See also the YMCA banquet that honored Nisei leaders, *Rafu Shimpo*, June 5, 1940, 3.

[50] *Nichi Bei*, August 23, 1941, 1.

Protestant churches and the Japanese were both broad and deep,[51] as the later experience of relocation would again demonstrate, and these connections paid off handsomely.

Christian churches were involved in almost every Nikkei endeavor to improve their public standing. Whether through their association with the Catholic Maryknoll group or with the mainline and Quaker Protestants, the Christian churches stood with the Nikkei. A 1941 speaking engagement illustrated this process. In July, Toru Matsumoto spoke to an audience of 800 at the Huntington Park Methodist Church in suburban LA "on a YMCA Forum program." As did many Nisei speakers of the time, Matsumoto sought to prove the undivided allegiance of the Nikkei to the United States. Unlike other immigrant groups who had proven their mettle in previous national crises, the Nikkei were still not well known to the broader public.[52]

Religion was not just a lever for group advancement. The Nikkei valued very highly the condition of religious freedom in the United States. Manabu Fukuda, president of the Young Buddhists Federation of America, stated his appreciation of "this land of religious freedom" and support for the defense program "of our nation which has given us the liberty to keep our faith in the teachings of Buddha."[53]

Although the Nikkei still complained of restrictive housing covenants that kept them out of certain areas, they were winning the residential turf war too. A mid-1940 *Rafu Shimpo* issue explained that at least 20 percent of the LA area housing stock was open to Japanese Americans. Since the Nikkei were no more than 40,000 of 1,500,000 Angelenos, this represented considerable access for them. Some barriers were breaking down and the Nikkei were overthrowing others by beginning to develop their own suburbs.[54] In LA alone, by mid-1940, the Nikkei had established beachheads in Boyle Heights, Belvedere, the Normandie and 35th area, Uptown, West LA, Sawtelle, and Hollywood.[55] Residentially, they lived all over the metropolitan areas, not just in the Japantowns of San Francisco or LA. Some scholars have emphasized residential segregation,[56] but quite a few of the memoirists resided outside the ethnic settlements.[57]

---

[51] Ibid., August 24, 1941, 2.   [52] *Pacific Citizen*, July 1941, 1.   [53] Ibid., June 1941, 5.
[54] *Rafu Shimpo*, June 13, 1940, 1.   [55] Ibid.
[56] K. A. Leonard, *The Battle for Los Angeles: Racial Ideology and World War II* (Albuquerque, NM: University of New Mexico Press, 2006), 26.
[57] J. Modell, *Kikuchi Diary: Chronicle from an American Concentration Camp* (Urbana, IL: University of Illinois Press, 1973), 42–64ff; J. W. Houston and J. D. Houston, *Farewell to Manzanar* (San Francisco, CA: San Francisco Book Company, 1973), 4; K. Murata,

Their acceptance or access is indicated by further evidence of cooperation with Caucasians. In June 1940, *Rafu Shimpo* attended the "Publishers
and Editors Banquet of the Los Angeles Chamber of Commerce," where the
English section of that paper was recognized as a "community press."[58]
Simultaneously, LA public schools dedicated a "Willis A. Dunn Memorial
Japanese Garden on the campus of Polytechnic High School." Not to be
outdone, the University of California at Berkeley started one of their own in
late 1937, and the San Francisco garden was one of long standing.[59] At the
same time, Nikkei youngsters held model plane contests in Rancho Cienega
Playground and seniors played golf in a tourney honoring a Nikkei principal of Compton Gardens School returning from Japan. The Nikkei seemed
to have wide access to public life all over the LA region.[60] This impressive
Nikkei advance and that portrayed in the next chapter have largely gone
unrecognized, even by scholars like Yuji Ichioka and the *Report of the
Commission on Wartime Relocation and Internment of Civilians* on
Japanese reparations. Instead, their story is mostly about discrimination
and racism.[61]

Yet the Japanese American experience was much closer to that of white
immigrants than it was to that of African-Americans, whom John Hope
Franklin characterized as "indelible immigrants." The Nikkei did not
come to America as involuntary immigrants, they were not effectively
segregated as were African-Americans, and their pre-1942 history did
not include a nadir, as did that of blacks from the 1890s to at least 1920
or the New Deal. Their story up to World War II is not really one of
victimhood – it is one of besting victimhood.

Historians have long debated whether it is good for immigrants to give
up a part of their culture and assimilate or to hang on to most of it.
The Nisei were convinced[62] that it was much better to give up *some* of

---

An Enemy among Friends (Tokyo: Kodansha International, 1991), 31; T. N. Ito,
*Memoirs of Toshi Ito: USA Concentration Camp Inmate, War Bride, Mother of
Chrisie and Judge Lance Ito* (Bloomington, IN: Anchor Books, 2009), 11; H. Egami,
"*Wartime Diary*" reprinted in *Topaz Times*, December 12 and 14, 1943, 37. Kikuchi
lived in Berkeley, Wakatsuki in Santa Monica, Murata in San Leandro, Ito in the Los Feliz
District of Los Angeles, and Egami in Pasadena.

[58] *Rafu Shimpo*, June 25, 1940, 1.   [59] *Sun*, September 27, 1941, 1.

[60] *Rafu Shimpo*, June 23, 1940.

[61] CWRIC, 27–46; Y. Ichioka, *Before Internment: Essays in Prewar Japanese American
History* (Stanford, CA: Stanford University Press, 2006), 1–126.

[62] This argument is based on the evidence of assimilation discussed in the next paragraphs as
well as evidence from the prewar Japanese American newspapers. These often featured
arguments between generations over dating, friendships across nationality lines, behavior, opinions about the Sino-Japanese War, and so forth. *Sun*, November 29, 1937, 2.

their parents' culture. They revered their Issei parents, especially the pioneer generation who laid the foundations for Nikkei existence in America. They respected their own pioneers as much as the Caucasians did theirs. But the Nisei wanted to stand out less, to become less visible as an ethnic enclave in American society. The Nisei, or the second generation, were already behaviorally assimilated. Although the anti-Nikkei had campaigned for school segregation since the Progressive Era,[63] the Nikkei young went to American schools and integrated with Caucasian Americans. There was no segregated system as in the south. They wore American clothes, sported bobby sox and saddle shoes, listened to radio programs (*The Shadow, Jack Armstrong, the All-American Boy, Batman,* and *Terry and the Pirates*), learned swing dancing, enjoyed sodas and milkshakes, attended Christian churches as well as Buddhist temples,[64] and played baseball and golf avidly. To be sure, there was a "generation gap" on the coast and in Hawaii,[65] and it was clearly widening.[66] Although "thousands of American Nisei were fluent in Japanese," most spoke English.[67] The Nisei were still heavily tied to the less prestigious economies of agriculture, nurseries, fishing, and small urban businesses, but they were beginning to make serious inroads into the more mainstream economic realm.

The Japanese never lacked for defenders as well as detractors. Just how all-encompassing each sentiment, biased or benevolent, was we honestly do not know – thus the need for systematic proofs. The late Henry Shapiro, distinguished intellectual historian at the University of Cincinnati, once famously remarked when discussing historical causation that "saying it, is not explaining it."[68] The same is true of proving it,

---

See the columns of "Deirdre" in the *Sun*. Hereafter the *Sun*. See also the *Sun*, November 30, 1937, 1; December 15, 1937, 2.

[63] Daniels, *Politics of Prejudice*, 85.

[64] Even the Buddhists were heavily Americanized. B. M. Hayashi, *"For the Sake of Our Japanese Brethren": Assimilation, Nationalism, and Protestantism among the Japanese of Los Angeles, 1895–1942* (Stanford, CA: Stanford University Press, 1995), 132ff, 28. Hereafter Hayashi, *For the Sake.*

[65] Stephan, *Hawaii*, 25.

[66] Professor Hayashi minimized the assimilation after the first interwar decade. Hayashi, *For the Sake*, 127–47.

[67] *University of Arizona Reader's Report*, May 8, 2012, 4. Some modern scholars believe that thousands of Nisei were fluent in Japanese. CWRIC thought that there were few; CWRIC, 39.

[68] Email conversation with my University of Chicago graduate classmate Professor Zane L. Miller, April 2009.

we might add. With a few exceptions, like John Dower and Ronald Takaki, who have systematically discussed the concept of race, historians of relocation have contented themselves with saying it; that is, saying that racism was universal, asserting it rather than explaining it or, more to the point, proving its extent. So if historians believe that total bigotry outweighed toleration, it is time for them to prove it by systematic studies dedicated to this purpose. A study of home front racism comparable to Dower's *War without Mercy* of the fighting front would indicate once and for all how prevalent the animus was, as well as its opposite. To my knowledge, historians of the "Race Paradigm" have not conducted such a study. The Gallup and Roper polls do not indicate this kind of bias.[69]

The words on the Manzanar Center commemorative plaque that the Japanese relocation was caused by hysteria, racism, and economic exploitation[70] may be illustrative of the views of the vast majority of historians writing about the episode of Japanese relocation in World War II, but it is hardly representative of the reality of that experience. As the Inyo County Superintendent of Schools explained, "Pearl Harbor and World War II caused Japanese relocation."[71] Whether hysteria existed on the West Coast would be an interesting inquiry for a psycho-historian. But neither racism, economic exploitation (greed), nor hysteria by themselves nor together could have caused the unfortunate episode of relocation.

Before the Imperial Japanese attacked Pearl Harbor, there was no significant movement to relocate the Nikkei away from their mostly West Coast homes, whether because of racism, hysteria, or economic exploitation.[72] The Japanese were adjusting to America culturally and

---

[69] For a discussion of the lack of bias, using the Gallup polls, and of the lack of systematic evidence in the "Race Paradigm," see R. W. Lotchin, "A Research Report: The 1940s Gallup Polls, Imperial Japanese, Japanese Americans and the Reach of American Racism." *Southern California Quarterly*, Vol. 97: No. 4 (December, 2015), 399–417.

[70] Quoted in full below on p. 175.

[71] A. A. Hansen and N. K. Jesch, editors, *Japanese American World War II Evacuation Project: Part V: Guards and Townspeople*, Vol. 2. (Munich, New Providence, London, and Paris: K. G. Saur, 1993), 427; Vol. 1, 201.

[72] The *Los Angeles Times* later became a vocal critic of the Nikkei, so their pages provide a good test of whether any significant relocation, anti-Nikkei movement existed before Pearl Harbor. See *Los Angeles Times*, November 1, 1941 through November 30, 1941.

economically and West Coast society was coming to accept them. As the famous "Deirdre" column of the *New World Sun* explained, "What 'problems' we Nisei face are nothing compared to the real obstacles which our parents were confronted with when they first came to these United States."[73]

[73] *Sun*, December 21, 1937, 2.

2

The Ballad of Frankie Seto

Winning Despite the Odds

An incident at a boxing match at the Hollywood Legion Stadium in August 1941 is illustrative of the process of accommodation. LA *Times* sports columnist Dick Hyland was at ringside when Japanese American boxer Frankie Seto crawled outside the ropes after getting badly mauled inside them. The reporter mused that as native Californians, "Traditionally we are not supposed to think too highly of the Japanese [Americans]."[1] But seeing Frankie Seto move slowly out of the ring bloody and beaten, but wearing a fighter's robe bearing the wording "I am an American" across the back, Hyland was moved:

As one American to another, I was proud of him. Proud that he thought enough of being an American to tell the whole cockeyed, and slanteyed, world that he, little Frankie Seto, of Japanese ancestry was an American. And I was proud, too, that an American could take that whipping he took and come back for more, round after round.[2]

The native Californian obviously still held to some stereotypes (of the slanteyed world) himself and did not quite understand what was happening in the Far East, but just as certainly he was trying to work his way away from those stereotypes to a personal appreciation of another American. As Hyland put it, Frankie Seto "had the skin, the build, the flat features of a Japanese. He is a Japanese. But he showed the courage that an American ought to regardless of his appearance."[3] In Frankie Seto's moment between the ropes, the reporter had an epiphany. In late

---

[1] One of the most frequent criticisms of the Nikkei was that they were not assimilable. For a sample, see General John L. DeWitt, *Final Report*, 34.
[2] Quoted in *Nichi Bei*, August 22, 1941, E2.   [3] Ibid.

1941, people all over the West Coast were having their own epiphanies, and would do so for three and a half more years.

Simultaneously, the Nikkei claimed a place in politics. The Japanese American Citizens League (JACL), a pressure group made up of American citizens to protect their interests, began with the founding in 1928 of the San Francisco chapter.[4] Historians have consistently underestimated it, partly because it cooperated with the government in carrying out relocation and even earlier in identifying the disloyal within their community. However, given all of the difficulties facing them, the JACL did exceptionally well. Since their Issei parents, who owned most of the property of the group, could not become citizens under the naturalization laws, second-generation Nisei born in the United States had to assume public political leadership. American politicians do not listen closely to those who cannot vote. The Nisei were often young to boot; one Japanese newspaper estimated the average age in 1941 at nineteen.[5] Thus, in a political sense the group was divided between veteran, seasoned Issei, who had the wealth, and young, inexperienced Nisei, who had the ballot. That meant the Nisei had to fight a two-front war, to wrest community leadership from the Issei and prove their loyalty to often skeptical American pressure groups.[6] This power struggle was culminating in a Nisei victory as the country lurched into the war.[7]

Despite their youth and political inexperience in politics, the JACL was doing a magnificent job of establishing their place in Nikkei society writ small and American society writ large. Their leaders, especially national president Saburo Kido, national secretary Mike Masaoka, Washington lobbyist, sometime editor Togo Tanaka, and journalist Bill Hosokawa, were able men who should be taken seriously by historians. They ran a textbook campaign to gain both acceptance and political power. As we shall see, they had many specific interests and policy aims, but their overall goal was to end the isolation of Japanese Americans by reaching out to the other Americans; then, "the 'self sufficient' psychology will vanish."[8] As Kenneth D. Ringle, their admirer and a Navy intelligence expert, put it, "They saw and feared the looming danger to the Nikkei in the Sino Japanese War raging in China and they sought to contain it by reducing their exposure to it." A turning point in their affairs came in 1935.

[4] *Nikkei Shimin*, October 15, 1929, 1, 12; *Sun*, February 6, 1938, 1.
[5] *Sun*, November 10, 1941, 1.   [6] Ibid., November 14, 1937, 1.
[7] To follow this drama, see the *Pacific Citizen*, 1937–1941 and *Sun*, December 16, 1937, 2.
[8] *Pacific Citizen*, April, 1935, 1.

Not the least of their achievements was to spread the JACL rapidly throughout the Pacific Coast and into the Intermountain West.[9] Moreover, like effective politicians everywhere, the Nisei sought favorable publicity. Mike Masaoka and Togo Tanaka ceaselessly traveled the country making friends and explaining that the Japanese Americans were loyal, mostly had no ties to Tokyo, and backed the American President in his China War.

One of their most effective accomplishments was to lay a foundation for Nisei leadership. Many commentators have complained that the Nikkei found it difficult to get a foothold in the mainstream economy, but they certainly had one in mainstream colleges and universities. This paid off politically in many ways, but especially in the training of young lawyers. As Jon Teaford has written, the law was usually one of the entry points for big-city immigrant generations to get into politics through election to state legislatures.[10] Access to lawyers and legislatures was crucial to the Nikkei to fight off attempts to pass legislation that would patch up the bedraggled alien land laws or restrict Japanese fishing rights.

In 1937 alone, there were four anti-alien bills "before the California legislature," and one before the Washington State legislature. They were evidence of the continuing opposition to the Nikkei, but more important, they were proof of the growing political influence of the Nikkei. The California bills did not pass and the Washington State bill was vetoed by Governor Clarence D. Martin. Nikkei lawyer Thomas Masuda led this fight.[11]

Despite these struggles, these young leaders were willing to mend fences with their erstwhile enemies, like the American Legion. The veterans' association was one of the four major components of the Immigration Restriction League, so their behavior was illustrative. Perhaps their most outstanding joint venture (along with the Veterans of Foreign Wars [VFW]) was the 1935 passage of Congressional legislation making aliens eligible for citizenship if they had served in World War I. *This* legislation took effect in 1937. The Nikkei put great store by that legislation, the first Issei breach of the citizenship law.[12] The Nikkei had accepted the Legion as its mentor on citizenship, marched with them in patriotic and local festivity parades, held meetings in Legion halls, and were accepted by the

---

[9] *Sun*, November 27, 1941, 1.
[10] J. Teaford, *The Unheralded Triumph: City Government, 1870–1900* (Baltimore, MD: Johns Hopkins University Press, 1984).
[11] *Pacific Citizen*, March 1937, 1–2.   [12] Ibid., November 1937, 1.

veterans in their scholastic activities. The May 1941 issue of the *Pacific Citizen*, the national voice of the JACL, informed the public that Miss Patti Okura, a senior at Lodi High School, had won the local, district, and state Legion contests on Americanism and was the nominee by the California Legion for national honors in that competition. Lodi High School voted her "runner-up for the honor of the most outstanding senior girl," and the Lodi *Times* described her as "one of the most talented young ladies in Lodi high-school history." The same issue informed the Nikkei public that June Wada, of Marysville High School, had gained first prize in a Legion contest on citizenship for Sutter and Yuba counties.[13] World War II shifted the Legion back to its original anti-Nikkei stance, but the direction before the war was positive and unmistakable.

The acceptance of Japanese Americans by the public at large and by the American prominenti, to use the wonderful Italo-American word for the aristocracy, highlighted the trend. They were quietly gaining both.[14] The JACL sponsored speeches, banquets, and meetings where the prominenti appeared in considerable numbers. For example, on one occasion the sheriff of San Francisco County, Daniel C. Murphy, served as master of ceremonies at a Japanese Catholic Youth Society festivity.[15] Other meetings featured a laundry list of local notables. The audience for an address by National JACL national secretary Mike Masaoka at Fresno included judges, county supervisors, the county district attorney, sheriff, health officer, draft board officials, the mayors of four towns, the leaders of the Fresno chamber of commerce, eleven educators, and one commander of the American Legion.[16]

Building on these successes, the JACL sought and gained access to influential people in the next higher level of political culture. Face time, to use the modern phrase, does not automatically create results, but at least the JACL was given the right to make its case to mayors, governors, the US Attorney General, and even to the keeper of the back door to the White House, Eleanor Roosevelt. Mrs. Roosevelt praised them, gave them an audience, and promised, in time, to help get them through the front door.[17]

Historians have emphasized the hostility of the western governors to the Nikkei after Pearl Harbor, but shortly before that event, Mike Masaoka was on a tour of the West, scheduled to speak to all of them. Not the least of his contacts was with former state senator William

[13] Ibid., May 1941, 2.   [14] Ibid., November 1942, 3.   [15] *Sun*, October 19, 1941, 2.
[16] Ibid., October 28, 1941, 1.   [17] Ibid., November 3, 1941, 1.

F. Knowland, scion of the powerful Republican family that controlled the Oakland Tribune and future leader of the US Senate.[18] And in an age of universal radio audiences, the Nikkei had gained that kind of face time with the public too.[19] It allowed them to press their claims with the general public, for example, against the anti-Japanese boycott of 1937.[20]

Moreover, just as they sought to speak to the powerful, they also sought to be spoken to. At least one of the 1940 LA County District Attorney candidates came to speak to them very politely.[21] Their enemies noticed this growing clout.[22] Alarmed at the prospect of an alliance between African Americans and the Japanese, the California Joint Immigration Committee warned of a bloc voting alliance between the two, which might garner 25,000 votes: "25,000 is a large number of votes." Indeed! A Chicago First Ward alderman could not have put it any better.[23]

The Nikkei succeeded in establishing mutually beneficial ties with a number of other influential, but lesser politicos. A full year and a half before the Japanese struck Hawaii, their relatives on the West Coast had found an effective ally in Los Angeles Assemblyman Fred Reeves of San Pedro (San Pedro was part of the LA harbor district). *Rafu Shimpo* characterized Reeves as a "real friend" to the "Japanese of California" who helped protect their fishing interests.[24] They had others in the same neighborhood. In early 1938, when the US Treasury Department tried to impound Issei fishing boats in the harbor, both the San Pedro Chamber of Commerce and Van Camp Sea Food Company asked Senator William Gibbs McAdoo to intervene to protect them.[25] In Hawaii, Delegate Samuel King was an equally redoubtable champion of the Nikkei.[26] Two other key defenders were lawyers Guy C. Calden and Albert H. Elliott of San Francisco. The *New World Sun* credited them with helping the Japanese Americans "manage" the 1913–20 alien land laws so that they could "continue their operations within the law."[27] Given the

---

[18] *Pacific Citizen*, November 1941, 12. The *Pacific Citizen* was a monthly at this point.
[19] Ibid., November 1937, 1.   [20] *Sun*, November 14, 1937, 1.
[21] *Rafu Shimpo*, June 13, 1940, 1.
[22] A wonderful Chicago political term for political influence.
[23] *Tolan Hearings, San Francisco*, pt. 29, 11086.   [24] *Rafu Shimpo*, May 21, 1940, 1.
[25] *Sun*, January 7, 1938, 1.   [26] *Pacific Citizen*, April 1941, 11.
[27] *Sun*, December 12, 1937, 1. Whether the 1920 law was enforced is debated, but I have privileged the primary source because it explained how the evasion was carried out and by whom. Except for Sandra Taylor, the race paradigm apparently fails to take account of the crucial role of Calden and Elliott. Hayashi *For the Sake*, 185n explains the debate among historians. Daniels, Modell, Sandra Taylor, and Robert Higgs thought that the

centrality of fishing and agriculture to the American-Japanese economy, one can hardly imagine more important help.

The JACL had such friends from its very beginning. Frederick J. Koster of the powerful Industrial Alliance of San Francisco gave the keynote address at the founding dinner of the JACL, and Mayor James "Sunny Jim" Rolph hailed the creation of the new organization in the year of its founding. Rolph welcomed them in a speech reprinted in the October 15 issue of the *Nikkei Shimin* to help develop San Francisco's ties with the East. "The Pacific is the ocean of the future. Its commerce grows by leaps and bounds," he said. Understanding the language of two of the most important Pacific peoples, and with a knowledge of their ways of thought, it would be possible to play a great part in the development of their common ideals and the commercial intercourse that would be of great advantage to both.[28]

Rolph's greeting was symptomatic of his own openness and a very significant acceptance of both the Japanese language and the Kibei cohort, each often the target of the anti-Nikkei.

Others, like publicist and historian Carey McWilliams, used their talents to advocate on behalf of the community.[29] Still other friends included Assemblyman John B. Pelletier and Judge Ben Rosenthal of Northern California.[30] In the arena of city politics, aided by their Los Angeles Maryknoll Catholic mentors and the LA or Oakland Young Democrats, the Nikkei learned the mechanics of politics, which they were putting into practice in San Francisco, Los Angeles, and elsewhere.[31]

Although not much noted, access to public and quasi-public spaces is an important aspect of influence. Groups need venues to make speeches and to hold meetings, banquets, round table discussions, rallies, and dances. Lack of such access often plagued the early labor movement, but it did not afflict the Nisei. Available spaces included hotels, civic centers, temples, churches, auditoriums, public and private, and university facilities (such as San Francisco State University and Columbia University). For example, in San Francisco, where the American Federation of Labor was supposedly so hostile, the Nikkei hired the dance hall at the prestigious Palace Hotel in 1934 and the St. Francis in 1938. The 1934 dance

---

law was evaded; Masakazu Iwata, T. Scott Miyakawa, Ivan Light, and Jūjii Ichioka, thought it was enforced.

[28] *Nikkei Shimin*, October 15, 1929, 1. This paper was the predecessor of the *Pacific Citizen*.

[29] *Sun*, December 8, 1941, 1.   [30] Ibid., September 18, 1941, 1.

[31] Ibid., November 4, 1941, 1.

attracted 600 people, and the 1938 grand Bay Area ball would attract another 1,000. So these were not events that could be hidden in a back room.[32] Nor could events in the equally prestigious Biltmore and Ambassador hotels in Los Angeles. Counterintuitively, these available venues even included the Native Sons of the Golden West auditorium and the "American Legion Memorial Ballroom," in San Francisco, as well as the Seattle Chamber of Commerce.[33] Major fiestas, festivals, and celebrations were other venues where the Nikkei were included and could claim membership in a community. The Lodi (California) Grape and Wine Festival was not a world-class event, but like local festivals all over the country, it was an important cultural and city booster event. The Italo American fairs in the Hill neighborhood of St. Louis and those of the North End of Boston are perhaps the most famous.[34] Lodi was celebrated for the Flame Tokai Grape, and its annual grape and wine festival was a major event for the northern San Joaquin Valley. It drew 100,000 to 150,000 people.[35] The Japanese won the float first prize at Lodi, but the Nikkei members of the iconic Future Farmers of America positively swept the field at the California State Fair.[36] The Lodi Fair was a local festivity, but the storied Rose Bowl, where the Nikkei float won the theme prize, was not.[37]

They also found a place before influential private clubs and in local newspaper columns. Nikkei-sponsored speakers were welcome at both the prestigious Commonwealth Club of San Francisco and the Advertising Club of Oakland.[38] The San Diego branch of the General Federation of Women's Clubs helped them to defeat a Chinese American Maritime Union boycott against Japanese goods and Japanese American shops as early as 1937. At the start of the Sino Japanese War in 1937, many Nikkei sided with the mother country, but the mainline newspapers did not back the Japanese in that sympathy. However, they could be counted upon to respect Nikkei interests in strictly local affairs. The *San Diego Union* supported them in fighting off the boycott, and both the *Sacramento*

---

[32] Ibid., January 21, 1938, 1; January 26, 1938, 2.

[33] *Pacific Citizen*, March 1937, 4; *Sun*, September 18, 1941, 1; November 29, 1937, 2.

[34] For ethnic festivals, see G. R. Mormino, *Immigrants on the Hill: Italian-Americans in St. Louis, 1882–1982* (Urbana, IL: University of Illinois Press, 1986), 148, 154–5ff.

[35] *Sun*, September 11, 1941, 1.   [36] Ibid., September 6, 1941, 2.

[37] *Pacific Citizen*, January 1942, 1; *Sun*, September 11, 1941, 1; September 7, 1937, 1. For the importance to minorities of claiming public space, see the wonderful biography of Louis Armstrong by Thomas Brothers, *Louis Armstrong's New Orleans* (New York, NY: W. W. Norton, 2006), 78–87. It is also a common theme for labor historians.

[38] *Sun*, January 27, 1938, 1.

Union and *Sacramento Bee* (a McClatchy paper) stood up for Nikkei rights in the face of a worsening international situation, as did other papers like the Woodland *Democrat*.[39]

By mid-1940, the Nikkei were moving to adopt pressure group tactics, modeled on those of African Americans, to gain work in the telephone and defense industries. And they began personally confronting neighborhood housing restriction groups through personal appearances and educational efforts.[40] More powerful pressure groups reinforced these. The Northern California Committee on Fair Play for Citizens and Aliens of Japanese Ancestry was a Who's Who of Northern California prominenti. Governor Culbert Olson was honorary chairman and General David P. Barrows was chairman, and the committee included the presidents of both Stanford University and the University of California, important businessmen, Christian missionaries, and leading Jewish rabbis.[41]

One of the few good things to come out of the Sino Japanese War was pressure to consolidate Nikkei pressure groups at an urban level. In San Francisco in early 1938, the Japanese Association and the Chamber of Commerce and Nippon Club moved to consolidate their efforts and to recruit Japanese businessmen to enhance that merger. They hoped this would combine the efforts of "uptown" and "downtown" groups in the city and lend added prestige by recruiting Imperial businessman Kazuo Takahishi as president of the former. The same period saw the creation of another pressure group, the Japanese American Public Information Bureau to help fend off the boycott of Japanese goods.[42]

Results seemed to vindicate the Nikkei approach. They were able to protect their fishing rights, apparently by agreeing to put the boats under American registry, a strategy comparable to that of putting land ownership in their children's names.[43] That protected the Issei and defused one of the loyalty issues that plagued the community. As a prominent Japanese American newspaper noted, it had become something of a "tradition to introduce bills against the Japanese fishermen" at each legislative session, and in 1935 several more were introduced to limit Issei rights to farm the land.[44] However, when war broke out, the Issei were still fishing and still farming. As early as mid-1935, the Nisei leadership also openly took a stand against dual citizenship, another sore point.[45]

[39] *Woodland Democrat* quoted in *Sun*, October 10, 1941, 1. See note 54.
[40] *Rafu Shimpo*, June 2, 1940, 4.   [41] *Sun*, October 7, 1941, 1.
[42] Ibid., January 27, 1938, 1.   [43] Ibid., October 4, 1941, 1.
[44] *Pacific Citizen*, March 1935, 1.   [45] Ibid., May 1935, 1; *Sun*, October 9, 1941, 1.

On October 10, 1941, the *New World Sun* reported the defeat of bills in the California legislature to "restrict operation of vehicles owned by aliens and to restrict schools teaching foreign languages."[46] These were important victories, because the Issei needed trucks to transport their farm products and language schools to convey their culture to some of their children. As part of their access, the JACL was able to testify at congressional hearings that affected their interests. These included the Fair Employment Practices Commission hearings held in Los Angeles to investigate job discrimination in the defense industry, the first congressional hearings at which the Japanese Americans had ever been allowed to testify.[47] The government pledged fair play and made a down payment on that promise by hiring several Nikkei. Unfortunately, the war began before the Nikkei could follow up on this opening. In late October, the US House of Representatives delivered an even greater victory when it rejected, on what one newspaper described as a bipartisan vote of 167 to 141, a "hotly debated measure to permit forcible detention without bail of deportable aliens."[48]

Even when they did not immediately succeed, as in the battle to eliminate residential discrimination, the Nisei went about it in a very shrewd way. As they put it, the key to home owning in elite areas was sponsorship (of Nikkei home buyers) by "leading white families who are economically related to a high degree with [Imperial] Japanese trade."[49] Not bad for a bunch of youngsters! They were learning fast.

Apropos of the modern poker adage of knowing when to hold 'em and when to fold 'em, the Nisei were learning quickly too. The issues of dual citizenship and the Sino Japanese War were two questions on which the Nisei had either to give ground or endure continual political embarrassment. One historian has explained Issei super nationalism in that war on grounds of discrimination. Since they had no hopes of gaining a political role here, their attachment to the mother country was all the more intense.[50] According to historian Yuji Ichioka, the Nisei never took to the war, remaining neutral, indifferent, or hostile.

This was a much smarter way to respond to the Far Eastern problem than that of their fathers. Whereas the Issei and their many associations trumpeted their ties to the Old Country, the Nisei steered clear of them.[51] However understandable their intense nationalism may have been, it

---

[46] *Sun*, October 10, 1941, 1.   [47] Ibid., October 16, 1941, 1.
[48] Ibid., October 20, 1941, 1.   [49] *Pacific Citizen*, November 1937, 2–3.
[50] Ichioka, *Before Internament*, 197–9.   [51] Ibid., 188–90.

made the Issei suspect and that suspicion eventually engulfed their children as well. When the security services began making lists of dangerous people, the lists were taken from these Issei organizations, not those of the Nisei.

They also took the shrewd side on the issue of dual citizenship. This matter gave endless ammunition to their opponents, and the JACL were not long in recognizing it was a lost cause. They decided that renouncing dual citizenship should be a test of their loyalty to the United States, and from 1935 campaigned to do so.[52]

Although not enfranchised in public politics, the Issei were often represented on private institutions that affected their interests. In 1938, Japanese Americans had prominent places on the Central California Berry Growers Association, Inc., which protected berry growers' interests. Five new Nikkei directors sat on the board of directors, one of which was the vice president. They also had access to quality lawyers who helped them circumvent restrictions like the Alien Land Laws. So not only were the Nikkei cooperating with Caucasians in economic matters, they also had a say in how they were managed.[53]

Although the enemies of the Japanese fishermen were still trying to secure congressional action to limit the fishing rights of the Issei, this was only because they had failed to get a state ban on alien fishermen.[54] The JACL was employing a full-time lobbyist in Washington and had made other notable gains at the national level. By the mid-1930s they had secured legislation to grant citizenship to Issei veterans of World War I. Partnering with the League of Women Voters and other Caucasians like Edith Walker Maddux, the wife of a San Francisco banker and president of the Republican Women's Federation of Northern California, they had secured the repeal of the Cable Law which discriminated against Nikkei women born abroad.[55]

As John Modell has summed up, the Japanese were a thrifty, entrepreneurial, family bound, gifted people, and they were rapidly swimming into the mainstream.[56] They were winning what one historian called the "Battle for Los Angeles" and those for San Diego, San Francisco, Seattle, the farming lands of Oregon, Washington, and the San Joaquin

[52] *Pacific Citizen*, May, 1935, 1, 4; January 1938, 1.   [53] *Sun*, February 8, 1938, 1.
[54] *Rafu Shimpo*, June 10, 1940, 1; *Tolan Hearings, San Francisco*, pt. 29, 11086.
[55] *Pacific Citizen*, November 1932, 3; F. Chuman, *The Bamboo People: The Law and Japanese Americans* (Del Mar, CA: Publishers Inc., 1976), 165–7.
[56] Modell, *Economics and Politics*, 95–123.

Valley. Their sometime enemies admitted as much. The California Joint Immigration Committee deplored this influence of the "Japanese Lobby," which they said was made up of "church people, idealists, foreign traders, employees of cheap labor, and uninformed government officials."[57]

The JACL helped to fashion other legislation that affected their vital interests. As the war drew near, the US House of Representatives considered a bill to tighten the responsibilities of dual citizens. The legislation required an oath of loyalty from those suspected of owing primary allegiance to another country. One of the principal goals in the second half of 1941 was to declare in no uncertain terms their loyalty to the United States. Historians have denounced these oaths of allegiance when later administered in the relocation centers, but in late 1941 they were an effective way to disarm another of the issues. The tactic of cooperating with the government seemed to work. As the paper proudly announced, "The League [JACL] has been established as the logical authority for accurate reports about resident Japanese."[58] There were all kinds of people working with the Nikkei at various levels in the struggle for influence. The JACL was going about this process in the right way, as Frank Chuman put it in a section title in his impressive constitutional history of the thirties, "The JACL Becomes Influential."[59]

They seemed to be making headway even with their former enemies. Although the American Legion was one of the components of the California Joint Immigration Committee, its representatives appeared at Nikkei-sponsored events on citizenship and patriotism, marched with them in preparedness parades, and mentored them about citizenship. By the same token, the San Francisco AFL, another constituent part of the Joint Committee, could nonetheless side with the Nikkei in the boycott dispute. The Committee itself also forcefully repudiated the concept of racial superiority. Within weeks of the outbreak of war, both the *Sacramento Union* and the *Sacramento Bee* published articles praising the Nikkei and supporting the Fair Play Committee.[60]

To supplement their pressure groups, by mid-1940 the Nisei were leaning towards the Democrats in party preference, active in the Young Democrats branch, and participating in the usual party rituals like the

---

[57] *Tolan Hearings, Portland and Seattle*, pt. 30, 11084–86. This is a very intriguing issue. Historians should investigate the size of this "Japanese Lobby."

[58] Ibid.   [59] Ibid.

[60] *Sacramento Bee* and *Sacramento Union*, quoted in the *Sun*, October 15, 1941, 1 and December 3, 1941, 1.

famous Jackson Day Dinner. In contrast to African Americans, there was no "white primary" to exclude them. When the alien issue arose, the Young Democrats sought to purge their ranks of communists, but not of Nisei. And their opponents had also tired or relented. As historian Alan Bosworth put it, "When war finally came, the [anti-Nikkei] pressure groups in California had been generally ineffective and inactive for a decade."[61] And their future looked bleaker still: the Nisei voters were becoming more numerous; Labor was split between AFL and CIO (pro-Nikkei); the Nisei had learned to work with the American Legion, and the Issei were aging out and dying off. The contention of Carey McWilliams that the period from 1900 to 1941 was one of unrelenting harassment of the Nikkei is not plausible;[62] neither is Jacobus tenBroek's notion of the enduring stereotype.[63] Nor is Yuji Ichioka's view of pre-war Issei exclusion.[64]

There was still some prejudice, and some of it was racial in the biological sense. Yet the progress was striking. In March 1941, a number of local and national institutions in Southern California held a meeting for an open discussion of the place of the Nikkei. It was a high-profile conference, including the sheriff of Los Angeles County, the secretary of the LA Chamber of Commerce, a spokesman for Fort MacArthur, and the 11th Naval District Commandant Admiral C. A. Blakely. Every one of them stated their faith in the loyalty of "American citizens of Japanese ancestry." They agreed that the Nisei would be tested in the coming months by the breakdown of US-Japanese relations. And Captain E. R. Riordan, speaking for Colonel [no first name given] Kimberly, Fort MacArthur commandant, said, "I don't think there's any doubt as to your loyalty." And he went on to state what the Nisei also frequently said, "However, you are going to be tried and tested, not because of you, but because of the position the country of your ancestry has taken in this crisis."[65]

Just before the crisis came, the *Pacific Citizen* summed up Nikkei progress very well. They knew the metaphor of the bottle half empty, but they appreciated the part that was half full.

[61] A. Bosworth, *America's Concentration Camps* (New York, NY: Bantam Books, 1967), 95; R. Daniels, *Concentration Camps USA: Japanese Americans in World War II* (New York, NY: Holt, Rinehart and Winston, 1972), 49, 138; Francis Biddle, In *Brief Authority*, 30.
[62] C. McWilliams, *Japanese Evacuation: Interim Report*, American Council Paper, No. 4 (New York, NY: American Council and the Institute of Pacific Relations, 1942), 1–6.
[63] tenBroek, et. al. *Prejudice*, 66–67.   [64] Ichioka, *Before*, 198.
[65] *Pacific Citizen*, April 1941, 1–2.

Its [the JACL] history is the story of the American-born Japanese and their growth into manhood. The achievements are reflected in the comparatively enviable status which we Japanese enjoy today as a minority group. Were it not for the League, prejudice, discrimination and jingoism might still be rampant – and we might still be subjected to such humiliations as separate schools and rooms, inferior instructors, inadequate equipment; such injustices as passport difficulties, loss of citizenship simply by reason of marriage to a Japanese national, special days and sections in theatres, dance halls, roller skating rinks, hotels, cafes, swimming pools, etc; such prohibitions as existed and still exist, for the colored folk.[66]

The JACL may have been beating its own drum a bit loudly, but these past discriminations are those that historians have insisted upon and that no longer existed.

If all of this were true, it suggests a seminal question. If the Nikkei was marching with and learning from the Legion, boxing and dancing at the Legion, lunching with the prominenti, testifying to the solons, legislating in Hawaii,[67] schooling with the Caucasians, lobbying the powerful, interviewing the First Lady, partnering with the League of Women Voters, marching before the thousands at Lodi and before many more in the Rose Bowl Parade, and rough water swimming with the Anglos, where does this leave our understanding of racism? Could all of these things be true of a completely racist West Coast, an American West, an entire United States, all of California, or all of LA, as Roger Daniels and Alan Leonard have contended?[68]

Although the idea of assimilation is a one-way street, accommodation to America has always been two-way. The Nikkei were affecting the host culture as well as being shaped by it. Their contributions to agriculture included finding ways to cultivate some 250,000 acres of hitherto useless land, new types of irrigation, new foods, new crops, innovative techniques of animal husbandry, and even Judo. In 1941, when California opened a "new prison without walls at Chino," every guard was trained in the Japanese self-defense art of Judo.[69]

Saburo Kido, in a talk to the San Francisco Parent Teachers Association, claimed that the Nikkei had imparted to other Americans a "love of nature and a new form of religion, namely Buddhism." Kido might have mentioned Japanese cuisine as well,[70] or food for the spirit, through an appreciation of Japanese landscapes introduced by artist Chiura Obata.[71]

---

[66] Ibid., November 1941, 1.   [67] *Sun*, September 20, 1941, 1.
[68] Daniels, *Concentration Camps*, 95.   [69] *Nichi Bei*, August 24, 1941, 2.
[70] *Sun*, January 20, 1938, 1.
[71] K. Silber, "Wood Blocks and Water Colors," *National Parks Magazine* (Summer 2013), 33–40.

Through their imports, they had also made silk clothing for women widely available. The point of the speech was to discuss the "meaning of cultural diversities for adolescents."[72] Kido spoke in the midst of the China War crisis caused by the Panay Incident and the generally brutal Japanese march to rape of Nanking. So despite the unpopularity of the Imperial Japanese action, important San Franciscans were willing to think about Nikkei contributions.

Much of the pre-war anti-Nikkei publicity was generated by Martin Dies and his House Un-American Activities Committee, mostly regarding Imperial Japanese espionage.[73] We know this from MAGIC intercepts of widespread espionage networks on the West Coast before the war.[74] Dies was probably feeding the LA papers information from these. Wherever he got them, these accusations were serious, but they did not lead to a widespread movement to remove the Japanese Americans, nor metropolitan newspaper support for doing so.[75] Some diehards like the California Joint Immigration Committee and some state legislators still pushed for the deportation of aliens ineligible for citizenship. However, that issue did not gain traction with the public, and its future was increasingly limited because of the die off of the supposedly offending aliens. Soon there would be none to deport. Some Nikkei feared that, in the event of war, they would be put into camps. As discussed elsewhere, there was very little support for that position in the pre-war San Francisco *Chronicle*, LA *Times*, LA *News*, LA *Examiner*, or *Sacramento Bee*.

And the Japanese American journals, *Pacific Citizen, Nichi Bei, Rafu Shimpo*, and *New World Sun*, were not reporting it either.[76]

Some people at the time and historians ever since have talked about hysteria, but there was virtually no public manifestation of it. Who exactly was hysterical? From my reading of Japanese American newspapers, it is evident that the charge of hysteria and racism came almost exclusively

---

[72] *Sun*, December 9, 1937, 1.

[73] 77th US Congress, House of Representatives, "Investigation of Un-American Propaganda Activities in the United States," *Hearings on H. Res. 282 Before a Special Committee on Un-American Activities* (Washington, DC: United States Government Printing Office, 1942), 1723–32; *Los Angeles Daily News*, November 27, 1941, 18. Hereafter HUAC, "Investigation" [1942].

[74] D. D. Lowman, *Magic: The Untold Story of U.S. Intelligence and the Evacuation of Japanese Residents from the West Coast during WWII* (Stanford, CA: Athena Press, Inc., 2000), 16–17ff.

[75] Dies called for removal of Japanese commercial agents and students, but not Japanese American, HUAC, "Investigation" [1942] 1731.

[76] *Nichi Bei*, August 23, 1.

from the Japanese themselves and their allies mostly from mid-1941. In my reading of the sources, friendly sentiments were more prevalent before the war began and well after Japan's attack on Pearl Harbor.

Before the war, West Coast whites were not, as a group, dedicated to biological racism. They were a community in which Japanese Americans were making progress. If one had to guess, and that is really all we can do, the Nikkei were about a half to one and a half generations away from the same kind of acceptance that other American ethnic groups already enjoyed. Unlike East and South European Slavs, Italians, or East European Jews, the Nikkei did not have massive numbers to back up their claims, but they were making them effectively nonetheless.

As early as December 1937, a columnist for the *New World Sun* acknowledged that progress in terms of generations: "What problems we Nisei face," he wrote, "are nothing compared to the real obstacles which our parents were confronted with when they first came to these United States."[77]

Kenneth D. Ringle, the Navy intelligence officer who knew the Japanese situation well, "categorically denied the need for mass evacuation," which the defenders of the Nikkei have often cited. But he also recognized the progress of the Asian-Caucasian accommodation, of the Frankie Setos and the Dick Hylands: "the 'entire Japanese question in the United States' had 'reversed itself' in the last ten years before the war," said Ringle.[78] "'The alien menace' was no longer paramount and was becoming of less importance almost 'daily as the original alien immigrants grow older and die, and as more and more of their American-born children reach maturity'." As journalist and historian Bill Hosokawa explained: "The anti-Oriental racism, largely dormant since the Exclusion Act [of 1924] slammed the doors to immigration less than two decades earlier,[79] was quickly whipped into life" by the war.[80] Historian Masuda Hajimu is only the most recent historian to note the same point.[81]

Another Nisei summed up the progress in early 1939, nearly three years before Pearl Harbor:

---

[77] *Sun*, December 21, 1937, 2.
[78] M. Grodzins, *Americans Betrayed: Politics and the Japanese Evacuation* (Chicago, IL: the University of Chicago Press, 1949), 188.
[79] In every case, except where otherwise explained, emphasis has been added by the author.
[80] B. Hosokawa, *Nisei: The Quiet Americans* (New York, NY: William Morrow and Company, Inc.), 263–4.
[81] See endnote 52 below.

We must never forget that this country has offered us opportunities which would have been denied us in the land of our ancestry [Japan]. It has given us a standard of living vastly superior to that in the lands from which most of us came. It has given us freedom to a degree unknown in many lands. It has given us educational opportunities offered us freely and without stint.[82]

What disrupted this progress was not racism, nor a "sudden revulsion" against the Nikkei triggered by racism, nor hysteria, nor greed, but World War II.[83] Without it, or something like it, there would have been no relocation because none was on the horizon before December 7, 1941, put it there.

---

[82] *Pacific Citizen*, January 1939, 1–2.
[83] The phrase is from H. W. Brands, "The Coils of Empire," *Diplomatic History*, Vol. 33: No. 1 (January 2009), 132.

3

The Chinese and European Origins of the West Coast Alien Dilemma

The exaggeration of race is underscored by the fact that the World War II origin of anti-alien sentiment in the West was neither racial nor western. Contrary to almost everything written on the subject, the story of relocation began in December 1937, and was triggered by the outbreak of Sino Japanese conflict. It was fueled further by events on the East Coast in early June 1940, triggered by the outbreak of war in Western Europe. In neither case did the rise of anti-alien feeling rest upon racism, greed, or anti-war hysteria against Japanese Americans. The Asian War was fought between peoples of the same race and so was the European one. Since the United States was not militarily involved in either, there was nothing to be hysterical about.

As we have seen, Nikkei-western Caucasian relations were improving from at least 1930 onward, but the Sino Japanese War created fresh complications. Certainly progress did not cease, but it was now accompanied by ill will over the China situation. When the Roosevelt government adopted the Chinese side in the war, the Nikkei home country became very unpopular. As the *New World Sun* put it, "The Japanese take an awful beating from American audiences when their activities are shown in American newsreels."[1] In 1938, *Time Magazine* declared Chiang Kai-shek and his popular wife, Song Mei-ling, "Man and Wife of the Year."[2] At this point, the Japanese Americans began to fear

---

[1] *Sun*, November 18, 1937, 2.
[2] K. Scott Wong, "War Comes to Chinatown: Social Transformation and the Chinese of California," in R. W. Lotchin, editor, *The Way We Really Were: The Golden State in the Second Great War* (Urbana, IL: University of Illinois Press, 2000), 171.

a backlash from this all-Asian war.[3] Ethnic politics added weight to the threat. Prior to the war, trade between the United States and Japan grew. It soon came to include US exports of crucial war-making materials, especially gasoline, oil, and scrap iron, plus machine tools, cotton, and food. In turn, Japan exported silks, food,[4] and retail goods often destined for Nikkei consumers. The war jeopardized this exchange. There wasn't much to choose between a Chinese regime that was corrupt, brutal, and militarily incompetent and an Imperial Japanese one which was corrupt, brutal, and militarily efficient.[5] Yet, as one would expect, some in both ethnic groups responded by supporting their own mother countries.

Thus, seeing their homeland in flames, Chinese Americans took to the docks, marching to prevent the export of military goods to Japan, picketing Nikkei stores, and boycotting Japanese merchants.[6] It started in November 1937. As *New World Sun* columnist "S. K." explained, "There is no doubt that the *Panay*[7] incident has stirred up the boycott agitation."[8] The Chinese on the West Coast were adamant about this national rivalry, while the Japanese were split between those who wanted to defend the fatherland and those who wished to remain neutral. The latter feared the wrath of the national government and a local backlash as well: "Anti-alien land laws, boycotts, and investigations of various types must be expected if conditions should turn for the worse," thought the *Sun*.[9] The Federal Government had just investigated the ownership of Japanese fishing boats and the Nisei took that as a word to the wise; stay neutral on the issue of the Sino Japanese War. But not all the Nikkei wanted to, criticizing American policy for putting the *Panay* in harm's way, demanding the immediate withdrawal of all American citizens from

---

[3] *Sun*, November 13, 1937, 2.

[4] For Japan's dire food shortages before and during the war see, Lizzie Collingham, *The Taste of War: World War II and the Battle for Food* (New York, NY: Penguin Books, 2011), 49–74, 228–47, 273–307.

[5] For Chiang Kai-shek and his army, see H. W. Brands, *Traitor to His Class: The Privileged Life and Radical Presidency of Franklin Delano Roosevelt* (New York, NY: Anchor Books, 2008), 729.

[6] The story of the Chinese American aid to the mother country is well told in K. Scott Wong, "War Comes to Chinatown," in Roger W. Lotchin, *The Way*, 164–86.

[7] The *Panay* was an American gunboat in the Yangtze River in China, which was bombed and strafed by Japanese airplanes. The boat was assaulted despite an American flag painted on the deck. The survivors were machine gunned in the water. Japan promptly apologized and individual Japanese did too. The Roosevelt Administration accepted the apology and considered the incident closed as a result. Brands, *Traitor*, 95–96, 505.

[8] *Sun*, November 25, 1937, 1.   [9] Ibid.

China,[10] and more shockingly, not acknowledging the atrocities of the "Sack of Nanking."[11]

In the main West Coast Chinese settlement, the struggle for power in Asia got tangled up with a tussle for urban commercial sway. Grant Avenue in San Francisco was the main artery of Chinatown, and South Grant Avenue was traditionally a part of that settlement, "our best bazaar section," said one newspaper. The Nikkei steadily encroached upon it, until by 1941 they had displaced a large number of Chinese American merchants. The *Chinese Digest* demanded in 1935, "Keep Chinatown Chinese."[12] The Chinese responded by picketing Nikkei shops, and they persuaded some of the unions to join them.

Though they would later support the Nikkei, the CIO picketed the docks.[13] The *New World Sun's* view of the matter was that the boycott was a sinister plot fronted by the communist-influenced maritime unions and communists and backed by money from Chinese merchants.[14] Tempted for a time, San Francisco Labor Council (AFL) eventually refused to endorse the boycott.[15] In San Diego, the Japanese American Citizens League (JACL) persuaded the Women's Clubs and the *San Diego Union* to oppose the boycott on silk and other Japanese goods, the Union with fifteen-inch banner headlines![16]

Though the Chinese picketed docks and besieged shops, only the government's measures against Imperial Japan in the fall of 1941 halted the Japanese trade. However, the fear of a Sino Japanese War backlash troubled Nikkei memory well into the fall of 1941. That anxiety had nothing at all to do with race, since both parties to the conflict were Asian.

[10] For the sack of Nanking by the Japanese Army see Iris Chang, *The Rape of Nanking: The Forgotten Holocaust of World War II* (New York, NY: Basic Books, 1997), 35–142ff. Japanese and Chinese national scholars remain at loggerheads over the death toll, estimating anywhere from 15,000 to 350,000 fatalities. The International Military Tribunal of the Far East put the number at 250,000. Chang, *Rape*, 4. For the argument over the episode, especially the numbers of atrocities, see D. Yang, "Convergence or Divergence? Recent Historical Writings on the Rape of Nanjing," *American Historical Review*, Vol. 104: No. 3 (June 1999), 842–65, especially 844, 850, 853.

[11] See the *Sun* for December 1937. For support of the Japanese assault, see *Sun*, column by their war correspondent Kamenosuke Suzuki, December 19, 1937, 1, "Grim tragedy of warfare and heroic fighting of brave Japanese soldiers in action on the Chinese warfront were told in the simple and colorful language of a newspaper men," by Suzuki.

[12] Wong, "War Comes to Chinatown," 170 and Charlotte Brooks, Alien Neighbors, *Foreign Friends: Asian Americans, Housing, and the Transformation of Urban California* (Chicago, IL: The University of Chicago Press, 2004), 137–9.

[13] *Sun*, November 10, 1937, 1.   [14] Ibid., November 14, 1937, 1.
[15] Ibid., December 12, 1937, 1.   [16] Ibid., December 7, 1937, 1.

It had everything to do with nationalism. Americans roundly supported one set of Asians over another, largely because of US and media policy. So those Nisei trying to shore up their standing in the face of growing national Far East tension proclaimed both their loyalty to America and their opposition to the Japanese in the China War.

One historian believes that the Nikkei were drawing closer to Japanese nationalism in the second decade of the interwar period. Supposedly, the Nikkei believed that "loyalty to Japan was not in conflict with American interests." If so, they were extraordinarily naïve. For example, the community usually turned out in force for visiting Imperial dignitaries. That included the likes of Foreign Minister Yōsuke Matsuoka, former head of the infamous South Manchurian Railway, the Japanese delegation that walked out of the League of Nations, and the architect of the Tripartite Pact between Japan, Fascist Italy, and Nazi Germany.[17] One could not have chosen a figure more likely to call their loyalty into question.

They had further reason in 1940 to avoid identifying with Japan' government. This was the dramatic Nazi victory over the Allies in Western Europe. The reputed role of fifth columnists in these victories, especially in Norway and France, put the status of aliens in the headlines and set the congressional wheels turning. Liberal Samuel Dickstein of New York State, chairman of the House Committee on Immigration and Naturalization, moved to counter the threat of supposed German and Italian subversives. To do so, he and his committee crafted the Nationality Act of 1940, derived from both liberal and conservative ideas. Dickstein intended to codify, rationalize, modernize, and systemize the oft-amended American nationality legislation. Among other things, the bill notably loosened the racial criteria for citizenship (see below), but the law also had an anti-alien intent.

Section 402 specified that if American citizens lived abroad in their parents' motherland for longer than six months, they would be considered expatriated.[18] The clause created endless bureaucratic headaches and had to be repeatedly modified in order to accommodate the needs of American diplomats, businessmen, and missionaries; yet the law remained on the books until 1945. The provision struck at the Japanese American Kibei

---

[17] Hayashi, *For the Sake*, 130–31.
[18] US House of Representatives, Seventy-Ninth Congress: First Session, *Hearings before the Subcommittee of the Committee on Immigration and Naturalization, Pursuant to H. Res. 52*, Part 5, August 31, 1945, 425. Hereinafter *Dickstein Committee; Dies Hearings*, November–December 1943, 10078.

and persons of German or Italian descent. Dickstein aimed the legislation at all potentially dangerous aliens, but the Nikkei certainly thought it was pointed straight at them.[19]

The rapid collapse of the western democracies in April, May, and June, 1940, was accompanied by bitter charges that a fifth column, especially in Norway and France, had facilitated the Nazi lightning storm. A *Rafu Shimpo* headline captured the impact: "FEAR OF 'FIFTH COLUMN' SPURS MOVEMENT TO PASS L. A. ORDINANCE," registering and fingerprinting local aliens, including 18,000 Issei.[20] The Nisei paper saw the writing on the wall in the registration forms:

> While the heat of public sentiment against potential "fifth columnists" is being directed primarily today against suspected Communists and German-American Nazis, an alarming trend in the direction of anti-Japanese and anti-Nisei feeling has been observed.[21]

The swift German victories vaulted the fifth column issue into the local political arena where both candidates for Los Angeles County District Attorney promised to do something about it. Sitting DA Buron Fitts said that his "campaign is intended to 'stop anything from happening here like has happened in Holland, Norway, or Poland.'"[22] He later promised a large Nikkei audience at the Catholic Maryknoll auditorium to take care of the problem while also praising the "exemplary citizenship" of his Nisei hosts.[23] The call to require the registration of all enemy aliens grew out of this initial surge of the "alien scare," as columnist and JACL national secretary Saburo Kido put it.[24] Los Angeles Mayor Fletcher Bowron warned against whipping up "hysteria" over the issue, but the question would not die down. If "hysteria" it was, it soon spilled over onto the Young Democrats, who set about purging their own pro-Soviet left wing under the cry that "there can be no Fifth Column in the Young Democracy."[25]

So the wars in China and Europe put the interests of the Japanese Americans – citizenship, dual citizenship, expatriation, registration, fingerprinting, fishing fleets, Bainbridge and Terminal island residence, espionage, fifth columns, and sabotage – into play. It did so one and

---

[19] *Rafu Shimpo*, June 2, 1940, 2.   [20] Ibid., June 9, 1940, 1.
[21] Ibid., June 5, 1940, 3. For the dualism, anti-fascism and anti-communism, see the remarks of Samuel Dickstein, Congressional Record, 76 Congress, 1st session, part 12, 13769–70.
[22] *Rafu Shimpo*, May 29, 1940, 1.   [23] Ibid., June 6, 1940, 1.
[24] Ibid., May 28, 1940, 1.   [25] Ibid., May 31, 1940, 1.

a half years before Pearl Harbor. The issue had to do with the calamitous defeats of the democracies of Western Europe. Maybe this "alien scare" was about nationalism, maybe about culture, maybe about ideology, maybe all three, but it was certainly not about race. All the actors on the European stage were white, but their actions made matters worse for some Californians who were not.

Conservative Democratic Congressman Martin Dies of Texas, and the revelations of his House Un-American activities Committee, was one of the prime movers behind this problem, which augmented fears of German and Italian sabotage and espionage and linked it to the Imperial Japanese espionage efforts on the West Coast. Several newspapers, including both the LAT and Hearst papers, picked this up and hammered away at the theme of Imperial Japanese spying on the West Coast and resident Nikkei aid to that effort.[26] Sometimes these concerns about spying were considered greatly exaggerated or even irrational, but some Issei groups had their own version. Although the Nikkei were never found guilty of espionage after the war began, their Imperial Japanese relatives certainly were trying. In the years just before Pearl Harbor, the Imperial Government ordered increased spying on the West Coast orchestrated by the Japanese consuls. We know this from the work of the American code breakers, who laid bare the espionage network.[27] How effective this network was is not known, but the spymasters certainly reported back home that the Japanese had agents in Los Angeles defense plants, the US Army, the Bremerton shipyards, and the Boeing plants near Seattle, working for the emperor. The consuls, in turn, were intimately connected to the American-Japanese, honoring friends of the Empire, lobbying against Roosevelt's economic measures, cooperating with the Nikkei chambers of commerce, and joining locals on ceremonial occasions. As one spy report assured Tokyo, "We shall, further-more, maintain close connections with the Japanese Association, the [Japanese] Chamber of Commerce, and the [Nikkei] newspapers." They were also working through "our own companies here" in the Seattle Area and reported that they had secured the services of a "second generation Japanese lawyer."[28]

---

[26] The Dies Report was published in the LA *Times* on January 28, 1942, but was a retrospective of its activities for a full calendar year. Special Committee on Un-American Activities of the House of Representatives, 77th Congress, First Session, *Investigation of Un-American Propaganda Activities in the United States, Hearings on H. Res. 282* (Washington, DC: US Government Printing Office, 1942), 1723–32ff.

[27] Lowman. *Magic* cited below is the source for my discussion of intelligence matters.

[28] Japanese communication is quoted in full in Lowman, *Magic*, 147–50.

None of this proves that the Nikkei actually helped the Japanese to spy, but the Imperial Japanese certainly thought so. As a modern Japanese historian put it, "The forced incarceration of Nikkei after the outbreak of war brought the United States an intelligence victory greater than the freezing of Japanese assets [in July 1941]."[29]

The war in Europe also made acute the festering issue of Japanese fishing. Pro- and anti-Nikkei had debated this question for several years, and the issue was resolved in favor of continuing to allow the mostly Issei fishing boats to operate from West Coast harbors. The problem was complicated by the fact that until at least mid-1940 Imperial Japanese company boats fished off the American West Coast, the Pacific Coast of Baja California, and in the Gulf of California. All of these company boats of Nippon Suisan Kaisya and Hayashi-Kane Shoten Kisen Kaisysa operated out of Southern California ports.[30] During their stay in the Western Hemisphere, these fleets were stationed at Los Angeles and were resupplied and reconditioned by the Nikkei of Southern California.

As the United States moved ever closer to war with Japan, that relationship necessarily became increasingly suspect to naval intelligence, to anti-Nikkei in the Southland, and to the Mexican government.[31]

Like the alien scare, other problems began before the shooting did. Government pressure began to hurt the Nikkei long before Executive Order 9066, at least as early as Roosevelt imposed the trade restrictions on Japan. The *Nichi Bei* reported in late August 1941, that Roosevelt's freeze order of July 26, 1941,[32] would put both Issei and Nisei out of work by denying Imperial Japanese goods to Japanese American wholesalers and retailers:

The Japanese Wholesale Grocers association of San Francisco freely predicts that if no goods are received within the next two months, they will have to close their doors because of the lack of goods to sell.[33]

Though this punitive diplomacy was intended to restrain Japanese aggression in the Far East, it landed hard on their relatives on the West

---

[29] The author is indebted to Professor John J. Stephan for this crucial information. Eizo Hori, Daihonei Sambo no Joho Senki [Imperial Headquarters Intelligence War Diary] (Tokyo: Bungei Shunju, 1989), 202. Citation and quote supplied to me by Professor John J. Stephan, May 7, 2012.

[30] *Rafu Shimpo*, June 11, 1940, 1.

[31] For Japanese geopolitical thinking about attacks on the United States, see J. J. Stephan, *Hawaii*, 168, ff.

[32] Brands, *Traitor*, 597, 622.   [33] *Nichi Bei*, August 22, 1941, 1.

Coast. It was the first adverse government economic action that progressively undermined the Japanese American economy, seven months before EO9066.

Between these economic measures, the Sino Japanese War, the fall of Western Europe, and worsening relations between America and Japan, the Nikkei began to worry. They spoke of the plight of the Japanese Americans and even of growing "hysteria" against them. As *Sun* columnist Ayako Noguchi put it in late September 1941, "For many years we Nisei have been enjoying the peace of this country and quite recently this peace has been threatened."[34] Within a week the JACL national secretary, Mike Masaoka, was calling on the Nikkei to fight "hysteria," and from then until December 7 that term appeared on various occasions in the Nikkei press.[35] To combat this supposed problem, in the first week of October the allies of the Nikkei established the Northern California Committee on Fair Play for Citizens and Aliens of Japanese Ancestry.[36] And yet despite all of this, the Issei remained in the good graces of the landlord community of the San Joaquin Valley at least up to May 1942.[37]

This tense period in the fall in 1941 also saw the first Nikkei press references to racism, that is, discrimination based on what could accurately be considered biological matters. As Mike Masaoka put it to the Fair Employment Practices Committee hearing in LA, "The lot of the Japanese-Americans in securing and retaining employment" is a difficult one, "largely because of certain physical characteristics" and a fear that the Japanese Americans would displace others from jobs.[38] Yet the problem of hysteria, in their minds, was not triggered by the outbreak of the Pacific War, but rather by the Sino Japanese War. A full three years and nine months before December 7, 1941, a Nikkei columnist clearly explained the connection between their fear of hysteria and the Sino Japanese War:

In these days of hysteria, [bold in the original] sound, logical arguments may fall on deaf ears. But the time is coming soon, when there will be more rational thinking as far as the Far Eastern problem is concerned.[39]

Contemporaneously, another Nikkei spoke "of the time of crisis such as the Japanese people are facing today" and of Americans "running wild" over the (Sino Japanese) war.[40] At the same time, presaging the

---

[34] *Sun*, September 10, 1941, 1; September 30, 1941, 1; October 7, 1941, 1.
[35] Ibid., September 16, 1941, 1; October 4, 1941, 1.   [36] Ibid., October 7, 1941, 1.
[37] Azuma, *Between*, 205.   [38] *Sun*, September 11, 1941, 1; October 22, 1941, 1.
[39] Ibid., February 3, 1938, 1.   [40] Ibid., January 30, 1938, 1; November 19, 1937, 2.

period from late January, 1942, the Nikkei also laid claim to the victim status. They believed that they were fighting "for fair play and against discrimination" because they upheld the Japanese side in the Sino Japanese War.[41] It is well to remember then, that the initial Nikkei claim to "fair play" did not originate with the famous Northern California committee of the same name. Rather, it surfaced in 1937 out of the Japanese Americans' attempt to avoid the unpopularity that came with espousing the territorial claims and conquests of the Tokyo fascists.

But the committee did arise from a growing sense of unease among the Nikkei and their friends. From at least the middle of 1941, more references appeared in the Nikkei press that they might be singled out. However, they were not being singled out by any kind of racial outbreak, but by the possibility of war. The *Pacific Citizen* feared a backlash against the Nikkei if war occurred, but at the same time gave the larger culture credit: "Here on the Pacific Coast public sentiment so far has been surprisingly sympathetic toward Japanese American citizens."[42] In early October the *San Francisco News*, the Scripps-Howard paper in that city, could report "no major outbreak of anti-Japanese feeling."[43] And one day before Pearl Harbor the *Sun* described the Caucasian mood as "calm," not hysterical.[44]

From the start of the Sino Japanese War I in 1937 until December 7, 1941, the Japanese Americans were claiming progress.[45] They had good reason to be. Despite interpretations that this period featured "wild rumors and tales of Japanese American treachery that had been launched over the months before Pearl Harbor,"[46] the absence of attacks in the vernacular press appear to support the assessment of the Japanese American press.[47] Things were holding up, the Japanese press thought, but a backlash was surely on the way.

---

[41] Ibid., November 27, 1937, 1.   [42] *Pacific Citizen*, September 1941, 10.

[43] Quoted in the *Sun*, October 9, 1941, 1.   [44] *Sun*, December 6, 1941, 1.

[45] *Pacific Citizen*, September 1941, 3.   [46] Robinson, *A Tragedy*, 71.

[47] Wild rumors and hysteria do not appear in the SF *Chronicle*, LA *Times*, *Los Angeles Daily News* for the six months before Pearl Harbor. Sometimes the Dies Committee reported problematical situations, but they were not wild rumors.

4

The Impact of World War II

A Multicausal Brief

The conduct of Japan and her military forces is irrelevant to the issues which the Commission [CWRIC] is considering.
Report of the Commission on Wartime Relocation and Internment of Civilians, 1982[1]

The baffling claim of the above statement is indicated by the conversion of State Senator John Harold Swan of Sacramento. He was a pre-war defender of civil liberties who had introduced a bill in April 1941 to protect California civil servants of color. Swan's bill, subsequently enacted, made it illegal to note in the civil service records anything *"indicating or suggesting in any wise or pertaining to* [emphasis added] the race,[2] color, or religion of any persons."

Yet when the war broke out, the same Senator Swan, together with Senator Jack Metzger of Red Bluff, introduced "a resolution urging special loyalty investigations of Nisei state civil-service employees."[3] Obviously, the Nisei had made pre-war progress or they would not have been in the civil service. It was the conduct of Japan and her military forces that produced this remarkable transformation of a civil rights champion of the Nisei into a foe.

Thus "the conduct of Japan and her military forces" had everything to do with relocation and internment. Before Pearl Harbor, there was no significant movement to evacuate the Nikkei from the Coast. And once the war began, every step in the relocation process was debated over how much of a war threat the "conduct of Japan and her military forces" were.

[1] *CWRIC*, 48.   [2] Note again the reference to "race" as something other than color.
[3] *Wartime Exile*, 104.

So how did the war disrupt the progress of these Nikkei? Historians have answered this question by emphasizing Executive Order 9066 (EO 9066), which authorized the removal from security zones of people thought to be dangerous, or some American failing, especially racism, greed, anti-war hysteria, or ultra-nationalism, or the persuasion of Walter Lippmann, or of behind-the-scenes manipulation of military officers like Karl Bendetsen or Allen Gullion.

While not wishing to ignore these war-related matters completely, the answer to the question of why the government decided on relocation is different. With the exception of EO9066, other things mattered more. They too were war induced, but they were different. Evacuation of Japanese Americans can only be understood as a step-by-step progressive process of political and military events and governmental responses to them. No single event or failing can explain it. Generally speaking, historians have begun this story too late. It began in December 1937, flared heavily in May 1940, subsided, only to flash again in late January 1942, and did not finally subside until March 18, 1942, when Washington made the decision to build centers into which to evacuate the Japanese.

In delineating this developmental process, one must answer several questions. First, did West Coast public opinion swing to an anti-Nikkei position because of the war or because of racism, hysteria, and greed? Second, how did the war affect military judgments about the vulnerability of the West Coast? Third, did the shift in public opinion against the Japanese Americans push the military into support for evacuation of the Japanese or did the course of the war lead them to favor evacuation on strictly national security grounds? In short, in signing EO9066 did the President act on racial or national security grounds? Finally, once the government decided to evacuate the West Coast, where would the Japanese go, to the interior on their own or into government centers?

The paradigm of racism is exceedingly appealing to contemporary historians, but to argue so is to put the effect, race, before the cause, war. To the extent that race, hysteria, and economic exploitation played a role, they were supporting ones, not leading parts. Not only were war and governmental policy the driving forces after the war commenced, but they were before the war began as well. It remains unclear why the Roosevelt Administration chose to stand in the way of Japanese ambitions to dominate China and Southeast Asia.[4] Perhaps the motivation was

---

[4] That statement is based on a scholarly lifetime of reading and more recently and specifically on H. W. Brands, *Traitor to His Class*, 477–526.

democratic; perhaps it was economic; perhaps it was nationalistic, but it was real.

Similarly, for their own reasons, the Imperial Japanese decided to attack Hawaii, Wake Island, the Philippines and other American possessions rather than simply bypassing them to seize the resources they wanted from the British, French, and Dutch empires. These two governmental policies, American and Japanese, led to war and war led to relocation. It was not, to borrow a phrase from historian H. W. Brands' discussion from another context, a "sudden racial revulsion" against the Japanese Americans that put them in centers.[5] After nearly ten weeks of disastrous losses in the Pacific, the clock ran out on the Nikkei.

A few historians of late have begun to question the validity of the race paradigm of the Nikkei story. The work of Japanese historian Masuda Hajimu, who wrote of the hostile period, from 1905 to 1913 is illustrative. He explained that "scholars who examine the role of culture – particularly racism – have tended to describe it as an ineradicable structured force, which is almost predestined."[6] This would include most American historians writing about relocation.[7] Instead he placed the explanatory burden on the ebb and flow of Imperial Japanese-US relations. When relations soured, so did domestic views of the Nikkei and Imperial Japanese views of Americans. When diplomatic relations sweetened, so did Japanese-Caucasian domestic relations. As he concluded:

Although anti-Japanese and anti-American sentiments in America and Japan respectively in 1905–1913 were for a time largely forgotten, they were abruptly and vigorously reconstructed in the mid-1920s and again in the early 1940s when the people of the two countries faced their crises, culminating in an all-out war after 1941.[8]

This dance, in turn, was heavily influenced by the blaring cacophony of the media. Hajimu's interpretation is persuasive because it tracks the movement of history, the succession of events – the Russo-Japanese War, the Alien Land Laws, immigration restriction, Japanese aggression against China, the *Panay* Incident, and finally the runup to and onset of World War II. Emphasizing a "structured," "ineradicable,"

---

[5] The phrase is H. W. Brands', "The Coils of Empire," *Diplomatic History*, Vol. 33: No. 1 (January 2009), 132.

[6] M. Hajimu, "Rumors of War: Immigration Disputes and the Social Construction of American-Japanese Relations, 1905–1913," *Diplomatic History*, Vol. 33: No. 1 (January 2009), 3, 37ff.

[7] For a historiographical discussion of interpretations, see Hayashi, *Democratising*, 1–11.

[8] Hajimu, "Rumors," Ibid.

"predestined" cultural force like racism maximizes the difficulty of achieving an understanding of cause and effect. The race paradigm, by emphasizing a universal and nebulous failing of racial bias, puts the blame on the culture which reacted to Pearl Harbor instead of on the culprits who bombed it.

The most nuanced study of FDR's EO9066 decision is contained in two books by Professor Greg Robinson. He argues that the decision to evacuate the Japanese was not based "strictly" on national security grounds. Robinson did not demonstrate that FDR expressed racial motivations when he signed the executive order, but rather that "his training, background, and personality" predisposed him to violate the Nikkei's liberties. This "training" derived from the Progressive Era, Roosevelt's time as Assistant Secretary of the Navy, and in the 1920s when Roosevelt supposedly spoke or published racist remarks, including two articles on "racial purity."[9]

To the contrary, in "Shall We Trust Japan" (1923) diplomacy, not race, was the principal subject. And the answer to the rhetorical question in the title was a resounding "yes," as Roosevelt sought to encourage American-Japanese rapprochement. FDR was highly complimentary to the "Japanese race," to Asians generally, and to recent Japanese foreign policy. His comments on race stated general American attitudes about race, *not his own*, and his remark about "racial purity" referred to possible American immigration to Asia. Here as everywhere in this story the reality of race is very complicated. He opposed Japanese immigration because he thought them "unassimilable," which in 1923 was politically correct.[10] FDR's point of view is as irenic as one could imagine, especially in view of the contemporaneous, heated battle to ban all Asians from entering America. It was a very statesmanlike, realistic, and courageous stand for a politically ambitious person at that point in American history.

In any case, what a person said in at a particular stage (1910s, 1920s) cannot explain his specific action twenty years later, as the race paradigm does. Finally, relying on Roosevelt's background, training, and personality to prove a case for racism ignores FDR's many multicultural experiences. These included his time in the New York State Legislature, dominated by the culturally pluralistic Democratic Party; his time as Assistant Secretary of the Navy, when he had to balance numerous

---

[9] Robinson, *Tragedy*, 91 and notes 1–2, p. 325.
[10] F. D. Roosevelt, "Shall We Trust Japan?" *Journal of the American Asiatic Association*, Vol. 23 (July 1923), 475–78, 526, 528.

conflicting demands for shipbuilding and basing between the polyglot North, the black, highly segregated, and white South; his witness of President Wilson's advocacy of national self-determination; his Vice Presidential candidacy in 1920; his party activism in the 1920s; and his governorship of multiethnic New York State, 1929–33. And finally they would take in his two terms as President and leader of the Democratic Party, not to mention his multi-year marriage to Eleanor Roosevelt, a champion of both African Americans and Nikkei.

Thus Roosevelt's background included many influences that would have predisposed him toward toleration rather than bias against the afflicted, not least because of his own partial paralysis. Anyway, Japanese American support for Roosevelt in the 1944 presidential election does not support the contention that the AJA thought he was a racist.[11]

A developmental interpretation is more realistic because it puts first things first and because it follows the story line more effectively. The 1940s outburst against the Nikkei occurred because, at specific points in time, it was whipped up by Pearl Harbor, and by politicians, intellectuals, elected officials, pressure groups, and pundits and tolerated by Roosevelt, but the war created the situations for them to exploit. There were specific actors, not Americans, Westerners, or Californians generally, who created the upheaval by hammering on the issue of national security.

Even when specific actors like John Costello or Martin Dies are discussed within the narrative, their motivations are made subservient to race. The race argument is largely frozen in time from the rise of scientific racism in the nineteenth century through the various crises of the twentieth. It assumes a direct connection between the former through February and March, 1942.

Milton Eisenhower, the first director of the War Relocation Authority (WRA), the government agency that administered the centers, understood relocation in a more holistic, nuanced, and multifaceted way than most of those who have explained American policy as a response to a "structured," "ineradicable," "predestined" cultural/racial force. He saw the decision as complex, the result of several competing factors, situations, and personalities. Ike's brother refused to search for scapegoats. As he put it: "Only after events had taken place could historians work their magic and reconstruct chaos into a neat, logical, linear chronology." As he continued: "At the time, many forces were at work –

[11] *Rocky Shimpo*, July 5, 1944, 1.

military, political, economic, emotional, and racial." One must add the importance of governmental policy, the significance of religion, and the role of individuals to Eisenhower's list, but his interpretation certainly restores the complexity of that history.

All too often historians have rejected this messy, multi-causal, nuanced, and complicated understanding of history for a one-dimensional predestined, racial explanation. Although their aims and behavior were obviously nationalistic, the Fascist Imperial Japanese framed the conflict as a race war, including their interpretation of American treatment of the Nikkei.[12] The fact that the modern historians' race assumption agrees with the Axis explanation of what the Far Eastern conflict was all about (i.e. race), is an irony that has yet to be fully recognized.[13]

---

[12] For the Fascist Japanese racial interpretation, see the *Tokyo Times*, from December 1941 through March 1942.

[13] For an imaginative, challenging, but unconvincing attempt to link the Japanese American experience to the Koreans under Japan, see Takashi Fujitana, *Race for Empire: Koreans as Japanese and Japanese as Americans* (Berkeley, CA: University of California Press, 2011), ix–xvii.

5

The Lagging Backlash

But for the Nikkei, the most astonishing thing about December 7 was the lagging backlash. Remarkably enough, it remained largely in abeyance for another seven weeks, until January 25, 1942. Instead of a hysterical response, the exact reverse occurred. Even the December 15 alarmist report on Pearl Harbor of Secretary of the Navy Frank Knox did not bring a reaction. Knox described no sabotage or espionage, but in a follow-up news conference the press quoted him as saying that very "effective Fifth Column work" had occurred.[1] Yet public sentiment remained overwhelmingly pro-Nikkei.

The newspapers, public officials, ministers, University administrators, professors, the Fair Play Committee, and others spoke out. They called for equitable treatment, insisting that the Japanese attack on Pearl Harbor was the work of the Fascist mother country and should not reflect on the Japanese Americans.

That response was one of the most heartening events of the war, and it presents an important challenge to the race paradigm. If America was so suffused with racism – West Coast racism, United States racism, racism of the West, racism of California, white American racism – how does one explain this support and its persistence, noted by many scholars, up to January 25, 1942?[2]

This lack of animus was despite the fact that the various prewar Japanese language newspapers in California often championed the Axis

---

[1] M. Eisenhower, *The President Is Calling* (Garden City, NY: Doubleday and Company, Inc., 1974), 100.
[2] Grodzins, *Americans Betrayed*, 377ff.

cause in Asia.[3] While the LAT and other mainstream English language newspapers refrained from baiting either the Japanese or the Japanese Americans, according to editor Togo Tanaka of LA-based *Rafu Shimpo*, the Japanese language press gave vent to "vicious anti-American expressions."[4] On December 7 the papers immediately changed their tune to pro-American, and the government closely supervised what they would print until all ceased publication in May 1942.

Nonetheless, despite the delayed backlash, the Nikkei were hurt by the post-December 7 roundup of dangerous aliens and other government actions. On December 8 the state authorities began checking all "Japanese operated automobiles" on the San Francisco Bay and Antioch bridges.[5] Simultaneously, the government detained all Japanese, German, or Italian aliens suspected of disloyalty and sent them off to true internment camps. Their story is beyond the scope of this book, but this roundup was not aimed specifically at the Japanese Americans. Nevertheless, it hit that community hard because it included several thousand males. These were generally fathers and husbands, so their loss was heavily felt by all the Nikkei.

The feared invasion that haunted the mind of Secretary Stimson seemed to portend on the remote Hawaiian island of Nihau. On December 7 a Japanese Zero pilot crash landed there, and with the help of a Nisei male, intimidated local residents until the pilot was killed by a Hawaiian.[6] It did not establish what the 157,000–160,000 Nikkei in the Greater Hawaiian Islands would have done in case of a broader invasion. But there were overseas colonies of Japanese throughout Southeast Asia, and these welcomed the Imperial Japanese Fascist occupiers. As historian David Lowman put it:

What happened in the countries overrun by Japan was not encouraging. In China, Hong Kong, and Southeast Asia the resident Japanese had sided completely with the attacking Japanese armed forces. Moreover, the conquering troops treated all resident Japanese as reunited brethren rather than part of the local population, and this was more than reciprocated by the local Japanese when they welcomed the troops with flags and nationalistic fervor. In the Philippines there were about 30,000 Japanese residents on Mindanao Island alone, almost all of whom

[3] The best sources for this are the Japanese American papers, like *Rafu Shimpo*, but see also the excellent B. Masaru Hayashi, *"For the Sake,"* 132ff.

[4] T. Mizuno, "Self-Censorship by Coercion: The Federal Government and the California Japanese-Language Newspapers from Pearl Harbor to Internment," *American Journalism* (Summer 2000), 31–57.

[5] *Sacramento Bee*, December 8, 1941, 22.   [6] J. J. Stephan, *Hawaii*, 168.

appeared to have completely gone over to the invaders, offering to serve as guides and interpreters, or be useful in other ways.[7]

Lowman summed up the disturbing information that the hard-pressed Roosevelt Administration was looking at as the relocation story unfolded on the mainland. That development seemed to be the writing on the wall and the context into which the minor incident in Nihau was put.

That context grew directly out of the dreadful course of the war up to the issuance of Executive Order 9102, as the Imperial Japanese simply swept aside every individual or collective Allied force. Pearl Harbor was an astounding feat of arms even if the Japanese had stopped there, but they did not. The next day they destroyed most of the American Far Eastern Air Force on the tarmac of its Philippines air base. In December, Japanese submarines torpedoed several tankers right off the coast of California. On December 10, 1941 to add insult to injury, they destroyed the British battle cruiser and battleship, *Repulse* and *Prince of Wales*, by air attack.[8] They next swept down the island of Luzon in the Philippines to bottle up and begin to strangle the American and Filipino army on the Bataan Peninsula. Earlier they had moved into the East Indies (now Indonesia) on January 11, 1942, with an airborne assault on Borneo and quickly subdued that resource-rich East Indies archipelago.

Simultaneously, the Japanese fought their way down the Malay Peninsula to capture Singapore on February 15, 1942, with many fewer soldiers than the number of men defending it. At the Battle of the Java Sea, February 27, 1942, the Japanese destroyed four Allied capital ships in one encounter. All of this happened on top of the terrifying Nazi parachute attacks on Norway and the Netherlands, the blitzkrieg rout of the famed French army in the spring and summer of 1940, and the gargantuan, murderous thrust of the Wehrmacht into Russia on June 22, 1941.

To people at the time, these were astonishing, and more importantly, *unprecedented feats* [italics added] of arms which the Axis had mastered and the Allies had not. Blitzkrieg changed many of the rules of land warfare overnight, and the use of airborne (vertical envelopment) changed them again. Likewise, the sinking of the British capital ships altered the rules of naval warfare at a single blow.

After World War I reached its sanguinary end, admirals of all nations had argued about the fighting potential of battleships versus carrier-based

[7] Lowman, *Magic*, 9ff.
[8] M. J. Lyons, *World War II: A Short History* (Boston, MA: Prentice Hall, 2010), 149.

airplanes. The destruction of two of Britain's great ships of war by Fascist Japanese airplanes seemed spectacularly to settle this debate in favor of carrier-borne airpower. Announced in alarming, bold headlines just three days before Executive Order 9066, the loss of the Singapore fortress, a state of the art bastion, confounded everyone.[9] Booster cities like San Francisco, seeking to capture naval resources to stimulate urban growth, could think of no higher aspiration than to call themselves the "American Singapore."[10] And yet the British one had fallen with hardly a struggle.[11]

Perhaps most alarming to West Coast residents, already in a state of shock over Pearl Harbor, was the sinking of American merchantmen in December, off the coast where the population and defense industry were heavily concentrated. America's first line of defense was supposed to be its Navy standing guard on its two-ocean moat, and yet Japanese Fascist submarines were assaulting American ships within sight of shore.

One sinking was especially shocking. Sometime after Pearl Harbor, just before dawn, the small city of San Luis Obispo was startled by a terrific "explosion off the coast that awakened the whole town." Residents tumbled out of bed and down to the seashore to learn that a Japanese submarine had just sunk an American tanker. "The crowd stayed down there talking about the thing, and when it got light, along came another tanker and up came a submarine in front of the whole town and sunk it right there."[12]

One of Earl Warren's lawyer friends from that city asked the local air base commander if it could protect them from further harm and was told it could not. So Abe Brazil called Attorney General Earl Warren to see if he had better news.

Warren did not; he had worse news. When Warren asked Admiral John Greenslade, Commandant of the Twelfth Naval District in San Francisco, if the coast was really that defenseless, that officer answered yes: "Confidentially, I have only two destroyers between here and Vancouver, British Columbia," he told Warren, "All the rest of the fleet that was not sunk at Pearl Harbor has gone out into the Pacific."[13]

---

[9] SF *Chronicle*, February 16, 1942, sec. I, 1.
[10] For the competition for military resources see R. W. Lotchin, *Fortress California, 1910–1961: From Warfare to Welfare* (New York, NY: Oxford University Press, 1992), 44, 74ff.
[11] In the end blitzkrieg, carrier, and airborne warfare were not as revolutionary as their first striking uses seemed to promise.
[12] Warren, *Conversations*, 1–2; Warren, *Memoirs*, 146.   [13] Ibid.

Historians of the Nikkei pay scant attention to these astonishing military losses. When they do, they treat this shocking military collapse as primarily a catalyst for white racism which triggered anti-war hysteria, a gateway to white greed (Manzanar plaque), and a rationalization for the centers. Yet it would have been fundamentally unrealistic to have ignored all of this military misfortune. Although the military leaders later assured the Tolan Hearings that an invasion of the West Coast was not possible, they also stated that an *air assault* was. Of course, that is exactly what the disastrous Pearl Harbor attack was, and even a partially successful air strike on the coast would have lit a firestorm.

Mayor Fiorello LaGuardia of New York City, national head of Civil Defense, and Eleanor Roosevelt, his second in command, warned of this danger of an "air attack" forcefully on December 10. They made a dramatic flight to LA "through rain and fog to warn the public they must take the Japanese more seriously."[14] His subordinates, John DeWitt, John Greenslade, and General Jacob Fickel, commandant of Hamilton Field north of San Francisco, stoked it by alarming statements that Japanese attacks were "imminent" and that "enemy planes" had actually flown over San Francisco the night after Pearl Harbor.[15] So the gloomy military situation up to the June 4, 1942, Battle of Midway provided the military component to the explanation of relocation. Just before Executive Order 9066 was drawn up, the outlook was bleak.

With the exception of Brian Hayashi,[16] most of the histories of Japanese American relocation have minimized this military context and treated their subject as simply a pretext for a massive civil rights violation. The American Civil Liberties Union (ACLU) eventually decided that evacuation was the greatest civil rights violation in American history.[17] Yet if it was a civil rights infringement, it occurred within a military context and that context cannot be divorced from that violation. West Coast residents were ultimately accused of "wartime hysteria." It would be much more accurate to say that they were very afraid and with very good reason.

Fear generated quick action. Even before the fires at Pearl Harbor had cooled, the FBI and other government agencies swooped down on the

---

[14] *Sacramento Bee*, December 10, 1941, 12.
[15] *Los Angeles Daily News*, December 9, 1941, 1, 23.
[16] Hayashi, *Democratizing the Enemy: The Japanese American Internment* (Princeton, NJ: Princeton University Press, 2004), 79–81.
[17] Grodzins, *Americans Betrayed*, 373–4.

alien communities to arrest those considered dangerous. They were taken to true internment camps run by the Justice Department, in Missoula, Montana; Bismarck, North Dakota, and Lordsburg, New Mexico. From that point onward, the national state lurched toward relocation without a set policy for the Nikkei minority nor a single set of policymakers to implement it. This lack of clarity would illustrate the government component of a complex explanation.

It might not have been inevitable to evacuate the Japanese Americans. But to prevent it would have required prompt and vigorous action by a president much distracted by the war. Roosevelt had to rally public support for the war, explain why he considered Europe the primary threat to America, despite the attack in the Pacific, and mobilize a reluctant business community whom he had systematically alienated since his class attacks in the 1936 election onwards.[18] He had a lot of other crucial matters demanding his attention besides the fate of the Nikkei.[19]

Lack of leadership is often offered as a reason for evacuation,[20] and that is probably true, but it would have been difficult for FDR to exercise that guidance in the context of the time. So the president let the Japanese American story slip from his grasp. That left the narrative to lesser politicians, media, pundits, and pressure groups. They were only too happy to compose it. It is often remarked that the press creates the first interpretations of history, and this media was no exception. Still, they could not have done so without the awful news from the fighting fronts. And almost every day there was more.[21]

By the end of February, the Japanese U-boats were even shelling shore installations, like the oil refinery at Ellwood, near Santa Barbara. This attack inflicted minimal damage on the refinery, but had a startling effect on West Coast imaginations. Two nights later (February 25) the Army Air Corps thought it discovered unidentified airplanes over Los Angeles, and anti-aircraft guns opened up on them full blast. Air wardens hastened to

---

[18] J. Maolo, *Cry Havoc: How the Arms Race Drove the World to War, 1931–1941* (New York, NY: Basic Books, 2010), 373–85: A. Herman, *Freedom's Forge: How American Business Produced Victory in World War II* (New York, NY: Random House, 2012), 64–84.

[19] Roosevelt's hostility to Japan is discussed at length by Greg Robinson, *By Order of the President* (Cambridge, MA: Harvard University Press, 2001), 8–44ff, especially 44.

[20] US Congress, 98th Congress: 2nd session, Subcommittee on Administration, Law, and Governmental Relations, Committee of the Judiciary, *House, Japanese American and Aleutian Relocation* (Washington, DC: Government Printing Office, 1984), 822.

[21] D. M. Kennedy, *The American People in World War II* (New York, NY: Oxford University Press, 1999), 102.

their posts as the well-organized Los Angeles civil defense organization swung into action. The military ultimately found no hostile aircraft and the responsibility for the "event" was still in doubt by the time General DeWitt began implementing EO9066.[22] Historians have ridiculed this "Great Los Angeles Air Raid" ever since it happened, as an example of the prevailing jitters gripping the West Coast.[23]

Perhaps "jitters" is a bit too weak a word to describe an urban populace sitting amidst an immense defense establishment – aircraft factories, shipbuilding, headquarters, aeronautical laboratories, test ranges, naval bases, and university nuclear research facilities, with sirens wailing, searchlights probing the night skies and exploded and unexploded antiaircraft shrapnel falling onto their streets, rooftops, and front yards. The Japanese certainly did not consider any of this a laughing matter. The assumption that an air raid on LA was possible was confirmed by the military authorities and by a prewar statement by a spokesman of the Japanese Navy Office who said that in case of war, "air raids on the enemy's territory will take place."[24]

In early January 1942, the *Tokyo Times and Advertiser*, the English language mouthpiece of the fascist Japanese government, called December, 1941, "The Month that Transformed the World."[25] The editors followed that sweeping assessment with one even more brash in an article entitled "Can the United States Be Invaded?" They answered confidently: "The plain truth is that the contention that the United States cannot be invaded is a myth – as much a myth as that the Maginot line could not be taken." The *Times* boasted: "We propose to fight this war until our enemy is crushed even if we have to go half way around the globe to do so."[26] And this threat of invasion by the *Times* was reprinted in coast newspapers and thus was known on the West Coast.[27] The paper

[22] A. C. Verge, *Paradise Transformed: Los Angeles during the Second World War* (Dubuque, IA: Kendall/Hunt Publishing Company 1993), 32–3. Abbreviations to save space.

[23] J. Smith, "The Great Los Angeles Air Raid," in John and L. Caughey, *Los Angeles: Biography of a City* (Berkeley, CA: University of California Press, 1976; Paperback ed., 1977), 364–6.

[24] *Sun*, October 17, 1941, 1.

[25] *Tokyo Times and Advertiser*, January 8, 1942, 6. Hereinafter *Tokyo Times*. The *Times* did not specify sections.

[26] *Tokyo Times*, January 9, 1942, 6.

[27] *Sacramento Bee*, January 8, 1942. However, had the press of the coast been hysterical, the story would have appeared on p. 1 instead of p. 17 in this paper published during the heart of anti-Nikkei agitation. Hysteria does not flourish on p. 17.

went on to brag of what the residents of San Luis Obispo needed no reminder:

The fighting craft of Japan's glorious Navy have already carried the war almost to the shadows of the Golden Gate. Air attack alarms have been sounded in many Pacific Coast cities, bringing panic among the frightened citizenry.[28]

With the benefit of hindsight, we now believe that the coast had little to fear from invasion. Yet given the record of the two fleets, which claim would have seemed more credible in January, 1942? As noted, *as late as February 10, 1942*, [emphasis added], Secretary Stimson believed an invasion was possible.

These defeats had a terrible cumulative effect on West Coast public opinion. It grew progressively afraid and increasingly worried about internal sabotage, espionage, and outright military assault on West Coast cities. The military especially stressed the "effectiveness of sabotage activities in the European Theater."[29] The roundup in December of the dangerous persons had somewhat diminished any chance of sabotage, but that was not immediately known to the general public or to the pundits.

General DeWitt's Final Report stressed the importance of shore-to-ship communications to explain the national security rationale for evacuation. There are two contrasting accounts of this activity. David Lowman, a trained American intelligence analyst, argued that according to military intelligence *the government did have* [emphasis added], the Japanese were operating off the coast of California with help from onshore. In the days after Pearl Harbor, "many hundreds of shore to ship communications through blinking lights" were reported. In 1944, the Federal Communications Commission reported that "there were no illicit radio transmissions," a matter that historians have duly noted. But this report was published more than two years later, and the intelligence that the military possessed at the time of EO9066 said the exact reverse.

On the outbreak of war, the FCC was bogged down in tracing hundreds of reports of illicit transmissions and "it was months ... before it was determined that illicit transmissions were not the problem that they were once thought to be." When General DeWitt wrote his Final Report to explain relocation, he did not yet have this information. The hard

---

[28] *Tokyo Times*, January 9, 1942, 6. The *Tokyo Times* presented a much more sophisticated analysis of the calamitous defeats of the Allies than historians of relocation have yet attempted. For statements of extreme Axis-Japanese designs on US territory, see J. J. Stephan, *Hawaii*, 1–11ff.

[29] Warren, *Memoirs*, 147.

information (from the FBI, MID, and ONI) that he did have was that "illicit signaling by shore radios to offshore Japanese naval units was rampant in Hawaii."[30]

The contrasting report from the CWRIC holds that the FCC found *"minimal"* [emphasis added] unauthorized shore-to-ship communications and that these were communicated to DeWitt on January 9, 1942. But the FCC also admitted that "minimal" would have included "ten to twenty-five cases of reasonably probable illegal operation of radio sending sets on the entire Pacific Coast."[31] So even if we privilege the CWRIC version over Lowman's account, that still leaves enough transmissions to have helped in the attacks or sinkings of five merchantmen and the submarine shelling of a Goleta/Ellwood refinery on February 24.[32]

If General DeWitt had read the FCC reports of January 9, he would not have believed them anyway. As he pointed out, it was devilishly difficult to catch signalers and one signal might wreak havoc, even if "999" were chimerical.[33] Incidentally, the now well known meeting on January 9, between DeWitt and James Rowe was not about race; it was about reconciling civil liberties and military necessity. Finally, the FCC refutation of DeWitt is not convincing anyway. If Japanese submarines could sink American ships within sight of land in broad daylight, they most certainly could have sneaked agents onshore under cover of darkness.

We have to understand and explain western motivations in the context of the times. Historians have emphasized that no known act of sabotage or espionage had ever been tied to the Nikkei in the western United States. Westerners had a ready answer to that critique. As a participant at the Tolan Hearings pointed out, no act of sabotage or espionage had been known in Hawaii before Pearl Harbor either. Even if the civilians had been informed of the opinions of the military experts, they clearly did not trust and openly scoffed at those military professionals because of their failures at Pearl Harbor and in the Far East.[34]

Civilians said over and over again that they did not intend to allow another Pearl Harbor on the West Coast. Not only were the military in Hawaii unprepared, so were the American authorities in the Philippines. The loss of American aircraft on December 8, 1941, would seem to have

---

[30] Lowman, *Magic*, 94–95; DeWitt, *Final Report*, 4.   [31] CWRIC, 63.

[32] Bosworth, *America's Concentration Camps*, 94.

[33] Transcript of a conference between DeWitt and Jame Rowe, January 4, 1942, Western Defense Command records, UNC microfilm copy, 7–8.

[34] Grodzins, *Americans Betrayed*, 73.

been more a matter of chance than military bungling. Still, American authorities consistently underestimated the threat of Japanese invasion of the islands and were therefore equally unprepared for that eventuality.[35]

West Coast civilians had more than Pearl Harbor to think about. Civilian authorities were not discussing racial theory or the "Yellow Peril"; they were discussing impending military assaults on the West Coast by an Axis power, fresh from an epic string of them. The military doubted the possibility of an invasion, but not of a raid. And after Pearl Harbor and the Philippines, a raid did not seem like such an inconsequential matter.

In a sense the argument over military necessity accepts a distinction, erroneous in wartime, between military and civilian realms. Most commentators accept that by the crucial period beginning on January 25, 1942, there were strong political forces building on the coast against the Nikkei, and the West Coast congressional delegation was not the least of them. The President was rightly worried at this early stage about public support for the war. He could not allow that situation to spin out of control. He was losing badly on the fighting fronts; he could not afford to lose public support for the war as well. *Maintaining* that mainland political support was a military necessity.

And the hard evidence at the time pointed to the unsettling conclusion that the local Japanese were capable of both espionage and sabotage. The most professional handlers of intelligence in the crucial period between Pearl Harbor and EO9066 were the FBI and Army and Navy intelligence. Of these, the FBI agents in coast cities were split over the espionage and sabotage potential of the Nikkei, and Director J. Edgar Hoover hedged on the matter as well. Frank Shivers, "The F.B.I.'s Special Agent in Charge in Hawaii," told the Roberts Commission that in case of a Japanese assault on Hawaii, "I think you could expect 95% of alien Japanese to glory in that attack and to do anything they could to further the efforts of the Japanese forces."[36]

The Office of Naval Intelligence (ONI) was convinced of the sabotage and espionage threat of the Japanese Americans. This included Kenneth D. Ringle, a Navy intelligence officer in Southern California, who is often

---

[35] For conditions in these camps, see F. B. Cogan, *Captured: The Internment of American Civilians in the Philippines, 1941–1945* (Athens, GA: The University of Georgia Press, 2000), 25–32.

[36] *CWRIC*, 58.

cited as one intelligence professional who did not agree with the majority of the ONI. But even Ringle did not disagree that the Nikkei were a threat, only over whether or not the threat should be handled by evacuation. He emphatically concurred that espionage was long standing. As he said, "Espionage has been going forward for many years." He continued:

As long as this colony [Terminal Island], which contains known alien sympathizers, even though of American citizenship, is allowed to exist in the heart of every activity in the Los Angeles Harbor, it must be assumed that items such as the above [convoys, shipbuilding, aircraft shipment, military cargo, dry dock activity, base defenses,] are known, observed, and transmitted to the enemy quickly and easily.[37]

His estimate is confirmed by the report of Curtis Munson, who shortly before the war was given the task of reporting, through a third party, on the Japanese American situation to Roosevelt. Munson emphatically stated that the Japanese were not enough of a threat to justify evacuation. Still, he thought that espionage was quite possible: "They [Japanese agents] will be in a position to pick up information on troop, supply, and ship movements from the local Japanese."[38] Of course, that is exactly the kind of information that was crucial to the Imperial Japanese navy in attacking Pearl Harbor. The same thing could be said of Bainbridge Island, in Seattle Harbor, which sits amidst Puget Sound, below its mouth and almost adjacent to the crucial Bremerton and other shipyards and the myriad defense works of the Thirteenth Naval District.[39]

Ringle also thought that 25 percent or 28,000 of the Nikkei "were of doubtful loyalty," that 3,500 might act as spies, and that 1,500 Kibei should be placed in detention, whether citizens or not.[40] Army intelligence shared these views. The most recent Army intelligence that Stimson received (January 21, 1942) before the EO9066 decision, said that "their espionage net containing Japanese aliens, first and second generation Japanese and other nationals is now thoroughly organized and working underground."[41] So whether or not any Nikkei had been convicted after Pearl Harbor is beside the point. The key military professionals and

[37] Lowman, *Magic*, 77.   [38] CWRIC, 53.
[39] That Bainbridge Island was actually considered more important than Terminal Island was indicated by the fact that it was evacuated a week before the latter. "Composite Chronology," WRA, Jerome Records, MC 452, Box 1, Griswold Papers, MC 733, series 1, Box 3, Folder 14, and War Relocation Authority, "Semi-Annual Report, January 1 to June 30, 1945," Special Collections, University of Arkansas. Hereafter "Composite Chronology." See also *CWRIC*, 60, 109.
[40] Lowman, *Magic*, 76–7.   [41] Lowman, *Magic*, 76–7, 79–80.

many civilian ones as well believed that espionage and sabotage were both possible and ongoing. And these were the estimates passed on to the decision makers before EO9066.

Those decision makers had plenty to worry about because the espionage/sabotage argument had another important dimension. Part of the reason that no Nikkei was ever convicted of espionage or sabotage in a court of law was that, during the critical period, government at all levels, plus neighbors, were keeping careful watch over them.

As Kenneth D. Ringle confirms, the government had reduced the sabotage potential to 20 percent through extensive protective measures; nonetheless, he also documented extensive potential sabotage targets in LA harbor.[42] Even if they had been caught red handed in espionage or sabotage, the government could not have prosecuted them anyway. The famous *Chicago Tribune* case of 1942 explains why. A *Tribune* reporter (hostile to FDR) published information that the American forces at Midway had advance knowledge of Japanese battle strategy. This information was obtained by American code breakers. If the Navy had prosecuted the reporter, the existence of the code breaking would have come out in court. So the *Tribune* got off because the Navy had to protect its own sources and by the same token the government could not prosecute any other spy whose activity would reveal such sources.[43] So this was a further part of both the military and political components of a complex explanation.

The espionage part of the explanation of relocation needs further study. The fact that spies were not caught is no proof that spying was not occurring. The famous British double agent Zig Zag remained undetected in Germany and the continent for several years. So did the British double agents who helped to perpetrate the Operation Fortitude ruse on German intelligence, who never discovered it.[44] And as the CWRIC itself admitted, it was quite possible that the Japanese continued their spying during the war by using Caucasian front men, whose activities would arouse less attention than Asians would.[45] That is also what Professor

[42] K. D. Ringle, "Japanese Menace on Terminal Island, San Pedro, California," Report, February 7, 1942, 4, in Lowman, *Magic*, 328.
[43] Dina Goren, "Communication Intelligence and the Freedom of the Press: The *Chicago Tribune's* Battle of Midway Dispatch and the Breaking of the Japanese Naval Code," *Journal of Contemporary History*, Vol. 16: No. 4 (October 1981), 663–90.
[44] B. Macintyre, *Double Cross: The True Story of the D-Day Spies* (New York, NY: Crown Publishers, 2012), 1–28ff; B. Macintyre, *Agent Zig Zag* London: Bloomsbury, 2007), 1–20ff. The insight about the archives is John Stephan's.
[45] CWRIC, 59.

Azuma found, as the Imperial Japanese shifted their espionage away from Nikkei and to other "citizens of foreign extraction aliens, communists, Negroes, labor union members, and anti-semites."[46] This entire aspect of the problem may not be clarified until more government archives are opened.[47]

In any case, wars are not civil rights exercises, where one side wins or is convicted in a court of law. They are military and political struggles where one side wins or loses on the battlefield and in the court of public opinion. We cannot be certain that an absolute majority of Americans or even West Coast residents ever favored mass evacuation of the Japanese.[48] Yet we can be certain that in the court of opinion, among major public figures, they had lost the verdict. Before the war Japanese espionage certainly was going on, directed by the consulates, and these were tied to the Japanese communities in countless ways. And the ties between the Nikkei, Japanese businesses, the consuls, and espionage were the very kind of damning and incontrovertible evidence that the Nikkei baiters like Martin Dies and John Costello were dying to get their hands on.[49]

The perceived Nikkei peril was worsened by the lack of planning for enemy alien control, another part of the governmental explanation. The Japanese conflict was foreseen many years in advance, but the Administration had done virtually nothing to prepare the West Coast for the eventuality. As early as the mid-thirties, FDR had planned to round up dangerous aliens but had not planned beyond that. Los Angeles authorities asked him to prepare programs to insure the loyalty of the Nikkei, and his government had not responded.[50]

Unwittingly, some California Japanese Americans had hitherto contributed to this uncertainty by following the Axis-Japanese line in foreign policy. So did those in Hawaii.[51] Since the United States supported China in the (1937) Sino Japanese War, that meant that these Nikkei opposed American policy in the Far East. Those on the West Coast usually did so very carefully, speaking from the high ground, but they backed the Axis Japanese nonetheless. In 1937 they opposed the boycott of Japanese silk products, because it would damage trade. "Among Asiatic countries that buy American goods, Japan buys fifty percent of all the commodities

---

[46] Azuma, *Between*, 266, n. 80. This passage is based on Record Group 38 of the ONI, National Archives and agrees with the research of David Lowman.
[47] The information about the Archives is Professor John Stephan's.
[48] Grodzins, *Americans Betrayed*, 112, 209, 221.
[49] See *Dies Hearings*, 1942, 1723–31.   [50] *Dies Hearings*, June and July 1943, 9201.
[51] Stephan, *Hawaii*, 27–30.

America sells," said *Rafu Shimpo*.[52] During the nearly two-month long, gruesome "Rape of Nanking,"[53] *Rafu Shimpo* accused the Chinese government of "hysterical war preparation," and contrasted that behavior to "the sagacious attempts of Japan toward conciliation."[54] All this led an anti-Nikkei Seattle publisher at the Tolan Hearings to wonder why the papers "have not denounced the depredations and enslavement by Japan of the Chinese, the Koreans and other Asiatics?"[55]

Instead, for several years, the Nikkei press supported the contemporary Japanese assault on North China and called the Chinese "terrorists."[56] This press praised "Nippon's crusade [that] has brought undeniable assurance of order and effective administrative rule over a vast area in North China."[57] They upheld the Japanese conquest of Manchuria; they opposed the dispatch of American aid to Chiang Kai-shek's Chungking government, and when the Nazis invaded the Soviet Union, the papers opposed sending American lend lease materiel through the port of Vladivostok to the beleaguered Russians. The Imperial Japanese government thought gasoline sent to that Siberian port could be used by American bombers in case of a war against Japan and would threaten Japanese interests in Manchuria.[58]

As war with America drew closer in 1940, *Rafu Shimpo* upheld the Japanese "new order" in Asia and deplored the misguided efforts of the US to stand in the way.[59] The paper went on to defend Japanese bombing of Chunking and to accuse the Chiang Kai-shek government of being "communist controlled."[60] In response to further complaints about Japanese aerial bombing of cities, a later issue quoted the Japanese authorities that "Japan was engaged in a war not a picnic."[61] In another column the paper carried an argument by a Japanese American which accused earlier US foreign policies of stabbing the Imperial Japanese in the back and another quoting a Nazi publicity agent blaming the war in Europe on

---

[52] *Rafu Shimpo*, December 24, 1937, 1.
[53] For the rape of Nanking, see Chang, *The Rape*.
[54] *Rafu Shimpo*, December 24, 1937. Where page numbers are not provided, they are not available. For Issei pro Japan politics, see also Hayashi, *For the Sake*, 127–47.
[55] *Tolan Hearings, Portland and Seattle*, pt. 30, 11536.
[56] *New World News*, November 17, 1937, 1; November 19, 1937, 1; November 18, 1937, 2; November 22, 1937, 1; December 20, 1937, 1. This pro-Japan stance continued up to the fall of 1941, when some editors began to back off of the argument and side with US policy.
[57] *Rafu Shimpo*, December 24, 1937, 1.
[58] *Nichi Bei*, August 20, 22, 23, 24, 1941, p. 1 in every case.
[59] *Rafu Shimpo*, July 7, 1940, 5.   [60] Ibid., July 7, 1940, 1.   [61] Ibid., July 14, 1940, 5.

the British.[62] Another urged on the Nazi war against Great Britain.[63] American immigrant groups have traditionally upheld their own father-land's foreign policies, but defending Nazi Germany and Axis Japan in 1937–41 was tempting fate. Japan's assault on China was very unpopular in America.

Although some Japanese American newspapers backed off of the pro-Japan line as war approached, many Nisei and most Issei held to that line even after Pearl Harbor. According to historian Brian Hayashi, who studied the Topaz, Manzanar, and Poston centers, "backing Japan" "probably" characterized "the majority at Manzanar, Poston, and Topaz."[64] One can certainly understand the plight of the Nikkei, but supporting Japan at this point confronted the government with a considerable predicament.

So did the Japanese intimate, long-standing cultural, social, religious, political, and economic bindings. The Empire frequently exploited the Issei on the West Coast and in Hawaii for their own imperial purposes. The American Issei did not go quite that far, seeing themselves in an "interstitial position," between two empires. They stressed the common-alities of both nations and tried to behave accordingly. Professor John J. Stephan saw the Hawaiian Japanese in somewhat the same position, tied to both sides of the Pacific, but more firmly to Hawaii.[65] The most explosive cultural bond was through the Kibei. Whether they were more important than the foreign-educated German or Italian second generation is not known, but they were numerous and well publicized.

The Kibei had perfectly understandable reasons for returning to the homeland, to appreciate the language, culture, and spirit of Japan.[66] Harold Jacoby found the Kibei a complex lot, some pro-Japanese and some not, including those brave men who used their crucial language skills in the Pacific War on behalf of the United States.[67] Nonetheless, their continual shuffling back and forth to Japan prior to the war made them suspect when hostilities began. Until at least 1943 many Nikkei were dual

[62] Ibid., July 14, 1940, 5.
[63] *Sun*, September 28, 1941, 1; October 5, 1941, 1; October 17, 1941, 1; October 19, 1941, 1; October 27, 1941, 1.
[64] B. Masaru Hayashi, *Democratizing the Enemy: The Japanese American Internment* (Princeton: Princeton University Press, 2004), 121–2.
[65] Stephan, *Hawaii*, 6. 11.   [66] *Rafu Shimpo*, June 2, 1940, 5.
[67] Harold Stanley Jacoby, *Tule Lake* (Grass Valley, CA: Comstock Bonanza Press, 1996), 28–9, 31, 72, 86–7, 107–8. Carey McWilliams echoed Jacoby's point that the Kibei were a complex lot. *Japanese Evacuation: Interim Report*, 37. D. Lowman, *Magic*, 14, 16ff rated them much more of a threat.

citizens of the United States and Japan, although many were moving away from that state. Morton Grodzins estimated that 25 percent of Nikkei were dual citizens as late as 1943.[68] David Lowman and John Stephan put the figure at 50–60 percent.[69] In any case, dual citizenship was an inflammatory issue for wartime Americans. And that was not simply hysteria. Even the moderate Kenneth D. Ringle thought that the Kibei were the "most dangerous class of persons of the Japanese race in the United States."[70]

The Nikkei had equally close economic ties to Japan. Many of them worked for Japanese companies, perhaps several thousand, and they served as middle men for much of the commerce with the Orient. When the Roosevelt Administration's export bans began to threaten trade with the Japanese, in July 1940, *Rafu Shimpo* complained that "scores of representatives and firms" of West Coast Nikkei would be damaged if America banned the export of "precision tools and machinery." A headline proclaimed: "Ban on Machine Tool Exports Deals Blow to Nippon Traders Here":

Machinery under ban [by the US] has been purchased in huge quantities during the past year by Japan, for the industrial development of Manchoukuo [sic] and China as well as for the use of Japanese domestic needs.[71]

In addition, by mid-1940, Japanese fleets often fished the waters of Southern California, Baja California, and the Gulf of California. Likewise, the Japan Society was lobbying for both the Nikkei and Imperial Japan:

The Japan Society [of Southern California] is made up of persons employed by Japanese interests, such as lawyers and other agents, representatives of transportation companies, import and export concerns, ministers, educators, peace advocates, and represents a cross-section of public men in communities where it operates. Some have been decorated by the Japanese Emperor for services rendered.[72]

The lobby strove to prevent the abrogation of the US-Japan trade treaty, which allowed the shipment of "large amounts of scrap iron and war materials" to Japan. The drive was organized by the Japanese consul working with the Mitsubishi Corporation and "included the employment of men who are [were] in high public office, including former Attorney

---

[68] Grodzins, *Americans Betrayed*, 154.   [69] Lowman, *Magic*, 12.
[70] Quoted in Lowman, *Magic*, 326.   [71] *Rafu Shimpo*, July 1, 1940, 1.
[72] *Tolan Hearings, Portland and Seattle*, pt. 30, 11538.

General [George] Wickersham" who defended "Mitsui and Co., which had operated two airplane plants in the United States."[73] These ties were the kind that occurred naturally in the American political system. Whether or not they seemed sinister would depend upon one's view of Japan's assault on China. The Pacific War made this connection seem dubious, a Fifth Column even.[74]

The Japanese Association of San Francisco illustrated the same point. It was a group of Nikkei, who were trying to persuade Japanese businessman Kazuo Takahashi, the manager of the NYK office (a Japanese shipping line), to run for president of the association. Until early 1938 the Japanese businessmen had stayed out of local affairs because they would ultimately be rotated home to Japan anyway. But the Sino Japanese War forced a reconsideration. The Japanese businessmen now became desirable partners for the Nikkei and they, for him. For larger issues, said the *New World Sun*, the Japanese Consul General "stands at the head of the Japanese people," but for local ones the Nikkei could use some help.[75]

Speaking of the Japanese Association of America, Eiichiro Azuma explained how. "Supported by Tokyo's *extraterritorial nation-building* [emphasis added] the apparatuses of immigrant control allowed a relatively cohesive ethnic collectivity to emerge in the American West during the 1910s," almost exactly coincidental with the California Alien Land Laws he said. "The Japanese Government and opinion leaders furnished funds, personnel, and general guidelines." He continued that Kinji Ushijima, president of the Japanese Association of America, stated to a California Issei gathering that the Issei stand "like a bridge between the two countries, ... representative of the Japanese national interests."[76] Nothing seemed more natural to them, but nothing could have made them more suspect.

Yet before the war, American code breakers did just that. They discovered that Japanese agents in the United States were trying to carry on espionage.[77] They planned to employ both Nikkei and Imperial businesses and orchestrate the operation through the Japanese consuls. So the Sino Japanese War forced closer local cooperation with Imperial businessmen; they were both tied to the consul, and the consul was leading a spy ring

---

[73] Ibid., 11540.   [74] Ibid., 11538.   [75] *Sun*, January 27, 1938, 1.
[76] Azuma, *Between*, 48, 43–8, 50–3ff., Roger Daniels argued that such ties arose in response to American discrimination. Daniels, *Prisoners without Trial: Japanese Americans in World War II* (New York, NY: Hill and Wang, 1993), 22–42.
[77] Azuma, *Between*, 266.

against the United States. These intercepted messages are printed in David Lowman's book.[78]

Other pan-Pacific connections were important as well. Perhaps half of the Nikkei were Buddhist. According to a leading scholar of the Asians, Buddhist priests were subsidized by the Japanese Government.[79] In wartime that too was problematical. And then there were the Japanese patriotic associations, sometimes veterans' organizations, which further drew together Americans of Japanese descent and the mother country. These have sometimes been discounted, but if the American and Asian Japanese worked together in business, banking, trade, religion, and cultural tourism (Kibei), there is little reason to believe that they were not involved together in patriotic societies, Japanese Chambers of Commerce, and other bi-national groups. As historians Persico, Lowman, Azuma, and Hayashi have shown, the home government sought to exploit these ties to its advantage through the Japanese consulates, also the fount of espionage against the United States.[80] In fact, the close connection between the homeland and the Southland was further evidence of the shrewd, heady economic sense of the Nikkei.

Employment by and commerce with the motherland companies, a kind of tie the Okies did not have,[81] gave the Japanese Americans a more diverse economic base beyond their agricultural pursuits, one more resistant to economic downturns. But like all of their other ties to the homeland, also one more vulnerable to political downturns.

---

[78] Lowman, *Magic*, 123–206.   [79] R. Daniels, *Prisoners*, 18
[80] Persico, *Roosevelt's Secret*, 190; Azuma, *Between*, 266; Hayashi, *Democratizing*, 39.
[81] For the Okies, see J. Gregory, *American Exodus: The Dust Bowl Migration in California* (New York, NY: Oxford University Press, 1989).

6

The Looming Roberts Report

An Adverse Fleeting Moment

The same coupling occurred on the Atlantic side. German Americans had extensive links to the Fatherland, and those ties brought down a torrent of criticism on their heads too.[1] Samuel Dickstein, the chairman of the House Committee on Immigration and Naturalization, was the anti-alien hawk in the East, whose activities were comparable to those of Los Angeles congressmen Leland Ford and John Costello. He published an extensive list of hundreds of German American names and organizations whom he accused, with virtually no corroboration, of disloyalty.

The point was to provoke the HUAC to investigate them. Dickstein was in a power struggle with Martin Dies for control of HUAC, so that may explain his intensity. Among other things, he accused the German consuls of "preparing the way for military attack by spreading propaganda and conniving with native Fascists."[2]

Most historians have believed that the Dies Committee was much too active, but Dickstein wanted it to be more energetic still, to "tell the country how many spies and saboteurs we have in this country that have not been subpoenaed by the Dies Committee."[3] If Dies had, the committee would have been swamped.

In September, 1940, the United States was fourteen months away from war with Germany. And as the Battle of Britain was then proving, the German navy could not even get across the English Channel, much less the

---

[1] For the political repercussions on eastern city politics, see works cited later by Ronald Bayor and John Stark.
[2] *Congressioinal Record*, September 19, 1940, 12379, 12372–80 ff.
[3] *Congressioinal Record*, September 19, 1940, 12372.

Atlantic Ocean. So an attack on the East Coast was much less probable than an Imperial Japanese descent on the Pacific Coast was later on.[4]

The spectacular Axis victories in Europe and Asia and the war-induced vulnerability of the Japanese Americans, put them under pressure. President Roosevelt might have been able to relieve it if he had been on top of the situation and if he had been willing to risk some precious political capital. Much of what historians write are counterfactual arguments that can never be definitively proven, but, given the great misfortune of Japanese American relocation, it is at least worth a try. If FDR had moved to control the West Coast Japanese story immediately after the post-Pearl Harbor raids, he could conceivably have calmed public opinion. He would have had to assert forcefully that the FBI raids had eliminated any serious threat of sabotage and espionage and that the Army and Navy had assured him that an invasion was not possible.[5] FDR did assert at the beginning of January, 1942, that he was "deeply concerned over the increasing number of reports of employers discharging workers who happen to be aliens or even foreign-born citizens."[6] So he was not unaware of what was happening. But the President would have taken a grave political risk if he had mounted a full-scale publicity campaign because he could not afford to rule out all other kinds of military assaults on the West Coast.

The commander of the Oregon Department of the American Legion and former mayor of Portland explained one kind. "The greatest menace that there is in the Northwest is the question of our forests," said Joseph K. Carson, Jr., "because nearly all of it belongs to the United States and practically half of the stand of merchantable timber in the United States lies here."[7] The Oregonians remembered the all-too-recent Great Tillamook Burn[8] of the 1930s which destroyed a huge swath of timber.

Californians also worried about incendiarism. "The first of June, the fire season is very, very acute in Tulare County," testified Wendell Travoli, representing the Tulare County Citizens Committee. There were large dry grasslands and brushlands leading up to the General Grant and Sequoia national parks: "The fire hazard in our territory is the main thing," said

---

[4] *Rafu Shimpo*, June 16, 1940, 1.
[5] Grodzins, *Americans Betrayed*, 176. For the lack of government control of information on the Nikkei story.
[6] *Tolan Hearings, San Francisco*, pt. 29, 11042.
[7] Ibid., *Portland and Seattle*, pt. 30, 11328.   [8] Ibid., *Portland and Seattle*, pt. 30, 11365.

Travoli. "The grass land does burn."[9] With the benefit of hindsight, a hit and run attack on the coast seems like a stretch, but so did an attack on Pearl Harbor or the destruction of the American planes in the Philippines only a day later. Fires, especially in California, where they occur every year,[10] along with Santa Anna winds to fan them, were no stretch at all.[11] Both for reasons of military realism or public safety, no responsible leader would have promised immunity from such a disaster.

Taking command of this situation would have posed grave risks to the President without much chance of commensurate political gain. As Doris Kearns Godwin, Walter Johnson, Thomas Fleming, Jon Meacham, William Leuchtenburg, H. W. Brands, Arthur Meier Schlesinger, Jr., and other historians have made abundantly clear, Roosevelt was a very calculating President. Though called upon to do so, he did not[12] and was not likely to take such a chance, so the Nikkei remained vulnerable. This leadership vacuum was a part of the political explanation.

Between December 7, 1941, and early March, 1942, the unintended consequences of government actions vastly undermined the Japanese American economy. However, the government blow against fishermen could not have been avoided. By commencing the war, the Imperial Japanese also struck at the Nikkei fishing industry, one of the principal pillars of their economy. Terminal Island in LA hosted the Nikkei fishing communities, the fish canneries where they sold their catch and where many worked, and a hefty and growing Navy presence. Therefore, the Navy felt it wise to eliminate all civilian residents from the Island. Though this involved the removal of the 3,000 Japanese American, another 2,000, or 40 percent of those evacuated, were Caucasians, some Italian Americans.

---

[9] *Tolan Hearings, San Francisco*, pt. 29, 11064, 11066, 11068. See also SF *Chronicle*, March 15, 1942, I, 10.

[10] This portion of the manuscript is being written as wild fires are raging from one end of the Pacific Coast to the other in the week of August 16 through August 22, 2015. The truth of what Wayne Travoli testified to the Tolan Committee has been illustrated in orange colors and dramatic news reports every evening.

[11] Grodzins, *Americans Betrayed*, 278. In 2015 they have been especially prevalent. It is presumed that, in part, they are caused by climate change. That is entirely possible, but West Coast fires have been a constant for as long as I have followed western history, 1959–2015. And the Tillamook Burn indicates that fires were a constant for a much longer period of time. For this year's fire season, see the *Economist*, September 12–18, 2015, 32.

[12] Grozdzins, *Americans Betrayed*, 245.

Others in the San Francisco, Pittsburg/Vallejo, and Monterey/Santa Cruz regions were Italian aliens who were grounded.[13] These boats went far out to sea, some as far as Panama, another crucial military zone, and carried high-powered radios.[14] Since many of these boats were owned by first-generation Issei, subjects of Axis Japan, the government thought that it would have been tempting fate to allow enemy aliens to cruise up and down the coast between LA and the Panama Canal. In fact, it would have been close to military lunacy. Some Issei were pro-Japanese, just as many Italians were pro-Mussolini or pro-Italy.[15]

Though understandable, the ruling hurt fishermen in both communities because the Navy did not allow the aliens enough time to dispose of their property without ruinous losses, at least Japanese ones, but the Navy did not really have time. Still, this action was hardly hysterical or racial because the evacuation of Terminal Island and Bainbridge Island came nearly two months after Pearl Harbor. These evacuations lagged as much as the political backlash.

Many AJA actually worked for the private companies of the mother country either in the United States or in the Japanese Empire. One estimate puts the number of Japanese Americans who spent the war in the Japanese Empire at 40,000.[16] And if we accept Professor Stephan's number of 40,000, this meant that a very large number of Nikkei had family (six per capita) ties to the enemy. The number working in the United States could not have been that large, but it was considerable. The war, not racism, nor greed, nor hysteria toppled that bond quickly and completely and thus another pillar of the ethnic economy with it.

The third and further blows could have been dodged, but again, only with forceful direction from the top and the bottom of the policy pyramid. Despite frequent assertions that the Nikkei were excluded from the mainstream economy, many worked civil service jobs (several hundred for the state of California)[17] and other non-Japanese American jobs. The justly famous Mitsui Endo, whose US Supreme Court victory in 1944 destroyed the legality of the relocation centers, was not the least of them.[18] Most

---

[13] *Tolan Hearings, Portland and Seattle*, pt. 30, 11057.
[14] Bosworth, *America's Concentration Camps*, 40.
[15] *Tolan Hearings, San Francisco*, pt. 29, 11057–58. Testimony of Ottorino Ronchi was a former San Francisco newspaper editor and University of California professor sent by Richard Neustadt to determine the impact of the prohibited zone exclusion on Italian-American fishermen communities.
[16] J. J. Stephan, note 29 above.   [17] Grodzins, *Americans Betrayed*, 122.
[18] R. Daniels, *Concentration Camps USA*, 40–41.

held onto their positions well into February 1942, but with the anti-Nikkei pressure building, state, county, and city officials began dismissing or furloughing these employees. Private employers followed suit, prompting the President himself to deplore these firings,[19] but they destroyed another pillar of the Nikkei economy.

Yet none of these actions or trends fully explain how the Japanese Americans ended up in centers. Nor did any media campaign against them. The editorials, venomous cartoons,[20] or manipulated information did not appear in the metropolitan media until well after December 7. Wars generate demonizing propaganda,[21] whether the "other" is portrayed as an ape or a dark complexioned, fat, jowly, slobbering bully like Mussolini. It was war that triggered such portrayals, but not for some time. The *Los Angeles Times*, the bête noir of the race school, did not portray the Japanese Americans as beasts or call them "Japs" until well after the attack on Hawaii. I found the term "Jap" employed to characterize Japanese Americans for the first time only on January 28, 1942, and it did not publish a racist cartoon until January 9, 1942, one month after Pearl Harbor.[22]

Neither of the two spikes, one upward and one downward, in public attitudes toward the Japanese Americans coincided with any racial matters. The first was overwhelmingly favorable to them, as the Reverend Harold Jensen noted to the Tolan Committee.[23] So, initially, even the military routs at the Philippines and Pearl Harbor did not trigger US official or public anti-Nikkei feelings – whether hysterical, racial,

---

[19] *Tolan Hearings, San Francisco*, pt. 29 11042.

[20] Perhaps the most famous anti-Japanese cartoonist was Theodore Seuss Geisel, later famous as Dr. Seuss in children's books, including those of my son. See Reeves, Infamy, 21 and photographs between 136–7. There is also a literature on Seuss.

[21] The propaganda of World War I is often portrayed as the ultimate exercise in demonizing the enemy and it is the worst example that this historian has read of. The practice in the United States is usually discussed in the activities of the Creel Committee. For an egregious example in Europe, see R. Briffault, *Europa in Limbo* (New York, NY: Charles Scribner's Sons, 1937), 172–96, 224–54ff.

[22] LA *Times*, January 28, 1942, I, 1 and 7, January 30, 1942, II, 4. For a sample of cartoons in US papers see LA *Times*, January 1, 1942, pt. 4, p. 4. The first and only *Times* cartoon which portrayed the *Imperial Japanese* as animalistic appeared in the paper on January 9, 1942, which showed a huge, buck-toothed gorilla attacking civilians. I found none that portrayed the domestic Japanese as animalistic before Executive Order 9066. LAT, January 9, 1942.

[23] *Tolan Hearings, Portland and Seattle*, pt. 30, 11565. So far as I am aware Morton Grodzins was the first historian to write about the favorable backlash to the Nikkei in the wake of Pearl Harbor.

nationalistic, cultural, tribal, greedy, or class motivated.[24] The LA *Examiner* did employ the term "Jap" with regard to the Nikkei on December 8, 1942, but did not call for relocation. That paper also allowed the Nikkei quite a bit of space to proclaim their undoubted loyalty to the United States.[25] The LA *Times*, the LA *Examiner*, and the SF *Chronicle*[26] hardly even mentioned, much less demonized, the Japanese Americans from November, 1941, until January 25, 1942.

Beginning on that date, a rush of events prompted an unfortunate public re-evaluation. These included the *Roberts Report* on January 25, 1942, a report by Congressman Martin Dies on January 28, 1942, the creation of prohibited and restricted zones by the government on January 29, 1942, and the organization of the West Coast Congressional delegation on January 30, 1942.[27] This combination proved fatal.

January 25, 1942, initiated the second and downward spike and marked the turning point of big-city official and much of public opinion against the Japanese Americans. This change was initiated by the *Roberts Report*. Supreme Court Justice Owen Roberts was tasked to chair a commission to inquire into the defeat at Pearl Harbor. According to Secretary of War Henry Stimson, Roberts privately expressed to Stimson on January 20, 1942, grave doubts about Hawaiian Japanese loyalty.[28] Although sometimes said to have revealed large-scale Japanese and Japanese American espionage before the Sunday attack,[29] in fact the report said hardly anything about any Japanese Americans or their race.[30] Yet the report aroused a public protest against the Nikkei.

So why was Roberts a turning point? As a *Sacramento Bee* cartoon demonstrated, the newspapers' response was neither racial nor hysterical. Instead, the *Roberts Report* was a scathing indictment of the military in Hawaii, and that set off the West Coast time bomb against Japanese Americans. From that point onward, the cry of national security arose from all quarters. The cry of "No more Pearl Harbors" could not be countered. Race was not mentioned in the Roberts Report.

---

[24] F. Biddle, *In Brief Authority* (New York, NY: Doubleday and Company, Inc., 1962), 214.
[25] LA *Examiner*, December 8, 1941, I, 1; December 8, 1941, I, 11; December 8, 1941, I, 10; December 8, 1941, I, 11; December 9, 1941, I, 8.
[26] Hereafter abbreviated.   [27] Godzins, *Americans Betrayed*, 67.
[28] H. L. Stimson *Diaries* (UNC microform copy), Vol. 37, January 1, 1942 to February 28, 1942, p. 3, January 20, 1942.
[29] A. Bosworth 215–16.
[30] *The Roberts Report* was published in full in both the SF *Chronicle* and the LA *Times*. See the *Times*, January 25, 1942, I, 1.

Military reassurances about it did not go down well with the official public. This is no surprise, because the Secretary of War himself feared an invasion as late as February 10, 1942.[31] The more officials and other civilians thought about it, the more they feared some kind of attack. The coast was literally clogged with defense establishments that were right on or near the water. In Southern California, for example, the aircraft assembly plant farthest inland was Lockheed-Vega in Burbank, possibly six minutes flying time from the Pacific Ocean. When the military pledged security, civilians answered that Pearl Harbor was supposedly secure too. Summing up a meeting with the California congressmen, the pro-Nikkei Justice Department lawyer, Edward Ennis, said that they (the delegation) believed that the "military were jackasses, that they had been proved wrong at Pearl Harbor, that there were no reasons to accept their testimony, and that the California congressmen were not going to wait for another Pearl Harbor in Los Angeles."[32]

That conviction was complicated by the fact that since Pearl Harbor the Japanese American predicament was linked to a serious morale problem. Historians have believed that the West Coast population was guilty of hysteria, which led first to racism, then to relocation. However, the supposed hysteria was also tied to the question of morale. Just as West Coast residents doubted the ability of the military to protect them, they also doubted the government's ability to manage public opinion. As one northwestern agriculturalist put it in speaking about hysteria, "We have before us a serious condition of public morale that should have the attention of the Government." Put a different way, he said that a "jittery populace" had created a "morale" problem caused by "a very serious lack of public confidence in the Government."[33]

On January 27, 1942, Admiral Greenslade warned San Franciscans that sub attacks on San Francisco were "probable" and air raids "possible."[34] The next day the Los Angeles County Board of Supervisors resolved that the 93,717 AJA in California constituted a national defense menace.[35] The same day the City of Los Angeles began pressuring its AJA employees into leaves of absence. The mayor tried to break their fall, but they either had to take the leave or be terminated.[36]

---

[31] Stimson, *Diaries*, UNC Microform copy, Vol. 37, Jan. 1, 1942 to Feb, 28, 1942, Vol. 37, February 10, 1942, 102.
[32] Grodzins, *Americans Betrayed*, 73.
[33] *Tolan Hearings, Portland and Seattle*, pt. 30, 11428–29.
[34] LA *Examiner*, January 27, 1942, sec. I, 4.
[35] LA *Examiner*, January 28, 1942, sec. I, 3.   [36] Ibid.

As though this was not a bad enough day for the Nikkei, the California Department of the American Legion weighed in with a call for "mass evacuation" into "concentration camps" in the interior in order to avoid another Pearl Harbor.[37] On January 28, 1942, HUAC published another damaging, sensationalist report, which expressed hostility to the Nikkei and laid charges of espionage against them.[38] Much of this biting indictment was hyperbole, but close Imperial Japanese-Nikkei ties were confirmed by the MAGIC intercepts of the time. On the heels of Dies' sweeping assessment, on January 29, 1942, California Attorney General Earl Warren agreed that the entire Nikkei population of the West Coast should be evacuated, and he later agreed to take responsibility (whatever that meant) for the action.[39]

All this uproar must have seemed especially disturbing and dangerous to West Coast residents because of the near silence about the Nikkei in the metropolitan press since Pearl Harbor. Instead of building to a crescendo, the issue exploded in their faces, between January 25 and January 30, 1942.[40]

Three days after Roberts, the LA *Times*, for the first time, called for the ouster of all Japanese aliens from Terminal Island. It is significant to note that the *Times* did not demand the ouster of all Japanese Americans, as members of a "race,"[41] or nationality, or a cultural or ancestry group. The demand was not for wholesale removal, but only the removal of Nikkei aliens; and not for removal from the West Coast, but only from proximity to sensitive installations. Exactly when the first calls for wholesale removal occurred is not certain, nor by whom, but the *Placerville Times* called for this as early as January 14, 1942.[42] On January 28, 1942, an LA

[37] Ibid.
[38] House of Representatives, Seventy-Seventh Congress, Committee on Un-American Activities, *Investigation of Un-American Propaganda Activities in the United States, Hearings on H.R. 282* (Washington, DC: US Government Printing Office, 1942), 1723–32ff.
[39] Grodzins, *Americans Betrayed*, 96.
[40] The only exceptions to the silence on the Nikkei came on January 23, 1942, from Mayor Bowron, who said that the city had a "program" for the Nikkei and from Congressman Leland Ford, who called for total evacuation of the Nikkei on January 24. LA *Examiner*, January 23, 1942, II, 8; January 24, 1942, I, 7.
[41] Literate people at the time habitually conflated the terms "race" and "nationality." See below discussion of the use of the conflation by Churchill, Mussolini, et al., p. 112. The Japanese and others habitually referred to themselves as the "Japanese race," although they obviously were not a race in the modern sense of the word.
[42] Quoted in Reeves, *Infamy*, 32. Earlier in his book Reeves cited the December 12, 1941, *San Luis Obisbo Independent* as the first call for evacuation of all Nikkei from the West Coast to concentration camps. Reeves, 29.

Times editorial reiterated the West Coast refrain "that there shall be no Pearl Harbor here."[43]

Also for the first time, they used the term "Jap" to apply to Japanese American. On the 18th, the LA County Board of Supervisors called for the removal of all Nikkei employees, not by dismissal, but by temporary leave.[44] They did so with regret. On the 27th Mayor Bowron closeted himself with his Board of Harbor Commissioners to assess the Terminal Island issue.[45] Walter Lippmann, a widely syndicated columnist based in Washington, DC, weighed in the same day, insisting that "what went wrong in Hawaii was that we let them strike first."[46] The implications for the increasingly hard-pressed Nikkei were obvious, and other *Times* correspondents made it more so. The first racist cartoon appeared on January 29, 1942 in the *Times*, and California Attorney General Warren demanded its removal.[47]

Spectacular events in the Southland and Washington seemed to provide a rationale for embracing the *Times*'s view. On January 29, 1942, page one of the *Times* headlined the news that back east three Japanese and three Nikkei plus three Germans and three German Americans had been indicted or arrested on national security grounds.[48] On page 6 columnist Henry McLemore made the first openly racist appeal: "Let's have no patience with the enemy or with anyone whose veins carry his blood."[49] On the 30th the headlines shouted that a Japanese sub had been sighted near LA by Army planes and attacked by Navy ones, the first sub sightings since December.[50]

On January 29, 1942, DeWitt and Biddle issued orders creating ninety-nine "prohibited" zones and two "restricted"[51] zones, from which enemy aliens were banned.[52] The Army located the prohibited zones in San Francisco, LA, Oakland, and San Diego, at sensitive points like the waterfronts, plus elsewhere at bridges, dams like Shasta, and power stations like

---

[43] LA *Times*, editorial, January 28, 1942, II, 4.
[44] LA *Times*, January 19, 1942, I, 1 and 6.   [45] Ibid., January 28, 1942, 1 and 7.
[46] Ibid., January 28, 1942, II, 4.   [47] Ibid., January 29, 1942, I, 6.
[48] Ibid., January 29, 1942, I, 1.   [49] LA *Times*, January 29, 1942, I, 6.
[50] LA *Examiner*, January 30, 1942, I, 1.
[51] Although General DeWitt's *Final Report* distinguishes between these two quoted terms, in practice the report itself sometimes equates the two. See *Final Report*, 23 ff.
[52] Since the territory in question was a civilian area, not under martial law, only the Attorney General could issue such orders, but only the military could decide what was a military security zone, so the zones were established by civilians, on the advice of the military (DeWitt).

those of the Pacific Gas and Electric Company.[53] The devastating 1928 collapse of the St. Francis Dam in Southern California was still fresh enough in people's memories to mandate the protection of dams, of which California had many.[54] Roosevelt's secret advisor Curtis Munson had reported the undefended state of dams, power stations, bridges, and so forth in November 1941 and at that time FDR had directed the Army to protect them.[55] The order did not ban all persons of a race or nationality, only enemy aliens near sensitive installations, and the order specifically excluded Nisei. DeWitt acted on military grounds; there was nothing racial in these geographic specifications.

Egged on by Roberts and Dies, the dormant immigration restriction forces sprang back into life and new pressure groups organized to assault the AJA position. The West Coast Congressional delegation organized on January 30, 1942, and they and the Los Angeles *Times* and *Examiner* pitched into the Nikkei.

Predictably, "There was much conjecture that this was the forerunner of a general enemy alien evacuation." General DeWitt later explained:

Mr. [Tom] Clark and his Anti-Trust Division staff [the Justice Department division tasked to handle these matters] were deluged with inquiries and comments. Public excitement in certain areas reached a high pitch, and much confusion, the result of conflicting reports and rumors, characterized the picture. However, in essence, there was no substantial dislocation or disruption socially or economically of the affected groups.[56]

This was the first step to evacuation, but the General's belief that the measures caused "no substantial dislocation or disruption" proved terribly inaccurate. As noted, the measures caused great disruption because they affected both Issei and Nisei.

The short-run consequence was to knock still another prop from under the Nikkei economy. Since thousands lived in cities and others farmed close by, the January 29, 1942, order and subsequent zone orders destroyed the jobs of farmers, landscapers, nurserymen, produce stand merchants, grocers, florists, Japanese restaurant owners, barbers, hotel keepers, money lenders, and other urban tradesmen. Some estimates of the

---

[53] For a description of the geographic areas and installations from which enemy aliens were banned, see *Sacramento Bee*, January 31, 1942, 4; February 4, 1942, 4.

[54] For St. Francis see M. L. Davis, *Rivers in the Desert: William Mulholland the Inventing of Los Angeles* (New York, NY: Harper Perennial, 1993), 171–4.

[55] J. E. Persico, *Roosevelt' Secret War: FDR and World War II Espionage* (New York, NY: Random House, 2001). 131.

[56] DeWitt, *Final Report*, 6.

Nikkei residents of Los Angeles ran up to 36,000 and in San Francisco, up to 5,000, more than one-third of the California total.[57] Thus, the problems and predicaments of the nation state were leading to even bigger ones for the Japanese ancestry minority.

This development was negatively compounded by the agricultural calendar. In the Northwest and in Southern California, specific Nikkei specialty crops had to go into the ground during a certain time frame in order to ensure an adequate growing season.

Traditionally, banks, shipping firms, fertilizer companies, and Caucasian landowners advanced credit to the Nikkei to finance their crops.[58] Since it was not possible to assure Caucasian lenders that the Nikkei borrowers would not be excluded from their farm lands, the investors could not be sure of their investments.[59]

Labor complicated the problems of capital. As Earl Warren explained of the "large scale" Japanese farmers, "They don't necessarily harvest them [their fields] with Japanese [labor]. They harvest them with Filipinos and Mexicans and even white People." This year, "the Filipinos and Mexicans have resolved that they will not harvest crops for Japanese."[60]

As if to give credence to Warren's words, "the French Sardine Company (on Terminal Island), one of the largest canneries," had already released their few Japanese employees "after Filipino workers had refused to work alongside them."[61] Filipino American conflict with Japanese growers went back to the 1930s when Filipino farm workers struck Japanese growers and boycotted businesses in the Japanese section of Stockton.[62] Confirmation of that enduring hostility came from the California State Department of Social Welfare, which wrote to Richard Neustadt about Imperial County that we "have had serious difficulties between Japanese and Filipinos in this county and the situation is so serious some Japanese have been killed." So great had the hostility between the two groups become that by mid-January, 1942, "Fisticuffs between Filipinos and Japanese have been almost a daily occurrence around the [fish] canneries since the Philippine Islands were invaded,"

[57] *Tolan Hearings, San Francisco*, pt. 29, 11151; Hayashi, *For the Sake*, 4.
[58] Modell, *Economics and Politics*, 95–123.
[59] *Tolan Hearings, San Francisco*, pt. 29, 11194–95. [60] Ibid., 11016; l 11090.
[61] LA *Times*, January 14, 1942, p. 1; *Christian Century*, March 25, 1942, 383.
[62] *Rafu Shimpo*, December 1, 1939, 1. For a more detailed discussion of Japanese-Filipino conflict see Azuma, *Between*, 187–207.

wrote the LA *Times*.[63] Gangs of the two groups were still battling it out with knives on the streets of Chicago well into the resettlement period.[64]

One historian went so far as to maintain that "Japanese consciousness" or "ethnic nationalism" among the Issei in the 1930s stemmed "as much or more" "from an image of a collective enemy [the Filipinos] and a sense of shared interests in the delta as from events in Asia or anger against [the] racist society."[65]

That twofold threat from above and below, from labor and capital, destroyed the last leg of the Nikkei economy. The lenders, including two of the three Seattle banking partners of the Nikkei, now shut off the flow of money. Although historians have long claimed that greed led competing agricultural interests to favor evacuation, neither greed nor racism is consistent with these events. White interests had worked with the Japanese Americans for years.[66]

Greed might explain the opposition of large corporate interests elsewhere, and in California, some agribusiness[67] lent their support to relocation.

Perhaps some Italo American market gardeners did too. One cannot know for certain that the Italian Americans, the Mexicans, and the Filipino Americans were motivated by nationality, race, greed, ethnic animosity, class conflict, cultural bias, or in the case of the Filipinos justifiable anger at the Fascist Japanese occupation of their country, but the same is true of whites. Charles Kikuchi noted in his diary the deadly hatred between Japanese Americans and Filipinos, and John Modell and Elliott Barkan have found labor difficulties that pitted the Filipino, Mexican, and white workers against their Japanese American agricultural bosses.[68] Filipino farmers sometimes took over the farms that the Nikkei

---

[63] LA *Times*, January 14, 1942, pt. 1; *Tolan Hearings, San Francisco*, pt. 29, 11068.

[64] C. Brooks, "In the Twilight Zone between Black and White: Japanese American Resettlement and Community in Chicago, 1942–1945," *Journal of American History*, Vol. 86: No. 4 (March 2000), 1655.

[65] Azuma, *Between*, 188.   [66] *Tolan Hearings, Portland and Seattle*, pt. 30, 11426–27.

[67] *Tolan Hearings, Portland and Seattle*, pt. 30, 11432. Perhaps this animus was class-based resentment, as one letter to the editor argued, corporations were discriminating against whites and favoring Nikkei in rentals because they could get them cheaper. *Sacramento Bee*, January 20, 1942, 18.

[68] Modell, *The Economics and Politics*, 123–6. Modell found that Japanese American growers employed the backing of the Associated Farmers, the LA County Sheriff's department "Red Squad," the LA city police, blacklisting, strikebreakers from the schools and the "breadlines" to fight the Mexican, Fillipino, white, and sometimes even Nikkei strikers. E. R. Barkan, *From all Points: America's Immigrant West, 1870s–1952* (Bloomington, IN: Indiana University Press, 1007, 272–9 for other examples.

evacuated, and the well-informed Toru Matsumoto implied that the animus against the Nikkei in Colorado came mostly from areas of Italian American market gardening. Certainly Mayor Angelo Rossi of San Francisco testified to the Tolan Hearings that Japanese enemy aliens should be evacuated and the Italian enemy aliens should not. And LA congressman John Costello (counterintuitively, an Irishman) was one of the most vociferous leaders of the movement to evacuate the Nikkei aliens and was the co-sponsor of Congressional Public Act 503, which provided fines and prison time for those who disobeyed Executive Order 9066.[69]

It would be hard to imagine that leaders as prominent as Rossi were ignorant of Nikkei alien economic competition. Thus, he would have been aware that rounding up the Issei would leave the realm of market gardening and fishing largely to his own, Filipino, or other non-Japanese ethnic groups. In the Monterey Area, that is exactly what happened. During evacuation, as historian Carol Lynn Mckibben explained:

> most Japanese were forced either to abandon property such as fishing boats or sell them for a fraction of their value to Sicilians and other fishermen who rarely gave them back when the Japanese returned [from relocation].[70]

The Japanese and Sicilians had competed for market share in the Monterey area since at least the 1920s.[71] It is worth noting in this respect that the Nikkei were excluded from "produce marketing" in San Francisco, where the Italians had a firm foothold.[72]

In raising this point, historians must not fall into the same trap as those who have assumed that the words of Earl Warren represented the beliefs of the majority of Caucasians. By the same token, we must not assume that the expressions of Rossi represented all or even many Italians. The ethnicity of this story is very complex.

In any case, the January 29, 1942, and subsequent zone orders forced the Nikkei aliens and other "enemy aliens" inland. It was this initial, sudden influx that created the hue and cry in the interior. Morton Grodzins and the JACL estimated that nearly three-quarters of the 70,000 Nisei were minor children under the age of twenty-one, and almost

---

[69] Grodzins, *Americans Betrayed*, 332.

[70] C. L. McKibben, *Racial Beachhead: Diversity and Democracy in a Military Town, Seaside, California* (Stanford, CT: Stanford University Press, 2012), 60.

[71] D. T. Yamada and Oral History Committee, MP/JACL, *The Japanese of the Monterey Peninsula: Their History and Legacy, 1895–1995* (Monterey, CA: Monterey: Japanese American Citizens League, 1995), 114, 116, 125ff.

[72] CWRIC, *Report*, 43.

none of them was much older. Roger Daniels put the figure at "a major-ity,"[73] but regardless of which figure we accept, a very large number of the Nisei were under age. Since many of the Nikkei families were headed by a resident male alien Issei, the January 29, 1942, and subsequent zone orders forced thousands of Nisei to leave with their parents, upon whom they depended.

Ironically, though understandably, the defenders of the Nikkei added to the certainty of this outcome. As they often said in their recommenda-tions to mitigate the burden of evacuation, the various friends of the Nikkei vehemently insisted that Japanese American families not be broken up. Louis Goldblatt of the CIO spoke for just about every defender of the Nikkei when he stated to the Tolan Committee that "under no circum-stances should families be broken up."[74] So, haphazardly, though the prohibited zone pertained only to aliens, it struck citizen and non-citizen alike.

Much the same thing happened to Italian American families. As Professor Carol Lynn McKibben explained of the Italians living near Monterey, the alien males had often gained citizenship because they had to interact with non-Italians in work, business, and civic affairs. However, the alien women had no role outside the home and therefore felt no need to become naturalized. Thus, when enemy alien restrictions hit the Italian mothers, their families refused to leave their matriarchs alone in distant, inland locales like, Salinas. So others, too, left the coast.[75]

The Nikkei expulsion destroyed the delicate political balance between them and the Caucasian community. After the 1924 national legislation banning further Asian immigration, the anti-Nikkei agitation died down and Japanese Americans were widely accepted residentially, economic-ally, religiously and in schools and colleges. But the January 29, 1942, decision and zone removals reopened the Nikkei question. Many interior people, especially in Fresno and Tulare counties, saw removal as an effort to solve the problems of the coast at their expense by dumping the Nikkei into their midst.

Historian and activist Carey McWilliams, the great champion of the Nikkei, estimated that the Issei expulsions numbered 10,000 in LA

---

[73] Daniels, *Concentrations Camps USA*, 64 105.
[74] *Tolan Hearings, San Francisco*, pt. 29, 11185.
[75] C. L. McKibben, *Beyond Cannery Row: Sicilian Woman, Immigration and Community in Monterey, California, 1915–99* (Urbana, IL: University of Illinois Press, 2006), 81–93.

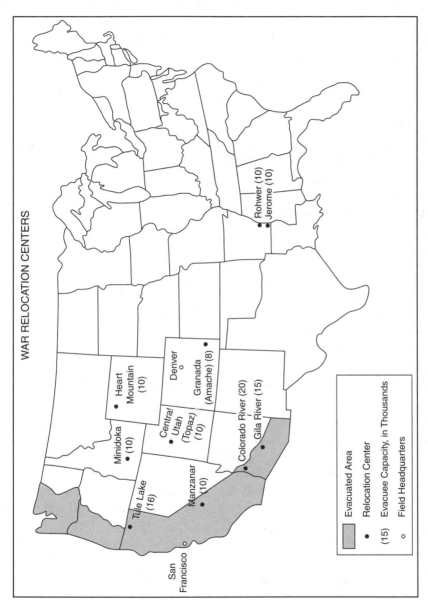

WAR RELOCATION CENTERS

San
Francisco ○

Tule Lake
(16)

Manzanar
(10)

Minidoka
● (10)

Heart
Mountain
● (10)

Central
Utah
(Topaz)
● (10)

Denver
○

Granada
(Amache) (8) ●

Colorado River (20)
●

Gila River (15)
●

Rohwer (10)
● Jerome (10)
●

	Evacuated Area
●	Relocation Center
(15)	Evacuee Capacity, in Thousands
○	Field Headquarters

FIG. 3. War Relocation Centers. With the exception of the Arkansas centers, all of them were located in the Dry West, where rainfall for agriculture was deficient, but irrigation was universally available. Note the huge shaded coastal area, which was only a part of what the Fourth Army had to defend.

87

County alone.[76] So 10,000 plus dependent children amounted to a large inflow of population (six AJA per family) into the interior. It was this expulsion of Issei and their dependents without a place to go that eventually led the government to their only possible solution, assembly centers, then relocation centers. The DeWitt zones, which preceded EO9066, set the stage; EO9066 was important, but by February 19, 1942, the deed had already been done.[77]

These evacuations emboldened the congressional delegation. They now demanded that the exclusions of January 29 be enlarged to ban all persons of "Japanese lineage" from the West Coast. They got their way when DeWitt asked Roosevelt on February 14 to evacuate all Nikkei and all subversives from the coast. On February 19, 1942, FDR issued Executive Order 9066, which authorized the Secretary of War to remove anyone from areas crucial to national security. This task fell to General John DeWitt, head of the Western Defense Command and Fourth Army. On March 2, 1942,[78] under this authority, the general excluded all Japanese Americans, citizens and aliens, plus "alien enemies other than Japanese aliens" and any other dangerous persons, from the western half of Washington, Oregon, and California (later changed to include all of it), and the southern portion of Arizona.[79] DeWitt labeled this area as Military Area No. 1 and labeled an ill-delineated area to the East as Military Area No. 2. Within Military Area No. 1 the General created specific prohibited zones and restricted zones, which are explained below.[80]

Initially, the government thought that it would need only two "reception centers," Manzanar, California (in the Owens Valley) and Parker, Arizona (south of Parker Dam which was, on the Colorado River), to house the displaced Nikkei. It quickly became apparent that "relocation facilities would have to be developed for virtually all evacuees."[81] This resulted in the well-known "assembly centers" where the Nikkei were initially housed. The peak assembly center population reached 89,320 of 112,000 ultimately relocated, and from there these centers declined as their populations emptied out into the evacuation centers.[82]

---

[76] C. McWilliams, *Japanese Evacuation*, 8.

[77] DeWitt, *Final Report*, Figure 15, following. 152.

[78] I am heavily dependent for chronology on the excellent chronology of evacuation presented in Bosworth, *America's Concentration Camps*, 253–6.

[79] DeWitt, *Final Report*, 16, 36–7ff.   [80] Ibid., 15–16, 32.   [81] Ibid., 44.

[82] DeWitt, *Final Report*, 371. The figures sometimes vary, see p. 381.

"Japanese American citizens" were initially offered "voluntary internment." If they declined voluntary internment, they too were excluded from Military Area 1 and were to be left to their own devices, but "encouraged to accept resettlement outside of such military areas."[83] The general recognized that the ultimate solution to the problem was a civilian responsibility; he recommended "that mass internment be considered as largely a temporary expedient pending selective resettlement, to be accomplished by the various Security Agencies of the federal and state governments."[84] Thus resettlement outside the relocation centers was an Army recommendation from the beginning.

Since there was no existing government agency to handle the confinement at the assembly centers, General DeWitt was forced to create one. This led, on March 11, 1942, to the creation of the Wartime Civil Control Administration. Tom C. Clark had been the Justice Department representative in charge of the January 29 and later exclusions under that order, so the Army borrowed him to run this new agency. This administration was also to aid the Nikkei who voluntarily left the sensitive zones by providing information about housing, employment, and so forth.[85] There are no Rooseveltian footprints in this bureaucratic thicket and none of the Secretary of War, Stimson. But the Army was not yet done; it had to guard the assembly centers, then to safeguard the evacuees on their train trips to their ultimate destinations in the relocation centers, supervise the building of those centers, and then guard them in turn.[86]

At first it was hoped that voluntary migration would give maximum opportunities to those Nikkei who rejected the centers.[87] When this failed, either because the evacuees declined to depart or inland areas refused to accept them, the government eventually established the relocation/evacuation centers on March 18, 1942, by Executive Order 9102.[88] It would seem that a government driven by racism or hysteria would not have

[83] Ibid. footnote 401. The term "relocation" is conflated throughout the Nikkei story with that of "evacuation." I have employed the terms evacuation and relocation when dealing with the process of removal and to denote the center experience. In addition the term relocation is often equated with the term "resettlement." The War Relocation Authority confused the issue by employing the term "relocation" to explain the process of leaving the centers even though the term "relocation" appears in the Authority's official title. So in order to avoid confusion, the term "resettlement" appears more appropriate for leaving. The term relocation cannot stand for removal, center experience, and leaving all at the same time. For purposes of clarity this seems the appropriate designation of terms.

[84] DeWitt, *Final Report*, 37.   [85] DeWitt, *Final Report*, 102.

[86] DeWitt, *Final Report*, 65–67.   [87] DeWitt, *Final Report*, 101.

[88] For the evolution of the government's actions, see WRA chronologies previously noted.

waited ten weeks to decide the fate of the people whom they were supposedly fundamentally biased against and hysterical about.

As with most of its Nikkei policy, the Roosevelt Administration more or less stumbled into the relocation solution. Los Angeles mayor Fletcher Bowron and his deputy Alfred Cohen had anticipated the Nikkei problem in case of war and had fruitlessly asked the government to establish some guidelines. As the Stimson diary shows, Washington was winging it, trying to create guidelines after Pearl Harbor and mostly concerned with Hawaii rather than the continental United States.[89]

This juncture again illustrates the crucial role of war-driven government blundering through the Japanese American misfortune and the problematic validity of the race paradigm. When DeWitt created the prohibited zone, he did not apply it to all Japanese Americans as a race, a nationality, or a cultural group, but only to Japanese national aliens. He also did not have another place to put the prohibited aliens. Attorney General Francis Biddle said it very bluntly, wise after the fact, to one of the Dies Hearings (House Un-American Activities Committee): "The Army was not interested with what would be done with the Japanese after they were excluded."[90]

However, in fairness to the Army, it was not their place to run centers for civilians on American soil. That was the administration's job, and Roosevelt simply had no place for the Nikkei to go either. So they naturally moved to the adjacent restricted zone and upset the balance in those areas, which in turn generated the demand for total removal.

De Witt's exclusion zones further bear out that the government did not blunder into the centers for reasons of racism, anti-war hysteria, or greed. His zones established on January 29, 1942 were created to protect bases, factories, bridges, headquarters, ports, and other sensitive installations. The orders did not include all Japanese, only enemy aliens and only those adjacent to sensitive areas. Japanese citizens and aliens[91] outside those zones were not excluded despite their race.

When the larger zones were created on March 2, 1942, they again did not include all Japanese. Only enemy aliens in the western half of Washington and Oregon, all of California, and the southern part of

---

[89] Stimson, *Diary*, Vols. 36–38, 1941–42, Nov. 1941–March 1942.
[90] *Dies Hearings*, November–December 1943, 10073.
[91] Technically they were subjects of an empire, not citizens. That status was created only in 1945. J. J. Stephan, referee's report on manuscript of R. W. Lotchin *Japanese American Relocation in World War II and the Reach of American Racism.*

Arizona were excluded. As we have seen, the other Nisei could leave and avoid the centers.

These areas coincided with security zones and were in no way racial. For example, Japanese Americans in Seattle were evacuated, but those in Spokane were not. Nikkei in western and southern Arizona were taken, but those in northern and eastern Arizona were not.[92] By the same token, the Nikkei in the remainder of the West or the United States as a whole were not uprooted. Nor, except for a few, were the 157,000–160,000 Japanese Americans in Hawaii, so the national security basis of the policy is evident. The Japanese on the West Coast and southern Arizona were considered a military threat; others were not.

So how can we sort out the sinuous path to relocation, employing Milton Eisenhower's complex mode of analysis, stressing racial, military, economic, emotional, and political influences, with some modification, to include individual, national, and governmental ones?

Historians have repeated the racist refrain endlessly, but Roger Daniels, Alan Bosworth, and Morton Grodzins, are illustrative of this race school of historical thought. Perhaps Daniels' interpretation is fully instructive of the race paradigm. As he explained, "it was the racism of the intermountain West which was the final determinant of WRA policy."[93] This is a breathtaking assertion of collective responsibility. In this manner, the racial school has bundled up Eisenhower's diverse causes into one toxic package and explained a complex and developmental question with a static and simple answer – racism.

Most important, there is no skein of racial planning running from DeWitt to Bendtsen to Gullion to McCloy to Stimson to Roosevelt. The CWRIC analyzed an extensive correspondence among the various parties to the relocation decision and found no such thread of biological race causation. The hard-pressed bureaucrats were trying to determine what to do with the Nikkei. They frequently talked of nationality and military necessity, but they were not discussing racial theory.

---

[92] The clearest delineation of these takings is contained in DeWitt, *Final Report*, 289.

[93] Daniels, *Concentration Camps USA*, 95. Almost every part of that statement is problematic in one way or another. Certain people on the West Coast may have been racist, but the West Coast as a whole was not collectively responsible for them. The same is true of Daniels' statement. Each is a breathtaking assertion of collective responsibility for which neither this author nor any other I have read offers any survey data or other proof. This body of literature is shot through with assertions of collective responsibility against Americans, whites, and Caucasians. Of course, to attribute this universal racism to the WRA is completely non-factual. The WRA, from start to finish, was pro-Nikkei.

Next we must answer questions about individual decisions of FDR, General DeWitt, and General Emmons. The stance of the President is easiest. FDR was a politician who shifted from a harsh view of the Imperial Japanese during the Progressive Era to a friendly one in the 1920s to a tougher one in the 1930s. By February 1, 1943, when he authorized Secretary Stimson to form an all-Nikkei fighting unit, he wrote that "Americanism is not, and never was, a matter of race or ancestry."[94] At the time that he signed EO9066, there is no evidence that he did so on racial grounds. His political background was fundamentally culturally pluralist.

He did not accept evacuation because the Nikkei were a yellow peril, inferior, subhuman, lice, monkeys, serpents, insects, or any other living thing at the bottom of the great chain of being. He was thinking about national security, the code breakers information about the prewar Japanese espionage network in America, the disastrous Allied defeats in the Pacific, and keeping public opinion behind the war effort.[95] He had fresh in mind the examples of how the Overseas Japanese, "in China, Hong Kong and Southeast Asia," had often jumped onto the victorious Axis bandwagon as the Japanese rolled over Southeast Asia.[96] The Great Chain of Being was less important to him at that moment than the great chain of Japanese island conquests.

Perhaps the President, as an individual, could have affected a different outcome if he had planned for shielding the innocent, in the immediate aftermath of December 7th as fully as he had for arresting the guilty. But by February 19, 1942, he would have had to go up against an increasingly hostile West Coast public opinion and his own fear of another Pearl Harbor. Needing the support of a confused and questioning public, Roosevelt was not likely to antagonize the Western Congressional delegation.

General DeWitt would have faced the same difficulties plus going against the intelligence reports and military recommendations of everyone but Kenneth D. Ringle. DeWitt could not have acted as General Delos Emmons did in Hawaii either. West Coast opinion certainly would not

---

[94] Chuman, *Bamboo*, 175.

[95] *Tolan Hearings, San Francisco*, pt. 29, 11428. A northwestern agriculturist expressed it as follows speaking of the "battle of morale on the West Coast," "It reflects what to my mind is a very serious lack of Public confidence in the Government."

[96] *Lowman*, Magic, 9, 16–17. The British evacuated the Overseas Japanese of Singapore to India and those from Fiji to New Zealand. For Mindanao, see Cogan, *Captured*.

have tolerated martial law. General DeWitt did not have the Emmons option.

And neither Ringle nor any other government individuals who offered an opinion of how dangerous the Nikkei might have been, were authorities on sabotage. They were not really expert enough to consider their opinions definitive proof of the ability of hostile Nikkei to commit sabotage. General DeWitt's January 29 directive specifying restricted areas seems quite sensitive to military espionage and sabotage. As the urban maps show, the Nikkei, especially those on Bainbridge Island in the Seattle urban area and those on Terminal Island in Los Angeles, were within plain sight of crucial military activities. Such easily obtained information set up the Pearl Harbor attack.

This was the very kind of information that the Allies depended upon getting from the Resistance in Europe as did the Allies in the Pacific from the islanders in the Solomons. DeWitt's enumeration of roads, railroads, dams, port facilities, aqueducts, and highways were wide open to sabotage. Railroad track from the World War II period were fastened onto metal plates and spiked through them onto wooden ties. Disengaging these rails would have been easy, as the D-Day landings proved. The Underground committed literally thousands of acts of sabotage against the French railroad system in the days before the D-Day invasion.[97] Arson would have been just as easy. Then as now West Coast fires rage every fire season.

Race, culture, and nationalism in general are harder to tease out from each other, especially because of the habitual custom of conflating race and nationality. But certainly the close cultural and nationality ties of the Nikkei to Japan helped put them on the bull's eye. The nationalist rivalry between the United States and Japan, up to and after the outbreak of war combined to keep them there.

Economics are even harder to assess, but certainly some commercial and farm interests, some small, some large, wanted an end to Nikkei competition. However, we do not have evidence that this factor was crucial to the decision makers. Some agricultural competitors demanded evacuation, but neither Roosevelt nor DeWitt said that the Nikkei must go in order to facilitate the profits of their white economic competitors. But the general's boss Henry Stimson condemned the California agricultural interests who wanted to beggar the Nikkei economically. Southern California florists opposed them as well. We need much more study also

[97] C. Kaiser, *The Cost of Courage* (New York, NY: Other Press, 2015), 136.

of the California AJA role in fostering the industrialization of Manchuria. If the former were the conduit for machine tools for Manchuria, a sine qua non of industrialization and their arms buildup, that could not have gone unnoticed by the US policymakers who had opposed Japanese possession of that province since the Stimson Doctrine.

Emotional tension built up gradually from the first appearance of the enemy alien issue in the eastern United States in June of 1940, through the Dies Committee "revelations" of July and August of 1941, to Pearl Harbor. Finally, the tension soared from the *Roberts Report* of January 25, 1942, and the subsequent events of the next few days, including the next Dies disclosures of January 28, 1942, especially the exclusion order of January 29, 1942, and the organization of the West Coast Congressional Caucus on January 30, 1942. All the while these were exploited by the bureaucratic politics of Provost Marshal of the Army, Allen Gullion and Karl Bendetsen.

Resentment was undoubtedly smoldering against the Nikkei beneath the surface. On the night of Pearl Harbor a continuous line of cars rolled through Japantown, LA, and for several weeks before Roberts, employers were firing or furloughing Japanese American employees. It is possible that race, nationality, war bitterness, or culture underlay this resentment, or even some combination of the four.

Americans would have reacted angrily, regardless of who attacked them. Still, before the *Roberts Report* and the several other contemporaneous developments up to January 30, the backlash was being held in check. So the *Roberts Report* supplied the emotional component to the complex explanation of relocation.

Hapless governmental policies maximized these personal, political, economic and emotional ones. Government policies deliberately or willy-nilly largely destroyed the Nikkei economy; its ad hoc approach, its regulations, and its deadlines muddled everything.

Specifically, its indecision broke the final leg of the Nikkei economy. From the first days of the war, Washington vacillated and delayed in establishing an enemy alien policy until it vastly undermined Japanese agriculture. Since Executive Order 9066 did not specify who should be evacuated, General DeWitt was tasked with that decision. So for almost two weeks after February 19, 1942, the political actors battled to see who must go – only those guilty of sabotage or espionage, all enemy aliens, or every Nikkei.

It should be emphasized that the governmental factor in a federalist country was not one-dimensional. Several of the measures to restrict the

Nikkei, short of relocation, were taken at a lower city, county, or state level. The civil service illustrates the point. Civil service posts were state, county, and city positions, and the Japanese had collected a considerable number. The continuing thaw in opposition to the Nikkei during the 1930s accounts for why the Japanese Americans had these positions in the first place. But the national state did not control all of these jobs, so Roosevelt could not have protected them. Nor could he have anticipated the unintended consequences of national actions, taken before relocation, especially the prewar trade restrictions against Imperial Japan. These too put some Nikkei out of work or business, as did the actions of their former economic allies, like banks or landowners.

The influence of the military factor, that is, the war and the government's response to it, hovered over everything, provoking ethnic discord, tearing at emotions, tempting the greedy, constraining anti-racists, limiting politicians' room for maneuver, forcing the government's hand, tripping up the bureaucrats, and scaring everyone.

War brought together these several crucial forces at the only, narrow, possible four-month window of opportunity in the twentieth century. Only between the *Roberts Report* and the American victory at Midway, were the Nikkei vulnerable to relocation. Before the war the Nisei were swiftly winning acceptance and after the war was over they went on winning it. Their Issei parents, closely tied to Axis Japan, were rapidly dying off. American policy was a response to an adverse fleeting moment in time, not the working out of a "structured," "ineradicable," "predestined," cultural/racial force. Inyo California County Superintendent of Schools Dorothy Cragen, had it right when she said, "Pearl Harbor set the whole thing in motion. Without the war, this misfortune would not have unfolded."

7

Races and Racism

In the early part of World War II, 110,000 [112,000] persons of Japanese ancestry were interned in relocation centers by Executive Order No. 9066, issued on February 19, 1942. Manzanar,[1] the first of ten such concentration camps, was bounded by barbed wire and guard towers, confining 10,000 persons, the majority being American citizens. May the injustices and humiliation suffered here as a result of hysteria,[2] racism and economic exploitation never emerge again.

Plaque of the National Park Service at the Manzanar Center Relocation site.

I think they [the Park Service] should have mentioned the bombing of Pearl Harbor, because after all, that was what set the whole thing off, wasn't it? . . . the way this [the Manzanar plaque] reads it looks as if the Americans were altogether to blame. As I say, I think that they should have said, "May the event of Pearl Harbor, and the resulting effect never emerge again." That way they [the Imperial Japanese] would have shouldered some of the blame. I don't think the Americans were altogether to blame.[3]

(Dorothy C. Cragen, Inyo County [site of Manzanar] Superintendent of Schools, during World War II.)

---

[1] The centers are sometimes referred to by more than one name. Central Utah was also Topaz; Poston was also called Colorado River; Gila River was Rivers; Amache was Granada, and Minidoka was Hunt. I apologize for any confusion that this may create or any mistake the author may have made.

[2] The term "hysteria" is a very problematical one to apply to a public in fear of attack. But in any case, it would be instructive to compare American West Coast opinion in the wake of Pearl Harbor with the concurrent "Victory Disease" portrayed so effectively in Stephan, *Hawaii*, 122–35 to determine which was the most extreme.

[3] A. A. Hansen and N. K. Jesch, editors, *Japanese American World War II Evacuation Project: Part V: Guards and Townspeople*, Vol. 2 (Munich, New Providence, London, & Paris: K. G. Saur, 1993), 427., Part V. Vol. 1, 201.

So where did the race argument originate? The first explanations are complex, as one might imagine, and derive from the facts on the ground. The second set of explanations stem from historians' misinterpretation and exaggeration of them. Several facts on the ground stand out. It would appear that the race paradigm flowed from traditional white biases against peoples of color, from DeWitt's *Final Report*, from the pressure group politics of the Nikkei and their allies, from the wartime argument of the Imperial Japanese that the war was a racial one against whites, from the different treatment of Japanese Americans versus German and Italian Americans, and from the semantic usages of the nineteenth and twentieth centuries. And the Nikkei themselves seemed habitually to employ the racial term "Caucasian" with regard to Americans.[4]

The Japanese Americans themselves helped craft the charge of racism, mostly in the second half of 1941. At least eight months before they were evacuated, parts of the Nikkei press began to claim discrimination based on "the way we look," or because "we are Americans with Japanese faces," or some other biological derivative/marker. They also employed other terms like nationality or Japanese ancestry; but for the first time, they came to stress race, in the modern sense, too. This was paradoxical because their accusation of biological racism came at the very point in time, 1937–41, when the Nikkei were making one political and cultural breakthrough after another.

So the timing of this racial plaint is puzzling. Certainly, they feared a backlash from the China War or the looming Pacific War or both. Perhaps they thought that charging racism in some way protected them. Or perhaps their jobs cauldron was just coming to a boil as average-age Nisei (nineteen to twenty-one) were reaching the employment stage just as the war threatened, producing more demand for work than the ghetto economy could satisfy. Second, whatever the motivation, their allies at the Tolan Hearings picked up the chorus of racism, and other allies like the Protestant churches and the *Christian Century* sang along.

The race indictment also derived specifically from several passages of DeWitt's *Final Report*. This account supplied ammunition for everyone from later historians to Justice Murphy's famous dissent in the Endo Case. Since the passages have been so heavily cited, this evidence should be made transparent. For most of the *Final Report*, General DeWitt did not use any racial terminology to refer to the Nikkei. In the vast majority of cases

---

[4] Nishimoto, *Inside*, 79.

DeWitt himself in the *Final Report* spoke of the Nikkei as a nationality, as "Japanese."[5]

The racial argument is almost always quoted out of context. Therefore when DeWitt used the term "race," it is important to understand the context. On pages vii, 9, and 15 of the *Report*, the general explained why the Nikkei were a military threat: "Because of the ties of race, the intense feeling of filial piety, and the strong bonds of common tradition, culture, and customs, this population presented a tightly knit racial group." In explaining his decision to single out the Nikkei, on page 15 he spoke in a similar vein:

It was, perforce, a combination of factors and circumstances with which the Commanding General had to deal. Here was a relatively homogeneous, unassimilated element bearing a close relationship through ties of race, religion, language, custom and indoctrination to the enemy.[6]

Two things are significant about this identification of the Nikkei. The terms "Japanese" or "Japanese ancestry" are used over and over again, and racial terms employed just a few times. Yet the defenders of the race paradigm, up to and including Justice Murphy, have seized on this very infrequently used DeWitt terminology to characterize the entire motivation of the United States government as "racist."

Even where the term "race" occurs, it often does so in the context of ancestry, culture, or nationality. As my article "The Conundrum of Race" explains, in the 1940s and well beyond, people conflated the terms "race" with "nationality."[7] They equated them. This equating was done by people high and low, by Franklin Roosevelt,[8] Eleanor Roosevelt,[9] George Patton,[10] Winston Churchill,[11] Benito Mussolini,[12] Adolf Hitler,[13]

[5] From pp. 1 through 114, of the *Final Report*, the term "Japanese" appeared eighty-six times and "Japanese ancestry" twenty-six times. No other term appeared as often as ten times.
[6] DeWitt, *Final Report*, vii, 9, 15.
[7] R. S. Hoyt, *Europe in the Middle Ages* (New York, NY: Harcourt, Brace and Company, 1957), 128.
[8] G. Robinson, *By Order*, 236.   [9] Reeves, *Infamy*, 31.
[10] T. Brighton, *Patton, Montgomery, Rommel: Masters of War* (New York, NY: Three Rivers Press, 2008), 229, 378, 380. Patton deployed the word "race" to mean both race *and* nationality.
[11] W. S. Churchill, *The Island Race* (New York, NY: Dodd, Mead and Company, 1964), 2, 4, 9, 23, 24, 35, 47, 57, 63, 72, 104, 140, 169. The term "race" meant "group" in Churchill's use and that of many others.
[12] For a sample of Mussolini's conflation of the terms race and nationality, see D. Mack Smith, *Mussolini* (London: Weidenfeld and Nicolson, 1981), 192–3, 206–8ff.
[13] A. Hitler, *Mein Kampf* (New York, NY: Reynal and Hitchcock, 1939), 29, 79, 80, 91.

J. A. Hobson,[14] the Gallup polls,[15] the Roper polls, *New York Times* correspondents,[16] the Imperial Japanese ("the Yamato Race"),[17] Radio Tokyo,[18] WRA analysts, the Nikkei themselves,[19] Chinese Americans,[20] big city mayors,[21] Protestant ministers,[22] Japanese American newspapers, the US Congress,[23] and California pressure groups.[24]

The Issei saw their conflicts with the Filipinos – strikes, boycotts, and picketing – "as a 'war' between the 'races'" (both were Asian).[25] Churchill's use, in his history of England, *The Island Race*, was prolific, employing the term "race" to characterize such diverse British groups as the English, Jewish, Scottish, Welsh, Plantagenet(!), Danish, Norman, German, Celtic, Irish, Saxon and cultural, ethnic, or nationality groups, *all of whom were white.*[26]

The practice endures today in modern journalism, in English language fiction, and throughout one of the outstanding modern books on relocation.[27] In fact, Professor Azuma's book is an excellent example of

[14] N. Ferguson, *The House of Rothschild: Money's Prophets, 1798–1848* (New York, NY: Penguin Books, 1998), 21.

[15] G. Gallup, "An analysis of American Public Opinion Regarding the War: A Confidential Report," (Princeton: American Institute of Public Opinion, 1942), 10.

[16] H. Abend, *Japan Unmasked* (New York, NY: I. Washburn, Inc. [1941]), 85, 96.

[17] 77th US Congress, 2d Session, House of Representatives, Special Committee on Un-American Activities (75th Cong.) and H. Res 26 (76th Cong.), *Special Report on Subversive Activities Aimed at Destroying Our Representative Form of Government*, Report 2277, Pursuant to H. Res. 282 (Washington, DC: US Government Printing Office, 1942), 5. *Tokyo Times*, January 16, 1942, 6. DeWitt, *Final Report*, 8; Dower, *War without Mercy*, 31.

[18] Stephan, *Hawaii*, 141.

[19] *Rafu Shimpo*, June 2, 1940, 1, 5, 141; June 2, 1940, see also T. Matsumoto speaking of Ancient Jewish dual citizenship, "Romans by birth right and of Jews by racial heritage." *Rafu Shimpo*, June 2, 1940, 7. See also Grodzins, *Americans Betrayed*, 299.

[20] For the Chinese see the LA *Examiner*, December 9, 1941, I. 8; *Sacramento Bee*, December 13, 1941, 2; Brooks, *Alien Neighbors*, 137.

[21] Mayor Edward Kelly of Chicago quoted in an editorial in the *Heart Mountain Sentinel*, February 26, 1944, 4.

[22] *Tolan Hearings, San Francisco*, pt. 29, 11205–06.

[23] 77th US Congress, 2d Session, House of Representatives, Special Committee on Un-American Activities (75th Cong.) and H. Res 26 (76th Cong.), *Special Report on Subversive Activities Aimed at Destroying Our Representative Form of Government*, Report 2277, Pursuant to H. Res. 282 (Washington, DC: US Government Printing Office, 1942), 5.

[24] tenBroek, et. al., *Prejudice*, 51.   [25] Azuma, *Between*, 187.

[26] W. S. Churchill, *The Island Race* (New York, NY: Dodd, Mead and Company, 1964), 2, 4, 9, 23, 24, 35, 47, 63, 104, 140, 169. For other frequent uses by historical figures, see Ferguson, *House of Rothschild*, 14, 17, 22, 23ff.

[27] Y. Hayawshi, "Anti-Korean Voices Grow in Japan …," *Wall Street Journal*, May 15, 2013, A16; Azuma, *Between*, 98–105, 113, 119, 120ff. On the other hand, Carey

the consistent conflation of the terms "race" and "nationality" on his part and that of the Nikkei. He describes the Japanese, white Americans, Chinese, Filipinos, Mexicans, and others by using the term "race." Although he sometimes employs the term "race" in the modern biological sense, he is usually talking about nationality. Americans, Mexicans, Japanese, Chinese, and Filipinos are not races in the modern biological sense; they are nationalities.

Naturally, if we accept a modern definition of race in preference to a 1940s one of the historical record, the forties will seem suffused by race and racism. In reality, it was steeped in nationality and nationalism. Contemporaries in the 1940s habitually referred to the Japanese as the "Japanese race."[28]

Space here does not permit extensive supporting quotations, but one by anthropologist John Embree, who was an admirer of the Nikkei, worked closely with them in one center, and was a WRA expert on the Japanese, will suffice to illustrate the conflation. As he put it in a discussion of race and culture, "The only thing evacuees in relocation centers have in common is their ancestry, i.e. their race."[29] He went on to explain that "The basic element in race is heredity," and that "A number of people of the same ancestry may be termed a race."[30] Notice that there is nothing here about color. Modern historians, such as European historian David Blackbourn, make a similar point:

Notions of racial difference were a commonplace of European culture [1780–1920]. The word race was used much more broadly (and less self-consciously) than it is today, as a synonym for ethnic group.[31]

Historian Matthew Pratt Guterl found the same usage for the United States in a forty-page discussion at the beginning of his 2001 book.[32] Exactly where and when this conflation originated is not certain, but it

McWilliams employed the term in the modern sense of race, not nationality, *Prejudice*, 134.

[28] P. Scott Corbett, *Quiet Passages* (Kent, OH: The Kent State University Press, 1987), 34.

[29] J. F. Embree, "Dealing with Japanese-Americans," 1, Griswold Papers, MC 733, Series 3, Box 3, Folder 1, Special Collections, University of Arkansas.

[30] Ibid. For Embree's more extended of discussion of Japanese and Asians, see his *The Japanese Nation: A Social Survey* (New York, NY: Farrar and Rinehart, Inc., 1945). He wrote the book to help Americans to understand the Japanese and Asians. See 3–11.

[31] D. Blackbourn, *The Long 19th Century: History of Germany 1780–1920* (New York, NY: Oxford University Press, 1998), 327.

[32] M. P. Guterl, *The Color of Race in America* (Cambridge, MA: Harvard University Press, 2001), 27–67.

dates back at least to Charlemagne.[33] So when encountering the term race, we must be aware that in the 1940s context, it usually meant nationality or ethnic group. That may even have been the basic meaning of the term, as it is explained here by Churchill, Embree and Blackbourn. The historian can determine when the term meant race or nationality only by the context in which the term is used. DeWitt's description is almost always quoted out of context. In the context that the general employed the term, it meant nationality. The Nikkei themselves employed this language, referring to themselves as Japanese and to the Caucasians as Americans.

Filial piety, tradition, culture, customs, religion, language, and indoctrination are not racial or racist markers; they are national or ethnic ones. They are hardly simplistic statements of blatant racism. Rather, they are assertions of a complex Japanese American identity, in exactly the way John Dower explains it for Imperial Japanese–culture, residence, language, customs, race/nationality, and history.

In the *Final Report*, DeWitt used the term "race" to denote a complex identity. Race/nationality was only one part of Japanese national identity, just as whiteness was only one part of the American 1940s national identity. DeWitt did not speak of biology – "Americans with Japanese Faces," "people who look like us," people with a certain facial structure, a Yellow Peril, vermin, insects, snakes, or biological inferiority, terms from Dower's race litany.[34]

Because the term "Jap" was often used after January 25, 1942, it is the basis for another of the race school's assertions of widespread racism. DeWitt is quoted in 1943 as opposing the return of the Nikkei to the Western Defense Command because "a Jap is a Jap" and will never be loyal to anyone other than Japan.[35] But that term is an abbreviation of the word "Japanese" and has no racial connotations. Nor does the Nikkei pejorative use of the word "chink" connote race.[36] Nor is all of this merely the parsing of sentences. Using such terms invariably to mean race multiplies the supposed prevalence of racism by all parties. Perhaps worse for our understanding of history, it obviates the influence of nationality and nationalism, crucial factors in understanding history since the French Revolution.

[33] R. S. Hoyt, *Europe in the Middle Ages* (New York, NY: Harcourt, Brace and Company, 1957), 128.
[34] For the view that DeWitt was a lifelong hater of Japanese Americans but simultaneously held that the general's earlier plan to remove the Nikkei from Oahu was based on "military necessity," see Taylor, *Jewel*, 46.
[35] Taylor, *Jewel*, 46.   [36] Hayashi, *For the Sake*, 134.

Moreover, DeWitt may not have ever uttered those words. His exact statement, from the Congressional hearings, which are usually quoted, is that, "It makes no difference whether he [a Nisei] is an American citizen, he is still a Japanese. American citizenship does not necessarily determine loyalty."[37]

In fact, DeWitt's sentiment was no more racial than that of the Imperial Japanese on the same subject. Paraphrasing the Japanese Foreign Minister, historian Eiichiro Azuma wrote, "To the Japanese elite, racial ties were innate and immutable, while citizenship was contingent and expedient."[38] And in any case, both West Coast and Hawaiian Japanese also used the term "Jap."[39] It does not refer to any of the specifics on Dower's litany. The term is certainly a slur, but it is a nationality slur, comparable to the words kraut, Boche, Heinie, guinea, and wop, used to demonize the other Axis.

To complicate the matter even more, DeWitt had previously opposed mass evacuation on grounds that "an American citizen, after all, is an American citizen. And while they all may not be loyal, I think we can weed the disloyal out of the loyal and lock them up if necessary."[40] Provost Marshal General Allen Gullion, often considered one of the architects of mass relocation, agreed with DeWitt.[41]

DeWitt stuck to these guns until the last week in January, 1942, when the Army and Justice Department agreed to evacuate only enemy aliens of all kinds from certain crucial military zones. This would have affected only about 20,000 Issei, perhaps half of that group. As journalist, historian and activist Bill Hosokawa put it, we do not know what made DeWitt execute a 180-degree change of mind[42] and accept mass evacuation. Unless racism is quite ephemeral and not enduring and can change day to day, then racism is the least likely explanation of DeWitt's transformation.

Nor is the different treatment of Japanese, Germans, and Italians a support for the race paradigm. Proponents of this view argue that since Japanese were taken to centers and the Germans and Italians were

[37] US Congress, House, Seventy-Eighth Congress: First Session, *Hearings before a Subcommittee of the Committee on Naval Affairs, Persuant to H. res. 30*: Part 3, San Francisco, Calif., Area, April 12, 13, 14, 15, 16 and 17, 1943, 40. I am indebted to Professor John Stephan for pointing out this widespread error.
[38] Azuma, *Between* (2005), 147. Azuma's book is an extraordinarily even-handed treatment of race and racism.
[39] Stephan, *Hawaii*, 26.   [40] Hosokawa, *Nisei*, 259–60.   [41] Ibid.
[42] Hosokawa, *Nisei*, 260.

not that the explanation for that discrepancy must be racial. That thesis is not plausible. To my knowledge, no responsible person ever said such a thing. Again, a broader political and military perspective is necessary. Richard Neustadt, the federal bureaucrat, who as head of the Social Security Board had sought to mitigate the plight of the Japanese Americans, was closer to the mark when he said, "They [The Nikkei] are obviously subject to more suspicion because the war, on this coast at least, is with Japan."

Race prejudice might also have entered into it,[43] but it was not the German or Italian Axis forces which were ripping apart the Western military position in Asia; it was the Japanese Fascists. The German Navy suffered grievously in the 1940 Norway invasion and was mostly bottled up on the German Coast and in the Norwegian fjords thereafter. The Italian Navy could not operate effectively outside the Mediterranean Sea and usually not safely inside it.[44] Also, the German Americans were not participants in market gardening on the scale of the Japanese Americans and therefore close to sensitive defense installations.

Although other groups like the Chinese and Italians also lived in ethnic settlements, "What's operative here isn't 'racial' prejudice but fear/concern about a potentially dangerous, but not yet assimilated, nationality group tied to a treacherous foreign power."[45]

Relocating the German and Italian aliens would have created other problems as well. They were much more numerous and therefore presented political, financial, and logistical problems that removing the Nikkei did not. Evacuating those other aliens to centers would have required a titanic effort. According to Attorney General Francis Biddle, there were 600,000 German aliens and 600,000 Italian ones.

As it was, the Roosevelt Administration had no agency in being capable of handling the 112,000 Japanese Americans. Many of the relocation memoirs complain that the centers were not even finished when the 112,000 Nikkei arrived. What would the situation have been like with an additional 1,200,000? At 10,000 per center such a program would have required 120 more centers!

---

[43] *Tolan Hearings, San Francisco*, pt. 29, 11053.

[44] R. Manvell and H. Fraenkel, *Goering: The Rise and Fall of the Notorious Nazi Leader* (London: Frontline Books, 2011, paperback edition of 1962 Simon and Schuster original), 240.

[45] Email conversation with independent scholar, historian, and linguist Burk Huey, Chapel Hill, NC, July 20, 2009.

The government also was not equipped to handle the political fallout from doing so either, a matter which most observers have ignored. Although many Italian Americans were not citizens, millions were and most Germans were. Citizens voted, and Roosevelt would not want to endanger political support for the war by singling out the numerous relatives of such groups. Eventually, he thought better of putting the Italians in the enemy alien category and took them off of it just in time for the November 1942 elections.

Being consistent in treating the Germans, Italians, and Japanese alike, as many law enforcement leaders urged the government to do, simply demanded too heavy a political and financial cost. Putting the Japanese Americans in centers was a painless way to pay attention to DeWitt and national defense without undermining national morale. The government could not solve all of its security problems, so it solved those which were both most pressing and most manageable. Biddle felt that FDR believed that in times of crisis, the government did what it had to do and sorted out the Constitution later.

Historians of Asian Studies have greatly hardened this preoccupation with race by their interpretations of the facts on the ground. That, in turn, has led to an upending of 1940s anthropological thought about race and loyalty, a near total misunderstanding of the meaning of the fifth column concept, and an unfortunate underestimate of the Tolan Hearings. It has also led to an unthinking dismissal of the threat of vigilantism, a misconception of the experience of the Hawaiian Japanese Americans, and a serious lack of awareness of the urban dimension. Since historians have written extensively about white biases against peoples of color, especially African Americans, Chinese, Hispanics, and Indians/Native Americans, it seems unnecessary to revisit that discussion.

The reversing of anthropological thought must claim our attention first. As Brian Hayashi has shown, by the 1940s, Franz Boas, Ruth Benedict, Otto Klineberg, Alfred Kroeber, Robert Lowie, Paul Radin, and other thinkers had "disconnected biological and cultural evolutions and ushered in a modern, liberal racial ideology making "race" unimportant in predicting human behavior."[46] Yet the race paradigm has restored this habit of using race to predict "human behavior" by using "racism," "white racism," "American racism," "institutional racism," and so forth to explain relocation; in short, to claim collective responsibility based on race for evacuation.

[46] Hayashi, *Democratizing*, 19–20.

One of the most oft-scorned rationales for evacuation was the fifth column fear of Earl Warren and others. The very fact that the Nikkei had not indulged in sabotage before EO9066, Warren said, indicated that they were just waiting for an invasion or attack to pitch in to help the aggressors.

Historians of the Nikkei consider this argument a howler,[47] yet like much of their canon, the objection indicates obliviousness both to military matters and the broader background of the war. What Warren contended was exactly the way a fifth column was supposed to work and did work. Historians have mistakenly argued from logic rather than history.

The term grew out of the Spanish Civil War, when Fascist rebel General Francisco Franco was asked how he could possibly hope to capture Madrid from the Republican forces when he had only four columns of men. Franco is reputed to have replied that he had a fifth column, disloyal to his Republican enemies, within the city waiting to aid his attack. That is how the fifth column worked in Norway when the Nazis attacked that country. As explained above in Chapter 4, the fifth column was feared throughout America, not just the West Coast.

These arguments played out during the West Coast hearings conducted by Congressman John Tolan of Oakland between February 12 and March 12, 1942. This testimony, from a very broad cross-section of the public, constitutes the most complete record of the evacuation story before the actual relocation. It included Congressmen, local elected officials, pressure groups, federal bureaucrats, city administrators, ministers, immigration restrictionists, ex-missionaries, Japanese Americans, Italian Americans, bankers, agriculturalists, chamber of commerce members, publishers, academics, and other interested parties. Fear of Japanese attack suffused the Tolan Hearings. The fearful witnesses were not talking about racism, biological or otherwise. They were discussing the implications of war, of national defense for the West Coast, especially Southern California.

The issue of removal grew into what developed into the Tolan destinations debate. In his capacity as California Attorney General, Earl Warren touched off the discussion by circulating several questions to California law enforcement officials. Warren's question number two asked: "Do you believe that the danger can be adequately controlled by treating all enemy aliens alike, regardless of nationality, or do you believe that we should

---

[47] M. N. Weglyn, *Years of Infamy: The Untold Story of America's Concentration Camps: An Updated Version* (Seattle, WA: University of Washington Press, 1996), 38.

differentiate among them as to nationality?" (Notice the use of the term nationality rather than race.) By the time of the San Francisco portion of the Tolan investigation, Warren had apparently decided that he wanted the Nikkei to be treated separately. If so, he was sorely disappointed by the responses to question two. These were usually conveyed on behalf of the counties by either the district attorney or the sheriff, although sometimes the answers came from the police chiefs of principal cities or county towns, or sometimes a mayor.

For the most part, the answers in the printed Tolan Hearings were very fair minded. Contrary to later interpretations, the law enforcement officials said that they favored treating Italian, German, and Japanese enemy aliens alike. Space does not permit extensive quotation of all of the responses, but a few of the most important ones will serve to make the point. Matthew Brady, the long-time district attorney of San Francisco City and County, said: "There should be no differentiation as to enemy aliens."[48]

Los Angeles City Police Chief C. B. Horrall agreed: "I can see no reason to differentiate between different types of aliens. In my opinion there is only one procedure to follow in handling this situation, which is the concentration of each and every one of the three classes of enemy aliens, and *I do not feel that any material difference exists in their potential danger to the internal security of this country"* (italics added).[49] Sheriff N. L. Cornell of interior Merced County arrived at a similar conclusion by a slightly different route: "I think that the danger can be adequately controlled by treating all enemy aliens alike, regardless of nationality, if they are placed in concentration camps under military guard. Too, that we should not try to differentiate among them as to nationality because I do not believe it can be done without running into a great deal of difficulty."[50] With some reservations, R. T. Wallace, Fresno city chief of police, echoed his colleagues:

There should in my opinion be no difference among them as to nationality, unless the possible Japanese American citizens who have at any time during the past 10 years been back to Japan [the Kibei] and in that case I believe they should be handled in a like manner as the enemy aliens themselves.[51]

The chief of police of Sacramento City took the other side: "I do not believe the danger can be adequately controlled by treating all enemy

[48] *Tolan Hearings, San Francisco*, pt. 29, 10992.   [49] Ibid., 10989.   [50] Ibid., 10998.
[51] Ibid., 10993.

aliens alike – I believe that we should differentiate among them as to nationality," argued A. K. McAllister.[52] "The Japanese aliens alone [not the mass, nor nationality] should be evacuated." His response was unsurprising since his jurisdiction included Sacramento City, home of the McClatchy newspaper chain whose opposition to the Nikkei presence was long standing. The executive secretary of the Joint Immigration Committee itself was V. S. McClatchy. Even a public figure like Mayor Angelo Rossi of San Francisco, who was not sympathetic to Japanese Americans, did not favor forcing out all of the Nikkei. Rossi's testimony primarily aimed to protect the Italian American aliens from evacuation. Thus he told the committee that removing Italian American aliens would undermine war morale, damage families, disgrace their sons in the armed forces, and undermine the ideals for which the country was fighting. Rossi continued:

The activities of the Japanese saboteur[s] and fifth columnists in Honolulu and on the battle fronts in the Pacific have forced me to the conclusion that every Japanese *alien* [emphasis added] should be removed from this community.[53]

A clearer statement that the problems and predicaments of the Japanese stemmed from the larger ones of the national state rather than race could hardly be found.[54] Still, even Rossi stopped short of calling for the ouster of all of the Nikkei on racial grounds.[55]

When advocates of evacuation favored removing all the Nikkei, they usually admitted the distinctions among them and therefore their potential danger. The American Legion was once one of the member institutions of the California Joint Immigration Committee, so its opinion is illustrative. As the *American Legion Magazine* put it in April, 1942, "It is generally recognized that a large number of our Japanese American citizens are loyal to this country *as is any Legionnaire*" (italics added) stated columnist John A. Sinclair. "In fact a considerable number of men of Japanese extraction served in the armed forces during the last war and the Department of California now has two Posts composed exclusively of those men." The magazine did see the war as both racial and national for

---

[52] Ibid., 10993.   [53] Ibid., 10967.

[54] Grodzins, *Americans Betrayed*, 322. Grodzins entire book is an argument that race was the primary motivating factor in the Nikkei story, and especially that military necessity was not.

[55] See also Kashima, *Judgment without Trial*, 16. For example, FDR singled out Hawaiian Nikkei who interacted enthusiastically with Imperial Japanese Navy visitors as potentially dangerous, not all Hawaiian Nikkei.

both the United States and the Empire of Japan, but it is clear that the Legion could tell one Nikkei from another.[56] The problem was not how to distinguish them, but rather how to vet them.

When the government decided on evacuation, the roundup was hurried along by this threat of physical violence. Some historians have minimized this problem, but it seems real enough.[57] The threat of mob or individual mayhem was often mentioned in the Tolan Hearings and many WRA documents, but no one would have had to point it out to the Nikkei. Morton Grodzins, who wrote one of the early accounts of relocation, published in 1949, included a survey of newspaper attitudes. Between Pearl Harbor and Executive Order 9066, the newspapers reported seven murders of Nikkei in the West, four of them supposedly by Filipinos. Contrary to historians who have minimized this rate, it would add up to a high murder rate of twenty-eight per 100,000 for a three-and-a-half-month period, at least quintuple the annual, modern murder rate of 5.5 in 2005.[58] And since these two groups were both Asian, the long-standing animus between Filipinos and Japanese again emphasizes the importance of war and nationality over race. So does the Japanese dislike of the Chinese. They referred to bad qualities within their own communities as "sinification."[59]

The Chinese reciprocated with a "spirit of revenge" for the Sino Japanese War. They shed few tears when the Nikkei were evacuated, slid effortlessly into the Grant Avenue stores that the Japanese were rooted out of, and according to one Chinese observer "hated the Japanese." Their hostility to the Japanese was, if not general, at least very widespread.[60]

Those who could not manage to kill someone did manage to shoot at them or into their homes. The LA *Times* reported four home shootings in

---

[56] J. A. Sinclair, "California on the Alert," *American Legion Magazine*, Vol. 32: No. 4 (April 1942), 29, 56–57.

[57] Grodzins, especially presented a long and spirited discussion discounting the threat of vigilantism, but the *Tolan Hearings* are literally full of this concern for violence against the Nikkei. See p. 1136o. The fear of the Nikkei themselves lasted until well after the war, delaying the departure from the centers for fear of what would happen to them on the outside. See also Grodzins, *Americans Betrayed*, 138–43 and 404–5ff.

[58] For discussions of historical American and English murder rates, see R. Lane, *Murder in America* (Columbus, OH: Ohio State University, 1997), 9–32ff and E. Monkkonen, *Murder in New York City* (Berkeley, CA: University of California Press, 2001), throughout. The latest figure from the *Statistical Abstract of the United States* is 5.5 for the year 2005 in Table 301.

[59] Azuma, *Between*, 38–40.   [60] Brooks, *Alien Neighbors*, 138.

just one edition in 1942. Charles Kikuchi also heard of several shootings. Violence was reported by others, including by some of the most staunch supporters of the Nikkei. Clarence Morris of the American Friends Service Committee noted the "bitterness which has developed on the coast during the years and has now flamed into overt violence."[61] Although the C.I.O. was later praised for opposing evacuation, that claim is not factual and their initial grounds for *favoring* relocation did not differ much from a host of others. Referring to the "hue and cry" against the Nikkei, spokesman Louis Goldblatt maintained, "In light of these developments no choice remained for the thousands of loyal Americans of Japanese parentage but to agree to general evacuation. To remain was to invite lawlessness and mob violence."[62]

What was especially ominous about these outbursts was that the authorities could not protect the Nikkei. In the immediate aftermath of Pearl Harbor, some cities did deploy more police in the Japanese settlements,[63] but usually the city police were 15 to 20 percent under strength. At the same time, the global conflict overtasked them by adding wartime duties to their regular peacetime roles. Supervising civil defense, making security checks for the numerous defense workers like the masses of shipbuilders (280,000 in the Bay Area alone), and chasing crooks left little time for anything else.[64] As the LA City Police Chief maintained, officers had to perform their regular duties, plus help with fire prevention, protect public utilities, and provide "the increased service of investigating suspects."[65] Short of placing a sentry at every house, the Army could not protect the Nikkei either. In any case, the Army was not trained for police work and the Shore Patrol and Military Police had their hands full with partying and law-breaking servicemen. Sometimes the latter had to depend on civilian jails to house their own exuberant, often drunken charges.

The terrible defeats in the war, the destruction of the Japanese American economy, the political protests against them, and the physical threat to them made their situation hopeless. Perhaps the lack of federal law enforcement was one of the shortcomings of federalism, but whatever

---

[61] *Tolan Hearinigs, Los Angeles and San Francisco*, pt. 31, 11747.
[62] *Tolan Hearings, Portland and Seattle*, pt. 30, 11187.
[63] *Sacramento Bee*, December 8, 1941, 1.
[64] Lotchin, *Bad City in the Good War: San Francisco, Los Angeles, Oakland, and San Diego* (Bloomington, IN: University of Indiana Press, 2003), 202.
[65] Grapes, *Japanese American*, 47.

the case, there simply were not enough available policemen for the Japanese Americans.

Counterintuitively, the war did not have a similar anti-Nikkei effect in Hawaii, the great staging ground for the American counterattack to the West, a site much closer to the fighting, and home to some 157,000–160,000 Japanese Americans. The different treatment of the Germans and Italians on the mainland is cited repeatedly as definitive proof that the taking of the Nikkei was racially motivated. But if that were so, then how does one explain that Hawaiians of the same race, nationality, culture, and ancestry were not taken?

Nor does the absence of racial, national, or cultural tension explain this discrepancy because identity hostility and distrust pervaded everything in Hawaii.[66] The reason the Hawaiians were spared the fate of their mainland brethren was that their labor was needed on the plantations of the powerful whites (haoles pronounced howlies) and in the Islands' defense industries by the even more powerful General Delos Emmons, commander of the Islands under martial law.

In Hawaii, Emmons followed an entirely different path to an utterly different outcome. He did not think the Nikkei were a security risk, and he was a much more decisive and sophisticated person than John DeWitt. Despite the support of both Stimson and FDR, Emmons managed to finesse the attempt at mass Hawaiian removal.[67] In an Eisenhower-like scheme of interpretive complexity, the importance of individual personality was crucial. Instead of letting the Nikkei story spiral out of control or abdicating to FDR or Stimson, Emmons declared martial law in Hawaii and acted promptly to spike any anti-Nikkei movement.[68] So the national security motivation was entirely consistent.[69] On the West Coast, the Nikkei were considered a military threat; in Hawaii they were an asset to national defense.

The canon also ignores most of the urban dimension and the urban dimension accounted for much of the threat of vigilantism to the Nikkei. On the one hand, it is universally assumed that hysteria explained the relocation centers, but on the other that the Nikkei were not in danger,

---

[66] Bailey and Farber, *The First Strange Place: Race and Sex in World War II Hawaii* (Baltimore, MD: Johns Hopkins University Press, 1992), 167–210, especially 191–205.

[67] Stimson, *Diary*, Vol. 36, November 1 to December 31, 1941, December 20, 1941, no page indicated. Robinson, *By Order*, 146–54.

[68] Bailey and Farber, *First Strange Place*, 4–6; Robinson, *By Order*, 146–58; Grodzins, *Americans Betrayed*, 299.

[69] Quoted in the *Heart Mountain Sentinel*, February 26, 1944, 5.

that is, safe if not taken into them. These two interpretations are not consistent and, in turn, they highlight the importance of the urban dimension. The term "urbanization" is employed by urban historians to indicate the degree to which (or percentage of) the total population of the United States lives in cities. And the term "urbanism" is used to explain what the quality of life in cities was like.

In 1940, this stage of the West Coast "process of urbanization" which concentrated people in cities and the demographic structure of urbanism placed the Nikkei in maximum danger. A large proportion lived in cities, enough to seem a threat to their Caucasian enemies, but not separated from their Asian ones. That meant that they would be beset by enemies both without and within Los Angeles, San Francisco, Seattle other urban places. Yet their concentrations in these cities were not yet sufficient to allow them to defend themselves.

The urban collective violence experience of African Americans is instructive. Until World War I, blacks were mostly concentrated in the southern countryside and small towns where they were tragically vulnerable to lynchings, debasement, and segregation. When the war pulled them to the North to war work, they were eventually attacked in race riots,[70] but here they fought back and after that war violent white encroachments on their "turf" virtually ceased. The war enhanced the Chicago black population from 50,000 to 100,000 and that was simply too many people to intimidate. As historians Jeffrey Sammons and Davarian Baldwin have demonstrated, concentration in cities not only provided protection for African Americans, but also the basis for the blossoming of black culture.[71] The post-war resurgent Ku Klux Klan also flowered all over the North as well, but not in northern cities.[72] World War I riots there were aplenty, but from that point on there were very few white-initiated urban race riots. Urban West Coast Japanese Americans had not yet attained this critical mass.

---

[70] For these riots see, among others, J. R. Grossman, *Land of Hope: Chicago, Black Southerners, and the Great Migration* (Chicago, IL: The University of Chicago Press, 1989), 5, 32, 55, 213, 222–3, 259–60ff; E. Rudwick, *Race Riot at East St. Louis, July 2, 1917* (New York, NY: Atheneum, 1972), 3–7ff; W. M. Tuttle, Jr., *Race Riot: Chicago in the Red Summer of 1919* (New York, NY: Atheneum, 1972), 3–73ff.

[71] D. L. Baldwin, *Chicago's New Negroes: Modernity, Migration and Black Urban Life* (Chapel Hill, NC: The University of North Carolina Press, 2007), 1–21ff.

[72] K. T. Jackson, *The Ku Klux Klan in the City, 1915–1930* (New York, NY: Oxford University Press, 1967), 3–24, 235–56ff.

This low density urban makeup made a stay-put policy equally unrealistic. In the bigger cities, especially San Francisco and Los Angeles, the Japanese' enemies suffused their settlements. There were Caucasians and others in the Fillmore District of San Francisco and Koreans, Chinese, and Filipinos in Los Angeles. The whites were angry about the Japanese attacks on Pearl Harbor, Manila, and other US possessions but the other Asians were angrier still. The Imperial Japanese had invaded and were brutalizing their homelands[73] and in the case of the Chinese had been doing so since late 1937. As historian Charlotte Brooks has shown, the Japanese and Filipinos were fighting even after they had resettled from the centers to Chicago later in the war.

The demographic structure of urbanism on the West Coast certainly worked against them. So did the urban housing supply. It is often said that after the Battle of Midway national defense was no longer a rationale for relocation, which makes a good point. But by that time the housing situation added to the Nikkei's woes. The war created a large-scale migration into a very limited number of defense boom towns. That was what Representative Ed Izak's famous congressional investigation was all about, how to decentralize war spending and provide more housing.

Returning the Nikkei to San Francisco, Los Angeles, Oakland, and San Diego would have worked against this policy. The Nikkei residences were the only large bloc of housing available to hard-pressed defense workers. By Midway this had already been taken over by defense workers, especially African Americans, which transformed settlements like LA Japantowns into Bronzevilles.

This also means that the process of urbanization had not taken enough of them out of their isolated and defenseless agricultural households and into defensible urban ones. They were vulnerable to attack on these farms and nothing that the national government could do would protect them. And even if the government had been inclined to do so, there was no available police force to carry out the task. Unlike France, where all of the police were controlled by the central state, the American national government had no such protective body. The American police have always been decentralized.

Is there a possible alternative explanation of relocation of a clear, specific racial nature? There is not. There was no sudden emergence on the West Coast of a racial demagogue like the infamous contemporary

---

[73] The Rape of Nanking and the brutal Japanese response to the Doolittle Raid were not the least of them.

congressman John Rankin of Mississippi. Rankin did consider the Pacific War a race war, but he could only offer up a voice from his own state or the Congress. He was not involved in the politics or relocation. Nor was there a notorious outbreak of collective racial violence like the Detroit Race Riot of 1943. The Zoot Suit riots of LA were more than a year in the future. Moreover, before the war, there had been no significant movement to dispossess and remove the Nikkei on racial grounds, no mass calls for expulsion. A lonely voice here and there, like that of Congressman Leland Ford, but no movement involving the majority of ordinary people, or even many influential people.

The race paradigm grew out of a number of ill-fated circumstances and equally mistaken interpretations of them.

PART II

CONCENTRATION CAMPS OR RELOCATION CENTERS?

8

Definitions versus Historical Reality

Concentration Centers in Cuba, South Africa, and the Philippines

Those parks and gardens [at Manzanar] lent it an oriental character, but in most ways it was a totally equipped American small town, complete with schools, churches, Boy Scouts, beauty parlors, neighborhood gossip, fire and police departments, glee clubs, softball leagues, Abbott and Costello movies, tennis courts, and traveling shows.[1]

Jeanne Wakatsuki Houston and James D. Houston in Brian Grapes,
Japanese American Internment Camps.

One of the most telling arguments against the race paradigm and for a more complex interpretation of relocation was the humane way in which the centers were administered. The WRA made a point of rejecting the concentration camp demand by the anti-Nikkei. They could not totally eliminate the eternal tension between majority rule and minority rights, but they could try. And try hard they did, mitigating the burdens of majority rule and upholding minority rights whenever they could.

Once the government decided to commit the Nikkei to more permanent centers, several possibilities existed, some better than others. One trial balloon was quickly punctured. Milton Eisenhower and others thought that it would serve both the national security interests and the agricultural war effort[2] if the Nikkei were scattered around the West, salt and pepper style. Getting them into the interior would calm fears of coastal states, break up Nikkei ghettos, and provide badly needed agricultural labor for the interior states. At a meeting in Salt Lake City, the western governors, with the notable exception of Colorado's, stormed all over this idea. They

---

[1] J. W. Houston and J. D. Houston in B. J. Grapes, *Japanese American*, 143.
[2] For the American agricultural war effort, see L. Collingham, *The Taste*, 75–88, 415–90ff.

loudly proclaimed that any individual Nikkei settling in the interior would be at risk and that they would only accept any if they were penned up in concentration camps. The Army could not protect dispersed groups either.[3]

Akin to the salt and pepper solution was one that might be termed the "wandering proletariat" plan. In this, the evacuees could be collected in centers close to where there was a need for "stoop labor." "They could migrate at various seasons in accordance with the labor needs of the different areas, again under the necessary supervision and control." This proposal would free up Filipino and Mexican labor to work in agriculture in the "more strategic [prohibited] areas."[4]

A third solution would have left the Nikkei in their isolated farmsteads and urban settlements, that is, to follow a partial ghetto strategy. Unfortunately, there was no one to protect them, especially those on isolated farms. Since those in cities lived mixed in with their wartime enemies, as in the South Central District of Los Angeles where they lived cheek by jowl with the infuriated Filipinos, Chinese, and Koreans. In these districts and the Fillmore neighborhood of San Francisco,[5] where they lived amongst other irate non-Japanese, an urban option would have been a "ghetto from hell."

Late in the game, Army Chief of Staff George Marshall sent General Mark Clark out to assess the military threat to the West Coast. Clark found it insufficient to justify mass removal. Instead he advocated removing "enemy aliens" from critical installations like the Boeing plants and Bremerton Navy Yard "and permitting the entry of all others by pass only. Civilian police and the FBI would be [the] responsible security forces." He would have enforced good behavior by threats of vigilantism.[6] Historians have characterized relocation as akin to the Nazi treatment of European Jews,[7] but the policy of urban concentration would have been much closer to a Nazi "solution" than the relocation centers ultimately were.

As they conquered Eastern Europe, the Nazis indeed herded East European Jewry into urban ghettos from which they had been freed during the nineteenth century.[8] There they remained as the old, invalids,

---

[3] M. S. Eisenhower, "Memorandum for Members of Congress," April 20, 1942, RG 210, Box 2, NA.
[4] *Tolan Hearings, Portland and Seattle*, pt. 29, 11195.
[5] For the Okinawans see B. Kobashigawa, *History of the Okinawans*.
[6] Daniels, *Prisoners*, 44.   [7] Daniels, *Prisoners*, 47.
[8] R. Bennett, Under the *Shadow of the Swastika: The Moral Dilemmas of Resistance and Collaboration in Hitler's Germany* (New York, NY: New York University Press, 1999), 206–7.

and very young were periodically "selected" for the death camps and the able-bodied young were sent off to slave labor camps. The rest festered in their newly reestablished ghettos drawing down their savings, if they still had any, starving, and bravely trying to keep their culture alive until their own "selection."

Although they did not describe it as such, this "ghetto solution," leaving the Nikkei in place, was advocated by some of their most ardent friends, who had not thought through the implications of that strategy, but it was a non-starter anyway. By early March, 1942, an aroused mass media and pressure groups would not have allowed it.

A fourth option was the out and back idea. In that, all Nikkei would be removed from the coastal zones. Then after loyalty checks, those who passed them could return.[9] That solution did not speak to the problem of Nikkei security, but it would have allowed a limited amount of return.[10] Of course, a loyalty check would have left the spies free to operate, since no spy in his right mind would voluntarily confess to being one.

A fifth option would have had other appalling side effects. During the destination debate between late February and mid-March, 1942, several parties suggested a literal concentration camp approach and one that was so called. Under this arrangement the government would have created agricultural "settlements" that would have set the Nikkei to farming for the national defense effort. This was proposed by the more determined Nikkei enemies, like the Pacific League. Congressman Leland Ford was one of the most vociferous advocates.[11] These critics argued that in this way Japanese Americans would contribute their "fair share" to national defense and would not get into anybody else's way. Nothing was said about disrupting communities, forcing people into defense work, or isolating them out in the tules.[12] One opponent of the agricultural ghetto plan aptly called it a "concentration camp type of serfdom."

Fortunately, the government opted for the evacuation centers. These were by far and away the most humane and realistic alternative once war and the attendant problems and predicaments of the nation state had destroyed the Nikkei economy, held hostage their property, destroyed

---

[9] *Tolan Hearings, Portland and Seattle*, pt. 30, 11094.
[10] *Tolan Hearings, Portland and Seattle*, pt. 30, 1087–92.
[11] Grodzins, *Americans Betrayed*, 65. Grodzins believed that T. B. Drake a Washington representative of the LA Chamber of Commerce was the initial organizer of the effort to evacuate the Nikkei. Grodzins, *Americans Betrayed*, 67.
[12] The term tules refers to tule rushes, which in a California context equates to the word "boondocks," in use elsewhere.

their good name, and eliminated their security. It has so far escaped the notice of historians of the Japanese American experience that the concentration camp solution was specifically considered and rejected. The principal actors in the drama understood very well the difference between a concentration camp and a relocation center.[13]

Still, it required a struggle to make the relocation center alternative an acceptable one. As already noted, many critics of the Nikkei, including Roosevelt himself, as Roger Daniels, Greg Robinson, and other historians have shown, wanted the Japanese Americans placed in "concentration camps." Nor did they mince words in describing them, employing that exact term. The fact that the centers did not turn out to be concentration camps was not because no one was trying to make them so.

The centers became more humane because a lot of people wanted them to be. These included both the center administrators and the precocious Nikkei themselves. Not the least of the former was Milton Eisenhower, the first head of the WRA. Eisenhower opposed the concentration camp solution on grounds of humanitarian sympathy and political realism. In a conflict where the Axis side was trying to portray the struggle as a race war, pitting Asians against whites, Eisenhower thought that harsh treatment of the Nikkei would hand a propaganda victory to the enemy.

Some historians believe that the American Government feared for the safety of Americans in Japanese camps if they allowed harsh treatment in their own.[14] That hostage theory may have been a factor, but from the establishment of the Fair Play Committee onwards religious spokesmen had emphatically stated their opposition to relocation itself, let alone concentration camps. The WRA itself was ubiquitous with people insisting on humane treatment. The American government knew by the time of Bataan Death March that the Japanese Army was quite capable of inhumanity, regardless of how the Americans treated the Nikkei in evacuation centers. They certainly knew about the worsening conditions in

---

[13] As Roger Daniels has noted, Japanese American contemporaries did not usually employ the term concentration camps to describe the centers. As he explained it the term was infrequently used by contemporaries and only came into vogue when historians much later came to accept it at the time of the campaign for redress. See Daniels, "Words Do Matter: A Note on Inappropriate Terminology and the Incarceration of the Japanese-Americans," in L. Fiset and G. M. Nomura, editors, *Nikkei in the Pacific Northwest: Japanese Americans and Japanese Canadians in the Twentieth Century* (Seattle, WA: University of Washington Press: 2009), 195–206.

[14] Hayashi, *Democratizing*, 11.

the Imperial camps in the Philippines housing some 5,000–7,000 American civilians.[15]

From Milton Eisenhower on down, many Americans felt that the relocation centers were an injustice to the Japanese Americans,[16] which, along with their religious convictions, is the main explanation for the humane conditions of the relocation centers.

The American opponents of camps had various reasons for opposing them, economic, religious, constitutional, and diplomatic. The Protestant churches are illustrative. Clarence Pickett, Executive Secretary of the American Friends Service Committee, wrote to a Quaker correspondent in Pasadena said that "without doubt the Japanese people are extremely keen to know what happens to their nationals who are in this country.... If they are put in concentration camps, it will contribute long-term, almost age-long bitterness."[17] The West Coast Protestants, along with some shippers, the American Civil Liberties Union of Southern California, the Fair Play Committee, and others were among those defending the rights of the Nikkei and opposing evacuation.[18] Even after General DeWitt and the government decided that military necessity required evacuation, the Protestant churches continued to oppose it.

However, if evacuation was absolutely necessary, the churches offered their services to help mitigate the blow to the Japanese Americans and, more important, urged a laundry list of guarantees that would help to lessen the shock. Protestant churches country-wide joined in this effort, sometimes on a denominational basis and sometimes as members of an umbrella organization, like the Federal Council of Churches of Christ in America. Their list of suggested guarantees varied from group to group, but it included many of the provisions that the WRA ultimately included in the relocation centers. For example, the Friends urged that families be kept together, that the government work to keep up morale of the Nikkei, to "improve their skills, to produce a part of their support," and to protect their "spirit of independence and self-reliance."[19] The Portland Council of Churches demanded that the "Federal Government" pay the entire expense of moving, protect and care for the evacuees' property, supply complete medical care, protect family integrity, and guarantee "the

[15] Cogan, *Captured*, 108–176ff.   [16] G. Y. Okihiro, *Storied*, 128.
[17] *Tolan Hearings, Los Angeles and San Francisco*, pt. 31, 11746.
[18] For a recent assessment of the Fair Play Committee, see C. Wollenberg, "'Dear Earl': The Fair Play Committee, Earl Warren, and Japanese Internment," *California History*, Vol. 89: No. 4 (2012), 24–61.
[19] *Tolan Hearings, Los Angeles and San Francisco*, pt. 31, 11746–47.

uninterrupted schooling of children of evacuees ... and adult education be offered in the reception centers."[20]

The government rejected the concentration camp idea and individual relocation in favor of centers run by the government operated on Judeo Christian principles and those of Western Civilization. As one former non-Japanese, Manzanar resident put it:

> It [the plaque of the National Park Service at the Manzanar Relocation site] shouldn't say "concentration camp." It wasn't one ... In a concentration camp the people are in horrible straits. I mean, in Europe you know, just terrible and all jammed together and no privileges, no means of keeping themselves clean or anything else. And this is not true of Manzanar. Manzanar was a war relocation center. The living conditions were pretty adverse at first, but after the camp was built and the people had a chance to, like I say to make themselves comfortable, it was pretty good. It wasn't bad at all. (Anna T. Kelley, resident of Independence, California, and former employee of the Pacific Indemnity Company, which insured the five companies that built the Manzanar Relocation Center.)[21]

To challenge the term "concentration camp" is not intended to belittle the injury that relocation did to Japanese Americans or to engage in semantics.

Although the vast majority of Americans of Japanese ancestry (AJA) never set foot in a center, many did and their injury was considerable. At the very least they lost two to three years of their liberty. Various prejudices against them were hardened, especially as the numerous Dies Committee attacks indicate. Many of them saved all or part of their property, but many lost much or all of it,[22] especially their household goods. Although 50 percent of the evacuees were able to return to the West Coast after the war, many drifted to other parts of the land. The word "Jap" crept into everyday usage by the newspapers, even liberal ones like the Los Angeles *Daily News*.[23] At least in the beginning, the Nikkei were forced to live in substandard, unhealthy conditions at the relocation centers.

For several months, many were uprooted and shuttled around between centers, as the WRA tried to cope with the rebel and pro-Imperial, Fascist Japanese disorder within the centers and the anti-Japanese agitation

[20] *Tolan Hearings, Los Angeles and San Francisco*, pt. 31, 11390.
[21] A. A. Hansen and N. K. Jesch, *Japanese American: Part V: Guards and Townspeople*, Vol. 2, 29.
[22] The CWRIC, held that only 27 percent of "farm operators" retained their property, *Personal Justice*, 241.
[23] *Los Angeles Daily News*, December 8, 1941, 29; December 9, 1941, 27.

without. They also had to bear the foolish and often condescending remarks of those who were curtailing their liberties. For example, Tom Clark, the civilian on loan from the Justice Department to General DeWitt to help organize evacuation, famously stated when only a few Japanese requested welfare to compensate for their property loss, he "praised the Japanese for solving their own problems."[24] Or the even more callous advice to the Nikkei that they should show their "patriotism" by accepting what was happening to them. They certainly did demonstrate their patriotism, vastly more than many other civilians involved in the war, but the gratuitous counsel could only have seemed wounding and ironic.

None of this justifies the use of the term "concentration camp" to describe the relocation centers. This kind of language does not fit the facts; moreover, it demeans those who had to endure unimaginably worse conditions in real concentration camps in Cuba, South Africa, the Philippines and above all, Nazi and Japanese Fascist camps in the 1940s. So we should begin with the question of whether the centers were anything like those in World War II, or any other earlier examples, or whether they were relocation centers, which was their official title during World War II.

The reader should be advised that the term, though widely used, is not universally deployed. Despite the decision of the Park Service to employ a term which equates these relocation centers with Nazi camps in World War II, many historians who write about this subject do not utilize that label. Still, the term is widely used in both titles and texts. One historian employed the phrase nearly fifty times in a book of under 200 pages.[25] Some historians who use the phrase simply state that the expression is fully descriptive without explaining why.[26] Others sometimes argue that the American centers were comparable to European ones, and on other occasions declare that they were not[27] while others consistently hold that the relocation centers were like some species of European concentration camps, that is, the "milder ones," if there was such a thing. Others deny the comparison to Europe but continue to employ the phrase. The most recent study insists the term concentration camp was widely used, so it uses that term along with "the officially sanctioned terms evacuation and

---

[24] SF *Chronicle*, March 10, 1942, 4.   [25] G. Okihiro, *Storied*, throughout.
[26] Taylor, Jewel, 88.
[27] R. Daniels, *Asian Americans*, 235; Daniels, *Concentration Camps USA*, 105. At one point, Daniels denies the centers were like European camps Auschwitz or Vorkuta, then goes on to say that "They were, in fact, much more like a century-old American institution, the Indian reservation, than like the institutions that flourished in totalitarian Europe."

relocation centers."[28] That is certainly an improvement, but we should instead judge the term by whether it parallels the historic concentration camps. Obviously it does not.

Historian Greg Robinson is one of the few relocation historians to question the term. He rightly thought it too reminiscent of the Nazi camps, as did the CWRIC.[29] But Robinson did not disapprove others' employing the expression.[30] Others did, and so did Robinson himself in a section entitled "Prewar Fears For Security and Preparations for Concentration Camps."[31] He also repeated the common charge that relocation was a euphemism, though it seems no more a euphemism than the term "confinement" that he preferred.[32] Still his discussion is an improvement. Some liken the American centers to Indian reservations, but continue to call the American centers concentration camps rather than Japanese American (AJA) reservations.

An apparent consensus and "generic" definition is that they were places where "minorities, identified by race, nationality, and/or ethnicity [were] concentrated or confined in designated areas known as concentration camps."[33] For many reasons this definition is not viable either, not least because it would exclude the original concentration camps in Cuba, South Africa, and the Philippines, which were created to confine majority populations, not minorities. The popular generic definition would also exclude the original Nazi camps, created to hold Germans, not minorities, and Soviet slave labor camps and Chinese or Cambodian camps, where majority people were confined for political reasons.

No matter how much we might argue about the phrase, in the twentieth century it has become unbreakably linked to Nazi Germany. And that is what is implied when used without specific explanation of the term. To investigate this point, I polled some 400 UNC students on the subject, asking their definition of a concentration camp, specifically the time, place, and circumstances of such. Almost every single one responded that a concentration camp was a Nazi World War II camp. A handful mentioned a generic definition of a concentration camp where a minority was held behind barbed wire for political, racial, or nationalistic reasons. Without exception, these latter specified the Nazi concentration camps as the foremost examples. Any supposed generic camp was based on the

[28] Reeves, *Infamy*, xx.   [29] CWRIC, *Personal Justice*, 27.
[30] Robinson, *Tragedy of Democracy*, vii–viii.   [31] Ibid., 47–50.   [32] Ibid., 141.
[33] Reader's report for the University of Arizona Press on *The Reach of American Racism*. Kristen Buckles, acquisitions editor to the author, September 18, 2012.

historic camps that bear that name. It lends a much greater discipline to the discussion to insist on historical standards rather than theoretical and semantic ones.

Yet since the term relocation has so often been called a euphemism, perhaps we should ask if that is a more appropriate expression. Euphemism is not a very satisfactory word, because it is too subjective and incapable of being tested. A better way to settle the issue is by usage and by historic standards. In the first place, the term "relocation" derives from the War Relocation Authority, the agency which ran the centers.

In addition, calling the centers internment camps, or the process, one of internment, confuses these centers with the real internment camps operated by the Justice Department. These were established to house the more dangerous cases, persons usually arrested in the first few hours after Pearl Harbor. That term would not only be confusing, but it would implicate the innocent Nikkei with the often not so innocent persons of German, Italian, and Japanese descent who were interned by the Justice Department.

One very important, additional difference is that the Nikkei could not easily leave the Justice Department internment camps. They *could* leave the relocation centers. So this is the more descriptive term, does not confuse one kind of center with another, and reflects the usages of the Nikkei themselves (if the term relocation or evacuation center is a euphemism, it is one that the Nikkei themselves used). It also coincides with the official name of the centers. They were not known as War Concentration Camps. And relocation was more appropriate because the centers were never intended as a permanent or long-term solution, only a waystation to a "relocation" away from the West Coast.[34]

Beyond these considerations, what is most troubling about calling these institutions concentration camps is that the term obscures both the precocious and courageous nature of the AJA adaptation to relocation and also the largely benevolent motivations of the centers' operators.[35] Hannah Arendt, in her definition of a Nazi concentration camp, argues that they were the key institutions of totalitarian systems and that the overriding purpose of the concentration camps was to break down the

---

[34] See http://dwightmurphy-collectedwritings.info/published/pub38.htm, p. 9.
[35] There is a wealth of evidence to support this statement, but a good place to see would be the semi-annual reports of the WRA, cited below.

individuality and spontaneity of the inmates.[36] Of course, the desert centers were not central to the American system; they were entirely peripheral to it. And they were not designed to break down the individuality and spontaneity of the Japanese. They were intended to promote them, to encourage the Nikkei to function successfully in a highly individualistic, spontaneous, capitalistic, and democratic world outside.

Historians have rightly called for comparisons of these centers across space, that is, especially the United States, Canada, and Latin America. The Canadian centers were more Spartan than the American centers of that period.[37] But we should also make comparisons across time. To get closer to the meaning of the term concentration camp, we must examine *historic camps*, of which there were at least three species in the history of western civilization before World War II. These were the 1890s camps in Cuba and those in South Africa and the Philippines at the turn of the nineteenth century. We should begin with the Cuban experience, since that is where the term apparently originated. Those camps grew out of the Cuban Independence Revolt against Spain in the 1890s. There the revolutionaries pursued a scorched earth policy designed to destroy the economic structure of the island, which would force the Cuban rural population either to join the insurrectionists or to flee into the Spanish-held towns and cities. This would reduce the Spanish towns' food supply, while increasing the numbers of people needing it.

The strategy worked gruesomely well, urbanizing thousands and then forcing the Spanish authorities to concentrate many others in order to protect them from the insurrectionists. So the policies of both sides led to a lethal, forced urbanization. Eventually a new Spanish regime ended this confinement, but by then it was too late. Some 170,000 out of a total Cuban population of 1,700,000 starved. Photographs from the period show soldiers sitting atop massive piles of skeletal remains. Others portray starving children whose appearance would have been indistinguishable from the inmates in the Third Reich lagers.[38]

This discussion does not take sides in what Professor Lawrence Tone describes as a very complicated situation, but merely tries to establish the outlines of what the Cubans called "reconcentration." Cubans were

---

[36] H. Arendt, *The Origins of Totalitarianism* (Cleveland, OH: The World Publishing Company, 1958), 237–59.

[37] Robinson, *Tragedy of Democracy*, 170–80.

[38] This discussion is based on J. L. Tone, *War and Genocide in Cuba, 1895–1898* (Chapel Hill, NC: The University of North Carolina Press, 2006), 193–224.

caught in the middle of a revolutionary situation; they were confined in towns, not in camps; they suffered enormous privation; and they eventually died in numbers sufficient to persuade an expert to describe their experience as "genocide." Their experience could not have been more different from the WRA relocation centers.

Nor could the camps in the Boer War, 1899–1902. Although the exact status of the Dutch Republics in South Africa as British colonies or independent states is cloudy, the conflict there was also a revolution. And the British military likewise employed the technique of concentration as a measure of war to counter it. They did so to deprive the Dutch (Boers) of sympathizers, suppliers, havens, food, and informants in the countryside. They also burned farms and killed livestock to impoverish the Dutch armies further.

Some would say that the British camps were refugee camps to succor those displaced, but for whatever reason they soon blossomed all over the areas of conflict. From the beginning, the camps were nasty and gendered. The British Army put mostly women and children into the camps, which totaled at least 137,000 and possibly 160,000 at their most populous. These women and children were crowded into tents, without adequate food, water, medical supplies, or doctors. As a result, 32,000 died, 20,000 whites and 12,000 blacks, of measles, typhoid, and other epidemics.[39] That was an appalling death rate of 20–23 percent, though the figure represents only the camp deaths, not deaths for the entire population as the Cuban figures do.

Like the Cuban camps, the horrifying British ones attracted public sympathy, especially through the work of, Quaker Emily Hobhouse and moderate suffragist Millicent Fawcett. Again, the camps were closed down, but not before thousands died.

Less is written about the concentration camps in the Philippine Insurrection/American-Philippine War, but the casualty figures are apparently higher than those in the Boer conflict. As in the other conflicts, this one was between a colonial power (the United States) and nationalist rebels. In order to separate the loyal from the insurgents, the Americans gathered Filipino populations into "fenced, guarded compounds." Anyone found beyond camp after curfew was considered a guerrilla and

---

[39] My discussion of the Boer War camps is based on T. Packenham, *The Boer War* (New York, NY: Random House, 1979), xxi–xxii and 522–49; F. R. Van Hartesveldt, *The Boer War* (Phoenix Mill, UK: Sutton Publishing Company, 2000), 71–76, 88–90; and D. Judd and K. Surridge, *The Boer War* (London: John Murray, 2002), 184–96.

liable to summary execution.[40] The camps spawned disease, killing off children and the elderly in "disproportionate numbers."[41]

Another historian claimed that the motivation for reconcentration was to win by the "isolation and starvation of guerrillas through the deliberate annihilation of the rural economy" and by forcing "peasants into garrisoned towns." Outside the towns troops adopted a "scorched earth policy" destroying everything of economic value: homes, crops, and livestock. One scholar put Philippine war deaths at 250,000, of which 50,000 were combat fatalities, so presumably, 200,000 died because of reconcentration, of which 150,000 came from the one province of Batangas alone.[42] None of these were like the American relocation centers.

However, to be fully comparable it is necessary also to include those camps in the 1940s Japanese Empire. The only civilian camps in World War II, that were similar to the historic concentration camps were those run by the Japanese Fascists in their conquered Asian territories. Those in the Philippines were camps for 5,000–7,000 American and British civilians picked up by the Japanese in their first triumphant months of war.[43] Space limitations preclude an exhaustive comparison, but a few matters can be addressed.[44]

The Japanese administrators ran a fairly loose regime to begin with. It frequently allowed inmates to leave camp, to secure food and supplies from the outside, and extensive privileges. However, as their war losses mounted, the Japanese progressively clamped down. This included some, but not extensive levels of torture, the shooting of four American camp leaders for their "stubbornness,"[45] and the revocation of most privileges. The Japanese did not provide food until well into the war, so the internees had to grow it or buy it from Filipino vendors, which exhausted their own resources. When the Japanese finally assumed that "burden," they fed the inmates according to an inadequate "soldier's" ration. They stole much of this before it got to the camp inmates.[46] Famine loomed by the end of

---

[40] H. W. Brands, *Bound to Empire: The United States and the Philippines* (New York, NY: Oxford University Press, 1992), 57.

[41] Brands, *Bound to Empire*, 57.

[42] P. A. Kramer, *Race, Empire, the United States, and the Philippines* (Chapel Hill, NC: University of North Carolina Press, 2006), 152–7. Brands did not provide a death toll and Kramer eschews a total estimate so my figure rests on his estimate of total deaths, minus those killed in fighting.

[43] Cogan, *Captured*, 1–9.

[44] Cogan, *Captured*. The book is not a specific comparison of American and Japanese camps, but it is a startling indictment of the Japanese camps.

[45] Cogan, *Captured*, 139.   [46] Cogan, *Captured*, 149–53.

1944, together with the attendant diseases triggered by it.[47] Like the Nikkei in relocation centers, the Americans and British civilians suffered huge property losses, and myriad postwar problems, everything from health to housing.[48]

Still, as historian Frances Cogan correctly explains, these camps did not completely replicate the conditions in Nazi camps,[49] nor one might add, of the historic centers either. Starvation would seem to be the most common denominator of real concentration camps. Thus perhaps the principal difference between these Japanese camps and the Nazi and historic concentration camps was one of time. The mostly American inmates in the Imperial Japanese camps were close to starvation, but they had not yet starved. Yet there was little question that it was Japanese policy to let the Allied prisoners starve.[50] The Japanese certainly understood that mass murder would be the outcome of their policy.[51]

Nor were the barbarities of the Japanese limited to either whites or prisoners of war. The Japanese treatment of other "peoples of color" is illustrative of the falsity of the Imperial war propaganda that the war was being fought to create an "Asia for the Asians." It is also testimony to the universality of the Japanese Army's[52] barbarity against peoples of occupied countries, regardless of race. Despite being Asians of color, residents of Guam were forced into agricultural slavery to feed the Japanese military. As the Japanese losses mounted in the war, they cheated, murdered, raped, and brutalized the Guamanians. The historian of the Japanese occupation of Guam repeatedly employs the term "slaughter" to characterize Japanese treatment of the locals. That drove the Guamanians into attacking the Japanese soldiers when they strayed from their bases.[53]

Historians[54] are right to remind us that words do matter; we should be reminded too that realities matter more. So what were the realities in the Americans centers?

---

[47] The Japanese soldiers, in turn, suffered stupendous privation due to the inefficiency of their services. Collingham, *Taste*, 273–316. Civilians did too.

[48] Cogan, Captured, 311–13.   [49] Cogan, *Captured*, 109.

[50] Corbett, *Quiet Passages*, 179. Corbett called it "the edge of extinction."

[51] Cogan, *Captured*, 197, 199, 201, 268–9, 281, 288.

[52] I have stressed the term "Army" here to avoid the implication that all Japanese were as barbarous as the Army.

[53] R. Mansell, *Captured: The Forgotten Men of Guam*, ed. L. Goetz Holmes, (Annapolis, MD: Naval Institute Press, 2012), 44, 155–60, 160–4ff.

[54] Op. cit., Daniels, 195–206.

9

Resistance or Cooperation?

When decorated Nisei war hero Ben Kuroki visited Heart Mountain, he was mobbed. The airman "was received at a public reception at the administration flag pole where thousands of residents gave him an inspiring greeting."[1] Then some 1,000 people packed the Heart Mountain auditorium to welcome Kuroki. He was wined, dined, toasted, hosted, danced, speechified, and sought out by almost everyone. Several celebrations were held in his honor; he was invited to speak to many clubs and organizations and was literally hounded for his autograph.

The relocation literature has emphasized the instances when the Nikkei did not behave cooperatively, but rather resisted the government, the WRA, and their own leaders, especially the JACL. The point of this approach is to question the "model minority" reputation of cooperation with the WRA that the Nikkei earned at the time. Some refused to sign the loyalty questionnaire demanded by the government in 1943; some refused to be drafted into the US Army; a few staged strikes; and still others still held mass demonstrations.[2] A small number demanded repatriation to Japan, although in the end, few followed through to self-exile.[3]

Professor Eric Muller's point that it was illogical and unfair to demand that the draft resisters risk their lives for a government that had evacuated them and their families to centers is well taken. Still, the draft resisters were not always well loved. Artist Miné Okubo did not fail to note the shortcomings of the WRA, but she was not deluded by the

---

[1] *Heart Mountain Sentinel*, April 12, 1944, 1.
[2] For the draft resisters see Muller, *Free to Die*.
[3] Hansen and Jesch, *Japanese American*, 427.

draft protesters either. When the issue arose, "Center-wide meetings were held, and the anti-administration rabble rousers skillfully fanned the misunderstandings," she remembered just after the war. "Strongly pro-Japanese leaders in the camp won over the fence-sitters and tried to intimidate the rest." In the end, she recalled "everybody registered [rather, most did]."[4] A Gila River resident found similar intimidation against the loyalty questionnaire. He and his wife had no difficulty answering yes to both questions, but "there were a few pro-Japan people there and they influenced a lot of the people who would have answered 'yes' if they had not been so aroused by these agitators."[5] By and large, the resistance literature[6] concentrates on the wrong end of the accommodation spectrum. The rejectionist literature implies that such people were submissive at best or inu, that is, dogs. They were often labeled collaborationist[7] at worst. The irony of historians applying the term collaborationist to Nikkei for cooperating with their own government is profound. Most Nikkei were more practical. They disliked their situation, but understood that they could do nothing about it, so they decided to make the best of a bad state of affairs. That was why they aided the American intelligence services before the war to weed out disloyal elements among the Issei. The Nisei were wisely striving to prove their loyalty in the face of growing signs of war between their homeland and that of their fathers.[8]

The years 1940–41 were no time to get on the bad side of a democratic government bent on provoking a war.[9] Although some historians have roundly criticized them for doing so, the Nikkei were behaving realistically in the centers too. To do so, they created an ethos that was spontaneous and protective of both individual and culture. At the same time, before and during the war, they sought to prove their loyalty, they also strove to explain their ties to their parents' homeland. As one Kibei member of the *Rafu Shimpo* staff explained, the Kibei returned to Japan to learn of its culture, its ideals, its language, and their roots.[10] Before the war catapulted them all into the maelstrom, Japanese Americans were

---

[4] Miné Okubo, *Citizen*, 176–77.   [5] Grapes, *Japanese American*, 158.
[6] Daniels, *Concentration Camps USA*, 105.
[7] F. T. Inouye, "Immediate Origins of the Heart Mountain Draft Resistance Movement," *Peace and Change*, Vol. 23: No. 2 (April 1998), 151.
[8] Kurashige, *Shifting Ground*, 99–100.
[9] For Roosevelt's strategy, like that of James K. Polk, of getting the enemy to fire the first shot see Persico, *Roosevelt's Secret*, 168.
[10] *Rafu Shimpo*, June 2, 1940, 5.

sincerely trying to fit into American society and to understand that of their
own fathers.

The relocation literature concentrates on the impact of the centers on
a people, but the people shaped the centers as well. The only way
the centers could have operated was cooperatively. Dorothy Cragen, the
Superintendent of the Inyo County School system, noted that the
Manzanar Nikkei teachers she worked with "were always sweet and
lovely. They made no criticisms whatsoever, never a negative word
about being there ... I am sure the students were happy because I would
have heard from the other teachers if they had not been and they had no
disciplinary problems whatsoever."[11] She discounted the more lurid stories circulating in Inyo County about upheaval at Manzanar. "I probably
was there more than anyone in the county, other than the employees, and
I saw no evidence of any trouble."[12]

FIG. 4. Early morning drill of Hokoku Seinen Dan, pro-Japan society, Tule Lake
Relocation Center, California. Tule Lake was the center for pro-Imperial Japanese
evacuees. Central Photographic File of the War Relocation Authority, 1942–45.
Record Group 210: Records of the War Relocation Authority, 1941–89. Courtesy
US National Archives and Records Administration.

[11] Hansen and Jesch, *Japanese American*, Part V, Vol. 1, 196.
[12] Hansen and Jesch, *Japanese American*, Part V, Vol. 1, 198.

That was a generous overstatement because there were troubles at Manzanar, Poston, Topaz, Tule Lake, the Arkansas centers, and elsewhere. Generally, historians have taken a positive attitude to these violent incidents, but they were much more troubling to people in the 1940s. Frank Chuman, a historian entirely sympathetic to the Nikkei, portrayed the uproar at Tule Lake in very unflattering terms. He said that the Kibei and other pro-Axis gangs barged into the women's shower rooms telling the terrified females that in Japan women and men bathed together. They frightened the other inhabitants into submission, intimidated the police, played loud Japanese martial music, bugled noisily in the morning, flew the Japanese flag, and marched about.[13] These gangs of Japanese nationalists, sometimes in uniform, "goose stepping" around, together with "threats and beatings,"[14] were seen as more sinister by that generation. That was especially true if the center bullies were pro-fascist or made up of those who had expressed their wish to be repatriated to Japan.[15]

So when trouble arose in the centers, it set off alarms among politicians on the outside and among administrators on the inside. Some trouble arose over the general attitude of the group to the WRA, some over resettlement, some over segregation of the troublemakers, some over the defense of Japanese culture, some over the struggle between generations, some over registration, some over the supposed informants revealing other people's secrets, and some over the different treatment of German and Italian aliens. Often, pro-JACL leaders were assaulted. For example, Saburo Kido at Poston and Dr. Thomas Yatabe at Jerome were beaten because of their counsels of moderation toward the WRA administration.[16] Some required no pretext at all, as when hostility arose against the Missouri Pacific Railroad which ran adjacent to both Arkansas centers. "Young men and boys repeatedly threw rocks and eggs at passing troop and other trains."[17] Of course, all of these incidents were reported by the press and created more animosity to the Nikkei.

One of the first of the larger incidents occurred at Poston in November, 1942. One historian explained that the episode grew out of "gang fights between alien and American-born Japanese." By the time the riot occurred, the beatings of JACL and other supporters of the administration

---

[13] F. Chuman, *Bamboo*, 268. [14] The phrase and quotes are Chuman's *Bamboo*, 268.
[15] The fights between "loyal" and "disloyal" Nikkei were "more or less common occurrences in every camp," especially Tule Lake, Manzanar, and Poston. Kobishigawa, *Okinawans*, 94.
[16] Bosworth, *America's Concentration Camps*, 150.
[17] Howard, *Concentration Camps*, 176–7.

were frequent. One such assault triggered the Poston Incident. It began when unidentified assailants attacked the sleeping Kay Nishimura with a "piece of pipe" and nearly killed him. The Poston police arrested two supposed attackers and held them pending the arrival of the FBI. One man was released, but when the second was not, a protest meeting demanded he be let go.

According to one account, the pro-Issei group then seized the city council and intimidated 6,500 workers, mostly women and children, into quitting work. However the center administrator thought that the pre-existing fundamental reason for the strike was a government failure. As Project Director W. W. Head uncomfortably admitted "the strike wasn't due to anybody in jail, but due to the fact that we [WRA] had failed to furnish some of the minimum necessities of life to them such as heating stoves and many other items."[18] The leaders barricaded themselves in the city jail and largely shut down unit number one, one of the three components of the Poston Center.[19] There they sat in the jail, flying banners printed in Japanese, blaring martial music, and waving Japanese flags. The strike did not spread to Poston units number two and three, but it featured considerable violence. Some 1,000, mostly Issei, gathered at headquarters and demanded the release of the prisoner. When the FBI refused, the protesters called a general strike. However, when the leaders flew the Japanese flag, the Nisei quit the strike. After considering several ways to terminate the incident, the administrators chose to negotiate. In the end they released the arrested party to the custody of his own attorney in return for a pledge to end the beatings. Center Director Wade Head called the disruptionists a "pro-Axis" group and participant observer Richard Nishimoto, called it a "coup d'état" of the Issei and some Nisei allies.[20]

Whether these pro-Japanists actually embraced fascism or whether they were just supporting the Japanese motherland is problematical.[21] Nonetheless, these pro-Japanists certainly behaved like fascists. In Italy where fascism was invented and Germany, where it later blossomed,

---

[18] WRA (W. W. Head and Harold Townsend). "Conversation between W. Wade Head, Project Director, and H. H. Townsend, Supply and Transportation Officer, on December 1, 1942.

[19] *Minidoka Irrigator*, November 25, 1942, 1; *Manzanar Free Press*, November 26, 1942, 1.

[20] R. S. Nishimoto, *Inside an American Concentration Camp* (Tucson, AZ: The University of Arizona Press, 1995), 139. Nishimoto confirms that the pro-Japan element at Poston was large, see 94–244.

[21] Hayashi, *Democratizing* 119–37.

bullying and thuggery were prominent features. Beatings of supposed informants in the centers for a time were endemic and, of course, a profound violation of civil rights.

The Associated Press labeled the upheaval a "reign of terror," but no one died.[22] Thus as American mass demonstrations go, the Poston "Reign of Terror" was not very terrifying and deserves no more than a minor footnote in the history of American collective violence.[23] Yet the incident gave the anti-Nikkei like the LA *Times* an opening to demonize the Japanese Americans and contribute to public misunderstanding of them. Historians have tended to treat these resisters favorably in their attempt to construct a "heroic narrative" of militant Nikkei bravely resisting the centers, in contrast to the supposedly spineless, accommodationist JACL who tried to work with the WRA. That view is not well founded. The upheaval gave the anti-Nikkei an opportunity to slow down the WRA's attempt to get them out of the centers as quickly as possible.[24]

At least through the middle of 1943 there were strong outside efforts to injure the Nikkei. For example, the security zone split the State of Arizona, so Nikkei living above the line never went to centers. In addition, the WRA freed some in the early stages of their resettlement program. In the spring of 1943, the Arizona legislature responded with a law which sought to prevent any but the most elementary economic contact between the AJAs and everyone else. This law went well beyond the better-known Progressive Era alien land laws to deny putative Japanese American farmers gasoline, hoes, shovels, tractors, autos, and everything beyond the bare necessities of food and medicine.[25] Politically, this was no time to be creating uproar. These relocation center upheavals border on the irrational. The Nikkei and the WRA had to function in a political world, which the Kibei and Issei nationalists seemed not to comprehend. They continued to supply ammunition to the ultras on the outside, and the outsiders continued to revile them, to demand exclusion from the West Coast for all the Nikkei, and deportation for the Issei.

---

[22] War Relocation Authority, "Extracts from a Report on the Poston Disturbance," undated, part 1, 1–12, part 2, 1–6. Record Group 210, Box 2. Hereafter WRA, "Extracts."

[23] For a general view of big city rioting see the works of P. Gilje, especially *Rioting in America* (Bloomington, IN: University of Indiana Press, 1996) and for rioting in individual cities see the works of G. Rudé, L. Richards, M. Feldberg, I. Bernstein, and E. Hobsbawm. And the classic works by G. Le Bon.

[24] B. Hosokawa, *Thirty Five Years in the Frying Pan* (New York, NY: McGraw-Hill Book Co., 1978), 19, 28ff.

[25] *Dies Hearings*, June–July 1943, 9195ff.

Close on the heels of the Poston "reign of terror," an "upheaval" occurred at Manzanar. According to historian Lon Kurashige, that center was literally seething with cultural, class, gender, generational, and racial animosities, so it is not surprising that the place exploded. It was typical of the struggles going on all over the system between Issei and Nisei with some Kibei trying to exploit the tensions between them. The Manzanar evacuees themselves precipitated this outbreak. They played a key role by inflicting a "severe" beating on Fred Tayama on "December 5, 1942, "on grounds that he was an informer, an inu." Tayama was a JACL leader and former LA restaurant owner who supported the WRA. The mugging led to the arrest of several people, including the cook Harry Ueno, who had been trying to organize the workers of one of the mess halls into a union. Ueno accused others in the mess hall of stealing sugar, but he was doing a bit of thieving too, he claimed, to bake "unauthorized treats" for the Manzanar kids.[26]

Ueno was taken to the county jail at Independence, which supposedly led to a crowd protest at the Manzanar administration buildings. The militants also urged further action against the injured Fred Tayama and "other informers." To provide a prompt, they "read off 'blacklists'" of supposed informers, including JACL leaders. "Resister" gangs[27] ranged through the center, singling out JACL members for beatings and others as well. "A handful of community leaders were marked for assassination by a small but influential group of internee protesters." These included Togo Tanaka, former JACL Washington lobbyist, former editor of the *Rafu Shimpo*, and current WRA supporter. Tanaka hid out by disguising himself, but it was a close-run thing with the crowd barging into his home and threatening his family. The "resisters" also beat up members of the miniscule Communist Party because they too supported the WRA Administration on grounds of sustaining the war effort.[28] However, when the resisters tried to tear down the American flag, a group of Boy Scouts confronted the resisters in turn and refused to give up Old Glory.[29] When

---

[26] L. Kurashige, "Resistance, Collaboration, and Manzanar Protest," *Pacific Historical Review*, Vol. 70: No. 3, (August 2001), 412.

[27] According to some disputed estimates, some of the gangs were pre-existing criminal gangs from before relocation. Whatever their status, the center authorities had them well under control before the culmination of the Manzanar incident. "Testimony of Congressman Herman Eberhalter to the Costello Sub-committee," August 26, 1943, 6.

[28] Kurashige, "Resistance," 415.

[29] House Committee on Un-American Activities, Seventy Eighth Congress: 1st session, *Investigation of Un-American Propaganda Activities in the United States*, Hearings before a Special Committee on Un-American Activities on H. Res. 282, June and July, 1943, 9215.

the crowd leaders violated a deal with the center director, part of the crowd set off to grab the "informers" and the other half to snatch Ueno out of the jail.

That brought in the military, which the crowd soon confronted. What happened next is disputed: either an attempt to run a truck into the soldiers or a tear gas attack by the soldiers followed by shots into the crowd.[30] Two died and several were wounded. According to one source, a month-long general strike ensued. The WRA deported several mob leaders to a center at Moab, Utah, and took into protective custody 60 "suspected" informers to a former CCC camp in Death Valley. That apparently quietened the Manzanar situation.[31]

The Heart Mountain episode followed Manzanar. The government first drafted young Nisei, then after Pearl Harbor, decided to exempt them from service, then changed its mind again in 1943 and made them subject to the draft. The JACL leaders were already urging the Nisei to volunteer, which many of them had done. More would have and told Army recruiters that their hesitation stemmed from their parents' opposition. Their parents were still subjects of Imperial Japan and feared retaliation if their sons volunteered to fight for America. For those Nisei, the draft was a way to serve their country and at the same time protect their parents.[32]

However, when the Roosevelt Administration decided to subject the non-volunteers to the draft, it gave an opening to malcontents in every center, especially those at Heart Mountain. The malcontents had a point. They did not refuse the draft; they merely asked that in return for their service they would be assured that at the end of the war their full citizenship would be restored. On the surface they seemed to be asking no more than restoration of their constitutional rights. Still, had they comprehended the true motives of the WRA and the Army, they would have understood.[33] The WRA was thinking of the Nikkei's postwar future and understood that no worse stereotype could be put on them than wartime

[30] Kurashige, "Resistance," 388. Bryan Hayashi's account also shows that the crowd initiated the shooting, singing Japanese national anthems and then pressing in against the soldiers, who then fired at them. Hayashi, *Democratizing*, 134–6.
[31] Bosworth, *America's Concentration Camps*, 148–56.
[32] A. W. Gullion, Provost Marshal General of the Army, Confidential Memorandum to Assistant Chief of Staff of the Army, November 2, 1943, Arthur C. Brown Papers, MC 946, series 2, box 1, file 1, Special Collections, University of Arkansas.
[33] United States Army, *Monograph on [the] History of [the] Military Clearance Program* (Screening of Alien Japanese and Japanese American Citizens for Military Service), Arthur C. Braun Papers, MC946, series 2, Box 1, File 1, Sp. Coll., U. Ark.

"draft dodgers."[34] Washington would not relent, nor would the resisters.[35]

Eventually sixty-three young men at Heart Mountain refused to be drafted, were arrested by local authorities in the surrounding communities, jailed, tried, and convicted.[36] They were eventually pardoned by various branches of government, judges, and in one final case, by President Harry Truman himself. However logical their case may have seemed, they were not fully aware of the motivations behind the government's action and, in any case, they represented only a small minority; just under 8 percent resisted, while another "758 men from Heart Mountain fought in Europe and the Pacific."[37] Support for the war was far more typical than draft resistance, even at Heart Mountain.[38]

The case of Army Air Corps Sergeant Ben Kuroki is illustrative. Supposedly the government sent Kuroki, a highly decorated winner of two Distinguished Flying Crosses, to the Wyoming center in order to counter the influence of the resisters. The historian of the center believes that the visit did not succeed. By contrast, the center newspaper found that the visit was highly successful. He ended up signing his autograph 2,000 times to 22 percent of the 9,000 Heart Mountain residents. That is an astounding figure and is itself testimony to the Nikkei enthusiasm at his reception.

Several mothers of Nisei soldiers were deeply stirred by the sergeant. Kuroki was not even a local boy, being a Nebraska farm lad who had never lived in a center. As with ethnic groups all over the country, Kuroki was embraced by this one. In their words, "To the Nisei, Kuroki is their first national hero."[39]

No draft resister, nor the group as a whole, ever gained such recognition from the residents of Heart Mountain. By and large, they felt sorry for the resisters and tried to dissuade them from evading the draft. Why Kuroki stood out as a hero in an ethnic group eventually extremely well represented with them is attested to by his dedication to duty. He flew the

---

[34] D. S. Myer's testimony to the Costello Sub-Committee, January 20, 1943, 20.

[35] The draft policy was a part of the government's attempt to raise enough men to make up an all Nisei combat regiment, which is discussed later.

[36] The story is sympathetically recounted in M. Mackey, *Heart Mountain: Life in Wyoming's Concentration Camp* (Powell, WY: Western History Publications, 2000), 111–19.

[37] Mackey, Heart Mountain, 128.

[38] The draft resistance movement can be followed in WRA, *Semi-Annual Report, January 1 to June 30, 1944*, 14–21. See also Inouye, *Origins*, 148–66; Muller, *Free to Die* 33.

[39] *Heart Mountain Sentinel*, April 19, 1944, 1.

requisite number of bombing missions in the European Theater, including one of the storied, but deadly Ploesti, Rumania, raids on the Nazi oil fields, and others against Wilhelmshaven, Danzig, Munster, and the submarine pens at La Pallice, France. Upon completing his European tour, Kuroki volunteered to fly more missions in the Pacific. The word hero does not quite do him justice, and the Heart Mountain residents were fully aware of it. The Nikkei newspapers were full of the experience of the Japanese American soldiers. They were very proud of them.

The WRA decision to segregate the disloyal from the loyal Nikkei precipitated an even more flamboyant series of events. This one spiraled out of control and never soared back in. Different historians have provided conflicting accounts of its origins. Bill Hosokawa, a relocatee himself and a journalist at Heart Mountain, well versed in the Nikkei experience, thought that segregation grew out of the painful exchange of views between WRA Director Dillon Myer and Secretary of War Stimson.[40]

By mid-1943 Myer had concluded that the centers had a destructive effect on the Nikkei and should be closed, especially since, with Japan now mostly on the defensive, no conceivable military threat remained. So, on March 11, 1943, he proposed this to Secretary of War Henry L. Stimson in three alternate plans. The Secretary, influenced by the resurgence of anti-Nikkei feeling, fueled, according to Hosokawa, by the press, politicians, and pressure groups, rejected them all. These latter proposed all kinds of anti-Japanese American measures, from perennial isolation of the Nikkei in camps to various deportation schemes, sometimes including both Issei and Kibei, too, despite their citizenship.

Stimson demanded a program to segregate the disloyal from the loyal before any kind of plan to close the centers could be considered. Myer countered that the Nikkei were already being segregated by voluntary resettlement in communities that willingly accepted them, but the Army would have none of it. Pressed by the directors of the WRA to accept a program of segregation, Myer finally and regretfully assented.[41]

As Hosokawa later explained, segregation was assumed from the start. Since the government did not have time to separate the loyal from the disloyal, they were all sent to centers. Still, it was taken for granted that ultimately "the sheep would be separated from the goats."[42] Both the friends and enemies of the Nikkei supported the idea. The friends wanted

---

[40] Myer was the second director of the WRA.   [41] Hosokawa, *Nisei*, 369–71.
[42] Hosokawa, *Nisei*, 362.

the separation of the disloyal because their tumultuous presence in the centers was preventing the larger Nikkei populations from resettlement into the wider world. The enemies wished to separate the "disloyal" for punishment and possible eventual deportation. The uproar in some centers created by the strikes, protests, and confrontation politics in the centers forced the WRA's hand. Stimson demanded that something be done, and therefore Myer agreed to segregation, in effect, to save the program of resettlement (permanent leave from center) and therefore a return to "normal life" for the Nikkei.[43]

In the meantime these events got entangled with those of the storied 442nd Regimental Combat Team.

Such a unit had been proposed as early as the ill-fated Salt Lake City conference of 1942, to decide the fate of the evacuees. Supposedly, the Army needed soldiers, and when they did not get enough Nikkei volunteers, they turned to the idea of an all-Japanese American unit to get more. It was also felt that such a force would allow the Nisei to demonstrate their loyalty to the country and thereby redeem the reputation of the Nikkei with the public.

On January 28, 1943, Secretary Stimson announced plans to create the all-Nisei force. Preliminary to doing so, the Army insisted on questionnaires to "evaluate" the Nisei suitability for military service. "Myer seized this as an opportunity to expedite WRA's leave clearance procedure and proposed that the questionnaires be presented to everyone – men and women, citizens and aliens – over seventeen years of age."[44]

As Hosokawa explained, that approach contained two mistakes. First, the questionnaire was labeled "Application for Leave Clearance." Many Issei did not want to leave because they feared for their safety on the outside. Second, Question 28 asked them to swear allegiance to the United States and renounce loyalty to any foreign power. Since the Issei could not become American citizens, the query asked them to become stateless persons by forswearing allegiance to Japan, the only nation of which they were subjects. Eventually Question 28 was quickly re-written to allow the swearing of allegiance to the US only, which the Issei found acceptable. By that time, the flawed process had created intense and widespread confusion and resentment.[45] Some 11 percent of the Nisei eligible for service answered no to the question, 3,000 at Tule Lake alone.

---

[43] Ibid.   [44] Ibid., 363–4.   [45] Jacoby, *Tule Lake*, 70–79.

They were probably "intimidated" by the gangs of Kibei bullies which the WRA could not control.[46]

Harold Stanley Jacoby, in one of the most fair-minded books about relocation, presented a different, but not totally antithetical version. At the time of the controversies over registration and segregation, he was serving as chief of police at Tule Lake, so he was in a position to understand the storm that eventually broke over him. For him, the Tule Lake upheaval also antedated the registration process set in motion by the government. It grew out of an inquiry by Dillon Myer as to the desirability of segregation. All over the system, but especially at Tule Lake, the militants were attacking those who wished to resettle because they considered it an act of "disloyalty if not to Japan, at least to the cause of the evacuees."[47] At Tule Lake an investigation recommended unanimously that separation take place.

So there was already acrimonious controversy over resettlement before the registration issue arose. According to Jacoby's understanding, the registration drive also originated from the outside communities which had begun to receive the first trickle of re-settlers. Not unreasonably, they asked if these newcomers had been vetted for security purposes. Most had not, so the WRA instituted the registration program to provide this measure of security and calm the fears of communities receiving re-settlers.[48]

Since the Army by this time needed more soldiers, it created a special combat unit for Nikkei and reinstituted the draft to get them. But they too wanted to be assured on the security aspect, so they piggybacked their military questionnaire onto the WRA registration process. It seems quite likely then that both of these pressures, one military and one civil, created the registration program, since there were pressures and legitimate interests on both sides.

In any case, registration at Tule Lake was mismanaged. The local administration of Harvey M. Coverly sprang the program on the residents instead of meeting with the block captains, the community council, and other interested parties to alert them and to pave the way for an understanding. But the Tuleans themselves, all over the center, met to discuss the implications, three of which seemed ominous to them.

---

[46] Ibid., 364–5. For the activities of these Kibei bullies, see the testimony of Dillon Myer. Subcommittee of the Committee on Military Affairs, United States Senate, 78th Congress: First Session *Hearings on S. 444, Part 4, Nov. 24, 1943* (Washington, DC: United States Government Printing Office, 1944), 235–6. Hereinafter, *Hearings on S. 444.*

[47] Jacoby, *Tule Lake*, 81.   [48] Jacoby, *Tule Lake*, 70–1.

Draft-age Tulean men who had already registered for the draft wondered why they had to register again. The Issei worried about the version of the registration form that they were asked to sign, which was labeled "Leave Clearance Application." They feared that the government was using this form to push them out of the center into a hostile world. They were even more startled by the famous question 28, which asked them to forswear allegiance to Japan.[49]

The WRA in Washington soon learned of the inappropriateness of question 28 and rewrote it, but by that time enough Tuleans feared the outcome of registration that only 42 percent signed up. The local WRA pleaded, cajoled, and finally threatened to arrest the non-signers. The center, led by Block 42, refused their signatures and the administration marched its security detail to the offending Block 42 mess hall and arrested the refusers. A group of Issei held back the crowd, and the WRA marched off the resisters to jail and to hero status. The WRA eventually gained enough signatures, but supposedly only under duress. Still, as Miné Okubo noted, the refusers were bullying residents to vote "no" as well.

If Myer's hands were tied on the registration question, those of the militants were not. It made sense in the first instance to weed out and eject the troublemakers from the centers, otherwise there would have been endless turmoil in all of them. The reverse side of that coin was that sending 9,000 suspect persons to a single center (Tule Lake) meant that the trouble avoided in the other nine centers would redouble instead at Tule Lake. But the cost was high and the outcome very burdensome to most of the Tulean residents. The uproar over registration split the community badly, with the opponents of registration calling those in favor inu or dogs, that is, traitors; but the words soon became more menacing, worsened by the government's decision to deport 1,000 Hawaiian Kibei troublemakers to the mainland centers.

When segregation occurred, almost every one of these ended up at Tule Lake, and these became the *enragées* of relocation, to borrow a French Revolutionary term. Many of the "Old Tuleans" had opted to stay there instead of being transferred to another center, not because they were disloyal, but because they did not want to move again, had upgraded their quarters to a satisfactory level, or were close to their former California homes.

---

[49] Jacoby, *Tule Lake*, 70–9.

The arrival of the Hawaii segregants created another division among the Nikkei because the newcomers did not think that the Old Tuleans were militant enough and because they wanted to take over the center. They did. Jacoby testified in his memoirs that his policemen "stood in awe – if not fear – of them."[50]

These new militants went much beyond the point of non-registration. They were openly pro-Japanese in the war, thought that the "Yamato race" would win it, and were convinced that they would end up in Japan after the conflict. And they openly played what moderns would call the "race card" against Nikkei who disagreed with them, labeling them "lily whites."[51] Hence they believed that they were better prepared to run the center and prepare the residents to live in postwar Japan. They battled the administration up to and beyond the end, then learning that Japan had lost the war, renouncing their renunciation and demanding to stay. In 1959 they won – a part of the story that goes beyond the scope of this book.[52] Yet the WRA tried hard to be fair even to the repatriates. At a Denver conference to create a just policy of separation, the meeting was told, "We must not take the attitude that, if they ask for repatriation, they are evil. They do not all happen to be troublemakers; they may be perfectly law abiding but just want to return to Japan."[53]

In the meantime, the militants singled out the Co-op, which supported the WRA Administration, as part of the opposition to them. As "a consequence of which the general manager of the co-op was murdered in July of 1944, an action for which no offender was ever apprehended."[54] One cannot be certain who the assassin or assassins were, but the Old Tuleans would not have had a motive to kill their own cooperative supervisor. Aside from encouraging street violence, intimidating the police, and murder, segregation also wrecked, or at least temporarily disabled the public school system. In order to accommodate the incoming malcontents, the center had to suspend school and turn the classrooms into residential barracks. More trouble still brewed.

Segregation meant ousting the loyal Nikkei to make room for the supposedly and blatantly disloyal. So for standing by the local administration, the loyalists, who had upgraded their apartments to a level of

---

[50] Jacoby, *Tule Lake*, 87, 89.
[51] WRA, "Summary Notes on [the] Segregation Conference of W. R. A. Officials," p. 4, Denver, Colorado, July 26–27, 1943, Griswold Papers, MC 733, Series 3, Box 3, Folder 1, Special Collections, University of Arkansas. Hereafter, WRA, "Summary Notes."
[52] Jacoby, *Tule Lake*, 105–10.   [53] WRA, "Summary Notes," 4.
[54] Jacoby, *Tule Lake*, 48.

comfort, now were rewarded with another uprooting and re-establishment in a new place. Many simply opted for resettlement at that point or refused to leave, changed their "yes" vote on loyalty to a "no" vote, faded into the crowd, and managed to hang on.

In addition, segregation worked a voluntary religious separation. Buddhists were the leading religious groups in the center and segregation brought about the loss of religious diversity as most of the Christians left. Historians have not yet given sufficient attention to the religious dimension of center life,[55] so we don't know how this aspect played out beyond strengthening the hand of the militants, who were more Buddhist and therefore less supportive of the center administration.[56] The whole situation was complicated, except that racism had nothing to do with it, since both parties to the disputes were of Asian ancestry. It would have taken the wisdom of Solomon to sort all of this out fairly, which no one at Tule had.

Yet the criteria for segregation were fair enough. They included those who had applied for repatriation to Japan, those who had failed to register or answered no to question 28, those denied a security clearance, and those who wished to follow members of their segregant families to Tule Lake. And to be certain that these guidelines did not fade, the WRA established review boards to insure that no one was segregated who had changed their minds about the above categories, such as repatriation to Japan.[57]

For the time being, segregation did head off several important sources for punitive action. United States Senator A. B. "Happy" Chandler of Kentucky had begun hearings about the centers which were producing sensational copy against the Nikkei. So Dillon Myer, through Eleanor Roosevelt, managed to get an audience with the President. Myer convinced FDR that Chandler was a threat to the WRA program of resettlement, and Roosevelt found a backchannel way to get Chandler to back off and issue an innocuous report.[58] That quelled one threat, and the program of segregation quenched another. Martin Dies, chair of the HUAC, had been holding equally sensational hearings and issuing similarly damaging publicity. When the WRA accepted segregation, Dies cancelled his latest round of hearings. As the *Rohwer Outpost* editor tersely put it: "The details of segregation and the news of the Dies Committee's calling

---

[55] UNC Department of Religion ... Blankenship is completing a PhD dissertation on the subject.
[56] Jacoby, *Tule Lake*, 51.   [57] Ibid., 83.   [58] Ibid., 375–8.

off [the] Nisei investigation were the highlights of press significance for the Nisei this week."[59] Those actions gave Myer a breather from the national political forces plaguing him, but the Tule Lake *enragées* did not let him enjoy it.

To centralize the "goats" in one place meant a complex population exchange of 15,000, thirty-three trainloads, moving out of one center and into several others. The exchange was carried out from September to mid-October, 1943. A total of 9,000 left Tule and 6,000 stayed, mostly for practical reasons. One figure puts the arrivals at 3,000 from Manzanar alone. Putting all of the radicals together and adding another 2,000 from Hawaii reinforced the militants' hand. Harold Jacoby said that they were "determined to play out their pro-Japan role in earnest."[60] Definitive figures are hard to come by and are mostly estimates, but Attorney General Biddle, a friend of the Nikkei who thought their relocation was unconstitutional, believed that the Tule Lake population included "a couple thousand of Kibei" who were "certainly disloyal."[61]

A US Senate hearing explained the result: "Immediately following the segregation movement, some of the evacuees at the Tule Lake center began to create difficulties." These generated several resignations among the Caucasian staff, including that of the fire chief, a retired fireman from Los Angeles. He charged that the militants "pursued a deliberate policy of sabotage by wrecking fire equipment and destroying fire hydrants." The militants made absurd demands like "midnight meals" for Nikkei firemen, and they spat on and cursed the soldiers.[62] The head of one of the machine shops testified that the Japanese American workers there were crafting knives on a large scale, "hundreds of knives," although he did not consider this unusual for a machine shop environment where knife making often prevailed.[63]

A traffic accident gave the militants a fresh opening. On October 15 a truck carrying twenty-nine workers and driven by one of the evacuees overturned while trying to pass on the road to the center. The accident injured all of the passengers, one of them fatally.[64] The next day no one reported for work. For ten days, the evacuees ceased harvesting the potato crop, but nothing else happened. The "leaders" wanted to stage a massive

---

[59] *Rohwer Outpost*, July 24, 1943, 6.   [60] Jacoby, *Tule Lake*, 87.
[61] *Dies Hearings*, November–December 1943, 10077.   [62] *Hearings on S. 444*, 208–09.
[63] US House of Representatives, 78th Congress: 1st session, *Hearings before a Special Committee on Un-American Activities on H. Res. 282*. November 29, 30; December 1, 6, 7, 8, 9, 20, 1943, 212–48. Hereinafter *Costello/Dies Hearings*, November–December 1943.
[64] *Hearings on S. 444*, Nov. 24, 1943, 215.

funeral for the truck death victim, hoping to capitalize politically on the event in classic European urban radical style.

WRA center director R. R. Best refused because the family of the deceased did not want a massive public event. He may have been thinking of the political implications of a huge funeral turnout, but he could hardly ignore the relatives' wishes in such a quintessentially family matter.[65] The refusal promptly became another issue for the militants. Then on October 26 a delegation approached the center administration seeking to demand POW status and to bargain about general center conditions.

As prisoners of war, they demanded exemption from work on behalf of a belligerent power which included harvesting crops to be eaten by the loyal members of the centers.[66] The administration told the radicals that they did not respond to demands and promptly set about finding harvesters (234) for the $500,000 potato and other vegetable crops, which were destined for consumption at all the centers. When Myer and the assistant WRA director, Robert Cozzens, arrived to investigate, the militants convinced the populace through false announcements in the mess halls that the director would make a speech to the Tuleans.[67]

That gave the militants a crowd which they then tried to exploit. Myer later said that up to this point the crowd of 3,000 to 4,000 was completely orderly.[68] With Myer in the administration building, seventeen "leaders" appeared, making demands, including that Center Director R. R. Best be fired. Of course, Myer refused. Best was no bigoted man.[69] He had been striving to make the turmoil of segregation as painless as possible by providing specific information to contradict the wild rumors circulating.

While this meeting was going on, a group of militants invaded the hospital and beat up the chief medical officer, Dr. Reece M. Pedicord. Why Pedicord was so unpopular remains unclear. The WRA Director refused to continue the meeting until assured that the hospital disturbance had ceased. The seventeen "leaders" were obviously embarrassed by the beating and agreed to send representatives to the hospital to quash the violence. They and the center chief of security went to the hospital and returned to say that Pedicord had been beaten, but that the violence in the hospital had ceased. Myer was asked to address the crowd and agreed to

[65] *Hearings on S. 444, Nov. 24,* 211.
[66] POW status would have given them certain rights under international law, which the neutral, but friendly Spanish Embassy supervised on behalf of POWs.
[67] *Dies Hearings,* November–December 1943, 10087.
[68] Estimates of the crowd varied significantly.
[69] *Tulean Daily Dispatch,* August 20, 1943, Supplement, unpaginated.

discuss any reasonable suggestions, but reminded the crowd that if they refused to deal reasonably with the WRA, they would have to deal with the Army.

Although he was later criticized by congressmen for addressing the crowd, the national director felt that with a large crowd outside the door and some violence already done, speaking to the crowd might help to defuse a dangerous situation. Center director Best believed that the Kibei had generated the crowd to help them pressure the administration and thus gain control of the leadership of the center.[70] Myer believed that they had produced the crowd "under duress" and that the situation had become tense, a word he employed several times in recounting the affair to the visiting congressmen. That was putting it mildly because the Army stood outside the gates ready to intervene if called upon or if they thought it necessary. He thought that "Kibei muscle men" were less irenic than the seventeen "leaders." Myer thought that the seventeen were under pressure to end the farm strike because the other Nikkei did not want to be deprived of food.[71]

While they met, minor damage occurred – a broken railing here, windshield wipers there, paint scratches, and broken auto antennae, but nothing serious. A couple of employees reported a knife or two in the hands of the crowd, but most WRA employees said they had seen no weapons. Still the crowd scared "a number of" Caucasian WRA employees out of their wits – Myer described them as "hysterical." One reason for them to be so, occurred at the gate. One of the doctors, Frank D. Fager, tried to flee from the hospital in his car, but found the center gate locked. Before he and the sentry could unlock it, three truckloads of young Japanese Americans arrived and prevented the doctor from leaving. They then staged what would later be called a sit in, camping down around their vehicles. The doctor appealed for Army protection, and a colonel and six soldiers armed with "tommy guns" arrived. The colonel directed the sit-in group to unlock the gate, which they did, and the doctor left.[72]

Still the whole situation was fraught with peril even if none turned into major violence. A massive crowd, militant Kibei and Issei agitators, a beating, a sit in, a vastly under-strength security force, and "touchy" soldiers armed with automatic weapons was ominous. Congressmen, at the 1943 Dies Hearing, raked Myer over the coals for deigning to speak to

[70] *Dies Hearings*, November–December 1943, 1943, 10116.
[71] *Dies Hearings*, November–December 1943, 00212–48.
[72] *Dies Hearings*, November–December 1943, 10090.

the crowd. Myer was acting responsibly in trying to defuse a dangerous situation. Whether because of, or in spite of the talk, the crowd dispersed.

In response to this close call, the administration began to enhance security. The director tried to hire an additional sixty-six security men, and the WRA began building a fence to separate its offices and employees living quarters from the evacuees. That evening about 400 young men "armed with clubs" entered the administration area. When an internal security person resisted the crowd, he tripped, went down, and was beaten. The crowd then surrounded center director Best's home, where-upon Best telephoned the Army to assume control. That second incident, which was closer to a riot because the crowd physically pushed the security forces out of their way and beat up a WRA person, grew out of a false rumor that two trucks were leaving the motor pool, taking food from the warehouse for the loyal evacuees in the center. Instead, the trucks were carrying loyal evacuees to Klamath Falls for farm work.[73]

When the soldiers took control of the center, Tule Lake became the only relocation center to be run by the Army. They ran it for ten weeks. The Army and the WRA had previously agreed that the WRA would control internal security. The Army would provide external security, including ingress and egress, unless a bona fide emergency arose. The strike and crowd activity ended that compromise, but it did not end Myer's Tulean headaches. The militants on the inside kept up their rumor mongering and bullying, and the anti-Nikkei on the outside kept up their media mongering and bullying, promised congressional action, and demanded that the Army assume control of all of the centers.

Neither Myer nor the Army wanted that.[74] General M. G. White explained repeatedly to the Senate Armed Services subcommittee that the Army intended to stick to their division of labor. Operating the centers would constitute a drain on Army manpower and it would breach a long Army tradition of the not operating centers in which civilians were detained. He steadfastly refused to be bullied into admitting the need for military control by Congressman Clair Engle of California, Senators Rufus Holman of Oregon and Robert Reynolds of North Carolina.[75]

It is difficult to divine what the militants expected to gain from these confrontations. Family control of its own funerals and the potato issue were non-starters. The center newspapers pointed out that the disputed crop was destined for consumption at Tule Lake and the other centers, not

---

[73] *Hearings on S. 444, Nov. 24, 1943,* 217; *Dies Hearing, Nov.–Dec., 1943,* 10115, 10117.
[74] *Hearings on S. 444,* 244–56.   [75] Ibid., 209, 213.

the Army. The overturned truck was driven by an AJA resident, not a WRA one. The centers normally traded food from one to another, so there was nothing sinister about this exchange.

Fearing loss of the winter supply, the WRA called for several hundred Nikkei volunteers from the other centers to harvest the offending potatoes. To portray this episode as a victory for the militants and to picture the 234 harvesters as "strike breakers" is not plausible. Rationing hit consumers rather hard in these years and the center residents suffered along with those outside. Food supplies per diem have often been described as minimal, so further squeezing them would not have been a "victory" for anybody, much less a heroic venture. In addition, the demand for repatriation was already acceptable to the WRA so there was no need for confrontation to secure that right.[76] By late July, 1943, some 6,300 Nikkei had asked to be repatriated.[77] In the end, most stayed in the United States.

The Tule Lake upheavals demonstrated exactly why the government had to investigate the resettlers carefully. Any incident outside the centers by militant Kibei or Issei would have touched off a fire storm, compared to which the embarrassments of the loyalty questionnaire would have been trivial. Recent literature about the resistance movement at Tule Lake has shown that those troublemakers were organized, determined, and quite capable of doing just that, causing trouble.

In describing the registration controversy, Miné Okubo noted the danger that the situation posed: "Strongly pro-Japanese leaders in the center won over the fence-sitters and tried to intimidate the rest." But they failed.[78] When "the program of segregation was ... instituted ... one of its purposes was to protect loyal Japanese Americans from the threats of the pro-Japanese agitators," said the artist. She pencil sketched the Topaz Japanese militants as uniformed, club wielding Axis bullies, not victims. No responsible government would have turned them loose onto a society, part of which was pumped up on anti-Nikkei propaganda and most of whom, from January, 1944, on, would have been receiving news of Japanese atrocities in the Pacific War.[79]

Some 1,300 from Topaz alone were segregated. If there were 1,300 "pro-Japanese" at the Topaz Center alone out of some 10,000, that must

[76] "Comprehensive Statement in Response to Senate Resolution 166," 33, RG 210, Box 2, National Archives [NA].
[77] "Comprehensive Statement," 32.   [78] Okubo, *Citizen*, 177.
[79] The prevalence of extreme newspaper stories about the Japanese and Japanese Americans is well known, but see M. Eisenhower, *The President*, 99–102.

have given the government pause. Ten times (i.e. the number of centers) 1,300 would have totaled 13,000. The idea of releasing that many pro-Axis militants in the midst of a bitter war, with growing public knowledge of Japanese Axis atrocities, was unrealistic. The politics of the situation have to be understood.[80] And the scheme worked. "For all the pain it caused, the loyalty oath finally did speed up the relocation [resettlement] program," noted Jeanne Wakutsuki Houston. That, in turn, notably reduced crowding in the barracks.[81]

Of course, the WRA had to seek the same security about the cities and towns to which the re-settlers went. "The WRA would obtain reasonable assurance that the coming of an evacuee to a community outside of the military [zones] would not disturb order and security there," noted Tōru Matsumoto.[82] The re-settlers had to be vetted, and so did their intended communities. That was simply an extension of the principle upon which the 1942 sugar beet workers were released.

The only ones to gain from uproar were Japanese American pro-fascists and the Senators, Congressmen, and media pundits who were provided with a wonderful opportunity to posture. Both Congressmen and Senators roasted the WRA mercilessly. Why were the internal security staff of the WRA not armed? Why did the director stoop to speaking to the crowd? Why were the evacuees of Tule Lake allowed to become internal security (police) personnel? Why were there not more white internal security people? Why did the Army not assume control of the entire system?

Representative Clair Engle of California criticized the evacuees particularly venomously, spreading absurd rumors all over the historical record of the hearings. In spite of this external uproar, Myer could not give them very much. Neither he nor the Army wanted full military control, and punishing the Tule Lake militants or any other evacuees carried international complications.

Myer was dealing with people who were famously loyal to Japan. Neither Issei nor the Nisei were ever considered to be universally loyal. There is little doubt that many of the Nikkei, especially the Kibei and Issei,

---

[80] The draft resistance movement is a different question. The majority of Nikkei answered the draft call by signing up, but a few in several centers refused to do so. I would not place them in the same category at the Tule Lake militants. The resisters could not be considered troublemakers. If the government wanted to put them into relocation centers because the military said that the Nikkei were a threat to national security, the government had no moral or legal right to expect these young men to risk their lives in return.

[81] Quoted in Grapes, *Japanese American*, 138.   [82] Matsumoto, *Beyond Prejudice*, 55.

were not merely alienated, but pro-Japanese, just as Miné Okubo said.[83] Charles Kikuchi found the same sentiment at Tanforan Assembly Center and later at the Gila River Relocation Center. Upon hearing of the fall of Corregidor to Japan, he quoted an Issei as remarking: "About time, no?"[84]

On June 19, 1942, nearly two weeks after the American victory in the Battle of Midway, he wrote of attitudes at the center that "the group radicals," (progressives, JACL, reactionary, and church elements) started to talk about the feeling of the Issei, and "I was disturbed to hear their opinions that the Issei still believed, strongly hoped for, a Japan victory, and influenced the Nisei accordingly." At another point he complained: "It gripes me no end to think of being confined in the same place with these Japanists."[85] When the United States Army released the information on Japanese atrocities in the Pacific War (early 1944), it created a fire storm of protest in the Gila River centers, especially among the Issei. As the opposition to a resolution condemning the atrocities explained, "The Japanese people could not possibly be guilty of such enormities." The resolution provoked "much violent resentment," noted a pro-Nikkei source.[86]

Buddhist Priest Kenko Yamashita, who chose to return to Japan after the war, told the Fullerton interviewers that it was only natural that many Issei cheered for their "motherland" and that the Kibei "despised America." When asked by his interrogators, after being rounded up in the first wave, if Japan could win the war, he answered: "Who should hope to see his mother country lose a war?" He continued: "You can't blame us for loving Japan and wanting Japan to win the war."[87] Those are statements of patriotism, not racism, nationalism, much less cultural chauvinism, and that is how most Caucasian Americans whose testimony I have read felt about their own "motherland."

[83] Modell, *Kikuchi Diary*, 138.   [84] Modell, *Kikuchi Diary*, 59.
[85] Modell, *Kikuchi Diary*, 50.
[86] WRA, Community Analysis Section, "Project Analysis Series No. 29, November 6, 1944," 13–14, Griswold Papers, Loc 733, Series 3, Box 3, Folder 2, Sp. Coll., U. Ark.
[87] Hansen and Jesch, *Japanese Americans*, Part I, Internees, 20, 25, 29, 31.

1 0

Bowling in Twin Falls

An Open Door Leave Policy

One of the most astonishing things about centers which have habitually been called "concentration camps" is the ease with which those confined in them could get out and when they were allowed do so. Although many good studies have been written about the constitutional cases like those of Mitsui Endo and Fred Korematsu, their impact on release was entirely after the fact. Neither case ruled on the fundamental constitutionality of the relocation centers and neither freed the Nikkei. In fact, it was WRA policy from the beginning to resettle the Nisei out of the centers "indefinitely" from July 1942 and the Issei from September, 1942. Either date was long before the construction companies had finished building the centers. As Charlotte Brooks and others have documented, beginning in January 1943, the Nikkei were leaving the centers in droves twenty-two months before the Supreme Court heard either of the iconic constitutional cases in December 1944.

Probably the most critical difference between a concentration camp and relocation/evacuation center was whether one could leave. Figures vary among historians, but by one means or another, by the end of 1944, the government had found ways to release at least 30,000, or 27 percent, of the original 112,000 evacuees. I have accepted the WRA figure of 30,000, for 1944, but that could be an underestimate because the WRA did not want to stimulate more uproar from anti-Nikkei politicians who opposed any release.[1] Historian Charlotte Brooks, who studied resettlement in

---

[1] This figure varies somewhat. The Dies Committee charged that "40,000 Japanese are at large in the United States." *Minidoka Irrigator*, June 5, 1943, 1. But the end of 1944 was more than eighteen months later.

Chicago, found that 60,000 (53.5 percent) had resettled by the end of the war, a seven-month longer period and the WRA estimate for that same period was slightly higher.[2] In July, 1945, WRA Director Dillon Myer put the re-settler total at 50,000, or 44.6 percent. Other estimates were dramatically higher. The demography was always dynamic.

There undoubtedly would have been more, but for the understandable Issei fear of leaving and therefore forcing their children to stay with them in the centers.[3] There are also some impressionistic qualitative estimates. When Miné Okubo left Topaz, she noted sadly that "only the very old or very young were left."[4] Whichever approximation we accept, some historians' idea that "only a small percentage of the internees were able to leave the camps" is a major miscalculation.[5]

In all, the WRA created at least three kinds of civilian leave policies. From the beginning, the WRA itself did not believe in the evacuation center solution for the "Japanese Problem," much less that it was an ideal one. They thought of the centers as a very temporary way out of a war and a government-created muddle. They realized that the centers were constitutionally suspect and internationally embarrassing. Therefore, they immediately began to conjure up ways to get as many Nikkei out of the western deserts and Arkansas lowlands as possible. Topaz was illustrative. Ruth Griffin, a WRA employee, explained in May 1943: "Since the gates of Topaz closed on the last new resident in October [1942], back out through the gates for relocation [resettlement] and normal work have gone 1200 evacuees to ninety-eight cities in twenty-one different states."[6]

Resettlement, or indefinite leave, began in earnest in January, 1943, a very quick turnaround, but it was a part of the WRA program from the very beginning. At 20,000,[7] Chicago ultimately claimed the most, with Salt Lake City second at 3,000.[8] Initially, the resettlers could move only to areas outside the Western Defense Command (WDC), which included the coastal states, plus Arizona, Utah, Nevada, Montana, and Alaska.[9] However, that restriction was honored in the breach, as resettlers soon appeared in Utah, Arizona, eastern Washington, Montana, and elsewhere

[2] Charlotte Brooks, "In the Twilight Zone," 1655–1687; WRA, "Semi-Annual Report, July 31–December 31, 1945," 1, Jerome Records, MC 752, Box 1, Sp. Coll., U. Ark.
[3] Okihiro, *Storied*, 121.   [4] Okubo, *Citizen*, 209.   [5] Robinson, *By Order*, 5.
[6] *Topaz Times, Supplement*, May 12 and 14, 1943, 8.
[7] I have accepted this lower estimate of the Chicago resettlement in order not to overstate my case, despite higher estimates by some experts.
[8] Brooks, "Twilight Zone," 1.   [9] *Pacific Citizen*, July 30, 1942, 1.

within the WDC. Utah was a very popular resettlement destination. Since the western governors and anti-Nikkei pressure groups were initially so hostile to the Nikkei, the WRA had to tread carefully.

So when the western governors demanded that the Nikkei be put behind barbed wire before they allowed the centers in their states, the WRA decided to test their resolve. They experimented with seasonal leave for Nikkei, who wanted the work, and western sugar beet growers, who wanted the workers. This approach put the ball in the governors' court. Were they more interested in saving the sugar beet harvest or bashing the Nikkei? Luckily, economics quickly won out over resentment. Out of that modest beginning came a program that allowed several kinds of leave, tailored to the needs of the evacuees.[10]

Nisei citizens were the principal beneficiaries of this leave program, which was overwhelmingly a movement of youth. It was more difficult for Issei families to exit the centers because of their language problems, because it was harder to find family housing on the outside than it was to find a single room for a lone worker, and because of fear. Nisei with children also faced housing shortages, plus selective service uncertainties, exaggerations of the outside cost of living, and fear generated by the rumor-mongering congressmen and newspapers. Other roadblocks loomed up for parochial reasons, such as California's lack of reciprocal professional licensing agreements with other states.[11]

Still, resettlement proceeded apace, but with great prudence. For example, before the "College Nisei" left for school,[12] the War and Navy departments investigated every institution, and eventually the two departments were "willing to clear most colleges and universities in the country which will accept Nisei students."[13] In addition, the WRA investigated resettlement communities to see if they would accept either students or those on indefinite leave.[14]

In order to facilitate this release, the Army and the WRA – while the Japanese Americans were still in the assembly centers – constructed very

---

[10] Leave procedures are spelled out in various WRA documents, especially, WRA, "Administrative Notice No. 54: Summary of Leave Clearance Procedures," 1–6, Griswold Papers, MC 733, Series 3, Box 3, Folder 2, Sp. Coll., U. Ark.

[11] R. Tajiri, "Relocation," *Topaz Times, Supplement*, May 12 and 14, 1943, 4–7; Griffin "Relocation: Through the Gates of Topaz," 8, 10–11.

[12] See below the discussion of education.

[13] O'Brien, *College Nisei* (Palo Alto, CA: Pacific Books, 1949; 1978 Arno Press reprint), 142–8.

[14] Ibid., 8, 11.

detailed guidelines that protected Nikkei, the employers, and the workers who might be affected by the Nikkei incursion into their labor markets.[15] Congressmen from both coasts seethed and shouted, but the WRA was always on solid ground and could counter the congressmen with hard facts about a carefully vetted program. So despite the anger, it continued to unfold, and after August, 1944, months before the Endo case, "all restrictions were removed."[16]

Short-term, episodic leaves allowed residents to take care of unusual economic, family, medical, or other personal business. Nikkei used these leaves to travel even to unexpected places like Los Angeles and the Bay Area, both in the prohibited military zone. For example, travel to specialized medical facilities allowed people like Bill Hosokawa's mother-in-law to journey from Heart Mountain to the Mayo Clinic for cancer treatment.[17] Hirosuke Inouye was given permission to leave the Topaz Center, almost as soon as it opened, to visit his sick wife at the Alum Rock Sanatorium in San Jose, and others left to visit the San Mateo Community Hospital.[18] Twenty-five received passes to attend a wake for a baby at McGhee, Arkansas.[19] These experiences were typical, as Nikkei shuttled in and out of the prohibited or restricted zones for the rest of the war.

Moreover, "unauthorized" daily leave supplemented all of the above. The Japanese at Rohwer were often "absent without leave," hunting *kobu,* and many others were outside the wire too. Heart Mountain historian Mike Mackey explained that lapse after some boys were busted by the *center police* for sledding outside where the yet unconstructed wire fence was to be built: "In the months that followed, however, such restrictions were relaxed. Moving through the front gate required a pass, so internees would simply climb through the barbed wire fence surrounding the center and freely roam the area from the Shoshone River up to Heart Mountain itself."[20] Historian John Howard summed up the permissive nature of the policy in Arkansas:

[15] Western Defense Command and the War Relocation Authority, "Employment of Japanese Evacuees in Agriculture Outside of Assembly Centers: Summary of Assurances Required by the Western Defense Command and the War Relocation Authority," no specific date, RG 210, Box 2, NA.

[16] WRA, "Education Program in War Relocation Centers, February 1, 1945," RG 210, Box 2, NA.

[17] Hosokawa, *Frying Pan,* 54.

[18] *Topaz Times,* September 26, 1942, 3; October 21, 1942, 2.

[19] WRA pass, November 7, 1942, Griswold Papers, no MC or Series no., Box 2, Folder 6, Sp. Coll., U. Ark.

[20] Mackey, *Heart Mountain,* 71–72.

It was easy to get out: people did it all the time. With a day pass, you could catch a bus into town and go shopping. Even without a pass, many Japanese Americans sneaked out to go fishing or to take a walk in the woods.[21]

The same was true all over the system. The Nikkei were much less intimidated, depressed, or oppressed by the supposedly ominous barbed wire, guard towers, and armed sentries than historians have believed. They restrained few evacuees, much less oppressed them.

Seasonal leaves allowed the residents to exit centers longer and earn better money. These leaves evolved in an ironic manner. When Eisenhower took up the reins of the WRA, he initially tried to put the Nikkei in small, temporary centers from which they would be recruited into the work force of the Intermountain West as required. In April, 1942, with the exception of Governor Carr of Colorado, every western governor had refused to accept such centers unless they were run and closely guarded by the Army. One governor powerfully expressed his opinion by saying that "if you [Eisenhower] bring the Japanese into my state, I promise you they will be hanging from every tree!"[22] However, by autumn the governors found that their crops might rot in the fields for want of agricultural labor. By fall, political hyperbole gave way to practicality, and the lynching governor decided that he was more interested in labor than lynching. So were his constituents.

To provide employees, the WRA tried an experimental program of taking men from the Portland Assembly Center to work in southeastern Oregon agriculture. Nobody ended up hanging from trees, and when a few lesser incidents occurred, Eisenhower told the local authorities that either these episodes must cease or the labor supply would. The harassment abruptly ended.

The WRA demanded that existing wage scales be paid and good conditions be provided. The experiment gradually expanded to include 10,000 men.[23] They were a godsend to American farmers stressed by the nationwide farm worker shortage. As early as the spring of 1942, hundreds of Manzanar detainees had already been out on work release to harvest the potato fields of Idaho.[24] Some settled at Keetley Farms in Utah or worked temporarily in other western agriculture and shopped

---

[21] Howard, *Concentration Camps*, 174. Since Howard is one of the severest critics of the centers, his admission here is useful. And his information is important in showing that bus services existed between towns and centers, not just between the Arkansas centers.

[22] Eisenhower, *The President*, 118.   [23] Eisenhower, *The President*, 118–21.

[24] *Manzanar Free Press*, September 17, 1942, 1. The Idaho potato crop in blossom is one of the most beautiful sights in the West, comparable to the lavender fields in Provence.

periodically in western towns.[25] These leaves sometimes involved surprising benefits beyond the money and freedom. Art Yorimoto and five friends worked for a Colorado farmer, who took them trout fishing during slack periods of farm labor.[26]

Another sensed "a feeling of freedom and relief from the routine of center life" en route to the beautiful Cache County, Utah, to farm. This Nikkei appreciated both the setting and the culture of his Mormon hosts, noting "the quiet, serene atmosphere of this valley community – a typical rural community, with large barns stacked high with golden hay." He continued, "The people are very friendly. They seem to be our kind of people, just believing in simple living, brotherhood and seeking of others' good."[27]

Despite western politicians' complaints about the Japanese Americans, they often found the other residents friendly. An agricultural worker reported from Idaho that "the people of Preston 'are real nice to us.'" Another from the same state said that "Shelley is a good town – something like Delta [Utah]."[28] James Satake, who had moved from Palo Alto California to Delta, ahead of evacuation, agreed: "The weather out here is pretty bad, but the people out here are nice so it makes up for it."[29] By October, 1943, 679 evacuees were out on seasonal leaves from Topaz alone (more than 7 percent of the center) in nearby agricultural regions of Utah and Idaho.[30] An Arkansas Presbyterian minister informed his Fayetteville flock of a "circular issued jointly by the states of Indiana, Illinois, Wisconsin, and Minnesota" which welcomed Nikkei resettlers.[31] The welcome mat was spread in many places.

Indefinite leaves were designed to get the Nikkei out of the centers permanently. Almost from the beginning, the WRA allowed families to leave centers to be reunited with their loved ones, and by June, 1943, this

---

[25] S. C. Taylor, "Japanese Americans and Keetley Farms: Utah's Relocation Colony," *Utah Historical Quarterly*, Vol. 54: No. 4 (1986), 328–44; Antoinette Chambers Noble, "Heart Mountain: Remembering the Camp," *Wyoming History Journal*, Vol. 68: No. 2 (1996), 38–44.

[26] R. Harvey, *Amache: The Story of Japanese Internment in Colorado during World War II* (Dallas, TX: Taylor Trade Publishing, 2004), 150.

[27] *Topaz Times*, October 14, 1942, 3.   [28] *Topaz Times*, October 14, 1942, 3.

[29] *Topaz Times*, October 24, 1942, 3.

[30] *Topaz Times*, October 19, 1943, 1. All of the center newspapers carried lists of residents on leave, the towns they left for, the kind of leave they were on, and the names of visitors of all kinds. It is an invaluable source.

[31] Reverend J. P. McConnell, "Understanding of Japanese-American Brothers," December 1943, 1–6, Griswold Papers, MC 733, Series 3, Box 3, Folder 1, Sp. Coll., U. Ark.

included the Justice Department internment camps, for those considered dangerous, like that at Crystal City, Texas.[32] Almost as soon as they opened, by the middle of 1942, the WRA began trying to resettle the Japanese Americans away from Manzanar and Tule Lake, California; Poston and Gila, Arizona; Topaz, Utah; Heart Mountain, Wyoming, and the Idaho and Arkansas centers.

The WRA saw clearly various shortcomings of its own centers.[33] "While all competent observers of the centers agreed that the management of the War Relocation Authority was humane and fair, the centralization of a people of one racial background could not be considered American," wrote Toru Matsumoto in 1946. They also recognized that the Nikkei were grossly underpaid and that barracks life was subversive of the family. Moreover, cooped up, it made them easier targets for their enemies within and without.[34]

The Japanese Americans had committed no known acts of sabotage from December 7, 1941, to March 18, 1942, and since the military no longer feared an invasion or attack, there seemed to be every reason to release the Japanese Americans. Yet until the government could be assured of their reception by host communities, it was understandably unwilling to let them go. The sugar beet harvest of 1942 broke the deadlock. Not only did hundreds of Nikkei help harvest this crop, which provided sugar for some 1,000,000 people, but it proved that the Nikkei could be well received outside the centers.

As Topaz resident Ron Tajiri explained it: "The initial seasonal work program in the inland west, necessitated primarily by a labor shortage on sugar beet farms, proved that individual resettlement was possible."[35] That experiment paved the way for the later program.[36] On October 1, 1942, the WRA, with the approval of the "War Department, the Department of Justice, and the War Manpower Commission" made public its procedures for resettlement. The Protestant churches then established the Committee on Resettlement of Japanese Americans, sponsored by the Federal Council of Churches, the Home Missions Council, and the Foreign Missions Council. The Friends had already established their own group for the evacuees, and several cities quickly joined the parade.[37] Permanent resettlement, although somewhat delayed by the segregation uproar, began in earnest thereafter, mostly beginning in early 1943.

---

[32] *Manzanar Free Press*, June 5, 1943, 1.   [33] Hosokawa, *Frying Pan*, 54.
[34] Matsumoto, *Beyond Prejudice*, 51.   [35] R. Tajiri, "Relocation," 2–7.
[36] Matsumoto, *Beyond Prejudice*, 50–53.   [37] Matsumoto, *Beyond Prejudice*, 55–57.

Even before that, as early as June 18, 1942, authorities began recruiting students for college.[38] By the 1945–46 school year some 2,870[39] young men and women eventually left the centers to enroll, mostly in the Midwest, where they were generally well received. Not so well known were the 3,800 primary and secondary school children who also left the WRA Centers (two in the author's home town).[40] Thousands of others departed to work in war industry. Settlements were founded in Denver, Salt Lake City, Des Moines, St. Louis, Chicago, and Cleveland, cities where housing was scarce, but work was plentiful.[41] Denver eventually drew 1,000 from the Amache Center alone.[42] By "war's end," Chicago claimed the largest number of resettlers at 20,000, "and [according to Charlotte Brooks] replaced the West Coast as the center of Japanese American life."[43] Families of persons in the Justice Department internment camps were allowed to reunite by taking up residence there.[44]

On a more macro scale, Secretary of the Interior Harold Ickes noted that 33,000 Nikkei had left the centers by the Christmas Season of 1944, and Charlotte Brooks put the figure at 60,000 by the Japanese surrender.[45] These resettlers made an "encouraging adjustment to their new homes." [46]

Periodic short-term leaves supplemented these longer term ones. These usually involved trips like shopping visits to the neighboring towns, hiking, wandering, exercising, and fishing. The degree of freedom in towns varied from one center to the next and at different times. Initially, the towns often limited or forbade Nikkei visits, but usually lifted these

---

[38] *Manzanar Free Press*, June 18, 1942, p. 2.
[39] R. O'Brien (New York, NY: Arno Press, 1978 [1946]), 92–108.
[40] WRA, "Education Program," 20.
[41] S. C. Taylor, "Leaving the Concentration Camps: Japanese-American Resettlement in Utah and the Intermountaion West," *Pacific Historical Review*, Vol. 60: No. 2 (1991), 169–94; M. Inoue, "Japanese-Americans in St. Louis: From Internees to Professionals," *City and Society*, Vol. 3: No. 2 (1989), 142–52; T. M. Linehan, "Japanese American Resettlement in Cleveland during and after World War II," *Journal of Urban History*, Vol. 20: No. 1 (1993), 54–80; R. Todd Walker, "Utah Schools and the Japanese American Student Relocation Program," *Utah Historical Quarterly*, Vol. 70: No. 1 (2002), 4–20; H. F. Smith, "The Battle of Parkville: Resistance to Japanese-American Students at Park College [Missouri]," *Journal of Presbyterian History*, Vol. 82: No. 1 (2004), 46–51.
[42] Harvey, *Amache* 152.
[43] Brooks, "Twilight Zone," 1; *Minidoka Irrigator*, November 11, 1944, 3–4; December 16, 1944, 2.
[44] *Topaz Times*, June 10, 1943, 1.   [45] *Minidoka Irrigator*, December 23, 1944, 1.
[46] Hosokawa, *Thirty Five Years*, 34.

restrictions. The Nikkei encounter with Lone Pine, California, was illustrative. At first the Japanese were allowed to enter and shop freely until someone complained that too many of them were coming at once. This led to restrictions, and a designated shopper period followed where six or eight came to purchase for everyone else. That too changed: "Later on, in the last part of the center experience, they were allowed to come to town quite freely."[47]

At Heart Mountain the story varied slightly, but came to the same happy ending. There, the narrative is carefully documented by historian Mike Mackey. The usual period of relatively free entry was followed by the common complaints and the imposition of restrictions. The mayor and city council of Powell, Wyoming, were especially insistent that the flow of Nikkei into town be severely restricted. At that point, some thirty-eight Nikkei were working as house servants in the town; many others labored on surrounding farms, and many more shopped at town businesses. This gave the Japanese Americans enough mutual interests with some Powellites to gain protection. It came from the business community, which united well nigh unanimously against the restrictions.

The issue went back and forth and eventually landed on the desk of the Governor of Wyoming. At least two studies of public opinion were conducted to determine whether the angry city council spoke for the majority of Powellites or a disgruntled minority. Both results showed that most residents had nothing against the Japanese. The Governor commissioned the second inquiry, and when it turned out favorably to the Nikkei, he advised the mayor to drop the matter, which he did.[48]

Mike Mackey aptly summed up the misapprehension that Powell residents as a whole were anti-Nikkei, "It was a very vocal, self-serving minority that continually caused problems for everyone concerned and led, wrongly, to the belief by many internees that a majority of the people in Powell and Cody were prejudiced against them."[49] By their responses to the public opinion inquiries and their support of the business community, the tolerant majority of Powell determined the outcome in a democratic manner. The merchants realized that an instant city of 10,000 plus, meant a great increase in trade for towns of 1,500 to 2,500 (Cody). Commerce won out over hostility, and evacuees often shopped there. At Heart Mountain "women [also] left the camp to work, shop,

[47] Hansen and Jesch, *Japanese Americans*, Part 5, Vol. 1, 140; Ito, *Memoirs of Toshi Ito*, 45.
[48] Mackey, *Heart Mountain*, 121–8.   [49] Mackey, *Heart Mountain*, 128.

visit family, and marry," traveling to Cody, Powell, Laramie, and Billings.[50]

The issue of daily release to the environs of the centers, as opposed to the town, ended in a similar Nikkei victory at Heart Mountain and everywhere else.[51] For months after the Japanese Americans arrived there, the government had neglected to build the fence around the center. When it finally got around to it, the Nikkei objected to it as "another government device to humiliate us." Since the barrier was only a three-strand barbed wire cattle fence, the residents pointed out that it could not restrain anyone and that there was no place to escape to.

The center administration insisted; the Nikkei protested in a giant petition to Dillon Myer and the columns of the *Heart Mountain Sentinel*. The two sides reached a compromise: the fence would stay, but the "residents could leave the campsite during daylight hours."[52] Thus ended the "Battle of the Barbed Wire." The government got a symbolic victory and the Nikkei got its freedom. At frequently embattled Tule Lake, the fence "was [initially] a *single* [italics added] strand of barbed wire," as police chief Harold Jacoby knew.[53]

However, in the Arkansas centers there seemed to be more feeling against the Nikkei. Still, they were allowed to enter town to shop, on trucks driven by the Japanese themselves.[54] They also enjoyed considerable freedom to roam the adjacent woods and swamps in search of cypress knees and mushrooms.[55] At Minidoka (Hunt, Idaho) Japanese American trips to town were frequent enough for the center to be "included in the regular itinerary of the major bus lines in and out of Twin Falls."[56] In Southeastern Arkansas, intercenter travel was frequent enough to support regular bus service between the two centers, running four times daily between 9:30 a.m. and midnight.[57]

Residents of Granada and Lamar, Colorado, initially also had reservations about Nikkei visits and sometimes held back some goods from sale to the evacuees. However, they too eventually warmed to these

---

[50] S. Mckay, *The Courage Our Stories Tell: The Daily Lives and Maternal Child Health Care of Japanese American Women at Heart Mountain* (Casper, WY: Mountain States Lithographing, 2002), 96–7.
[51] *Pacific Citizen*, July 23, 1942, 1.   [52] Hosokawa, *Frying Pan*, 52–53.
[53] Jacoby, *Tule Lake*, 15.
[54] Hansen and Jesch, *Japanese American*, Part 5, Vol. 1, 293–4.
[55] *Rohwer Outpost*, December 24, 1942 and January 1, 1942.
[56] *Rohwer Outpost*, January 23, 1943, 6.   [57] *Rohwer Outpost*, May 23, 1943, 3.

customers.[58] At Tule Lake, after the first few months and after a part of the center had been turned into a center to hold troublemakers, Nikkei residents were forbidden to visit towns like Klamath Falls at will. At Amache/Granada residents got weekend passes to go to town. And everywhere, the Nikkei went on temporary leave to visit relatives, even those in the supposedly hard-core internment camps, like the one at Lordsburg, New Mexico. Visitors from other centers came and went as well.[59] School children often went on extended weekends to visit children at schools outside the centers, and Caucasian children from nearby towns visited them.[60]

Periodic leave likewise allowed the Nikkei to take advantage of the magnificent western environment. At Poston, they could satisfy their fondness for fishing at the nearby Colorado River, only three miles away. As one Caucasian construction superintendent explained: "They would go over and stay all night and camp around by that river by the hundreds."[61] At Manzanar, one night could be stretched into one week to ten days. "Everybody around here knew it – that is the game wardens knew, nobody ever bothered them." The authorities were well aware of the custom.[62] The general lack of restraint was highlighted by the Topaz center boundaries. From sunset to sunrise, the Nikkei were confined to the barbed wire, but during the day they were free to go beyond the wire anywhere within the larger boundaries of the center.[63]

At the Poston Center there were no guards in close proximity to the centers. Some guards were posted about a mile outside the center at a gate, and none was at the actual entrance.[64] The point is re-emphasized by the redefinition of the Manzanar center boundaries in the summer of 1942. In order to facilitate "roving, ... picnicking, and outings, the center boundaries were extended four miles west into the foothills of the Sierra Nevada Mountains," well beyond the barbed wire and guard towers that have populated memory and many histories.[65] At Topaz, Japanese American youngsters left their barracks to play basketball against Mormon high schools, sometimes staying overnight after the time clock

---

[58] Harvey, *Amache*, 127.   [59] *Gila News-Courier*, February 9, 1943, 3.
[60] *Manzanar Free Press*, June 11, 1942, 2.
[61] Hansen, and Jesch, *Japanese Americans*, Part V, Vol. 2, 705.
[62] Hansen and Jesch, *Japanese American*, Part V, Vol. 1, 214.
[63] *Topaz Times*, October 10, 1942, 4; Okubo, *Citizen*, 202.
[64] *Dies Hearings*, June–July 1943, 9182, 9186, 9191.
[65] *Manzanar Free Press*, July 7, 1942, 2.

expired. On Saturday night, Topaz women and children shopped and attended movies in Delta.

At turbulent Tule Lake Segregation Center, a neighbor remembered that "they were allowed to roam at will in the hills out away from the camp." They also roamed into the famous Lava Beds, and although they could not go into the towns of Tulelake and Clear Lake, they rambled up to seven miles outside the center.[66] As the same witness said of Tule Lake, "Now they did have towers around this area but I don't know why, because actually the Japanese could have gone anyplace they wanted."[67] As a Nikkei editor explained the general permissiveness:

We Minidoka center residents today stand in a favored position, of being permitted to traverse beyond the barbed wires into nearby towns upon presentation of legitimate reasons. This arrangement, which has made it mutually beneficial for us as well as for the nearby towns which trade with us – and made our living here much more pleasant than if we were at some other center.[68]

Photographs of women walking their children outside the center make the same point.[69]

Limited transfers from center to center were also possible. At Minidoka, and presumably everywhere, residents could move to other centers at government expense if the reason was to reunite families.[70] On January 10, 1943, the first evacuees left Manzanar permanently for Chicago to work in war industry. At Minidoka the temporary and permanent release programs had reduced the center population by 2,278, or 24 percent, in the first six months of 1943 alone.[71] The exodus caused a severe labor shortage in both places. In the European Jewish ghettos, marriage was forbidden on pain of death. At Manzanar, for Tomiko Kato, it meant a bus trip to Mojave, California, to catch a train to Grand Rapids, Michigan, to join her fiancé John Nitta.[72]

It must be emphasized strongly that this laissez-faire regime was not as open to the Issei.[73] Since many of these still spoke only Japanese or broken

---

[66] Hansen and Jesch, eds., Japanese American ... Part V, Vol. 2, 472.   [67] Ibid.
[68] *Minidoka Irrigator*, June 5, 1943, 4.   [69] McKay, *The Courage*, 1.
[70] *Minidoka Irrigator*, June 5, 1943, 1.   [71] *Minidoka Irrigator*, June 5, 1943, 3.
[72] *Manzanar Free Press*, July 22, 1942, 1. A sample of leaves appeared in most papers. On one day in April 1943, at Gila River, Nikkei left for Omaha, Fort Leonard Wood, Missouri, Salt Lake City, Phoenix, Winfield, Kansas, Glendale, Arizona, and visitors appeared from Poston, Santa Fe, and Ogden for college, work, and family visits. *Gila News Courier*, April 13, 1943, 4.
[73] I am indebted to Professor Robert Cherny for this distinction.

English, leaving the centers required a Nisei, Kibei, or Sansei family guardian. Nonetheless, many Issei did venture beyond the wire. Still, because they feared going home or elsewhere in the United States, several thousand Japanese Americans chose to remain in the centers. However, these had pretty free range within them.

The multiplicity of leave destinations calls into question the fundamental convictions of relocation historians that the Nikkei met widespread rejection outside the centers, especially in the West. Fortunately, the center newspapers kept lists of the people who were out of the centers on seasonal, student, military, and indefinite leave. For example the *Topaz Times* reported in May, June, and July, 1943, indefinite leaves for Provo, Salt Lake City, Bingham, Delta, Cedar City, Utah; Caldwell, Idaho; Carson City, Nevada; Spokane, Washington; Minneapolis, St. Paul, and Detroit Lakes, Minnesota; Chicago, Maywood, Mendelein [Mundelein?], Des Plaines, and Rockford, Illinois; Gary, Indiana; Columbus, Ohio; New York City; Madison, Wisconsin; Estes Park and Denver, Colorado; Detroit, Ann Arbor, Kalamazoo, Michigan; and Philadelphia, Pennsylvania. On October 14, 1943, the paper noted indefinite leaves for Salt Lake City and Ogden; Denver, Cincinnati, Detroit and Ann Arbor; Palos Park and Chicago; Pennington, New Jersey; Milwaukee, and New York City. Two weeks later, residents had left for Salt Lake City; Omaha; Kansas City; Elcelsior Springs, Missouri; Chicago and Highland Park, Illinois; Cleveland and Cincinnati; Detroit, Ann Arbor, Richland, Michigan; and Lewiston, Maine.[74]

These were the lists from just a few days for one center. And the seasonal leaves on any given day reported more people leaving for at least as many destinations. The same October edition reported seasonal leaves for Provo, Alta, Spanish Fork, Ogden, Delta, and Springville, Utah; and Lewiston and Idaho Falls, Idaho – forty-eight people on that one day.[75] Two days later a "Chicago Special" train left the Amache Center with thirty-eight evacuees bound for the Windy City.[76] Obviously there were a lot of places willing to accept Nikkei into their communities and where Nikkei felt safe enough to go.[77]

So these young people waited with their WRA identity cards and suitcases "on desert roadsides and in dust-beaten stations" for transportation to "take them away from the watchtowers and sentries," wrote the

---

[74] *Topaz Times*, October 28, 1943, 3. The names of states are mentioned when the town names are not familiar.
[75] *Topaz Times*, October 14, 1943, 2.   [76] *Topaz Times*, October 16, 1943, 2.
[77] *Topaz Times*, June 3, 1943; July 17, 1943.

eloquent Larry Tajiri.[78] They would ride trains like the "Sunshine Special" of the Missouri Pacific line, from Houston to St. Louis, which would scoop up resettlers at sidings at Rohwer and Jerome, where they rode with friendly soldiers, helpful seatmates, and old ladies. "No questions are asked. No one stares." They could originally have been headed for a nearby farming community like Abraham, Utah, or the "cosmopolitan city of New York,"[79] or to Cincinnati or Chicago in the Midwest, to a hostel or boarding house, to a waiting home, to a nursery in Ohio, to an aircraft plant in the Mid-Continent, to a sweetheart in St. Louis, to some place in the forty-four states who would accept them by mid-1943.

"Except in the far west," wrote Tajiri, the former San Francisco newspaperman and foreign correspondent, "national sentiment appears definitely favorable to the resettlement of all loyal evacuees."[80] They would be met not by brass bands, but by friendly people from religious or social agencies, who would help them through the maelstrom of a wartime metropolitan railroad station and into a new life.[81] And the WRA helped financially to facilitate indefinite relocation from the centers. The agency provided a transportation allowance and a five-day subsistence allowance of $25 for every family member. In addition, the WRA ran a series of training movies, like "This is Chicago," to help the process of adaptation along.[82]

Of course, it could be argued that these Nikkei were not really liked, but just tolerated to ease the widespread labor shortage. A like scarcity existed on college campuses, whose majority white male students were called to the colors. So we must examine the Japanese Americans' own perceptions of their acceptance. "On the whole, I think no student will have much trouble regarding racial discrimination," wrote Yoshi Hibino from Austin. "Feeling against Nisei just doesn't seem to exist in Texas." From Syracuse University, Kiyoshi Nishikawa agreed: "The people here are very nice. The educated persons and the clergy are very friendly and kind whereas the average person on the street seems to take us for granted. They don't stare at us like curios. Thank God."[83] From Chicago, came the same message. A Nikkei who had successfully resettled there, wrote that "his neighbors treat him fine, [he] likes his employers and fellow employees." Another analysis of Chicago conditions summed up the situation similarly:

---

[78] L. Tajiri, "Relocation," *Topaz Times*, May 12 and 14, 1943, 4.
[79] Griffin, "Relocation," 8.   [80] Tajiri, "Relocation," 7.   [81] Tajiri, "Relocation," 3–7.
[82] *Topaz Times*, November 4, 1943, 1.   [83] *Topaz Times*, June 3, 1943, 4; July 7, 1943, 4.

Against isolated cases of discrimination, however a young machinist earning $250 monthly, a factory worker saving $50 out of his $165 earnings, a young secretary receiving $100 – all made new homes, found friendly neighbors, went on their way, happy to be out of the camps. These were the more typical of success stories receiving no mention in newspapers. [84]

The analysis concluded that 95 percent of the 300 so far located in Chicago had successfully adjusted, and most were saving money. Some historians of the Nikkei claim that the WRA requested that the center papers publish favorable responses, but that argument does not give the Nikkei credit for good judgment and honesty. Even such historians agree that the Nikkei were much better off in their new post-center homes.[85]

To be sure, some Nikkei received hostile treatment or were subjected to discrimination in some places and at some times, including the "Provo Incident." The *Topaz Times* explained that a "Provo camp (where Nikkei volunteers worked at farms and canneries) raid climaxed a series of unlawful demonstrations by the boys, which included stoning the camp and the home of a Japanese in Oren [Utah]."[86] The incident began with the "hurling of stones and epithets and ending with the use of guns." The October 9 *Pacific Citizen* considered the incident a racial one, and the Provo Nikkei workers refused to come to work the next day. The paper went on to say that "the citizens of Provo were quick to take steps to rectify the damage." The October 12, 1943 issue of the *Topaz Times* reported three men charged "with assault of the Provo FSA" center were convicted and sentenced to the sixty days in the county jail. One was given the choice of jail or joining the army and chose military service.[87]

This hostility was not representative. The same paper reported two days later that forty-nine Nikkei had left on seasonal leave for various Utah, Oregon, and Idaho destinations, *including nineteen for Provo*. The AJA were obviously welcome in many places and felt safe enough to go there.[88] More representative was the case of two Nikkei who resettled in Cleveland. "We sure miss camp," admitted Ted H.[89] In Europe, resettlement was more sinister. Admittedly, wartime Cleveland, where the Cuyohoga River was so polluted that it occasionally caught fire, was no country club. Still, it was a far cry from Buchenwald. When evacuees left the American desert centers, they might have felt a pang of guilt, but they mostly felt joy.

---

[84] *Topaz Times*, May 29, 1943, 7.   [85] C. Brooks, "In the Twilight Zone," 1655–1670.
[86] *Topaz Times*, October 12, 1943, 1.   [87] *Topaz Times*, October 12, 1943, 2.
[88] *Topaz Times*, October 21, 1943, 3.   [89] *Topaz Times*, October 19, 1943, 2.

11

Food, Labor, Sickness, and Health

The nature of the centers was critical because it allowed the Nikkei to exist and gave them a sphere of their own that they could pretty much mold to their liking. Many of the complaints against the centers both within and without arose because of the daily life inside them. And there were many, as for example the failure to get stoves into the Poston barracks until well into the fall of 1942. Again the context must be considered. The WRA and the Army Corps of Engineers faced the daunting task of building, in effect, instant cities or towns from the ground up. Unlike other planned cities or parts thereof, these desert locales required not only the basics of the physical city of 112,000, but employment as well. The WRA centers provided most of their own food supply, a feat not even the rapidly built cantonments of the two world wars did. Despite shortcomings, the Corps and its contractors accomplished this magnificent feat in seven months.

So what were the conditions of the American centers for those staying instead of leaving? Another critical distinction between a concentration camp and a relocation center is the stark omnipresence of starvation. Crucially, evacuees of American centers were eventually fed amply and well. No one starved. Initially the food sometimes was not Japanese style, too much beef and mashed potatoes and not enough tofu. But the tofu quickly appeared, although it may have taken the non-Japanese cooks a while to learn to manage it. That phase did not last long, however, because Japanese chefs soon replaced them.

For example, at Tule Lake each of the residential blocks hired their own cooks from among the residents and mostly controlled them. Unlike food for the staff, that for the evacuees was free. Nonetheless, food gave the residents some anxiety. Some believed that the mess hall staffs were stealing food instead of providing all of it to the residents. Since the evacuees temporarily lost control of their food supplies, they were anxious about its regularity.[1] Because of rationing, food angst gripped most of the nation except for farmers, who provided some of their own, so the Nikkei anxiety was part of the wartime predicament. Other Americans certainly shared the same angst.

Nonetheless, food shortage rumors circulated widely in the centers, just as rumors circulated on the outside that the Nikkei were evading rationing and thereby taking food off the tables of others. Sometimes the food was monotonous and on one occasion prompted a strike by the Topazians, who were served liver "for several weeks."[2] And food rumors were the cause of the November 4, 1943, uprising that brought military control of Tule Lake. But by 1942, residents of Poston and Minidoka enjoyed turkey on Turkey Day. Minidoka residents devoured 7,000 pounds of it.[3] When government rationing eliminated the availability of baby food at Minidoka, the residents simply grew and processed their own.[4]

Allegedly, the cafeteria-style dining regimen undermined the Japanese American family because families did not have tables that they all shared. This problem, too, did not last forever. As early as May, 1943, the Topaz dining service "inaugurate[d] family style service for the convenience of the residents."[5] A Nikkei-friendly person familiar with the situation noted "that they were well fed. I know because I usually ate lunch there every time I went down to visit the school," Doctor Dorothy Cragen remembered of Manzanar. "They had very good food and, in fact, they had some things that we didn't have. We were short on butter and coffee and many commodities like that, and they had plenty of everything, so they were never mistreated."

Many Nikkei got around the mess hall regimen by buying hot plates from Sears and cooking at home.[6] On Christmas Eve, 1942, the Rohwer canteen offered California Sunkist brand oranges and Yakima Fancy Delicious apples for sale, so universal liver was not the rule.[7] Residents often complained about their diet, but they were no more disadvantaged

---

[1] Jacoby, *Tule Lake*, 17–19, 25.   [2] Okubo, *Citizen*, 143.

[3] *Minidoka Irrigator*, November 25, 1942, 1; D. H. Estes and M. T. Estes, "Letters from Camp: Poston, the First Year," in M. Mackey, guest editor, *Journal of the West*: Special edition, *Japanese Relocation in the American West*, Vol. 38: No. 2 (April 1999), 31, 29–32.

[4] *Minidoka Irrigator*, June 5, 1943, 3.   [5] *Topaz Times*, May 29, 1943, 1.

[6] Hansen and Jesch, *Japanese American*, Part V, Vol. 1, 195. Ito, *Memoirs of Toshi Ito*, 45.

[7] *Rohwer Outpost*, December 24, 1942, 3.

in the wartime rationing system than were the people on the other side of the wire.

As many ultras on the outside criticized the food as Nikkei on the inside complained. The critics charged that the AJA hoarded food and had more of it because they were not subject to rationing as were other Americans. In fact, rationing governed the Nikkei in the same way it governed the rest of America.[8] They might have benefited marginally because the centers could purchase in bulk for populations of 10,000 and could benefit from government surplus. Or certainly they, like farmers all over wartime America, grew much of their own food in their omnipresent Victory Gardens. Each center was an agricultural commune which produced both meat and vegetables. The food flap had very little substantive truth and was often whipped up by anti-Nikkei newspapers like the Hearst *Denver Post*, which published the complaints of disgruntled employees who quit or were fired.[9]

In Europe, starvation and "hunger stalked the ghettos"; it haunted the camps; it beset even POW lagers.[10] When prisoners withered away under their vile diet, Jews and Christians alike were sent to death camps and more slaves replaced them.[11] More than 3,000,000 Soviet prisoners died in these and other camps in what historian Michael Neufeld called "one of the forgotten holocausts of the Third Reich." Soviet camps were similar.[12]

In the relocation centers, Japanese Americans worked to build the settlements, to supply the centers with food, to administer and maintain them, to produce some government defense items, especially camouflage nets (for a time), and to provide such professionals as doctors, teachers, retailers, beauticians, journalists, or dentists.[13]

Labor on war work, like the camouflage nets, was not required. Nor was any work of any kind required! "Whereas compulsory labor was very much a part of life in the Nazi and Soviet prisons, it was wholly nonexistent in the relocation centers," wrote Harold Jacoby.[14] Historians have found the wages, which ranged from $12 to $19 a month, to be inadequate.

---

[8] *Manzanar Free Press*, June 5, 1943, 1.   [9] Hosokawa, *Frying Pan*, 54.
[10] Bennett, *Shadow of the Swastika*, 196.
[11] Michael Marrus wrote that "nearly one-fifth of Polish Jewry [died] from starvation and disease." M. R. Marrus, *The Holocaust in History* (New York, NY: Penguin Books, 1987), 117.
[12] M. Neufeld, *The Rocket and the Reich: Peenemunde and the Coming of the Ballistic Missile* Era (Cambridge, MA: Harvard University Press, 1995), 209–13, 185. See also N. Troller, *Theresienstadt: Hitler's Gift to the Jews* (Chapel Hill, NC: University of North Carolina Press, c. 1991), 2.
[13] *Topaz Times*, September 26, 1942, 1.   [14] Jacoby, *Tule Lake*, 56.

FIG. 5. Workers in field, Tule Lake Relocation Center, California. Farm Security Administration – Office of War Information Collection. Courtesy Library of Congress Prints & Photographs Division, LC-DIG-fsac-1a35013.

That is especially true for doctors and other highly qualified personnel. If this had been the only means of Nikkei support, it would have been dreadful, but the WRA was seriously constrained by congressional politics. Milton Eisenhower initially attempted to pay "prevailing wages, that is wages competitive with those outside the centers, for all positions" in them. That idea "brought a storm of protest from members of Congress, who demanded that pay not exceed that provided for privates in the army. Politically, we had to accept that," noted Eisenhower.[15]

To offset those limits, other Nikkei working outside the centers received the going wage in their localities.[16] Reminiscent of the First African American "Great Migration" to the North during World War I, labor recruiters swarmed into the centers from near and far. As early as June 9, 1942, AJA went to Idaho to harvest sugar beets, for which they were paid a flat fee and bonuses.[17] At Topaz, labor recruiters from Provo, Salt Lake City, Logan, and Cache County arrived at the center before it was fully operational, begging for white and blue collar workers.[18] Others, from the Hotel Sherman in Chicago, joined them.[19] All the histories of the Nikkei have emphasized the alleged antipathy of West Coast agribusiness to the Nikkei. But that was not true in many other western places, especially in Iowa. The "President of the Iowa State Vegetable Growers' Association" in mid-1943 was begging the Japanese Americans to come and compete.[20]

"The evacuees also voluntarily worked to make camouflage nets for the military."[21] Historians have frequently missed the difference in pay scales for those working inside the centers and those working outside. To them, the standard wages, which ranged from $12 for laborers to $19 for doctors, have seemed unusually severe. However, for those willing to labor outside the centers, wages differed. For example, at Topaz, the Nikkei engaged in sugar beet farming within the centers worked for $16 per month, but those who did the same work outside the center earned the prevailing wage in their area, such as in the Cache Valley.[22] The WRA also paid workmen's compensation to those injured on the job.[23] That allowed the outside workers to earn considerably more than those who did not venture outside. The government also supplied the Nikkei a monthly allowance for clothing and food, plus housing,

---

[15] Eisenhower, *The President*, 122; The government eventually raised privates' pay to $50, but war anger prevented the WRA from raising that of the evacuees, Nishimoto, *Inside an American*, 39.

[16] *Minidoka Irrigator*, June 5, 1943, 3.

[17] *Manzanar Free Press*, June 9, 1942, 1. The Free Press took it upon itself to monitor the conditions of work in Idaho and to report and to its readers that it was good.

[18] *Topaz Times*, September 26, 1942, 1.   [19] *Topaz Times*, June 19, 1942, 1.

[20] *Rohwer Outpost*, June 23, 1943, 5.   [21] *Manzanar Free Press*, June 23, 1942, 2.

[22] *Topaz Times*, October 14, 1942, 2.   [23] *Rohwer Outpost*, January 9, 1943, 2.

education for their children, adult education, and free medical care.[24] AJA did not pay taxes of any kind. So the monetary face value of center wages was only part of the compensation package.

However, given congressional opposition, it is impossible to see politically how salaries could have been raised above those paid to army privates. Congress and public opinion would not have tolerated it. Historians of the Nikkei have been virtually oblivious to the significance of political pressures on the WRA, except to present them as other examples of racism and discrimination. The WRA was already plagued with major political problems without touching off a firestorm over paying wages higher than those of Army privates.

Once Army pay was raised to $50, the government did not have the funds to match raises for the evacuees. Yet the various leave policies and the numerous allotments did allow the Nikkei to compensate for congressional insistence on low pay. So did the socio-economic class divisions within the Nikkei. As Ansel Adams noted in 1944, "quite a few of the citizen evacuees have property and various sources of income."[25] Other observers noted that many of the Japanese Americans invariably paid for their purchases in cash, so these monies also helped to mitigate congressionally dictated wages. The centers must have had something close to full employment. When the Topaz and Rohwer center populations topped out at about 8,000, 2,827 and 2,800, respectively, were employed within those centers, not to mention those employed outside.[26]

Pay for those who relocated permanently varied, but outdid the center scale by a great deal. Medical employers in Baltimore advertised for student nurses for $40 per month, plus cash allowance, full board, room, uniforms, laundry and medical services. New Haven wanted Japanese language trainees at $150 per month. In Chicago they needed addressograph operators for $110 per month and dieticians for $150 per month and maintenance. In the same city a machinist made $250 per month; a factory worker gained $165; a secretary, $100, and a couple to tag team as domestics, $135, plus room and board.[27] Cleveland employers sought screw machine operators for $1.40 per hour. In Oak Park, Illinois, they needed workers in the laundry business from $32 to $46 a month and

---

[24] *Topaz Times*, October 24, 1942, 1.
[25] A. Adams, *Born Free and Equal: The Story of Loyal Japanese Americans Manzanar Relocation Center, Inyo County, California* (Bishop, CA: Spotted Dog Press, 1944).
[26] *Rohwer Outpost*, January 13, 1943, 2; July 24, 1943, 6; *Topaz Times*, October 21, 1942, 1.
[27] *Topaz Times*, May 29, 1943, 7.

housing.[28] Historian Robert Higgs has shown that the idea of workers' wartime prosperity is problematical, but at least the Nikkei outside the centers earned more than those within.[29]

Many have noted that the Nikkei saved sugar beet growers in 1942 (not to mention consumers) and beyond that helped others by their contribution to business, which was also significant. It is a modern cliché that small firms are the inventive engine of American business. And the Nikkei were especially significant for hard-pressed wartime small enterprises. Scarcely had the smoke cleared from Pearl Harbor when Chicago Congressman Adolph Sabath was protesting about "hard hit little business" being "forced to the wall because of material shortages and curtailment of civilian goods production."[30] Despite the best efforts of Sabath and Congressman Maury Maverick, the problem lasted until war's end. Almost every company that advertised with the Nikkei center newspapers was a small firm. This Nikkei contribution to the business war effort deserves more study.

Farmers benefited even more, especially sugar beet growers, whose crops the Nikkei saved in 1942. The Sugar Beet Company of Lovell, Wyoming, employed AJA labor and stated that "most of the Japanese appear to be very fine people."[31] Some of the potential employers and their political backers apparently believed that they would enjoy the benefit of Nikkei labor on a concentration camp basis. If so, they were sorely disappointed. Beginning as early as the assembly centers, the Army and WRA minutely regulated the conditions of work. Employers were required to pay prevailing wages and to supply food, housing, and medical care, plus transportation to and from the place of work. A part of the wages was to be deducted for workers' families.

Employers could not employ the Nikkei if doing so would displace laborers already working in the area and no workers would come to the job until the governor of the appropriate state and the local law enforcement officials certify that "law and order will be maintained in the event that Japanese evacuees move into a specified area."[32] As we shall see later, the government did care about Nikkei safety. So those who worked outside the centers enjoyed most of the perks that those inside them did, plus

---

[28] *Topaz Times*, May 27, 1943, 3; June 3, 1943, 3; October 16, 1943, 3.
[29] R. Higgs, Depression, *War, and Cold War: Challenging the Myths of Conflict and Prosperity* (Oakland, CA: The Independent Institute, 2006), 79–104ff.
[30] *LA Daily News*, January 26, 1942, 25.   [31] Mackey, *Heart Mountain*, 25–34.
[32] WRA, "Employment of Japanese Evacuees in Agriculture Outside of Assembly Centers," 1–2, RG 210, Box 2, National Archives.

higher wages. Acceptance was not always automatic. In mid-1943 a group of Nikkei returned to center after "negative community acceptance" in Cedar City, Utah, plus disputes over working conditions. However, these were exceptions to the rule of acceptance and adjustment.[33]

The Nikkei often earned every cent of their wages. Those unaccustomed to beet work or turkey preparation came away from their first day on the job bone tired and sore of limb. The boys killed turkeys, the girls plucked turkeys, and everybody smelled of turkeys. A young Nikkei woman described the beet harvest:

It was the first time some of them ever had a sugar beet in their hands. Sunday ... all were resting with swollen hands, aching muscles and limbs, stiff backs, etc. The husbands are lucky for they have their wives who do the cooking, washing, shopping ... but I do feel so sorry for those boys who have to cook for themselves ... after a hard day's work in the beet fields.[34]

At the end of the eight-hour shift, they just collapsed. But a Topaz resident wrote back that "even if the work is hard, it is worth the freedom that we are allowed, I think. There is no limit to the ice cream and coca cola and shows [movies] here." A beet worker noted the same hard work and stiffness, but "it certainly feels grand to be in the wide open spaces again." She wrote that "Preston [Idaho] is a small nice town."[35]

The Nikkei especially prized the Utah capital: "The atmosphere in Salt Lake City is very friendly, undoubtedly influenced by the Mormons. There is no evidence of hostility towards us, but contrarily many are openly sympathetic." She explained further that "the absence of economic competition without a doubt aids our position no[t] a little. Labor is very scarce, and jobs are plentiful." She noted excitedly, "Practically everyone is working and enjoying life in general with the usual theatre jaunts and dances." [36]

Some of the work was dangerous. Among the many jobs that Nikkei took were those of merchant seamen, which tasks were considered as dangerous as combat. In June, 1943, the *Topaz Times*, quoting the *Gila News-Courier*, reported that several Japanese American seamen had lost their lives. "Several others have gone through the experience of being torpedoed and bombed, and are going back for more."[37] Not all Nikkei heroism took place in land battles.

---

[33] *Topaz Times*, June 12, 1943, 2.   [34] *Topaz Times*, October 24, 1942, 3.   [35] Ibid.
[36] *Topaz Times*, October 28, 1942, 3.   [37] *Topaz Times*, June 12, 1943, 2.

The resettlement program meant that Japanese Americans were now employed in more diverse places than before the war. The *Sentinel* summed up this move away from the ghetto economy:

He's [the Nisei] driving trucks and growing and delivering the products for America's table. He's building houses and herding sheep. He's tending poultry and milking the cows. He's recapping tires and keeping America's automobiles rolling as a mechanic. He helps maintain the tracks over which the overburdened rail flows ... the Nisei is on the high seas and on river barges, ... in government service, hotels, food and service industries, newspapers, and classrooms, in short everywhere.[38]

Much of the Japanese American labor was for themselves or their families. In many of the centers, residents planted personal gardens between the barracks and some did so as early as the assembly centers. The aridity of the West necessitated the use of the extensive irrigation canals to grow these products. Finally, the evacuees quickly created their own highly successful cooperatives to supply themselves with things that the WRA did not.[39] Those who worked outside the centers suffered from being away from their families, but shared that experience with 15,000,000 other civilian wartime migrants and 16,000,000 military ones.

Although recent historians have complained of center health conditions,[40] the primary sources show the reverse. Topaz had a 175-bed hospital.[41] A brand new, $150,000 hospital designed to handle 250 patients was opened at Manzanar in July, 1942, with all new equipment, including ex-ray, fluoroscope, and radiographic machines.[42] Ansel Adams, the renowned artist who photographed the Manzanar Center in 1944, said that "one of the most spectacular achievements is the Manzanar Hospital.[43] He called it a "complete health-service enterprise," staffed by 13 Caucasians and 280 evacuees. It included dental clinics, school health services, a teaching staff for "educating children with special problems or chronic diseases," and a handicapped children's clinic. Center health was such that only a third of the hospital beds were occupied and "the death rate is one-half the national average."[44]

[38] *Heart Mountain Sentinel*, August 2, 1944, 4. [39] *Minidoka Irrigator*, June 5, 1943, 6.
[40] *Congested Areas Hearings*. These provided testimony from the health authorities of the various congested urban areas. For complaints of substandard health, see L. Fiset, "Health Care at the Central Utah (Topaz) Relocation Center," *Journal of the West*, Vol. 38: No. 2 (1999), 34–44.
[41] Okubo, *Citizen*, 162. [42] *Manzanar Free Press*, July 22, 1942, 1.
[43] Adams, *Born Free*, 73. [44] Adams, *Born Free*, 73.

"There was a beautiful center hospital, well staffed with Japanese doctors and equipment," agreed Donald Branson, a plumber at Manzanar.[45] Similarly the *Outpost* reported that "the [Rohwer] center hospital is up-to-date and satisfactory in every way" according to "a committee of block managers" (Nikkei responsible for managing each block).[46] Harold Jacoby, the pro-Nikkei chief of police at Tule Lake, called its hospital "the best hospital in the northern part of the county," staffed "primarily" by Japanese American doctors and nurses.[47] The Army provided for "fully equipped" hospitals at each center.[48] Because Manzanar drew its population heavily from Los Angeles, it gathered in some very high quality medical personnel.[49] Other famous Japanese American doctors labored at the other centers, like Tule Lake, as well and they too had "large hospitals."[50]

Not that it made up for relocation, but health care was free. They had very good doctors, both Caucasian and Japanese. In fact, "the Japanese doctor working for the Public Health Service in Parker was in attendance with my wife when my second child was born," noted one Caucasian observer.[51] At least 6,000 babies were born in the relocation centers, most under sanitary arrangements. The Poston, Arizona, center newspaper boasted that "one baby was born on the average of every twenty hours for the month of September," 1943, and Miné Okubo agreed that the "birth rate in the [Topaz] center was high."[52]

Despite the swampy surroundings of the Arkansas centers, they too had very good Japanese doctors and facilities.[53] The bottom line is that the center death rate was low and childbirth was healthy.[54] At Rohwer in early 1943 every single child was given a physical examination paid for by the National Society for the Benefit of Crippled and Deformed Children of Little Rock.[55] At troubled Tule Lake, the Public Health Service "established a home nurse for every block" in order to make nursing care available whenever necessary." By September, 1942, the *Manzanar Free*

[45] Ibid.   [46] *Rohwer Outpost*, December 24, 1942, 6.   [47] Jacoby, *Tule Lake*, 14.
[48] "Statement in Response to Senate Resolution 166," 16.
[49] Hansen and Jesch, *Japanese Americans*, Part V, Vol. 1, 34.
[50] Hansen and Jesch, *Japanese Americans*, Part V, Vol. 2, 509.
[51] Hansen and Jesch, *Japanese Americans*, Part V, Vol. 2, 727–28.
[52] Quoted in the *Topaz Times*, October 16, 1943, 2; Okubo, *Citizen* 163.
[53] Hansen and Jesch, *Japanese Americans*, Part V, Vol. 1. 305.
[54] For births and deaths in the assembly centers, which saw the worst health problems, see L. Fiset, "Public Health in World War II Assembly Centers for Japanese Americans," *Bulletin of the History of Medicine*, Vol. 73: No. 4 (1999), 565–84.
[55] *Rohwer Outpost*, January 6, 1943, 3.

Press was claiming that "the Japanese people as a whole [at Manzanar] were getting much more – far more – and better medical attention than they ever had before."[56] That is not surprising because many AJA lived on isolated farms.

How much it contributed to ill health in the centers is not known, but the centers shared the problem of prostitution with the wider world of war. The world's oldest profession seemed to thrive on war in all of the congested centers and it did in relocation centers as well. The single men's barracks would seem to have provided them a literally captive market. In discussing theft and gambling at Tanforan, Kikuchi noted that "a more serious problem is the reported solicitations by Japanese prostitutes in the single men's dormitory."[57]

The contention of recent historians that health care in the centers was deficient must be placed within a 1940s wartime context and a western local context as well. The centers certainly enjoyed better medical facilities than those found in the small towns surrounding them. Because of lingering poverty and geographic isolation, medical care in the 1940s was none too good in many American places. The war exacerbated those conditions by drawing medical personnel, including doctors, into military service.

Towns of 1,000 to 2,500 did not have hospitals, much less renowned physicians, but the relocation centers did. They had distinguished physicians, nurses, hospitals, medical technology and other advantages that populations of 10,000 to 18,000 could support. Since the Army considered it more risky from an epidemiological perspective to concentrate so many people in centers and in barracks, it provided more hospital beds than "is customary in most normal communities."[58] Parker, Arizona, is illustrative. Before the conflict, at Parker near the Poston center, there was "no medical doctor here, there was one chiropractor," remembered a Bureau of Indian Affairs Superintendent.[59] One can only guess what conditions were like in the Ozarks, the Pine Barrens of New Jersey, Eastern Kentucky, or Appalachia.

During the war, all kinds of wild rumors circulated, charging the WRA with coddling the Nikkei. The Dies Committee was especially shameless in spreading such gossip. Those rumors that claimed that the Nikkei enjoyed better diets than outsiders seem to have had no validity. However, most of the centers enjoyed better medical care than the surrounding small towns.

---

[56] Reported in the *Rohwer Outpost*, January 16, 1943, 6.
[57] Modell, *Kikuchi Diary*, 60.   [58] "Statement in Response to Senate Resolution," 17.
[59] Hansen and Jesch, *Japanese American*, Part V, Vol. 2, 672.

Poston not only had dentists, but a "dental clinic."[60] Larger towns like Twin Falls, Idaho, or Phoenix, Arizona, might have possessed personnel and facilities comparable to Manzanar, but Delta, Lone Pine, Independence, Cody, Powell, Granada, Parker, Tulelake, or Clear Lake did not have hospitals, much less distinguished physicians from Los Angeles General Hospital. To compare the health matters of these American centers to those in Nazi concentration camps is farcical.

[60] Hansen and Jesch, *Japanese American*, Part V, Vol. 1, 412.

12

Wartime Attitudes toward Relocation

The attitudes of diverse groups toward the Nikkei cannot be understood within the race paradigm. These opinions were nuanced, complex, and eminently situational. Racism was only one of a very graded spectrum of feelings. These ran the gamut from outright racism to profound respect and varied according to motivation. Because of their distinctive analytical and methodological boundaries, the upholders of the race paradigm maximize the importance of race and racism and thereby overlook the complexity of American attitudes.[1]

The outlook of the Native Sons of the Golden West is a good place to begin. The closest one can come to biological racism is in the attitude of the Native Sons. For years, this organization was in the forefront of the struggle to ban Japanese immigration to the United States.[2] They even claimed to have been responsible for inserting the controversial ban on Asian immigration into the 1924 national restrictive immigration legislation. In the Tolan Hearings, the Sons explained their opposition to Japanese immigration and their support of wartime mass evacuation. They referred to "Japanese faces," and said that they were tainted by their own "blood." It is clear that the group was referring to race in the modern color-coded sense. But it was not referring to racism in the sense that Dower defined the term. They specifically *eschewed the idea of racial superiority* and did not accuse the Nikkei of being like snakes, insects,

---

[1] Okihiro, *Storied*, 137.
[2] The Joint Committee was made up of the state Grange, the Native Sons of the Golden West, the state AFL, and the state American Legion, plus some high-profile individuals like V. S. McClatchy.

vermin, or lice. Nor did they characterize them as childlike, savage, or lunatic, much less the basest links on the Great Chain of Being.

Of course the Sons' specific repudiation of white superiority eliminates the possibility of biological racism. As they said in explaining their opposition to the Nikkei, "These conditions, while unfortunate, are the result of the determination of Caucasians to keep their country and their blood white, and involve no claim of superiority." But their opposition involved many other claims, including unfair competition against white farmers. The Nikkei were overly "aggressive," accepted "low living standards," "lived in unassimilated racial blocs," worked absurdly long hours, put their women and children in the fields, ran language schools that inculcated Japanese culture,[3] and up to 25 percent of them were dual citizens. Above all, they were "unassimilable" because they, like the Caucasians, were so strongly oriented to their own nationality and culture that the two groups could not merge.[4] So beyond race, the Nikkei were opposed on grounds of class, culture, labor standards, business habits, proto feminism, and family practices. It was not exactly racist to oppose overly long hours or the use of child and female labor, since Progressive Era and New Deal reformers had also been trying to enact such protective legislation for years.[5]

Significantly, their view of assimilation was widely shared, internationally so. National identity was proving intractable throughout twentieth-century western civilization for the principal reason that the Sons urged. National identity and the nationalism that grew out of it, tore up the European part of the Ottoman Empire, then prompted World War I, and then imposed a peace based on self-determination, which destroyed the Austro-Hungarian Empire. That in turn led to endless nation state hostility, including most tragically the destruction of Czechoslovakia by the Nazis, aided by newly formed nations or historical ethnicities, the Sudeten Germans, Hungarians, Poles, and Slovaks.[6]

---

[3] Including "reverence for the emperor." See Murphy *Writings*, 17.

[4] *Tolan Hearings, Portland and Seattle*, pt. 30, 11069–11087. The renunciation of racial superiority is on p. 11085.

[5] Brands, *Traitor*, 343, 496–7.

[6] G. Weinberg, A *World At Arms: A Global History of World War II* (Cambridge: Cambridge University Press, 1994), 26–28, 31–35, but especially his *Hitler's Foreign Policy: The Road to War, 1933–1939* (New York, NY: Enigma Books, 2005), 484–692; and R. Manvell and H. Fraenkel, *Goering: The Rise and Fall of the Notorious Nazi Leader* (New York, NY: Skyhorse Publishing, 2011), 124–65.

As is well known, at the conclusion of both world wars a whole series of agonizing "population exchanges," ethnic cleansing in modern parlance, from Sudeten Germans to Pomuk Turks worked out this trend and created a fresh set of nationalist rivalries.[7] Assimilation, American style, was the great exception rather than the rule.[8] Belief in assimilation is an American conceit, one the author profoundly believes in, but a conceit nonetheless.

The Jewish experience with relocation should be seen in this same larger national identity context. According to historian Ellen M. Eisenberg, the vast majority of American Jews did not hold racist views against the Nikkei and did not favor mass relocation. Their "sin" was one of not speaking out against mass evacuation. One prominent Jewish group alone, the Los Angeles Jewish Community Committee, cooperated with anti-Nikkei groups to bring relocation about. This included cooperating with the government and the Dies Committee before the war to identify and combat pro-Japan groups in the United States.

Still, many high-profile Jews, including several rabbis, opposed mass evacuation.[9] As fascism took over Japan and one European country after another, Jewish identity was profoundly threatened. That menace clearly took precedence over the Japanese American problems. Nor could they have ignored the openly racial appeal of Imperial Japanese of "Asia for the Asians," nor the close association of some Nikkei with them.

Other religious groups had their own distinctive ways of looking at the problem. The Ministers Association of Boulder, Colorado, admitted the necessity of relocation, while praising the Nikkei, who they said had "a well–deserved reputation for industry and thrift; are law-abiding and have through the years conducted themselves well."[10] "A large number of ministers of Santa Barbara, California," agreed:

You have added greatly to our resources and to our moral and religious culture. The tragedy of a war between our country and Japan which is not of your making

---

[7] For the full reality of this European inability to "assimilate," see K. Lowe, *Savage Continent: Europe in the Aftermath of World War II* (New York, NY: St. Martin's Press/Picador, 2012), 12–60ff.

[8] L. S. Stavrianos, *The Balkans Since 1453* (New York, NY: Holt, Rinehart and Winston, 1958), 216–412; Glenny, *The Balkans*, 135–544ff.

[9] E. M. Eisenberg, *The First to Cry Down Injustice? Western Jews and Japanese Removal during WWII* (Lanham, MD: Lexington Books, 2008), 1–40ff. For Jews see also C. Greenberg, "Black and Jewish Responses to Japanese Internment," *Journal of American Ethnic History* Vol. 14: No. 2 (Winter, 1995).

[10] Reverend Rufus C. Baker to Governor of Colorado Ralph W. Carr, April 17, 1942, Governor's Collection, The Japanese Internment Camp Records, Colorado State Archives.

nor of your choosing makes it necessary that we be separated for a time, but we assure you that our friendship has not been disturbed.

Many diverse groups and individuals opposed the idea of mass evacuation, none more so than mainstream Protestants.[11] The Federal Council of Churches of Christ in America had resisted the 1924 exclusion legislation, and they and other Protestants continued to lead. When the Reverend Harold V. Jensen, of the Seattle branch of the Council, was asked at the Tolan Hearings whether the Council statement against race prejudice represented the view of "their clergy and the lay membership," he responded: "It is a fairly accurate statement of the attitude of the Protestant ministers and "of the majority of the participating membership of my church."[12]

At the Tolan Hearings on February 23, 1942, the California and Seattle Protestant church representatives opposed mass in favor of "selective evacuation."[13] As the Los Angeles Catholic Interracial Council report of December, 1944, said of their fellow Christians in a very ecumenical statement, the Protestants had led the way. But by the end of the war the Catholic Interracial Council was besieging some of the most anti-Nikkei doctrinal bastions.

The Quaker representative at the Tolan Hearings rejected race-based behavior just as unequivocally. He wrote, "Those who have known them [Nikkei] well have confidence in them. We have come to value them as neighbors, as friends, and as business associates."[14] U. G. Murphy, Superintendent of the Methodist Church in Seattle, insisted: "The manner in which minority groups are handled is a final criterion of the standard of national civilization."[15] When that benchmark was not met, much of the explanation was situation specific rather than racial, nationalistic, or cultural.

Before the centers were built, several of the town populations near the sites expressed their opposition to them. This response might well have

---

[11] For an argument that Protestants were responsible for growing intolerance in Southern California, see Eisenberg, *The First to Cry down Injustice*, 105ff. That argument smacks of collective responsibility, and the book in general is too harsh toward both Protestants and Jews.

[12] *Tolan Hearings, Portland and Seattle*, pt. 30, February 26 and 28, March 2, 1942, 11568.

[13] T. Matsumoto, *Beyond Prejudice*, New York, NY: Arno Press, 1978 [1946], 14–15. Primary source, since originally published in 1946 by a leading participant in the WRA resettlement program.

[14] *Tolan Hearings, Portland and Seattle*, pt. 30, 11527.

[15] *Tolan Hearings, Portland and Seattle*, pt. 30, 11598.

been a natural reaction of a small town people whom the government had not prepared for the momentous changes that the centers portended. The center populations varied from 8,000 to nearly 20,000, and these were unceremoniously "dumped" next to small, drylands communities (except for Arkansas) of 1,000 to 2,500, who had been pumped up on anti-Japanese and anti-Nikkei media news and opinion pieces for weeks before construction began. It is not surprising that these greatly outnumbered communities felt threatened.

Attitudes also depended heavily on residents' often heartbreaking experience with the war. For example, before the conflict, a Boise construction company contracted with the government to fortify Wake Island. When the Japanese subsequently seized that islet, several American workers became casualties, and the Japanese swept up the rest into their brutal slave labor camps. So considerable hostility emanated from Boise against the center at Minidoka on that account.[16] Others who had no sons in the islands did not necessarily feel such hostility.

Sometimes the resentment was individual, not group. In Parker, Arizona, population 2,000, near the Poston Center, a decorated, Nisei soldier was refused a haircut. Another Parker resident dismissed the incident because she said that the barber was the town curmudgeon and did not represent the sentiment of the majority. The barber also had four sons in service.[17] Although the incident was published far and wide, it did not represent the community's attitude toward Japanese Americans.[18]

Frontline news also created general spikes in anti-Nikkei sentiment, as when the resettlement program freed some 200 Nikkei from Poston, some of whom wished to settle in the Phoenix Area. Attempts to put down roots there would lead to "bloodshed and violence," said the undermanned sheriff of Maricopa County, Lon Jordan. After each atrocity, such as the

[16] T. Matsumoto, *Beyond Prejudice*, 31–32, 79.

[17] Hansen and Jesch, *Japanese American*, Part V, Vol. 2, 702: Part V, Vol. 1, p. 296.

[18] Hansen and Jesch, Part V, Vol. 2, 579–80. And the incident looked suspiciously like a politically contrived one because the boy was not really denied a haircut. All of the evacuation centers had cooperatives with both barber shops and hair salons. In choosing the town barber over the coop ones, the soldier was obviously playing politics with the issue, politics which might not have benefited other Nikkei, anxious to settle or resettle in Arizona, a rapidly growing area and expanding market for agricultural and nursery products that the Nikkei excelled at growing. For Phoenix and the rise of the Sunbelt, see B. Luckingham, "Phoenix: The Desert Metropolis," in R. M. Bernard and B. R. Rice, editors, *Sunbelt Cities: Politics and Growth since World War II* (Austin, TX: University of Texas Press, 1983), 309–27.

Bataan Death March, against American soldiers became public "the telephones at my office are kept hot, demanding that we get 'those damn Japs out of the country.'"[19]

Counterintuitively, given historians' assertions about the universality of racism, many Caucasians had little knowledge of the Nikkei. Instead of nursing a headful of racial stereotypes, "they [like the people of Owens Valley, California] hadn't associated with Japanese people; they didn't know anything about them." "Those of Japanese ancestry are still quite unknown to the public," noted a WRA spokesman in 1943.[20] Baptist Missionary Royal H. Fisher testified to the same unawareness.[21] Journalist Bill Hosokawa thought that the Nikkei misfortune derived more from ignorance than bias and Roper polls backed him up.[22] Many of the Fullerton interviewees did not believe that the Nikkei should have been relocated at all, as one interchange shows.

Question [from the interviewer]: So you think they [the Nikkei] should have been in the camps?
Answer: No, not really. Maybe some of them should've been in the camps. I think there is a certain percentage of any group that just doesn't follow orders and they probably should have been interned.[23]

Of course, selective evacuation was exactly what some of the Nisei themselves, like Charles Kikuchi, or the representatives of the West Coast Protestant churches favored, as did ONI specialist Kenneth Ringle. Whether the Nikkei were in danger of vigilantism is hotly refuted by historians, who claim that they were not in danger, and that only racism can explain their evacuation. However, some Caucasians certainly favored relocation to protect rather than to persecute the Nikkei, and their side of the argument makes more sense. When asked why the Nikkei were evacuated, Donald Branson, a former Manzanar plumber, said, "It was partially for their own safety, because people down there [Southern California] were quite bitter toward them."[24]

Historians nearly universally hold that war generated a wave of West Coast "hysteria" against the Nikkei. Thus the protective custody rationale for relocation[25] was not that implausible. During the period between Pearl

[19] *Dies Hearings*, July 1943, 9184.   [20] *Rohwer Outpost*, June 23, 1943, p. 5.
[21] *Rohwer Outpost*, January 23, 1943, p. 3.
[22] B. Hosokawa, *Thirty Five Years*, 18, 19, 28, 30.
[23] Hansen and Jesch, *Japanese American*, Part V, Vol. 1, p. 161.
[24] Hansen and Jesch, *Japanese American*, Part V, Vol. 1, p. 141.
[25] Biddle, *Brief Authority*, 224; Grodzins, *Americans Betrayed*, 29–30, pp. 119–21ff.

Harbor and Executive Order 9066, seven Nikkei were murdered by various races, none of whom was white.[26] That would work out to a rather high murder rate, over five times the 2005 murder rate of 5.5 per 100,000.

A series of other, less violent episodes accompanied these lethal ones. Attorney General Biddle later noted "no tale of vigilante action" against the Nikkei in the months just before EO9066. But that must have been cold comfort to the AJA victims of "robberies, extortion, rape, murder, assaults with deadly weapons, [and] the destruction of property," which he also noted.[27] On January 6, 1942, alone, the LA *Times* reported three separate shootings.[28] Two weeks later Charles Kikuchi lamented that:

there have been houses stoned in Placer County, and some of the newspapers are raising hell and making all kinds of wild statements about even the Nisei. Kenny [his friend] showed me a lot of clippings, and it is very dangerous ... There is a lot of hysteria going on[29] [even in his own family]. His sister Mariko says that the Japs [her word for the Imperial Japanese!] are going to invade California ... and she says she is going to get a Chinese card [student club card] too.[30]

Kikuchi soon got one himself, identifying himself as "Shar Lee" (possibly an ironic and mocking use of the stereotype "Charlie" to designate the Chinese). With the card "Shar Lee," he could evade the curfew for Japanese.[31]

Tōru Matsumoto, an administrator of the resettlement program, noted the peril of those trying to flee individually. "Soon it became dangerous for persons with Japanese faces to travel, as signs of active hostility appeared along the routes of evacuation."[32] The inability to buy gasoline and their fear of mob violence, vigilantism, or personal attacks[33] were widely shared by those well-informed parties who testified at the Tolan Hearings. The Washington Commonwealth Federation, in demanding evacuation, nonetheless urged that "the Japanese should be resettled in communities where they would be safe from vigilante action."[34]

Their fears were given ominous confirmation by California Attorney General and soon to be governor, Earl Warren. Speaking at the Tolan Hearings, Warren sounded the alarm of vigilantism:

[26] Grodzins, *Americans Betrayed*, 138–43.   [27] Biddle, *Brief Authority*, 224.
[28] LA *Times*, January 6, 1942, pt. I, p. 11.
[29] For other assertions see F. Oles, *Tolan Hearings, Portland and Seattle*, pt. 30, 11424.
[30] Modell, *Kikuchi Diary*, 47.   [31] Modell, *Kikuchi Diary*, 50.
[32] Matsumoto, *Beyond*, 16.   [33] R. Daniels, *Prisoners*, 49–50.
[34] *Tolan Hearings, Portland and Seattle*, pt. 30, 11614; 11607; 11421.

My own belief concerning vigilantism is that the people do not engage in vigilante activities so long as they believe that their Government through its agencies is taking care of their most serious problems. But when they get the idea that their problems are not understood, when their Government is not doing for them the things that they believe should be done, they start taking the law into their own hands.[35]

Californians had invented vigilantism in the American Dry West, shortly after the Gold Rush.[36] The year 1942 was a long way from 1849–56. However, given that heritage, still often praised in history books at the time, and given Warren's status in California and the supposedly hysterical, anti-Japanese bitterness that the press, politicians, and pundits had whipped up, his words were menacing.

Even undoubted friends of the Nikkei like Congressman Jerry Voorhis feared that the Imperial Japanese could attack California, and if they did the vigilantes would "indulge in mass murder."[37] That comment seems over the top, but Quaker leaders also feared "overt violence."[38] Future US Senator Samuel Hayakawa agreed.[39] Finally the Reverend Lester Suzuki, a decided opponent of evacuation with wide experience in the centers, admitted that "all too many of the Japanese-speaking Issei evacuees express the feeling that perhaps they were safer that way and more secure."[40]

Experience bore him out. By mid-1943 enough Nikkei had resettled in Arizona, some 200, mostly in the Phoenix Area of Maricopa County, and were trying to buy or lease land to get back into agriculture or, alternatively, urban domestic work. The restrictionists struck at both. They got the Arizona Legislature to enact a law that stated that anyone doing business with a restricted person or one of Japanese birth had to precede this trade with publication of their intent three times in a newspaper. Food, hardwares, medicine, and liquors were excepted from the banned items, but spades, hoes, shovels and gasoline were not. The restrictionists added an economic boycott to enforce the law and threats of physical violence, as a state legislator put it, "even to the point of

[35] Testimony of Earl Warren, *Tolan Hearings, San Francisco*, pt. 29, 11016.
[36] R. W. Lotchin, *San Francisco: From Hamlet to City* (New York, NY: Oxford University Press, 1974), 245–75; *City*; Robert Senkiewicz, S. J., *Vigilantes in Gold Rush San Francisco* (Stanford, CA: Stanford University Press, 1985), 155–202.
[37] Grodzins, *Americans Betrayed*, 79.
[38] *Tolan Hearings, Los Angeles and San Francisco*, pt. 31, 11746.
[39] Lowman, *Magic*, 74.
[40] L. E. Suzuki, *Ministry in the Assembly and Relocation Centers of World War II* (Berkeley, CA: Yardbird Publishing Co., 1979), 354.

bloodshed."[41] Even the agriculturally precocious Nikkei could not farm without implements and with mobs looking over their shoulders.

Later experience confirmed this threat. Dorothy C. Cragen was a racially tolerant person. She admired the Nikkei, worked with them, ate with them, and valued their culture. She opposed mass evacuation in the first place and said so publicly. Yet once the Nikkei were in centers, she came to understand the need to keep them there temporarily. She remembered that toward the end of the war, a young Japanese American was allowed to go to Los Angeles to buy wedding rings for his bride to be. While there, he was mugged of his rings. "He came back to the camp," recalled Cragen, "and said that he never wanted to leave it again."[42] She added that "there came a time when . . . many of them wanted to be there." They felt safer in camp because there was an awful lot of resentment in this county [LA], she said, "and, of course, there was resentment in other places all along the West Coast."[43] William Schindler of Tulelake agreed: "I think for their own protection they needed it."[44]

The protection issue resurfaced when the centers were closing, in late December, 1944, and 1945. The problem for the WRA then was getting the residents to leave their desert safe havens because of their fear of West Coast hostility. Their hesitation was fueled by several hostile episodes, including the famous Hood River, Oregon, Incident. There were thousands of Nikkei in January, 1945, who did not believe that the protective custody was a bogus issue. As usual, the *Manzanar Free Press* captured the sentiment perfectly when it spoke of "California extremists" who were practicing "outrageous terrorism against returning Japanese Americans."[45] Finally, the various release programs were predicated on the firm assurance that the Nikkei would be safe in them.

As in so many areas of investigation WRA policy directives make it crystal clean that protection of the Nikkei was fundamental. It is argued in *Personal Justice Denied* by a military figure, in the apology and restitution movement of the 1980s, that he found no such statement in reams of material that he had examined. Yet WRA policy stated clearly in May 1942 that the centers were not to be locations of "internment," but rather "places where evacuees from the West coast might live and work in

---

[41] *Dies Hearings*, June and July 1943, 9187–9210.
[42] Hansen and Jesch, *Japanese American*, Part V, Vol. 1, 199.
[43] Hansen and Jesch, *Japanese American*, Part V, Vol. 1, 194.
[44] Hansen and Jesch, *Japanese American*, Part V, Vol. 2, 538.
[45] *Manzanar Free Press*, February 3, 1945, 4; for the fear of returning to California, see also Hirasuna, *The Art of Gaman*, 123.

security until an orderly program of infiltration and resettlement in normal American communities could be developed."[46]

Historians who have contended that protective custody was unnecessary if the authorities would safeguard the Japanese, have not explained who was available to do that. The urban police were already overloaded,[47] and there was no national police to protect a people scattered over seven states from California to Arkansas, much less a way to fend off the vagaries of state legislatures, like Arizona. Given these conditions, temporary protective custody did not seem so indisputably inappropriate.[48]

Moreover, military necessity, not racial caprice, was overwhelmingly the most frequent justification for evacuation, even if people cited class or nationality. Robert Jones, who formerly went to school with Nikkei, had a Japanese American Sunday School teacher and respected the Nikkei, nonetheless backed evacuation because the government told him that it was a military necessity: "I felt pretty much the same as I believed most people on the West Coast did: that the camps were necessary." He continued, "That's what we were told, read, and heard, so we felt that it was necessary to have the camps; it was something that we didn't question."[49] The government claimed military necessity and that was that. Both pro-Nikkei Quaker and CIO leaders regretted the necessity of the centers, but nonetheless agreed to them because the Army claimed they were a national security necessity.[50]

A Port of Astoria Oregon, official summed up the security concern to the Tolan Committee well:

looking at the above [the militarily vulnerable parts of the economy] and the fifth column in mind, and supposing that the Japanese fleet can get a few carriers off our coast loaded with bombers, fires could be started to guide them, and it is impossible for any city on the coast to take care of more than a few fires at once.[51]

The cities also were very combustible.

Most Americans were in no position to exercise an independent judgment on the strategic or realpolitik diplomacy of either Washington or Tokyo, so support for evacuation did not necessarily imply hatred of Japanese Americans, racial, national, or cultural.[52] Even Christian

---

[46] Myer, "Relocation Program," 2. After note 822.   [47] Lotchin, *Bad City*, 202.

[48] Ibid.   [49] Hansen and Jesch, ed., *Japanese Americans*, Part V, Vol. 1, 470.

[50] *Tolan Hearings, Los Angeles and San Francisco*, pt. 31, 11746.

[51] *Tolan Hearings, San Francisco*, pt. 29, 11395; 11613.

[52] Morton Grodzins admits that the security concerns of those in favor of evacuation were genuine, but then proceeds to explain evacuation not by military necessity, but on

ministers who rejected mass evacuation, admitted the seriousness of the national security situation.[53] Yet to the race school, that is merely a rationalization ("a fig leaf") for the true motivation – race.

This theory also speaks to the oft-repeated charge that because of racism the Government evacuated the Nikkei and not the alien Germans and Italians. A Seattle banker's explanation was more contextual:

I think I am correct in concluding the whole coast – are more disposed to consider the Japanese as a problem for the reason that that they, differing from the Germans and Italians, remain in blocs, so to speak. They preserve a group identity which you will not find generally to be the case with other nationalities. Therefore, I think that we are more disposed to think of them, not only in terms of numbers, but in their adhesiveness as groups.[54]

The Japanese faced housing discrimination and were following a "ghetto strategy" of advancement at the time, so their "adhesiveness" is not surprising.[55] But their clannishness was often remarked upon by the Nisei resettlers,[56] who hoped their brethren would settle as individuals to avoid being singled out again.[57]

Both the German and Italian communities were more assimilated politically. Both were mostly citizens who voted. Evacuating their alien relatives would have angered a much larger bloc than the 112,000 Nikkei. FDR did not want to contemplate the political backlash against such a policy, witness his taking the Italians off of the enemy aliens list just before the 1942 off-year elections. The Germans are today the largest ancestry group in the nation and the Italians are one of the largest. In California in the 1940s, the Italo Americans were the most numerous foreign stock

grounds of race. "It cannot be doubted that the great majority of those who urged evacuation sincerely believed in evacuation as a measure of national defense." *Americans Betrayed*, 179.

[53] *Tolan Hearings, Los Angeles and San Francisco*, pt. 31, 11764–70.

[54] *Tolan Hearings, San Francisco*, pt. 29, 11421.

[55] Horace Cayton and St. Clair Drake, of the famous Chicago School of Sociology, provided the classic elaboration of this strategy when speaking of African Americans. They believed that this group was split between those who wanted to win equality by integration and thus securing their legal rights to compete fairly and those who favored a ghetto strategy of massing black numbers and creating their own society and power and prosperity based upon them. H. Cayton and St. Clair Drake, *Black Metropolis* (New York, NY: Harper and Row, 1945), Vol. I, 77–98.

[56] The War Relocation Authority intended to get the Nikkei out of the centers as soon as possible, hopefully by resettling them into non-West Coast communities. War Relocation Authority, "A Comprehensive Statement in Response to Senate Resolution No. 166, July, 17, 1943, 30," National Archives, Record Group 210, Box 2.

[57] *Rohwer Outpost*, January 23, 1943, 3.

group – over 300,000.[58] Their kin on the East Coast were largely working class, with power in unions, the voting booth, and the batter's box, but the California unit was often quite wealthy.

Each had star power as well. Many excelled in banking, including A. P. Giannini, the founder of Bank of America. He was also busily creating branch banking, financing the growth of California suburbia, investing in movies, and generally leading the economic development of the state. "A. P." also nurtured war industries large and small. Giannini not only helped to fund the big munitions industries, like Kaiser, who revolutionized shipbuilding. He also helped popularize subcontracting, which allowed small businesses to share in the war boom by providing components for shipbuilding and aircraft.[59]

The other Italo American prominenti included the owners of the Del Monte packing giant, large-scale farmers, two-thirds of the state's wineries, Mayor Angelo Rossi of San Francisco, the sans pareil Joe DiMaggio, his brothers and other high-profile professional baseball players, the legendary director Frank Capra, then making propaganda movies for the government, and Arturo Toscanini, the equally renowned conductor. On the East Coast Mayor Fiorello LaGuardia of New York City was also fleetingly head of Civilian Defense, and the crooner Frank Sinatra was one the nation's finest.[60]

The German Americans had their own star power. Henry Kaiser was not the least of them.[61] Nor were the Spreckels family, whose sugar empire rested in San Francisco and Hawaii and whose real estate interests stretched to San Diego. City politicians took up the rear. If evacuation had been applied to their alien relatives, it would have swept up the renowned novelist Thomas Mann, polymath Albert Einstein, and a host of Hollywood directors and actors. Babe Ruth and Lou Gherig and lots of other German American baseball players also had alien relatives. So did Senator Robert Wagner, author of some of the most important New Deal legislation.[62]

[58] R. W. Lotchin, *Bad City*, 249ff.
[59] G. D. Nash, *A. P. Giannini and the Bank of America* (Norman, OK: University of Oklahoma Press, 1992) (Bloomington, IN: Indiana University Press, 2003), 249–56.
[60] G. R. Mormino and G. E. Pozzetta, "Ethnics at War: Italian Americans in California during World War II," in Lotchin, ed., *The Way We Really Were* (Urbana, IL: University of Illinois Press, 2000), 143–63.
[61] Mark S. Foster, *Henry J. Kaiser: Builder of the Modern West* (Austin: University of Texas Press, 1989). In addition to the works of Mark Foster see Stephen B. Adams, *Mr. Kaiser Goes to Washington* (Chapel Hill: University of North Carolina Press, 1997).
[62] J. Joseph Huthmacher, *Senator Robert F. Wagner and the Rise of Urban Liberalism* (New York, NY: Atheneum, 1971), 3–11, 87–129ff.

East European and German American Jews had their own prominenti, in banking in Los Angeles and San Francisco, in San Francisco politics, not to mention the founders of Hollywood, all but one of whom were Jewish immigrants. The "moguls," as they were called by their enemies, included their leader, the legendary Louis B. Mayer, one of the most powerful conservative Republicans in the state. To argue that only a racist motivation could have explained why aliens of these nationalities were not taken to centers is downright dubious.

In addition, the historians of relocation have generally minimized that other political reality of relocation, the military one. For example, if all German and Italian enemy aliens were rounded up, the total would have amounted to some 600,000 of each or 1,200,000 total.[63] One of the principal American advantages of Lightening Warfare (island bypassing) in the Pacific Theater, was the ability of the CBs and the Army Corps of Engineers to establish staging areas quickly – supply bases, landing fields, barracks, and port facilities for the next leap forward.[64]

Diverting supplies from each leap would have been damaging. Moreover, 120 more centers would have required enough matériel for a European Theater army group. To have dedicated such resources to relocation centers would have been preposterous.

Not only were the German and Italian aliens spared relocation, but so was almost the entire Japanese American population of Hawaii.[65] The fact that masses of Japanese were taken into temporary protective custody on the West Coast and not the Germans and Italians is endlessly cited as definitive proof that the taking of the mainland Nikkei was racially motivated. But if that were so, then why were the 157,000–160,000 Hawaiian Japanese not taken? How does one explain that people of the same race, nationality, ancestry, and culture in a different locale experienced such different treatment? Race cannot.

---

[63] F. Biddle, *In Brief Authority* (Garden City, NY: Doubleday and Company, Inc., 1962), 207, 230. The figure may have been even higher since the Justice Department itself released figures, printed in the newspapers, that put the total at just over 1,400,000 counting the aliens of Italy, Germany and Austria Hungary, which must mean Austria, since Austria Hungary no longer existed. *Sacramento Bee, December* 8, 1941, 12.

[64] For the Army Corps of Engineers and Seabees' ability to create staging areas for the next leap forward, see *Eric M. Bergerud, Fire in the Sky: The Air War in the South Pacific* (Boulder, CO: Westview Press, 2000), 55ff.

[65] Only those Hawaiian Japanese of doubtful loyalty, some 2,000, were sent to the relocation centers on the mainland. Reader's report B on this manuscript, Cambridge University Press, c. April 11, 2016, 1.

The absence of racial, national, or cultural tension does not explain this discrepancy either because there was plenty of each in Hawaii. As historians Beth Bailey and David Farber have famously explained, "Race played a role in virtually every aspect of relations between men and women in Hawaii."[66] General identity hostility and distrust pervaded everything.[67] The reason that the Hawaiians were spared the fate of their mainland brethren was that their labor was needed on the plantations of the powerful haoles [whites, pronounced "howlies"] and essential to the Island's defense industries by the even more powerful General Delos Emmons, commander of the Islands under martial law. The security challenges in Hawaii and the American West Coast plus Arizona, were entirely disproportionate. Hawaii was a very small place that, as the great staging ground for the American counterattack in the Pacific, was literally swarming with soldiers and sailors. In contrast, the West Coast had several thousand miles of coastline, not to mention the hundreds of thousands of square miles of territory (WDC) to defend against sabotage and espionage. The total square mileage of the four mainland prohibited states is 437,775 compared to 6,450 square miles in Hawaii.[68] Leaving aside the equally mammoth population differences, espionage, let alone sabotage (virtually no railroads), would have been enormously harder in Hawaii.

And parenthetically the policy of taking the West Coast Nikkei while exempting the Hawaiian Japanese was strictly consistent with US mainland policy. The West Coast Nikkei were taken, but not those in eastern Washington and Oregon; northern Arizona, and the remainder of the continental United States.

Still, Stimson's Diary reveals that, two weeks after Pearl Harbor, the cabinet had actually agreed to remove all alien Japanese from the Islands or to centers within the Islands.[69] As historians Greg Robinson and Tetsuden Kashima have shown, despite the support of both Stimson and FDR, General Emmons managed to finesse the attempt at mass Hawaiian removal.[70] Emmons declared martial law in Hawaii and

---

[66] B. Bailey and D. Farber, *The First Strange Place: Race and Sex in World War II Hawaii* (Baltimore, MD: Johns Hopkins University Press, 1992), 167–210, especially 191–205.

[67] Ibid., 91.

[68] Webster's Ninth New Collegiate Dictionary (Springfield, MA: Merriam-Webster Inc., Publishers), 1437, 1445, 1464, 1489, 1514.

[69] Stimson, *Diary*, Vol. 36, November 1 to December 31, 1941, December 20, 1941, no page indicated.

[70] Robinson, *By Order* 146–54; T. Kashima, *Judgment without Trial: Japanese American Imprisonment during World War II* (Seattle, WA: University of Washington Press 1993), 75–78.

acted promptly to spike any anti-Nikkei movement. That meant that he could suspend the right of habeas corpus and depend on the hordes of servicemen to prevent sabotage and espionage. Emmons defended the Nikkei from the beginning and had the tools to prevent mischief by anyone.[71]

He pointed out that the Japanese Americans were a large part of the labor force, particularly of the skilled portion [90 percent of the carpenters] and of the general population, that they had given blood extensively and bought war bonds, that they were lined up around the block to volunteer to fight, and that they were by and large loyal. Any who were not trustworthy could be dealt with on a case-by-case basis, not .one of collective responsibility.[72]

The Japanese fleet lends further weight to the reality that military necessity trumped race on evacuation and further explains the differential treatment of Japanese, Germans, and Italians. Neither the Germans nor the Italians possessed the military power to menace the West Coast, but the possibility of another Pearl Harbor was realistically invoked again and again. As historian Dwight Murphy reminded us, the West Coast was defenseless because the Imperial Japanese had destroyed most of the US Pacific fleet there.[73] With the specter of Pearl Harbor hanging over them, it did not take much to persuade people on the West Coast that the threat was real. No one stated this rationale better than Dr. George Gleason, Executive Secretary of the Los Angeles Committee for Church and Community Cooperation, a county-wide group of prominent citizens devoted to religious tolerance:[74]

Dr. [George H.] Bender [Representative of Ohio, member of the Tolan Committee]:
   Doctor, do you feel that Germans and Italians deserve different treatment than the Japanese aliens; or do you think that they are all of the same group and should be handled in the same way?
   Dr. Gleason: I think they are all the same group, but I think that there is a difference in the importance of dealing with the Japanese at this time, because we, on the coast, feel that our war is with Japan just now. You see, if the Japanese Navy should come over to this coast, the Japanese who are loyal to Japan and disloyal to the United States would, and could do something ... So I think on account of our nearness to Japan, the subversive elements among the Japanese are

---

[71] For a concise discussion of the adverse logistics of putting the Hawaiian Japanese in centers, possibly on Molokai Island, see Lowman, *Magic*, 18.
[72] Bailey and Farber, *The First Strange Place*, 5–9.   [73] Murphy, *Writings*, 13.
[74] Eisenberg, *The First to Cry Down Injustice?* 61, 94ff.

a little more dangerous to us immediately on this coast than the subversive elements among the Italians and the Germans.[75]

To elucidate, Gleason's committee was in favor of selective evacuation, carried out by the Army, consistent with the needs of national security, but with due concern for the evacuees, whoever they might be. In stating as much, he explained: "I don't think that means evacuation of every alien, or every child of aliens in the Pacific Coast States." His star-studded committee was overwhelmingly sympathetic to the Nikkei and wanted them treated fairly, but still he saw Japan as the greater threat. The evidence is clear that the Nikkei were considered a threat on the West Coast on national security grounds and in Hawaii they were not. Those different outcomes were entirely consistent with the security requirements of the nation state, not those of racial profiling.

Finally, any action against the German and Italian populations had another very problematic aspect that Japanese relocation did not. Many of the former were already refugees in the United States, a fact that is often overlooked in explaining the different treatment of nationality groups. These included German Jews fleeing the Nazis in the thirties, German Gentiles escaping because of their anti-Nazi attitudes, or Italian expatriates opposed to Fascist Mussolini. Jewish rescue groups were already hard pressed, often unsuccessfully, to get more Jewish refugees into the country and would not have tolerated putting in centers those who were already here.

I am not aware of any Issei refugees from Imperial Japan who were fighting Fascism in Japan from their position in California as the alien German gentiles and Jews and Italians were. It does not require a belief in the biological inferiority of the Nikkei to explain why such a huge group, with such great political and cultural star power as the Italian and German American aliens, were not relocated. Like everything else about the Japanese American story, their selection and the omission of the other two groups was complex. Race might have played a minor role in the taking of the Nikkei, but the leaving of German and Italian aliens was a nearly pure war measure.

Some of the enemies of the Nikkei were also motivated by economics. That part of the traditional interpretation is valid, but the influence of greed is not always uncomplicated, and it is not the same thing as racism. Those two sentiments together may have helped aggregate widespread

[75] *Tolan Hearings, Los Angeles and San Francisco*, pt. 31, 11628.

demand for evacuation, but they are not identical. As was documented as early as the work of Morton Grodzins and in many of the primary sources, some of the aversion to the Japanese Americans grew out of their economic competitors' dislike of contending against them in the fishing, produce, nursery, florist, or hotel businesses. One Nikkei family who moved to Arizona "found Christians ready and willing to help ... [but] such social contacts as these might have been more numerous but for the attitude of the people of Arizona, led by the organized farming industry."[76] As John Modell demonstrated, the California Nikkei were very good market gardeners, fishermen, and nurserymen; they had a very strong work ethic; they were entrepreneurial, and they had strong family ties.[77] They were robust contenders in the marketplace.

Some Northwest Washington growers harbored similar covetous sentiments. "Applications are being made to various agricultural agencies," noted Henry B. Ramsey, chairman of the United States Department of Agriculture War Board (State of Washington), "by bona fide American farmers who desire an opportunity to farm land which has previously been operated by Japanese."[78] Floyd Oles, who was chief executive of both the Washington Produce Shippers Association and the Washington State Taxpayers Association and who opposed mass evacuation, was emphatic about it. "I have been approached by quite a number of interests who have a commercial motive in seeking the evacuation of the Japanese [Americans]," he explained to the Tolan congressmen. The typical small farmer producers from his region also competed with the big operators in California, and they considered the Washington producers a thorn in their side. "I receive in the mail every day now, from these people in California, considerable volumes of propaganda on this point, eagerly seeking evacuation for commercial reasons."[79] As witness to the Nikkei's extraordinary ability plus the openness of the prewar Northwest economy as well as the toleration of their wartime competitors, the Seattle AJA operated over half the hotels in Seattle.

But, once in the centers, economic interest could also offset hostility. In Cody and Powell, Wyoming, Granada, Colorado, and Twin Falls, Idaho, the residents were at first opposed to the Nikkei coming into town to shop, but eventually changed their minds. In Parker, Arizona, there was little

[76] Matsumoto, *Beyond Prejudice*, 36–7.
[77] J. Modell, *Economics and Politics*, 95–123.
[78] *Tolan Hearings, San Francisco*, pt. 29, 11606.
[79] *Tolan Hearings, San Francisco*, pt. 29, 11432.

opposition to the Nikkei presence and they came into town from the beginning.[80] In Independence, Lone Pine, and Tulelake, California, hostility prevented access initially. Nikkei could roam the countryside, but for a time, could not stray into town. Ultimately, however, when the residents saw how much business the centers generated for everybody, from the banks, post offices, clothing stores, and lumber yards, many relented. Almost everywhere economics won out over hostility, to allow the Nikkei commercial access.

As the war wound down, the primacy of economics surfaced again in the controversy over the right of return. For economic reasons pressure groups in California and Idaho, reacted to the WRA resettlement program in diametrically opposed ways. The Los Angeles Produce Exchange had bitterly supported the mass evacuation in the first place. The question now was should the Nikkei be dispersed over the entire country or be allowed to return to California? Bill Hosokawa explained the economic interests in his column in the *Heart Mountain Sentinel*:

In other words, the dispersal which California congressmen in particular favor (because Japanese Americans are property owners and operate their own or leased farms) is looked upon with disfavor by the Idaho representative because the vast majority of the evacuees in Idaho do not operate their own farms and therefore do not constitute competition, but are a valuable source of badly needed seasonal labor.[81]

The Heart Mountain Nikkei labor supply alone totaled 2,500 men and the nearby, cross-border Montana growers prized it highly. The war had created an agricultural labor shortage all over the country. And this was true even before any relocation center had opened its doors. So economic interest cut both ways, for and against dispersal.

As historian Mike Mackey has documented, many towns actually lobbied the government to locate evacuation centers nearby. The townsmen hankered after the construction spending and jobs during the building phase of the centers. They also wanted the retail sales from the Nikkei and labor of every kind, from harvesters to "houseboys." As he explained, the presence of the Nikkei shoppers in town or at work as domestics generated some friction, but nowhere were they banned absolutely.[82]

The most striking figures on this cooperation come from the realm of agriculture. It had long been known that the allegedly infamous California alien land laws were unenforceable, but the degree to which they were not is instructive. DeWitt's *Final Report* indicated that only 25 percent of Japanese farms, presumably Issei, were owned by them; in other words, 75 percent were owned and rented by Caucasians.

Since "greed" or "economic exploitation" is so often cited as the prime motivation for evacuation, we need to know how specific entities, like florists, wholesale grocers, produce dealers, fishermen, or Grangers, who wanted the Nikkei off the land and out of the boats, were able to overcome the interests of the 4,587[83] Caucasian landowners plus the banks, seed companies, implement dealers, fertilizer merchants, shippers and fish canneries, who wanted the Japanese on? Greed, if that is what it was, is a mean impulse, but hardly a simple one.

Or indeed, a universal one. Attorney General Francis Biddle, an astute and well-informed observer, summed up the widespread popular support for the Nikkei, or to put it another way, the widespread opposition to mass evacuation:

It may be even doubted whether, political and special group pressure aside, public opinion even on the West Coast supported evacuation. A confidential report from the Office of Facts and Figures on March 9, 1942, showed that, outside of Southern California, less than one-half of those interviewed favored internment of Japanese aliens, and only 14 per cent of the internment [relocation] of citizens of Japanese ancestry.[84]

That statement by a well-qualified, decidedly pro-Nikkei observer is a truly astonishing testimony that disproves most of the assertions of universal anti-Nikkei sentiment, much less racism. Other public opinion polls showed the same pro-Nikkei results.[85]

As Biddle's statement attested, many people on the West Coast had already ingested the cultural pluralism that modern historians claim that they lacked and did not give it up under pressure of war. The photographs of the crowds of Caucasians who came to the train stations to bid farewell to their Nikkei friends should have told us that, and anecdotal evidence should have too. When asked of her attitude to the Nikkei, Bette Kelly agreed with other Fullerton interviewees: "Well, really they were just the same as any other people. I was raised with all nationalities and I knew no difference," she said. "I mean, they were the same; they were human beings the same as I was."[86] Mrs. Claude H. Eckhart, president of the

[83] DeWitt, *Final Report*, 85.   [84] F. Biddle, *In Brief Authority*, 224ff.
[85] "Majority Favors Return of US Citizens in Gallup Poll," *Heart Mountain Sentinel*, January 16, 1943, 1.
[86] Hansen, ed., *Japanese American*, Part V, Vol. 2, 481.

Seattle Young Women's Christian Association, echoed this same cultural pluralism in opposing mass evacuation:

Since our constituency is made up of different racial and nationality groups, we are concerned with minority members of our membership. In this problem of evacuation facing the Government, we hope it may be possible to carry it out on an individual basis considering each case on its own merits.[87]

Even more prestigious American institutions sought to encourage this sense of cultural legitimacy. The Smithsonian Institution commissioned a study by experts of the countries or cultural groups that the US was fighting amongst or against and whose peoples an insular American public would not have been familiar with. These were mostly in the Pacific Theater, but, except for Icelanders, they were universally "peoples of color," to employ the modern terminology, that is, racially different from an America that was 93 percent white. The groups or countries included Siam; Polynesian Explorers of the Pacific; "The Far Eastern Civilizations;" Native Americans; the Philippines; Egypt; peoples of the (East) Indies, Micronesia and Melanesia; India; French Indo-China; China, and Japan. The studies were quite favorable to these peoples of color. Many Americans were trying to get it right culturally.[88]

A Tulelake male resident recounted: "I went through a grade school where over a third of the school's enrollment was Japanese; that was during World War I."[89] His brother responded in kind: "I didn't have anything against them. I used to live by them up in Washington, on Bainbridge Island, and they were always good people."[90] Fanny Ryckman, a resident of the town of Tulelake, was asked what her attitude to the Nikkei was before the war. "I was very much interested in them and was anxious to become better acquainted with them," she responded, because of "their way of living and their family life ... I was always interested in the children."[91] She visited the center often with her daughter. "I felt sorry for them," not because their living conditions were bad, but because they had been "unceremoniously uprooted from their homes."[92] "I found them lovely, I really did," said Victoria Thaler. "I

---

[87] *Tolan Hearings, San Francisco*, pt. 29, 11613.
[88] Smithsonian Institution, "War Background Studies" (Washington, WA: Government Printing Office, 1943), nos. 1–14, 16–20.
[89] Hansen and Jesch, *Japanese Americans*, Part V, Vol. 2, 529.
[90] Hansen and Jesch, *Japanese Americans*, Part V, Vol. 2, 537.
[91] Hansen and Jesch, *Japanese Americans*, Part V, Vol. 2, 517.   [92] Ibid., 518.

never had them up to tea like some Caucasians did; I know the people next door would have them up to tea on a Sunday afternoon."[93]

Many Americans in other parts of the country had internalized cultural pluralism long ago, as the Nikkei letters back to center explain. "My business was not affected in the least by the start of the war," wrote New York City businessman Shigeo Mayeda; "none of my customers have inquired about my nationality." He advised Nikkei still in the Manzanar Center that postwar business prospects in New York City were "excellent."

Rinpei Okuno explained that opportunities for small business were especially good and spoke forcefully to the frequent argument that Nikkei opportunity was limited to a "ghetto economy." "There is little field here for businesses depending entirely upon the *patronage of Japanese people* [emphasis added]. I have never encountered any prejudice in New York and that is why I live in this city."[94] New York City was only one such American place. The JACL was correct in urging the Nikkei to break up their West Coast colonies and try their luck elsewhere because there was no universal American racism here.[95] Migration has always been the wayfarers' answer to their economic problems.

Even those who supported mass evacuation did not necessarily embrace collective guilt. The Portland City Council in demanding evacuation of all Nikkei, nonetheless admitted that "many such Japanese nationals and persons of Japanese descent irrespective of American citizenship are not in accord with the aggression" of Japan.[96] F. M. Sweet, vice president of the Port of Astoria, Oregon, made the same point.[97]

Mayor Bowron accepted the same distinction that "only a limited portion of [the 40,000 Angeleno Nikkei] might be expected to do something dangerous."[98] This is a far cry from the assertion that the Tolan

[93] Hansen and Jesch, *Japanese Americans* Part V, Vol. 2, 546.
[94] *Manzanar Free Press*, February 3, 1945, 4. These quotes are contained in letters to the Free Press written by the men cited above.
[95] Historian John Howard believes that the Japanese were victimized by being forced out of the centers. He thought that they should have remained in the centers as agricultural colonists, basing their lives on the successful cooperatives that they had operated in the centers. Howard, *Concentration Camps*, 220–40.
[96] *Tolan Hearings, San Francisco*, pt. 29, 11388.
[97] *Tolan Hearings, San Francisco*, pt. 29, 11392–93.
[98] Grodzins, *Americans Betrayed*, 105.

Hearings demonstrated that "for Europeans, guilt was individual;[99] for Asians, it was collective."[100]

Perhaps a statement by the head of the supposedly hostile Washington State American Legion will serve to solidify the point. Floyd Fueker, Department Adjutant, Washington State American Legion, explained:

We have had a number of connections with the young citizens of Japanese origin. We know that among these younger citizens, *that any number* [emphasis added] of them are real Americans, but we also know, or at least suppose, that included among that same class, there *are a number* [emphasis added] that aren't, and those will have to be weeded out."

A number with dual citizenship were Kibei, he continued, whose loyalty was sometimes suspect.[101]

Witnesses to the Tolan Hearings almost universally held that many Nikkei were loyal. One of the congressmen, in advocating total removal, fully understood that removal of all Nikkei "will involve some mighty fine people who are 100 percent loyal."[102] Congressman Curtis spoke for many, if not most of the Tolan witnesses.

One of the most trenchant criticisms of American culture put the race paradigm in boldest perspective. In discussing the Heart Mountain draft resisters, lawyer Eric Muller spoke of "white America's common view of Asians that 'they all look alike.'"[103] Another historian of the period speaks of "the typical California contempt for Japanese Americans."[104] It is obvious from the foregoing that whites held no "common view of Asians." Still, more recent studies echo the same sentiment, employing terms like "white America," "American racism," "white racism," "white American racism," "racist American West," and so forth.[105] The idea of a "white America" is itself fundamentally ahistorical. In his monumental

[99] I removed the famous "a Jap is a Jap," comment widely attributed to General DeWitt, because I learned recently that it is not certain that he made it. His exact statement at a Congressional hearing was, "It makes no difference whether he is an American citizen, he is still a Japanese. American citizenship does not necessarily determine loyalty." US Congress, House, Seventy-Eighth Congress: First Session, *Hearings before a Subcommittee of the Committee on Naval Affairs, Pursuant to H. Res. 30*: Part 3, San Francisco, Calif., Area, April 12–17, 1943, 40.874. Greg Robinson repeats the charge against DeWitt, saying that the remark occurred after a press conference following the above congressional hearing. Robinson, *A Tragedy*, 248.

[100] Daniels, *Concentration Camps, USA*, 75.

[101] *Tolan Hearings, San Francisco*, pt. 29, 11447.

[102] *Tolan Hearings, San Francisco*, pt. 29, 11422.   [103] Muller, *Free to Die*, 109.

[104] Modell, *Kikuchi Diary*, 16.

[105] Azuma, *Between*, 76, 78, 83, 95, 209, 214; Hayashi, *Democratizing*, 5.

work on immigration in the American West, historian Elliott Barkan explains that his study "is a narrative about peoples" [not a people]. Barkan's book describes the "mosaic of rich hues and variations representing its [the West's] myriad populations."[106]

Barkan did not study African Americans and Indians, but it is clear from his book that the melting pot still had its work cut out for it in 1940 and that cultural pluralism dominated the West. A glance at big city ethnic politics in the East yields the same conclusion and illustrates the shortcomings of cultural pluralism rather than its strengths previously referred to. Fiorello La Guardia was the acknowledged master of the genre of ethnic politics, and he had plenty of imitators/rivals.[107] To assert that there was some coherent group called "white America" or "whites" beggars the language. Indeed the phrase "white America" is an ironic and preposterous reversal of the "they all look alike" slur against the Japanese American.

Certainly the Japanese themselves did not think so. Sometimes they railed against whites as a group. "I resent the term 'white bastards' which I hear many of the Nisei using," wrote Charles Kikuchi some two weeks after the Battle of Midway.[108] Still they usually fine sorted other people and were very specific about whom they were victimized by.

As Kikuchi surveyed the scene of a forlorn and derelict Japantown just before evacuation, he singled out a vocational group rather than a race or nationality. "The junk dealers are having a Roman holiday, since they can

---

[106] E. R. Barkan, *From All Points*, xii.

[107] For the bitter ethnic rivalries of eastern big city politics, dip into any of the historical literature on machine politics. In Chicago the Irish first fought the Jews, Poles, and Czechs and then united with them to fight the northern Europeans, English, and Africans Americans. In New York, the Irish fought off the other immigrant-derived groups until Fiorello La Guardia came to the mayoralty in 1933 and then the Irish, Italians, Jews, and Germans squared off against each other in an ethnic free-for-all. In Boston, it was the Yankees and Jews against the Irish. The persistence of political ethnicity in 1940 is beyond dispute. See R. H. Bayor, *Neighbors in Conflict: The Irish, Germans, Jews, and Italians of New York City, 1929–1941* (Baltimore, MD: The Johns Hopkins University Press, 1978); C. H. Trout: *Boston, The Great Depression, and the New Deal* (New York, NY: Oxford University Press, 1977); J. F. Stack, *International Conflict in an American City: Boston's Irish, Italians, and Jews, 1935–1944* (Westport, CT: Greenwood Press, 1979); J. A. Tarr, *A Study in Boss Politics: William Lorimer of Chicago* (Urbana, IL: University of Illinois Press, 1971); J. M. Allswang, *Bosses, Machines, and Urban Voters* (Baltimore, MD: The Johns Hopkins University Press, 1986). There is an extensive literature on bosses and machines and most studies are tied to ethnic politics to one degree or another, but the foregoing are specifically devoted to immigrant-derived politics as opposed to the structures and practices of machine politics.

[108] Modell, *Kikuchi Diary:* 146.

have their cake and eat it too," he noted. "It works like this! They buy cheap [from the Nikkei] and sell dear to the Okies coming in for defense work."[109]

Since racism is so central to the argument about evacuation, some comparison with the South is appropriate.[110] From slavery times onward many white Southerners believed in the *biological inferiority* of African Americans. And from the 1890s they created a vast, intimidating system of discrimination, accompanied by a wave of lynchings to enforce it, and Northerners constructed a not so blurry reflection of it as well.

Japanese Americans faced no such system on the West Coast. There were the unenforceable alien land laws but the Nikkei had acquired land anyway through their citizen children or corporations.[111] The Imperial Japanese had their own version, as Earl Warren, the California Attorney General, reported in discussing American restrictions against the Japanese: "On the other hand, Japanese citizenship was not open to Americans nor were our citizens free to buy land in Japan."[112] Of course, this did not justify the American outlook, but it does give us some comparative perspective. Nikkei residential areas were not universally segregated, and their children went to school with Caucasians.[113] It would be many years before an African American would enter the University of Alabama and then only under Federal coercion.

By the time of Executive Order 9066, 3,530 Nikkei students (3.2 percent of 112,000), attended a host of western colleges. Seventy-two percent of all Japanese college students attended California colleges, and 92 percent enrolled in the supposedly bigoted West Coast.[114] The 1942 valedictorian at the prestigious University of California at Berkeley was a Nikkei; so was the 1936 valedictorian at the famed California Institute of Technology.

With the exception of John Howard, antagonisms based on nationalism have generally been missed by historians. Some emanated from Filipinos and Mexicans.[115] Near the end of the war when many

---

[109] Ibid., 50.

[110] C. Greenburg has addressed African American and Jewish responses to relocation. See Greenburg, "Black and Jewish Responses to Japanese Internment," *Ethnic History*, Vol. 14: No. 2 (Winter 1999). 4.

[111] *Dies Hearings*, June and July 1943, 9179, 9197.   [112] Warren, *Memoirs*, 149.

[113] For the mistaken view that the Nikkei attended racially segregated schools, see CWRIC, 28.

[114] O'Brien, The *College Nisei*, 135–37.

[115] *Tolan Hearings, Portland and Seattle*, pt. 29, February 21 and 23, 1942, 11016.

communities were rolling out the welcome mat to the returning Japanese Americans, one of them reported back from Stockton that the Nikkei could stay in the best hotels there, eat in good restaurants, and attend the movies. George Hatanaka added "that the only warning note was sounded by a few Caucasians who felt that some of the Filipino residents might not be friendly and might not be willing to relinquish farm property leased from Japanese Americans."[116]

Historians from Morton Grodzins (1949) and Roger Daniels (1972) to Eiichiro Azuma (2005) and Yuji Ichioka (2006) have assumed the existence of a white America, white racism, white western racism, and so forth, either an implied or outright statement of similar opinions and attitudes about race. This book asserts that there was vast variety, diversity, and complexity in western attitudes about Japanese Americans. There was no such thing as a generic Caucasian or Japanese attitude. These were situational and personal.

Yet all of this complexity has been mostly bundled up by historians into a sweeping assertion of collective responsibility. Phrases like "white racism," or "West Coast racism," admit of no exceptions. We should remind ourselves that when General Delos Emmons approached the problem of the AJA' loyalty in Hawaii, he emphatically rejected the doctrine of collective responsibility. Historians of the Nikkei should do likewise for whites. We should stop asserting the collective responsibility of all whites for the racism of one, or a few, or some, or many. Historian Gary Okihiro argued persuasively that both Japanese and whites have been stereotyped in the literature.[117]

Since they have made such sweeping claims about the ubiquity of racism, it is incumbent upon these keepers of the race paradigm to suggest ways to prove systematically the quantity of racism, the mass of it, the universality of it, as opposed to piling up more anecdotes, mostly from politicians. There are as many anecdotes on one side as on the other. The Gallup polls of the 1940s are methodical and they do not support the idea of monolithic bias against Japanese Americans.[118]

The anecdotes nonetheless show that ethnocentrism flowed in both directions. For example, John Modell, the editor of the Charles Kikuchi

[116] *Manzanar Free Press*, January 13, 1945, 1.   [117] G. Y. Okihiro, *Storied*, 137.
[118] For an initial effort to pin down systematically the incidence of racism or the lack of it of the mass of Americans rather than the anecdotal evidence of an unknown number, see R. W. Lotchin, "Research Report: The 1940s Gallup Polls, Imperial Japanese, Japanese Americans, and the Reach of American Racism," *Southern California Quarterly*, Vol. 97: No. 4 (Winter), 399–417.

diary, spoke confidently that the WRA "believed from the beginning that at least eight in ten Nisei were thoroughly trustworthy" and a comparable statistic is often cited by other historians and contemporary observers.[119] Just 20 percent of the 70,000 Nisei would add up to over 14,000 persons, not including the Issei. Moreover, many of the Issei were just as sympathetic to the cause of their motherland. Undoubtedly more so. More than enough to confirm that ethnic and national hostility worked both ways.[120]

Skin color and culture did not always explain why. Certainly they did not always make the Nikkei sympathetic to other "persons of color," to what historians often called the "Other." Some mainland Japanese Americans, like some Caucasians, were ethnocentric. Several historians have found that when the Nikkei relocated to cities like St. Louis and Cleveland, under the WRA resettlement program, they often assumed an attitude of superiority to the resident African Americans.

In some cases, these attitudes, antedated encountering African Americans personally.[121] The *Manzanar Free Press* spoke in such a vein when it announced a Nikkei presentation of "Minsky's real minstrel show." It featured some standard pop and blues music, including "St. Louis Blues" and "Summertime," and an all-Nikkei female group, "who drew the crowd [in] with black magic, alias charcoal, for the 'blacky' effect." The gathering was packed like "sardines."[122]

Apparently this kind of humor was popular and expected. The week before the *Free Press* had advertised a gala "'Darktown Plantation Jamboree'." With "Cunning Pickanninies" in a one act play entitled "Silvuh Slippahs."[123]

Some of the Issei elite had an equally searing view of the Chinese. Like earlier migrants to American cities, the Issei elite were both embarrassed and threatened by the rowdy and bawdy behavior of their own lower class

[119] Modell, *Kikuchi Diary*, 35.
[120] For an apologia for the pro-Imperial Japanese fascists, see Ichioka, *Before Internment*, 153–71ff.
[121] S. Davidson, "Aki Kato Kurose: Portrait of an Activist," *Frontiers: A Journal of Women Studies*, Vol. 7: No. 1, 92.
[122] *Manzanar Free Press*, April 14, 1943, 4; April 7, 1943, 4; *Rohwer Outpost*, June 23, 1943, 5.
[123] For a scholarly treatment, see M. McAndrew, "Japanese American Beauty Pageants and Minstrel Shows: The Performance of Gender and Race by Nisei Youth during World War II," *Journal of the History of Childhood and Youth*, Vol. 7: No. 1 (Winter 2014), 42–64, 191. McAndrew believed that minstrelsy and beauty pageants were attempts to demonstrate patriotism to America in time of war. They are more likely examples of ethnic bias, omnipresent in the world in the forties and unfortunately widespread up to 2016.

groups. These Issei referred to the latter's failings as "sinification."[124] General DeWitt found similar ethnocentrism, in the assembly centers.

Because of their Americanization and their awkward social position, life in the Japanese [assembly] Centers proved a trying and often humiliating experience [for Caucasians, Chinese, Filipinos, Negroes, Hawaiians, or Eskimos]. The adults were ostracized and the half-caste children ridiculed. Their presence in the Assembly Centers was a source of constant irritation to the Japanese.[125]

Bias was not necessarily based on color or even nationality. It could be cultural as well. On June 23, 1942, Kikuchi spoke of a Japanese friend who "refers to the Jewish people as the 'Kikes' who supposedly gypped hell out of the Japanese in the evacuation,"[126] a reference to some used furniture dealers who took advantage of the Nikkei.[127] How many, if any, were Jewish is not known, but the implication of the word "kike" is well known. Imperial Japanese culture at the time was also famously ethnocentric. Their bias against their own countrymen, the Ainu and Okinawans, as well as Koreans, was pronounced, so it is not surprising that some Japanese Americans should have been prejudiced too.[128]

This failing of a few should not be projected onto the many because there is no systematic evidence that the Nikkei as a group were prejudiced against or hateful toward any other group, including whites. If the Pacific military theater of this conflict was a race "war without mercy," to use John Dower's phrase, the homefront was not. The story is full of examples of Nikkei praise for whites in the states of Utah, Idaho, Montana, Wyoming, Iowa, and the cities of Chicago, Cincinnati, Des Moines, Madison, Salt Lake City, Cleveland, and New York City.

An especially poignant example comes from Pasadena. Hatsuye Egami greatly revered her hometown, had a wonderfully close relationship with her female white neighbor, had her kids in mostly integrated schools, and was seen off from the railroad station by crowds of white friends.

I shall never forget this beautiful green city, even beyond the grave. Refined, religious, cultured Pasadena. A city famous for its dignified Rose Bowl graduation exercises held in the quiet of June evenings ... Verdant Pasadena. I shall love thee to the very end.

---

[124] Azuma, *Between*, 38–41, 48, 50, 100.   [125] DeWitt *Final Report*, 145.
[126] Modell, *Kikuchi Diary*, 146.
[127] E. Eisenberg refutes the charge in *The First to Cry Down Injustice?* 71–102.
[128] G. Feifer, *The Battle of Okinawa: The Blood and the Bomb* (Guilford, CT: The Lyons Press, 2001), 70, 438; P. R. Spickard, *Almost All Aliens: Immigration, Race, and Colonialism in American History* (New York, NY: Routledge, 2007), 24.

"Along the [railroad] tracks I notice people taking off their hats and waving to us."

She was "profoundly moved." Her train trip was especially poignant: her coach companion offered to hold her baby while she moved about; the "faces of sympathetic salesgirls" appear as the train passes the department stores; and the soldiers take care of the Nikkei en route. "Several girls are engaging in friendly conversation with the soldiers and laugh guilelessly as each humorous remark is made." "Such friendly and amiable soldiers – We would not like to see them sent to war to be maimed."

She felt sorry for these bored young men, "far away from home, separated from people they love; these young men must certainly feel lonely," she said of the Tulare Assembly Center guards. "In their spare moments when they look at us – especially pretty Nisei girls – wouldn't they think of us, not as enemy aliens, but rather as pitiful and touching captives?" Apparently so, because "in this way the seed of love began to germinate between a soldier and a certain girl. At dawn around four or five o'clock, the girl went to the fence [of the assembly center] where the soldier was to meet her."[129]

Such occasions do not find much place in the race paradigm. This one-sidedness has dominated discussions of relocation, and indeed much of the story of the domestic end of the Pacific War for so long that it has become canonical, an orthodoxy.[130] Yet both the 1940s primary sources and the later oral history testimony attest to exactly that toleration that Mrs. Egami found in "verdant Pasadena."

All of this reminds us that we need to question the determinist and dogmatic basis of relocation history. Historians have situated the hostility to Asians into a long narrative of bias against the "Other." To them, it began in the nineteenth century and was merely working itself out up to the point of Executive Order 9066. Primo Levi, the famous social thinker and concentration camp survivor, argued that no historian or epistemologist had "yet proven that human history is a deterministic process." Instead he spoke of "History's miscellany," of the need to resist the characterization of history as black against white, of "heroes and villains," and for the complexity of history, of the irreducibile individuality of much of human experience, of the anomalies of history. His fellow

[129] H. Egami, *Wartime Diary*, 34–39.
[130] Email letter from Professor J. Stephan to the author, July 18, 2012, who called the canon an "orthodoxy." Okihiro, *Storied*, 1–137. The whole book is about white "anti-racism, but see 65, 68–69, 70–71, 76–77, 78–79ff."

philosopher Karl Popper believed that "doctrines tend to beget fatalities, and the more absolute the doctrine, the less moderate the followers."[131] Richard Serra, another camp survivor, "deplores our tendency to simplify complex events and trends."[132] If there was ever an "absolute doctrine" of history, an orthodoxy, where the complex is made simple, it is the story of race in Japanese Relocation.

[131] For Primo Levi see his *If This Is a Man* and *The Truce* (London: Everyman's Library, 2000; joint publication of two books) and R. Franklin, *A Thousand Darknesses: Lies and Truth in Holocaust Fiction* (New York, NY: Oxford University Press, 2011), 45–68.
[132] J. Ahr, "Primo Levi, Richard Serra, and the Concept of History," *Journal of the Historical Society*, Vol. IX: No. 2 (June 2009), 361–90.

13

Family Life, Personal Freedom, and Combat Fatigue

Ostensibly the centers imposed strains upon the AJA family. Supposedly, the patriarch no longer controlled work, and the mess hall arrangements encouraged eating at any hour instead of with the family. Also, for a small number of family heads, the security roundups in the wake of Pearl Harbor deprived some Nikkei families of their patriarchal heads.

However, other aspects mitigated these disruptions. The WRA tried hard to respect family and group arrangements. For example, when the initial taking separated them, the WRA sought to reunify the family units. Even those families separated by the security roundups were allowed to move at government expense to the Justice Department internment camps. If the dinner hours tended to separate family members, the residential stove tended to congregate families around them in the cooler months. If the mess halls inclined to separate families, they also provided a place for community where people could meet, gossip, plan center life, hold meetings, and socialize. The WRA also attempted to respect the wishes of neighborhood or other Japanese groups to be sent together to the same centers.

The mess hall decline of the Nikkei family has been exaggerated. The Nikkei themselves had complete control of the mess hall schedules. It seems unpersuasive to blame the WRA for the lack of family unity at dinner if the AJA themselves controlled the feeding schedule. Other things must have been more important. One of the corrections the Nikkei made was to encourage family dining.[1]

---

[1] Ito, *Memoirs*, 44–45.

FIG. 6. Mr. & Mrs. Richard Izuno and children, Manzanar Relocation Center, California. This photo is somewhat idealized, but housing was better than usually described. Photograph by Ansel Adams. Courtesy Library of Congress Prints & Photographs Division, LC-DIG-ppprs-00252.

Not everyone liked the stronger patriarchal family. Historians, like Valerie Matsumoto, have argued that the weakening of parental control was a good thing for young women, who were excessively controlled to begin with.[2] It might well have been so for older women also: "The women did not have the three meals to prepare which gave them time to attend art classes, knitting and crocheting classes, etc ... Some said it was the first time they had experienced vacation time."[3] It probably was for children in general. Some center memoirs deplored the fact "that parents pretty much lost control of their teen-age children." The Issei males opposed the precocious leisure system in the centers. They thought that kids devoted too much time to leisure "and that life in the center should not be made too pleasant for the young people."[4]

[2] V. Matsumoto, "Japanese American Women during World War II," *Frontiers*, Vol. 8: No. 1 (1984), 447ff.
[3] Ito, *Memoirs*, 44.   [4] Jacoby, *Tule Lake*, 43.

Both the freedom within the centers and their departure for college represented an awakening for them. It might have been for youth in general, who left the centers to work on their own and fled the tight-knit AJA communities. It certainly gave them control of many aspects of center life that they might not have had on the outside in the prewar Nikkei settlements. Jacoby, a close observer, thought that "For many of the children, particularly adolescents, life in the camp was a 'ball'."[5] However, many fathers did not find useful work to do,[6] but many families found ways to maintain the household. Nancy J. Gentile noted that despite strains, "Japanese-American family culture was stronger than before [relocation]."[7]

Personal freedom within the American centers prevailed. The WRA did not subject residents to humiliating and wearying lineups and roll calls; they did not impose a lights-out policy, nor a curfew. They did not even impose dinner hours for the mess halls. The Nikkei imposed these on each other as well as other mess hall rules. Military police were generally not allowed inside the centers, which were "policed" by the Nikkei themselves.[8] Nazi camps imposed all of these burdens.

The Nazi vision constantly sapped the mental health of prisoners. Michael Neufeld noted that in the Mittelwerk camp the authorities periodically performed public hangings, often several people at a time. They left these unfortunates twisting in the wind, with urine and feces dripping down their legs, to remind the slaves of the consequences of resistance or sabotage. Between these examples and the routine beatings of those who had faltered physically, the inmates were continually reminded of how close they were to death. World War II was the first conflict in which combat fatigue was widely recognized professionally. Inmates of the concentration camps and ghettos had an infinitely worse version of combat fatigue and no doctors, rest, nor medicine to mitigate it.

It was fueled by "the pitiless process of natural selection" that destroyed the bonds between prisoners. Levi described existence as akin to Hobbes' war of all on all. Every person had to guard against thieves, informers, inmate bullies, absurd rules, and sadistic guards. As he wrote, "in the Lager things are different: here the struggle to

---

[5] Ibid., *Tule Lake*, 65.   [6] Ito, *Memoirs*, 44.
[7] N. J. Gentile, "Survival behind Barbed Wire: The Impact of Imprisonment on Japanese-American Culture during World War II," *Maryland Historian*, Vol. 19: No. 2 (1988), 15–32.
[8] Jacoby, *Tule Lake*, 59–60.

survive is without respite, because everyone is desperately and ferociously alone."[9] In the American centers the residents belonged to any
number of organizations that protected them from being "ferociously
alone:" families, churches, clubs, cooperatives, councils, and work
groups, like the newspaper staff.

[9] Levi, *If This Is a Man*, 65, 103.

14

Economics and the Dust of Nikkei Memory

Almost all of those who left personal memoirs of the relocation centers remembered the omnipresent, choking dust of their desert locales.[1] "All ten sites can only be called godforsaken," one historian noted. "They were places where nobody had lived before and no one has lived since."[2] However, both memory and history served to obscure reality, which was one of remarkable productivity. The centers were usually in deserts because that is what much of the Trans-Missouri River American West was and where there was unpopulated space. However, these deserts were eminently irrigable, and in some cases, perfect for agriculture. But even where the soil was supposedly not so suitable, the Nikkei pitched in: "Despite reports that the alkaline soil was not good for agricultural purposes [at Topaz], in the spring [of 1943] practically everyone set up a victory garden."[3] Nor was the climate challenging to everyone. The Nikkei had long worked in the roasting Imperial and Central valleys.[4]

Water was available everywhere. The picturesque Owens River irrigated Manzanar; canals from the Arkansas River watered Amache; the Gila River nurtured its namesake center; the Snake River wet Minidoka (which was adjacent to the local "Big Canal"); the Sevier River irrigated Topaz from the Gunnison Bend Reservoir; the Shoshone River watered Heart Mountain; the Colorado wet Poston, and so forth.[5] According to the historian of Heart Mountain, "The camp was to be built on land

---

[1] Miné Okubo thought that the dust was inescapable, *Citizen*, 184.
[2] Daniels, *Concentration Camps*, 96. See also Hosokawa, who should have known better, *Frying Pan*, 49.
[3] Okubo, *Citizen*, 13660, 192.   [4] Kobashigawa, *Okinawans*, 311–16.
[5] *Topaz Times*, September 17, 1942, 2; September 30, 1942, 4.

which was part of the Heart Mountain Federal Reclamation project half-way between Powell and Cody, Wyoming," that is, on land already targeted for irrigated agriculture.[6] And quite a few people lived near the Heart Mountain center and farmed extensively outside the center. The area around Cody and Powell was sugar beet country whose growers were desperate in 1942 to acquire labor.[7] By the same token, the Japanese Americans left the Parker Valley of Arizona a thriving farming area when they went home.

Far from being unsettled, all of the centers were located near smaller, existing towns and communities. The Arkansas centers coexisted with McGhee and Dermott; Manzanar was just outside Lone Pine and reasonably close to Independence; Gila River was near Phoenix; Poston was hard by Parker, Arizona; Tule Lake sat next to Tulelake (the spelling of the town name differs); Heart Mountain lay between Cody and Powell, Wyoming; Topaz was close to Delta, Utah; Amache was near Lamar, Holly, Wiley, and Granada, Colorado, and Minidoka was in the well settled and intensively cultivated Snake River Plain of Idaho and within commuting distance of Twin Falls.

The Amache Center existed in a particularly complex agricultural, pastoral, and hunting and gathering country. The Cheyenne, Arapahoe, Kiowa, and Comanche tribes had roamed the area before the whites, followed by the famous Bent's Fort on the Arkansas River, and later by the Goodnight-Loving and several other cattle trails. Then came local ranching and farming, especially sugar beet cultivation. The Santa Fe Railroad touched Lamar and Granada. So when the Nikkei arrived, the four towns (Granada was one mile from the Amache Center) dotted the country surrounded by a prosperous sugar beet industry, where many Nikkei labored seasonally during the center's tenure.[8]

The skill and determination of the Nikkei was such that even at the assembly centers victory gardens sprouted all over the landscape.[9] Every single one of the centers produced a wide variety of foods, as had others before them in some of the same locales. For example, the Owens Valley, which held the Manzanar Center, had formerly been a thriving farm valley before the City of Los Angeles diverted most of its water to its own San Fernando Valley. American Indians had irrigated crops in the valley 1,000 years earlier. As Manzanar resident Jeanne Wakatsuki Houston described it, rather than godforsaken, "The soil around Manzanar is alluvial and

---

[6] Mackey, *Heart Mountain*, 27.   [7] Ibid., 28–34.   [8] Harvey, *Amache*, 64–69.
[9] Okubo, *Citizen*, 97.

very rich." In the hands of the precocious Nikkei agronomists, "Gardens had sprung up everywhere, in the firebreaks, between the rows of barracks, rock gardens, vegetable gardens, cactus and flower gardens." With water borrowed from the Los Angeles city aqueduct, "a large farm was under cultivation just outside the center, providing the mess halls with lettuce, corn, tomatoes, eggplant, string beans, horseradish, and cucumbers."[10] Ansel Adams' and other people's photographs of the Manzanar farm picture a communal field that was close to huge.[11] All over the system, even at troubled Tule Lake, the Japanese gardeners made the desert blossom.

At Topaz, the Japanese farmers started out with the irrigation canals originally dug by the Mormons. Topaz is especially illustrative of Nikkei gardening skills, because the soil there was not promising and because the Mormons there apparently had already tried and failed at agronomy. Yet in the summer of 1944 the Japanese had 700 acres of grain and 166 acres of vegetables growing.[12] To provide a perspective 640 acres equals one square mile, so these agronomists farmed more than one.

Today one of the richest of agricultural cornucopias in the world is the Central Valley of California. Many of the San Joaquin Valley fields have only recently been reclaimed from deserts, and much of the wealth and power of the modern agribusinesses derive from these former wastelands.[13] When not working outside the centers on seasonal leave, Nikkei provided their own labor force. As Miné Okubo remembered: "At harvest time everyone pitched in to help."[14]

The Arizona deserts around the Poston and Gila River centers were positively bountiful. There, as in the nearby Imperial Valley, the growing season was long. In virtually no time, these experienced agriculturalists made the deserts yield a wide variety of crops. In the case of Topaz, a part of the proposed 10,000-acre farmland had to be reclaimed from the greasewood foliage upon it. On the other hand, that project benefited from the irrigation ditches already dug by earlier Mormon pioneers.[15] The Gila River Center raised enough produce to send at least one carload lot of vegetables to every other center in the system.

---

[10] Jeanne Wakatsuki Houston is quoted in Grapes, *Japanese American*, 140–1.
[11] G. Robinson. *Elusive Truth: Four Photographers at Manzanar* (Nevada City, CA: Carl Mautz Publishing, 2002), 67.
[12] *Heart Mountain Sentinel*, July 15, 1944, 5.
[13] The author viewed some of the last desert land in the San Joaquin Valley in October 1979 with fields of cotton all over it.
[14] Okubo, *Citizen*, 197.   [15] *Topaz Times*, September 30, 1942, 4.

Just to provide some diversity and self-sufficiency to their local economy, Gila River purchased 700 longhorn cattle from Mexico to start a ranch beside their agricultural domain. The arrival of the longhorns was reminiscent of western roundups, as the air smelt of burned cattle flesh when Nikkei cowboys branded the first lot in February 1943.[16] Pigs, chickens and other farm fowl followed cattle. Other centers followed this diverse ranching and livestock model.

The Amache/Granada settlement was one of the smallest centers, but it was large enough to stage its own agricultural fairs. In 1944, the second annual fair drew 3,500 spectators, including 500 visitors from the small towns around. In fact, the Amache record was close to prodigious in both quantity and quality. In 1943 alone, the center produced from its commercial acreage, 3,838,600 pounds of alfalfa, barley, sorghum, pyrethrum (for fly spray), potatoes, lima beans, spinach, sugar beets, and celery. They also introduced exotic crops never grown before in southeastern Colorado.[17] Since the excellent history of the center describes the land as a "barren, windblown desert" (modern photographs do not bear this out), the Nikkei feat was all the more impressive. Like Gila River, several of the centers provided a surplus, which helped support the other centers in the system. Even the troubled Tule Lake Center produced an excess.

The Amache output was astonishing, but Poston Nikkei perhaps surpassed even that. Parker Valley of Arizona was prewar, or more accurately pre-Nikkei, undeveloped land. The Bureau of Indian Affairs owned much of it, but had done little to improve its desert domain. The AJA changed that condition overnight.

Fullerton interviewee: They [the Nikkei] developed different foodstuffs – lettuce and the beets, carrots, peas, beans and all of that. I think they did a great deal in promoting the entire valley in an agricultural way to the extent that it is today [1993], which is very thriving, a very wonderful thing belonging to the Indians. Of course almost all that land down there, a majority of it is leased, which the Indians, or the Bureau of Indian Affairs, gets a pretty good revenue for it because they're producing a great amount of alfalfa, and a great amount of cotton, or ship thousands of carloads of cantaloupes and honey dew melons.
 Interviewer: Prior to the war, what did they grow.
 Answer: Nothing.[18]

The Japanese used their fields to demonstrate their industry and also to acquaint their neighbors with their character and skills.

---

[16] *Gila News-Courier*, February 20, 1943, 3. [17] Harvey, *Amache*, 124.
[18] Hansen and Jesch, *Japanese American*, Part V, Vol. 2, 676.

Interviewer: Was there any contact by yourself or the townspeople with the internees [evacuees].

Answer: Oh, yes, a considerable amount. They had a field day, where they invited us all to see their crops and then invited us down to the camp and served dinner. It was a very social affair, I thought, and a good dinner.[19]

Possibly the most laudatory praise of Nikkei agronomy occurred at Poston and Tule Lake. As word spread of their great agricultural skills, people from around Parker actually dropped by to watch the Japanese Americans work their crops.[20] That feat should find a prominent place in the annals of American yeomanry, where farming became a spectator sport. The land was hardly godforsaken.

The comparison with modern agribusiness is well founded because these farms were not primitive operations. Modern photographs show huge, well-tilled fields (nearly every center had one); thriving crops; irrigated grounds; large cattle, hog, and chicken pens; numerous harvesters; thriving growing crops; bulging, crop-laden wagons, and surprisingly modern machinery. Mechanization seemed omnipresent and caterpillar tractors were not the least of it. Overhead, the iconic American hot linemen brought power from the numerous hydroelectric dams to light and power towns from 8,000 to 18,000. These were not mom and pop operations.

Charles Kikuchi summed up the work ethic of the Japanese Americans at the Tanforan Assembly Center when he noted with surprise the "number of victory gardens being planted; these industrious Japanese! They just don't seem to know how to take it easy – they've worked so hard all of their lives that they just can't stand idleness – or wasted time."[21]

Although it is not as well known as their agricultural production, the Nikkei also produced considerable handicrafts. Sherry Turner, who worked in the Tule Lake Center, remembered that the Japanese Americans "would go through our offices selling the different things that they made in the colony, such as pins, cigarette holders, pictures, and various things which were just beautiful works of art."[22] And at Tule Lake at least, this production reached factory level. At one point, five buildings there were devoted to a "furniture factory." "Because of the fine workmanship, demand for the furniture has spread to other centers and to the outside."[23]

[19] Hansen and Jesch, *Japanese American*, Part V, Vol. 2, 530.
[20] Hansen and Jesch, *Japanese American*, Part V, Vol. 2, 461.
[21] Kikuchi, *Diary*, 55. The author's immigrant father had about the same work ethic.
[22] Hansen and Jesch, *Japanese American*, Part V, Vol. 2, 504–5.
[23] *Rohwer Outpost*, July 31, 1943, 6; for photographs, see Hirasuna, *The Art of Gaman*, throughout.

FIG. 7. Benji Iguchi driving tractor, Manzanar Relocation Center, California. Every center had a big, mechanized field, like contemporary agribusiness. Japanese were already accustomed to large, mechanized spreads. Photograph by Ansel Adams. Courtesy Library of Congress Prints & Photographs Division, LC-DIG-ppprs-00320.

Over the last forty years American historiography has heavily emphasized the conflicts in American history: slave rebellions, labor upheavals, Red Scares, gender conflict, Zoot Suit Riots, relocation, race riots, and the like. Of late, so has the historiography of relocation, emphasizing various center disputes.

There has obviously been conflict in American history and at the centers as well, as examples from the murder at Tule Lake, the shooting at Topaz, the Harry Ueno Incident at Manzanar, or the 1943 WRA questionnaire illustrate. However, this conflict paradigm misses the larger narrative of relocation and that is one of cooperation and voluntarism. Japanese American culture in the 1940s was extremely cooperative to begin with, and the center experience brought out this collective spirit strikingly. The highly successful consumer cooperatives that the Nikkei established everywhere make this point, but so do their records of achievements in agriculture.

The other side of the coin was the impact of the centers on the neighboring communities. These were both short term and long term, but both were economically stimulating to the tiny, mostly small town and farming communities. The short-term effects arrived with the construction industry. The government was building military camps all over the country, so it was well organized and experienced in cantonment construction by the time Executive Order 9066 demanded more. Since 112,000 people were initially relocated, the construction industry faced a substantial undertaking. The task would have been comparable to building a new town of 112,000 in about nine months.

All over the country, men commuted to these jobs if they were close by or migrated long range if not. They came in the thousands from all over the California, Oregon, Washington, and other parts of the United States, including the territory of Hawaii. These construction workers provided the first economic impetus to the towns. As in heavily impacted large cities such as San Francisco, Seattle, Portland, Los Angeles, and San Diego on the West Coast and Mobile, Wilmington, North Carolina, and smaller ones like Panama City, Florida, to the east, housing shortages also plagued these small towns.

As one resident of Tule Lake remembered it: "Until they got their quarters built they [the government] almost demanded everyone of us in the valley to take in two or three boarders and paid us a big room rent . . . Naturally that brought a lot of prosperity."[24] Construction workers were in great demand, and local underemployed people – "a lot of these fellows hadn't had a solid week's work in a long time" – could suddenly make $1.35 per hour ten hours a day and overtime. The influx also created a greater demand for food and commodities. Much lumber was purchased by the government for the centers and by the Nikkei to complete their housing or make furniture. "It was a good economical boom, I'll tell you that," testified one Lone Pine businessman. "I mean that boosted the economy of our area here in Lone Pine immensely."

The same boom and bust occurred at Heart Mountain and Amache.[25] The influx of workers and soldiers to staff the center did too. The construction worker boom wore off in about three or four months, but the stimulus from the influx of thousands of Nikkei remained until the centers closed. Despite the productivity of the centers, they represented a considerable loss of property and time for the Japanese Americans.

[24] Hansen and Jesch, *Japanese American*, Part V, Vol. 2, 451.
[25] Mackey, *Heart Mountain*, 27; Harvey, *Amache*, 69.

First, there was the loss of some or all of their earnings for periods from six months for those who resettled and found work quickly, to three-plus years for those who remained in the centers until they were forced out in 1946. This loss fell particularly hard on the Issei, who were both older and less confident about going out into what now seemed like a very hostile American community. As Miné Okubo remembered her departure, "I looked at the crowd at the gate. Only the very old or very young were left."[26] So the Issei income loss usually ran up to more than three years' worth. They also suffered considerable property loss. After the Nikkei had settled into the centers, they were able to have their furniture shipped to them at government expense, but many suffered loss before that point.

Again the problems and predicaments of the national state became the problem for this minority. "The Treasury Department, acting through the Federal Reserve Bank," was assigned to care for "urban evacuee property," and the "Farm Security Administration" was assigned the same function for farms. On paper, the government provided warehouses for personal property and procedures for disposing of land. This included helping those who took over the AJA farms.

The FSA provided 650 loans to these "succession farmers," who inherited 258,000 acres of Nikkei property. Sometimes the warehouses of the Federal Reserve District kept secure control of the property and sometimes they did not. Warehouses were broken into or not protected in the first place, and vandals helped themselves. Sometimes the frightened Nikkei sold before they learned of the warehouses. But even before the two agencies assumed control of their property, many Nikkei felt under pressure to sell it. Since it was months before they knew where they were going and under what conditions, the Nikkei often felt obliged to sell for whatever they could get because they thought that wherever they were going they would need handy cash. Others stored their goods with neighbors, churches, or private parties.[27] The results were predictable.

Roger Daniels quoted JACL leader Bill Hosokawa about the way in which the Navy unceremoniously evicted the Nikkei from Terminal Island. Upon hearing of their eviction:

Near panic swept the community, particularly where the family head was in custody [Justice Department internment]. Word spread quickly and human vultures in the guise of used-furniture dealers descended on the island. They

---

[26] Okubo, *Citizen*, 209.
[27] WRA, "Comprehensive Statement in Response to Senate Resolution 166," 34–39, RG 210, Box 2, NA.

drove up and down the streets in trucks offering $5 for a nearly new washing machine, $10 for refrigerators ... And the Japanese, angry but helpless, sold their dearly purchased possessions because they didn't know what to do.[28]

As Kenko Yamashita, a witness not hostile to America, explained: "It's true all the fortune they had made, in some instances over a forty or fifty-year period, was gone suddenly."[29] One infamous episode illustrated the Nikkei plight. When an opportunistic dealer offered one woman an insulting price for her family heirloom china, she refused and simply broke every piece before the dealer's horrified eyes. Perhaps the "College Nisei," in the words of their historian, best evaded the loss of income because they spent the war years preparing for a later life of work while not incurring economic loss in the meantime.[30] Many were too young to be previously employed or property owners. The property story is not well investigated by historians so far, and since the resettlement stretches well beyond the war, the story is beyond the scope of this book. Still, it seems irrefutable that the Nikkei suffered considerable and grievous property loss.

[28] Daniels, *Concentration Camps*, 86.
[29] Hansen and Jesch, *Japanese American*, Part I, Internees, 30.
[30] For the college Nisei see R. W. O'Brien, *College Nisei*, especially the list of colleges who accepted Nisei students, 135–48. O'Brien presented many fascinating charts showing who went where and when. In 1945–46, the Midwest was far and away dominant with 1,332, and Illinois led the list with 397. Populous New York lagged at 166. Nationwide in 1945–46, some 2,870 Nisei were in college. In the mostly prewar year of 1941, 3,530 attended, over 1,000 in California.

15

Consumerism

Shopping at Sears

Historians have emphasized heavily the importance of consumerism in American culture, as both a right and a ritual.[1] The Nikkei were not cut off from this right either. The cooperatives they founded everywhere were also based on sharing and were just as remarkable as other AJA achievements. The coops should have drawn more interest from historians because they were successful, capitalist, and cooperative. All showed a profit every month from the beginning, but interestingly they rested on very collectivist principles, which might not have been unexpected for a group of small-time entrepreneurs. The cooperatives were the modern Circle Pine variety seen for years in Berkeley and Chicago and patterned after the famous cooperative of Rochdale, England, and its imitators. The group ruled the coops democratically and received dividends based on the dollar amount of goods purchased. Membership was open to all except certain Issei who were still on the Roosevelt Administration's enemies list.[2]

At the instigation of the Caucasian administrators, outright market capitalism was forbidden. As the *Outpost* editor explained: "In recent weeks criticisms and comments concerning the growth of private enterprise in the centers have come up." It seems teachers of handicraft were charging "twice or thrice the WRA wages." "WRA administrative

---

[1] For the importance of consumerism, see L. Cohen, "Is There an Urban History of Consumerism?" *Journal of Urban History*, Vol. 29: No. 2 (January 2003), 87–106. See also F. Trentmann, *The Empire of Things: How we Became a World of Consumers, From the Fifteenth Century to the Twenty-First* (New York, NY: Harper Collins Publishers: 2016), 174–271; È. Zola, *Ladies Delight* (Oxford University Press: Oneworld Classics, 2008); G. Barth, *City People: The Rise of Modern City Culture in Nineteenth-Century America* (New York, NY: Oxford University Press, 1980), 110–47ff.

[2] *Rohwer Outpost*, March 27, 1943, 4; March 31, 1943, 2.

instructions state that no evacuee may establish and manage any indus-tries of [a] private nature," the editor reminded his readers.[3]

With the exception of John Howard, historians have frequently and unaccountably been uninterested in these Nikkei economic institutions.[4] But the Nikkei were very interested in them. In Arkansas, the chief administrator, Ray D. Johnson, was instrumental in creating the organi-zation, taking the initiative, and helping to get funding.

The Manzanar Cooperative was one of the earliest and most successful. The government helped set up the cooperative, "but the supplies and products it offered were minimal at best."[5] So the cooperatives developed thereafter under Nikkei tutelage as soon as the Japanese Americans set foot in the centers. Drawing on their already developed business skills and commercial contacts, the Nikkei developed their own coops. The government never exited the coops and continued to support them in various ways, beyond their initial stocks of goods. That included free use of the necessary buildings, electricity, and phone service.[6]

The coops proved profitable from the beginning to an entrepreneurial people. Membership cost $5 and quickly reached nearly 100 percent of the Manzanar adult population. In the first seven months, the coop generated $342,979 worth of business, a figure that grew to over $1,000,000 in the last year of operation. It came to include a "department store, a dry-goods store, a newspaper and magazine stand, a mail-order desk, a shoe-repair shop, barber shop, a beauty parlor, and a laundry and cleaning depot."[7]

Someone remarked that every Nikkei family entered the centers with a Sears or Montgomery Ward catalogue under someone's arm, and Japanese used the catalogues often. The coops competed with both Sears Roebuck and Montgomery Ward, the two mail order retailing giants of the era, and turned a considerable profit in the process. During the first complete year, the Manzanar coop earned a profit of $79,180 for the membership. In addition, it extended credit to its customers, thereby engaging in banking, and most coops included movie theaters as well.[8]

As early as October, 1942, the Rivers Community coop enterprises of Gila River reported total assets of $142,000 and a monthly profit of

[3] Ibid., April 3, 1943, 6.
[4] Among the prominent historians of the Nikkei whose works are cited elsewhere, whose books do not index the cooperatives are Roger Daniels, Sandra Taylor, Richard Nishimoto, Lane Ryo Hirabayashi, Richard Drinnon, Alan Bosworth, Robert Harvey, Michi Weglyn, and Eric Muller.
[5] Armor and Wright, *Manzanar*, 97.   [6] Jacoby, *Tule Lake*, 47.
[7] Armor and Wright, *Manzanar*, 97–101.   [8] Ibid.

FIG. 8. A concentration camp? Drawing of canteen at Tule Lake Relocation Center. The relocation centers developed many social hubs like this one and barbershops, beauty salons, mess halls, cooperative stores, and fire stations. Courtesy Oregon State Archives, Gov. Sprague Records, Daily Tulean Dispatch, October 1, 1942, folder 2, box 5.

$15,000. This seemed a remarkable feat for a center just barely off the drawing board, where workers were making $12 to $15 per month![9] By mid-1944 the small Amache/Granada Center had about 2,500 coop members, almost one-fourth of the population, which meant that virtually every family belonged. The Topaz Center Cooperative offered about the same services and goods as Manzanar. The storeroom also served a social function, thought the artist Miné Okubo. It "was like a country store where people gathered to discuss family and community problems."[10] In early 1943 the Rohwer cooperative boasted a membership of 4,000. Since its membership fees were low at $1.00, the coop shares totaled only $4,000 as compared to others whose total shares added up to $25,000.[11]

[9] *Gila News-Courier*, January 5, 1943, 1.   [10] Okubo, *Citizen*, 164.
[11] *Rohwer, Outpost*, April 3, 1943, 2.

The Heart Mountain coop was another very successful one. "The Heart Mountain Business Enterprises had its beginning on the afternoon of August 12, 1942, within a matter of hours after the arrival here of the first evacuees," wrote the former Center Superintendent. By the end of its first year, the Heart Mountain coop was an $820,000 business,[12] a remarkably rapid startup. As usual, the Heart Mountain coop began with WRA aid, but evolved into its own in an overwhelmingly decisive vote on the matter.

This entity had the usual departments and was a rather large multi-state business operation. They gained their initial stock from Rice-Stix of St. Louis and then reached out to Butler Brothers of Minneapolis for dry goods; to Ryan Fruit Company and Ryan Grocery Company and Meadow Gold of Billings for groceries and ice cream; and to Steward Creamery of Themopolis, Wyoming, and eventually Montgomery Ward for much else. Merchants of both Cody and Powell initially wished to establish desks at the coop like the two that Montgomery Ward operated, but ultimately found too little business to maintain them. Yet the merchants of these two towns ultimately reaped a considerable profit when the Japanese Americans came to town to shop. Still, it was important for Nikkei purchasing power that the towns did not monopolize retail trade because it kept a portion of the AJA retail money inside the center rather than draining all of it outside.[13] In October, 1943, the coops had moved to establish a central purchasing agency in New York to purchase for all coops.[14]

One of the perennial complaints of outsiders, often to the Dies Committees, was that there was a surfeit of food and products in the centers, to a degree that was unobtainable elsewhere. The accusation is difficult either to prove or disprove. At Christmas time in 1944 when supplies were stretched elsewhere both because of rationing and the season, the Manzanar-Coop offered girls' knee high sox for 24¢, men's jackets for $8.79, windbreakers for $3.00, and ladies' sweaters for $2.45. Perhaps their ability to purchase in large lots allowed them to bargain for better prices. For whatever reason these seem like bargain values.

Concentration camp inmates were quickly reduced to wearing rags, but the Topaz evacuees did much better. That coop advertised "boys' polo shirts, coats, shirts and nightwear; ladies', misses' and infants' hose; misses' and children's anklets; campus and athletic sox, half hose; and

---

[12] *Heart Mountain Sentinel,* August 12, 1944, 8.   [13] Ibid.
[14] *Topaz Times,* October 16, 1943, 2.

FIG. 9. Mrs. Ryie Yoshizawa, teacher of fashion and design, Manzanar Relocation Center, California. Young Nikkei women heavily fancied fashion. Photograph by Ansel Adams. Courtesy Library of Congress Prints & Photographs Division, LC-DIG-ppprs-00303.

men's jeans, overalls, shoes, work shirts, collar shirts, underwear, shorts and work gloves." [15]

Even in the lowland Rohwer Center, the coop turned a profit and extended a wide range of services, not the least of which were barber and beauty shops. The beauty shop offered the following services:

Machine permanents	$1.50
Machineless permanents	$2.50
Oil shampoos	$ .20
Oil shampoo & finger wave	$ .35
Plain facials	$1.00
Incl hairdress	$1.50
Scalp treatment incl hairdress	$1.50
Manicures	$ .35 [16]

[15] *Manzanar Free Press*, December 23, 1944, 2.   [16] *Rohwer Outpost*, April 7, 1943, 1.

All of the center adult residents shopped in the towns of Cody, Powell, Delta, Twin Falls and others and at retail outlets established by retailers from the surrounding communities, which were allowed, where profitable, to establish stores within the centers to sell shoes, laundry and dry-cleaning services, funeral arrangements, groceries, or other services the coops could not. Local creameries grew up to serve the Nikkei, and the center residents all told contributed $25,000 to $50,000 per annum to Powell alone.

The ability to shop directly from the Sears mail order house in Los Angeles and the Montgomery Ward one in Denver was a godsend for the Jerome Center because their nearby options were so limited.[17] "They had a commissary where they could get the necessities," said a Jerome post office employee, "but when it came to real shopping, the catalogue companies certainly did a big business ... nearly everyone of them brought the catalogue."[18] The Caucasian postal workers at Tule Lake thought that the Nikkei could obtain goods from the mail order houses that the townsmen could not. "It was surprising the things they were allowed to get through the mail that we couldn't buy, such as towels and sheets ... The American people [sic] couldn't buy a lot of things the Japanese were privileged to buy."[19] Arline Campbell remembered that she got around this problem by ordering under a Japanese name and receiving the goods where she worked at the center post office. "That isn't very nice," she confessed.[20]

Nor was the black market. Since they were out of the centers on so many pretexts, Nikkei participated in the same kind of illegal trading that existed all over the country.[21] The Nikkei were a model minority, but not a perfect one. Robert Jones farmed adjacent to the Tule Lake Center and remembered that large numbers of Japanese went by his farm to do their own work. At first a few would stop for a drink of water, probably feeling him out for anti-Japanese sentiment. When they found none, "they asked me if I would purchase things for them, like chickens and stuff that they could use to supplement what they had." He did: "I would buy the chickens and sell them to the Japanese and they actually plucked the chickens there at my place."[22]

---

[17] *Topaz Times*, October 28, 1942, 2.
[18] Hansen and Jesch, *Japanese American*, Part V, Vol. 1, 291.
[19] Hansen and Jesch, *Japanese American*, Part V, Vol. 2, 448.   [20] Ibid.
[21] For the US and other black markets, see Collingham, *Taste*, 432ff.
[22] Hansen and Jesch, *Japanese American*, Part V, Vol. 1, 470.

The Japanese markets were well stocked enough to draw Caucasian shoppers. Victoria Thaler, city clerk and judge in Tule Lake for many years, remembered: "I used to go down there and buy wool and fish; they had a beautiful fish market. I went down there and bought everything I wanted."[23] She also used the beauty parlor to get her hair fixed in the six-person salon. In turn, she supplied them with them with bananas, which they could not get.[24]

It would appear that the Nikkei had access to retail goods that the surrounding towns did not. That fact was often remarked upon by Caucasians who had occasion to visit the centers. Thaler recalled that "I knitted a lot and I couldn't come up to town and buy yarn, but they had it. So I went down to the compound and bought it, all I wanted." Thus, the economy of the centers supported the residents, provided a surplus for other centers, supplied food for outside parties, generated profits and benefits for the cooperative members, and generally benefited the evacuees. Not the least of its assets was employment. The Manzanar enterprise eventually employed 222 persons.[25]

In real concentration camps, like the ones in South Africa during the Boer War, women did not have enough water to wash their faces, hair, or bodies, much less to enjoy a shampoo, facial, or fingerwave. If they had water to wash their hair, it was usually inadequate and often polluted.

---

[23] Hansen and Jesch, *Japanese American*, Part V, Vol. 2, 546.
[24] Hansen and Jesch, *Japanese American*, Part V, Vol. 2, 551.
[25] Armor and Wright, *Manzanar*, 100.

16

The Leisure Revolution

Mary Kagoyama, the Sweetheart of Manzanar

Many historians have written of the "Leisure Revolution" in the United States and other western countries. They coined the term to indicate that modern Americans enjoy more recreational advantages than kings and queens centuries ago.[1] That may be an exaggeration, but the contrast between centuries is sharp. Dedication to sport and recreation is one of the distinguishing features of modern American culture.

Like education, recreation struggled against the odds to begin with. Just as evacuee turnover posed problems for the school systems, resettlement upset programs by withdrawing contestants. There was much less funding and many more shortages of equipment. Programs were cramped for space initially because some of those set aside for recreation had to be devoted to more pressing purposes. But the evacuees responded to these challenges well, making their own equipment available for program use and enthusiastically participating. Like everything else about center life, the evacuees pitched in. So did the coops, which took over the presentation of films which were as popular inside the centers as

---

[1] D. Q. Voights, *American Baseball: from Gentlemen's Sport to the Commissioner System* (Norman, OK: University of Oklahoma Press, 1966), xii–xxviii. For the literature on US sports, see N. J. Sullivan, *The Dodgers Move West* (New York, NY: Oxford University Press, 1987); S. A. Riess, *City Games: The Evolution of American Urban Society and the Rise of Sports* (Urbana, IL: University of Illinois Press, 1991); (New York, NY: Oxford University Press, 1987); M. L. Adelman, *A Sporting Time: New York City and the Rise of Modern Athletics, 1820–1870* (Urbana, IL: University of Illinois Press, 1990); and especially W. J. Baker, *Sports in the Western World* (Urbana, IL: University of Illinois Press, 1988); and many more.

outside.[2] By one means or another, the evacuees created an impressive network of leisure activities.

Although the predominant historians' stance about the environment of the centers has been a tale of woe – dust, heat, snow, wind storms, mud, and cold – the centers were ideally situated to take advantage of the wonderful geography of the American West, the natural environment. Heart Mountain is a case in point. It was within walking distance of the Shoshone River, which prompted hiking to that spot by church groups and sororities. And being close to Cody, the eastern gateway to Yellowstone National Park, added an even greater attraction. For example on July 15, 1944, a troop of 100 Nikkei Boy Scouts left for a grand encampment in the nation's first national park, and the Camp Fire Girls were slated to follow shortly thereafter.[3] Use of the park by the Scouts was a godsend for the Park Service because wartime travel restrictions had greatly reduced its normal patronage.

Astonishingly, at a time when most American kids could not even dream of summer camp, Topaz had one, in the House Mountains above the scorching desert. It was tucked away into the peaks at 7,300 hundred feet above sea level, thirty-nine miles west of Topaz, in an abandoned Civilian Conservation Corps (CCC) camp. The altitude meant that it was cool in summer, and the camp featured "flat recreation areas, [and] mountains ideal for hiking, and a swimming pool."[4] The Manzanar WRA officials immediately recognized the health and recreational potential of the natural environment by redefining the Manzanar camp boundaries in the summer of 1942 almost as soon as the center opened. In order to facilitate "roving," "picnicking and outings," the *Free Press* explained, the camp boundaries were extended four miles west into the foothills of the Sierra Nevada Mountains, well beyond the barbed wire and guard towers of inmate and historians' memory.[5] As a Japanese American editor explained it: "At Manzanar, elderly Japanese went fishing or rock hunting in the Owens Valley." Hiking was popular with both Nisei and Issei at Manzanar with its splendid backdrop of Mount Williamson and the Sierra Nevada Mountains.

---

[2] WRA, *Guide Lines on Community Activities*, pamphlet (Washington, DC: US Government Printing Office, 1943), 1–17. RG 210, Box 2, National Archives. Hereafter WRA, "Guide Lines."
[3] *Heart Mountain Sentinel*, July 15, 1944, 3. [4] *Topaz Times*, June 8, 1943, 2.
[5] *Manzanar Free Press*, July 7, 1942, 2.

Jeanne Wakatsuki Houston remembered that her father loved to hike up the creeks that coursed down from the mountains into the Owens Valley.[6] As she explained in her classic relocation memoir, Manzanar young people walked right past the barbed wire for hiking and overnight camping in the Sierra.[7] "Once the first year's turmoil cooled down," recalled another Manzanar resident, "the authorities started letting us outside the wire for recreation." At Tule Lake others tramped to or bobsledded on Castle Rock. Even in the more hostile Arkansas area, men "would go out to gather unusual pieces of wood and then they would bring them back into the camp and carve them, or make them, into beautiful things."[8] The Nikkei at Rohwer were especially diligent seekers of cypress knees, so much so that they planned cypress knee (i.e. kobu), hunting and Boy Scout hiking parties to the neighboring marshes. Others ranged over the woods and wetlands in search of mushrooms.

Because of their frequent presence in the woods, the landowners adjacent to the centers complained of the Nikkei presence on their forested property. The *Outpost* explained, "During the past few weeks many Centerites have been searching for cypress knees without permits and without escorts."[9] On one occasion, one of the mushroom seekers, Koiji Yano, got temporarily lost, which prompted a two-day search.[10] The "numerous lakes and rivers abounding in this part of the country" made fishing trips another possibility.[11]

World War II was noted for its dancing at USO affairs, the Stage Door Canteen, the Hollywood Canteen, night clubs, and officers clubs. The custom was omnipresent. Still, no one out-danced the Nikkei, who enjoyed a dance a week, if not more. Young men and women created their own dance orchestras, trios and quintets, choruses, choirs, classical music orchestras, brass bands, and every other kind of musical group imaginable. They danced and danced. For example, the "Bojangles"[12] group played to 275 dancers in Mess Hall 35 at a Rohwer Saturday dance in early 1943.[13] The following week "Las Amigas" sponsored a dance for members of the High Fliers, the Mr. Smiths, and the Free Lancers.[14] Often these dances were sponsored by clubs, and club life grew at least as fast as dancing.

---

[6] Grapes, *Japanese American*, 139.   [7] Houston and Houston, *Farewell*, 77–78.
[8] Hansen and Jesch, *Japanese American*, Part V, Vol. 1, 298.
[9] *Rohwer Outpost*, January 16, 1943, 1.
[10] *Rohwer Outpost*, December 21, 1942, 4 and January 1, 1943, 1.
[11] *Rohwer Outpost*, January 9, 1943, 3.
[12] The reference is to Bill "Bojangles" Robinson, the famous African American tap dancer.
[13] *Rohwer Outpost*, January 27, 1943, 4.   [14] Ibid.

FIG. 10. High school girls' glee club, Granada Relocation Center, Amache, Colorado. Central Photographic File of the War Relocation Authority, 1942–45. Record Group 210: Records of the War Relocation Authority, 1941–89. Courtesy US National Archives and Records Administration.

Seven hundred girls attended their Hi-Y and Girl Reserves at the beginning of one week at Rohwer.[15] The variety of these clubs was literally astonishing. Bill Hosokawa thought that the Japanese were the most organization-minded people imaginable, and club life in the centers bears him out.

Surprisingly, the Nikkei also introduced Hawaiian music to the western high country! After trying out in one of the small town radio stations near the Wyoming center, "Alfred Tanaka and his Surf Riders Hawaiian orchestra, were signed as a regular feature at the Powell station, KPOW." One can only imagine what the cowboys thought of the strains of Hawaiian music drifting over the sagebrush of the high plains.[16] The centers also put on mainstream plays and musicals. Six hundred Manzanar residents turned out to the auditorium to watch and listen to the contemporary hit musical *Oklahoma*.[17] Although some center dissidents like Harry Ueno, who triggered an upheaval that claimed two Nikkei lives, have been praised by historians since 1980, Mary Kagoyama was much better

[15] Ibid.　[16] *Rohwer Outpost*, March 24, 1943, 4; April 3, 1943, 6.
[17] *Manzanar Free Press*, December 6, 1944, 1.

beloved by the Manzanar Nikkei in the forties. In "Oklahoma," the "'Sweetheart of Manzanar' sang to an enthusiastic music-maddened crowd which applauded loudly."[18]

Although golf was still thought to be an aristocrats' game,[19] several of the centers sported courses.[20] Golf was widely played by the Japanese Americans on metropolitan courses near their prewar homes, but the resumption of the custom in the deserts is surprising. Manzanar, Topaz, Heart Mountain, and Tule Lake had nine-hole courses[21] with sand greens.[22]

Other sports likewise thrived. Topaz and several other centers enjoyed the other aristocratic game of the era, tennis.[23] At Topaz and elsewhere, the Nikkei liked ice skating in winter, baseball, tennis, golf, and football outdoors and ping pong, badminton, cards, basketball and Sumo wrestling indoors.[24] At Minidoka, residents had completed an ice rink and planned an ice carnival on it, at Heart Mountain residents enjoyed both ice skating and sledding. At the Amache/Granada Center, the evacuees competed widely in baseball, basketball, and football, and at Minidoka and Heart Mountain they participated in baseball and other sports. Several of the centers had new gyms, including Heart Mountain, Poston, and at least some others.

Sports brought considerable interaction with Caucasians. It occurred everywhere though the degree varied. At Manzanar, the Nikkei baseball teams played against teams made up of construction workers who remained at the center.[25] Also at Manzanar the residents played six-man touch football against "Caucasian" teams from the surrounding towns of Lone Pine and Independence.[26] One of the Fullerton interviewers discovered "At Rohwer, . . . and at Poston . . . the MPs [military police pictured as menacing by many historians] played softball against the Japanese inside the camp."[27]

---

[18]   Ibid., November 11, 1943, 2; December 6, 1943, 1.
[19]   Steven A. Riess, *City Games*, 59.   [20]   Murphy, *Writings*, 7.
[21]   *Rohwer Outpost*, March 27, 1943.
[22]   Adams, *Born Free*, 70. Sand greens were commonplace at small town Midwestern golf courses until they could afford to plant grass ones. The author caddied at one such in Shelbyville, Illinois, in the summer of 1950. For a more extensive discussion of sand greens see J. Paul, "A Game Lives on in the Great Plains; Roll, Putt, and Rake on Oiled Sand; Stop Your Chip Dead; $5 a Round. It's Sand-Greens Golf," *Wall Street Journal* (Online) (New York) May 31, 2013: n/a.
[23]   *Rohwer Outpost*, March 3, 1943, 6.   [24]   Okubo, *Citizen*, 158, 170–1.
[25]   Hansen and Jesch, *Japanese American*, Part V, Vol. 1, 33.
[26]   Grapes, *Japanese American*, 143.
[27]   Hansen and Jesch, *Japanese American*, Part V, Vol. 1, 324.

FIG. 11. Children ice skating at Heart Mountain Relocation Center, Wyoming. A colder climate allowed a wider variety of sports. Central Photographic File of the War Relocation Authority, 1942–45. Record Group 210: Records of the War Relocation Authority, 1941–89. Courtesy US National Archives and Records Administration.

As at Topaz, the high school athletes played outside high schools, beginning with a football game in mid-October of 1943.[28] Heart Mountain players competed against other interscholastic teams as well, losing only one football game.[29] The "Eagles" played nineteen games in 1943–44 against high school basketball teams from all over Wyoming.

[28] *Topaz Times*, October 16, 1943, 6.
[29] S. O. Regalado, "Sport and Community in California's Japanese American 'Yamato Colony,' 1930–1945," *Journal of Sport History*, Vol. 19: No. 2 (1992), 130–43; M. L. Mullan, "Sport, Ethnicity and the Reconstruction of the Self: Baseball in America's Internment Camp," *International Journal of the History of Sport* (Great

FIG. 12. Baseball game, Manzanar Relocation Center, California. Nikkei kids played both American and Japanese sports, often quite well. Photograph by Ansel Adams. Courtesy Library of Congress Prints and Photographs Division, LC-DIG-ppprs-00369.

Despite being outsized, the internee kids more than held their own. At Denson, Arkansas, the local all stars competed against the Pine Bluff Cardinals, "a semi professional team."[30] Amache High participated in the interscholastic high school league of Southeastern Colorado through the 1944–45 season. The 1944 football team looked forward to the climactic game against undefeated Wiley High School.[31]

Interscholastic sports could lead to other ties as well. When Topaz High lost in football to Wasatch Academy 19 to 12, "after the game the [Topaz] Rams were feted at a banquet in the high school cafeteria by the Wasatch team."[32] Sometimes one hears asides from historians *soto voce* that the centers provided sports opportunities for the Nikkei that they did not enjoy on the outside. At Topaz, the leisure revolution provided lots of new

Britain), Vol. 16: No. 1 (1999), 1–21; Mamoru Inouye, "Heart Mountain High School, 1942–1945," *Journal of the West*, Vol. 38: No. 2 (1999), 56–64.
[30] *Heart Mountain Sentinel*, April 29, 1944, 5.   [31] Harvey, *Amache*, 110–12.
[32] *Topaz Times*, November 6, 1943, 1.

FIG. 13. Basketball game, Manzanar Relocation Center, California. This must have been one of the earliest examples of a perfectly executed jump shot, long before it became a standard "weapon." Central Photographic File of the War Relocation Authority, 1942–45. Record Group 210: Records of the War Relocation Authority, 1941–89. Courtesy US National Archives and Records Administration.

experience. As the sports columnist of the *Topaz Times* explained, only three of the twenty-nine members of the 1943 Topaz HS team had any previous football experience. Topaz High played tackle football against Delta and other Utah high schools, in addition to competing in an eight-team industrial league within the center. Such teams were organized around their jobs – commissary, hospital, Coop, firemen, and so forth.[33]

[33] Ibid., October 16, 1943, 6.

The racial/nationality interaction at Minidoka was perhaps the most fully developed and most interesting. There the Twin Falls American Legion[34] sponsored baseball leagues for youngsters, just as Legion posts did all over America. These leagues allowed Nikkei kids to participate in the Junior Legion league, and these Nikkei youngsters won that Championship in the summer of 1944. An all-star team of Caucasian youths from Twin Falls participated against the Hunt [Minidoka] league champions in August. On August 20 the press announced that the Caucasian Rupert Boosters "a strong semi-pro outfit" would take on a Twin Falls Legion all-star team, "augmented by the best of the Hunt team." The Hunt team was scheduled to be honored at a Legion banquet when "a trophy will be awarded to the evacuee nine, emblematic of [the] league championship."[35] How often these teams were racially/nationally integrated is not known. Sometimes it was only a pickup basketball game as at Poston, but interracial sport was commonplace.[36]

Wyoming girls played both basketball and volleyball.[37] Women played softball and other sports in the centers as well.[38] Beauty pageants were especially popular with young women.[39] The Nikkei embraced traditional Japanese sports like sumo, judo, and kendo in addition to the American ones.[40] Poston and Heart Mountain had swimming pools, the envy of other centers.[41]

The Topaz Nikkei often ingeniously combined recreation with community building. In October, 1942, the residents welcomed a new contingent from the Santa Anita Assembly Center by staging a record dance in their honor. Then the center administrators were introduced, followed by "the appearance of Claude C. Cornwall, chief of the Employment and Housing Division, in his rendition of Irish ballads."[42]

---

[34] Ordinarily heavily criticized, but fundamentally misunderstood by historians.

[35] *Minidoka Irrigator*, August 12, 1944, 4.

[36] Hansen and Jesch, *Japanese American*, Part V, Vol. 2, 795.

[37] M. Inouye, "Heart Mountain High School," 61–62.

[38] S. O. Regalado, "Incarcerated Sport: Nisei Women's Softball and Athletics during Japanese American Internment," *Journal of Sport History*, Vol. 27: No. 3 (2000), 431–44.

[39] McAndrew, *Japanese American Beauty*, 42–64, 191.

[40] *Gila News-Courier*, January 14, 1943, 2. (This news was reported in the *News Courier*, although the item was about Minidoka. Camp newspapers commonly reported each others' news.) See Also, Mackey, *Heart Mountain*, photo 71.

[41] *Topaz Times*, May 27, 1943, 2; Mackey, *Heart Mountain*, 70.

[42] *Topaz Times*, October 10, 1942, 21.

Other social occasions brought Americans to the centers. "They had a Sunday social pretty near every Sunday, and ice cream festivals and what not . . . a lot of local people we've talked to did go out there," recalled one resident.[43] "There were a great many" programs at Manzanar, "and a lot of people did go," said Anna Kelley.[44] Manzanar, Topaz, Heart Mountain and most of the centers had new auditoriums/gyms where movies, music, talent shows, drama, and beauty pageants were presented.[45] At Manzanar the Japanese constructed a "traditional Japanese Garden from materials scrounged from the desert."[46]

Music and dancing suffused every recreation that Japanese Americans did. Poston Number 1 and perhaps other centers shared the World War II gaming boom. There it derived from pre-war Japanese syndicate gambling run by the famous Tokyo Club, though it subsequently declined.[47] The Club sheltered a number of Nikkei activities and as in almost any 1940s big city, gaming and politics were tightly intertwined.[48]

Nazi camp administrators did not welcome new arrivals with Irish ballads. In the real concentration camps, the SS employed music in an entirely different manner. It was used to entertain the guards or to force the prisoners to march in step to speed them to and from their slave labor jobs. One inmate remembered "the brutal rhythms that ruled our tired steps every morning and evening."[49] In the centers the rhythms were not brutal, they were "Fascinatin'."

---

[43] Hansen and Jesch, *Japanese American*, Part V, Vol. 1, 14.   [44] Ibid., Part V, Vol. 1, 38.
[45] *Topaz Times*, October 26, 1943, 1; Taylor, Jewel, 96.
[46] Adams, *Born Free*, 70; Okubo, *Citizen 13660*, 173.   [47] Nishimoto, *Inside*, 94–162.
[48] Ibid., 133.
[49] Levi, *The Truce*, 234; M. Waseda, "Extraordinary Circumstances: Music in Japanese American Concentration Camps," Densho Encyclopedia (September 2013), 171–209.

17

Of Horse Stalls and Modern "Memory"

Housing and Living Conditions

Horse stalls have haunted the memory of the evacuees and their historians. Recollection after recollection has chronicled the indignity of living in horse stalls at the race tracks or state and county fairgrounds which served as assembly centers.[1] Housing certainly was inadequate to begin with, but rapidly improved. Whether the assembly centers were actually located at race tracks or other sites, barracks quickly replaced the animal shelters.

There is overwhelming anecdotal and photographic evidence that the legendary horse stalls memory was near pure myth. Toshi Ito remembered that only the first arrivals at Santa Anita lived in horse stalls, but her family went straight into newly constructed barracks.[2] Miné Okubo sketched the same barracks that replaced the horse stalls at the Tanforan Racetrack near "The City" and DeWitt's *Final Report* contain photographs of row on row of barracks at Santa Anita Racetrack near Los Angeles, which at about 19,000, was the most populous of the assembly centers.[3] As teacher Toyo Tuyemoto Kawakami of Topaz remembered, "We had grown accustomed to barracks living at Tanforan."[4] Evacuee Monica Sone remembered the housing at the Puyallup Assembly Center, as a "camp of army barracks."[5] Others found similar housing at the Fresno Assembly Center in the California Central Valley, Tulare, and Pomona. And

[1] Grapes, *Japanese American*, 162–3; R. Daniels, *Prisoners*, 55.
[2] Toshi *Ito, Memoirs*, 37.
[3] Okubo, *Citizen*, 49, 61; *Tolan Hearings, Los Angeles and San Francisco*, pt. 31, 11804-M (photograph section); Mackey, *Heart Mountain*, 21.
[4] Grapes, *Japanese American*, 146.   [5] Grapes, *Japanese American*, 111.

assembly centers like the one on Van Ness Avenue in San Francisco were not at race tracks or fair grounds.[6]

The huge centers at Poston, Manzanar, and Tule Lake began life as assembly centers and then morphed into relocation centers, so there were no horse stalls there.[7] The assembly centers at Turlock, Sacramento, Marysville, Pinedale, and Portland also were not located at race tracks and were built from the ground up as assembly centers. General DeWitt's *Final Report* on the evacuation contains aerial photographs of fifteen of the assembly centers which show clearly neat rows of barracks, some on race track grounds, but most were not horse stall housing.[8] For years, historians have used DeWitt's *Report* to document the importance of racism, so it is somewhat surprising that they could have overlooked these photographs. In any case, none of the race track centers had enough horse stalls to put even the smaller center populations into, much less the 19,000 at Santa Anita.[9] Contrary to "modern memory," most Nikkei never set foot in a horse stall.[10]

A near universal complaint about both the assembly centers and the relocation centers is that they did not provide privacy in the showers and latrines. That undoubtedly was bothersome for some Nikkei, but it was scarcely out of line with shower and restroom facilities at American public institutions like schools and colleges of the time. Toshi Ito, raised in America, hated the lack of privacy; her mother, reared in Japan, "where public bath houses were a common thing," was not fazed.[11] Workers at the shipyards used open urinals and the custom did not generate the kind of complaints that the centers latrine facilities did. No one had much privacy in a public restroom or shower in the 1940s. Certainly servicemen did not.[12]

---

[6] Mackey, *Heart Mountain*, 16–18; Kobashigawa, *Okinawans*, 93.
[7] Egami, *Wartime Diary*, 37.
[8] DeWitt, *Final Report*, 167–81; Ito, *Memoirs*, 36–7. For the horse stall argument, see Howard, *Concentration Camps*, 14. Howard takes the position that because some contemporaries employed the term "concentration camps," that practice must validate the idea. His dissociation of the western centers from those of the Nazis is from Auschwitz and Nazi death camps, not Nazi concentration camps. Same page. My argument is not about the death camps, but rather the concentration camps, which were a different species.
[9] For the assembly center populations, see DeWitt, *Final Report*, Figure 15, following p. 52.
[10] For an example of the enduring horse stall myth, see Howard, *Concentration Camps*, 14. DeWitt, besides publishing the barracks photos, also explained in detail exactly where the assembly centers were located. See *Final Report*, 151–2.
[11] Ito, *Memoirs*, 39.
[12] Katherine Archibald described shipyard urinals in her book and the author can vouch for the other statements from public grade school, high schools, and both public and private

FIG. 14. Building first house at Tule Lake Relocation Center, California. The centers had to be constructed overnight, and the iconic American balloon frame helped carpenters cope with the instant city demand. Central Photographic File of the War Relocation Authority, 1942–45. Record Group 210: Records of the War Relocation Authority, 1941–89. Courtesy US National Archives and Records Administration.

Large, big city construction firms built the relocation centers under the supervision of the Army Corps of Engineers. These included the Morrison Knudsen Company of the Pacific Northwest, which built the Tule Lake Center; Griffith and Company of Los Angeles, which put up Manzanar; the Del Webb firm, of Phoenix, which constructed Poston, and the R. E. Rippe Construction Company of South Pasadena, California, which built parts of Amache.[13] Webb went on to build signature suburbs like Sun City, Arizona. Apparently the Poston job was one of the legendary firm's first/largest.

colleges. He played basketball and football in any number of towns and cities in Illinois and never once found showers that were individual. Nor in his experience in the Army Reserve and summer camps, 1957–63. Such a demand would have been considered absurd.
[13] Hansen and Jesch, *Japanese American*, Part V, Vol. 1, 29–30; Part V, Vol. 2, 726; Harvey, *Amache*, 105.

FIG. 15. Mud from rain and melting snow, Minidoka Relocation Center, Idaho. Central Photographic File of the War Relocation Authority, 1942–45. Record Group 210: Records of the War Relocation Authority, 1941–89. Courtesy US National Archives and Records Administration.

The centers sprouted overnight and drew a lot of workmen, in the case of Poston, 3,500 initially and close to 5,000 later. The evacuees also shared in the construction of the centers, which were often not finished when they arrived.[14] When the construction workers piled out of the Greyhound buses and trains, there was often no place to sleep, so the locals rounded up several empty boxcars where they stayed until tents were erected for them.[15] Earl Ager remembered that the Nikkei "were brought in here by train before anything was ready for them at the camp. They slept in camps," he said, "made up of tents like those in big fire camp . . . but I heard no complaining among them."[16]

One historian maintained that the centers "were built like prison camps,"[17] but the fact is that they were built like standard American

[14] Ito, *Memoirs*, 39.   [15] Hansen and Jesch, *Japanese American*, Part V, Vol. 2, 726.
[16] Ibid., Part V, Vol. 2, 436.   [17] Muller, *Free to Die*, 34.

army posts. Except for the main entry gates, the relocation centers were constructed of wood, with row on row of barracks, which the Corps of Engineers was good at assembling. Aside from the barbed wire surrounding the centers, the wooden and frequently unoccupied guard towers, and the Nikkei residents, the relocation centers could have doubled for the standard army posts all over the country from World War I onward.[18] The centers, like the equally rapidly built army posts, were not prison camps; they were instant cities.

"Every Block had its own mess hall, recreation hall, and combination laundry, showers, and toilets," said Mine Okubo of Topaz.[19] Officially the Central Utah Project, Topaz contained 17,500 acres (27.3 square miles), forty-two city blocks, of which thirty-six were residential.[20] Each block had a laundry with plenty of hot water,[21] but the one washroom made for considerable crowding in the morning.[22] None of the centers was completely finished when the Japanese Americans moved in, so for a time, the residents had to improvise. Army blankets became room partitions until the Caucasian and Nikkei carpenters finished the job.[23] In addition, the WRA truck fleet shipped Nikkei furniture free to the centers from the assembly centers or their former homes. Still, the residents were forever scrounging for wood to finish their own apartments and furniture.[24] At first the water at Topaz was hardly drinkable.[25] Each family received one pot-bellied stove, which on cold days tended to center the family around its iron perimeter.[26] Although little vegetation existed before Topaz was constructed, sizeable trees were brought in from the mountains, transplanted, and began producing green the next spring, and shrubs followed in the fall.[27] Fencing had to await the winter with the ironic outcome that the Nikkei actually helped construct the tardy fencing to enclose themselves.[28]

[18] For a discussion and photos of contemporary 1940s prisons see Ellen Baumler, "Justice as an Afterthought: Women and the Montana Prison System," *Montana: The Magazine of Western History*, Vol. 58: No. 2 (Summer 2008), 41–59. For nineteenth-century prisons see T. J. Guilfoyle, *A Pickpocket's Tale: The Underworld of Nineteenth Century New York* (New York, NY: W. W. Norton and Company, 2006), 47, 51, 74, 103, 128, 176, 198; R. Lane, *Murder in America: A History* (Columbus, OH: Ohio State University Press, 1997), 151. The photos of the barracks-style housing of the relocation centers are legion, but besides DeWitt, see D. Lange; J. Woods and P. Wright, *Manzanar* (New York, NY: Times Books, 1988), frontispiece, xix, 2, 8, 45, 73, 79, 84, 88ff; Ansel Adams, *Born Free:*, 38–9. See also Okubo, *Citizen*, 122.
[19] Okubo, *Citizen*, 124.   [20] Okubo, *Citizen*, 135.   [21] Okubo, *Citizen*, 159.
[22] Okubo, *Citizen*, 161.   [23] Okubo, *Citizen*, 132, 135.   [24] Okubo, *Citizen*, 137.
[25] Okubo, *Citizen*, 143.   [26] Ibid., 146–7; *Ito Memoirs*, 43.   [27] Ibid., *Citizen*, 149–50.
[28] Ibid., *Citizen*, 155.

Historians have often complained about the housing in the relocation centers,[29] and initially it was deficient, especially in view of the roasting summer climate of places like Topaz or Gila River or the frigid winters of Heart Mountain or Minidoka.[30] In addition, the floors were dusty when the Nikkei first moved in.[31] At Manzanar, Jeanne Wakatsuki (Houston) remembered waking up the first morning covered with dust because of the insufficient insulation.[32] At Topaz, winterizing did not begin until Christmas, 1942.[33] "In the first winter … they had no fire, no stoves, no nothing … and [they] would be up to two or three o'clock in the morning to keep warm," David McCormick reminisced. "They would build a fire in one corner of the block, a big bonfire, and that was the only way they had to keep warm."[34]

Still, housing generally became adequate. Stoves appeared in late winter and remained thereafter. Housing rapidly improved at Poston with barracks built of Number 1 grade lumber. It was of such good quality that when the camp disappeared, the lumber was sold off to whites and Indians in the Parker Valley to build homes of their own.[35] At Manzanar, and elsewhere, the quality of housing was rapidly improved as early as the summer of 1942.[36] Insects proved a special trial at Topaz until screens arrived to protect the evacuees.[37] Although many evacuees came from San Francisco, Los Angeles, San Diego and other windy coastal places, the desert winds were a hardship, literally blowing away the Easter ceremonies at Topaz on one occasion and generally chasing the residents about. Like Chicago in winter, Miné Okubo remembered that at Topaz "the wind blew from all points of the compass most of the time."[38]

Internees were cramped for space, but they managed to make their new homes congenial. For example, once they had arrived, they were allowed to ship their furniture to the centers at government expense.[39] The missing

---

[29] See, for example, U Yoshiko, "Topaz, City of Dust," *Utah Historical Quarterly*, Vol. 48: No. 3 (1980), 234–3.

[30] R. Bearden, "Life Inside Arkansas's Japanese-American Relocation Centers," *Arkansas Historical Quarterly*, Vol. 48: No. 2 (1989), 169–96. For a contemporary view of the desert heat, see Okubo, *Citizen*, 189.

[31] Okubo, *Citizen*, 128; Grapes, *Japanese American*, 147.

[32] Houston and Houston, *Farewell*, 17.   [33] Okubo, *Citizen*, 154.

[34] Hansen and Jesch, *Japanese American*, Part V, Vol. 2, 753.

[35] Ibid., Part V, Vol. 2, 732.   [36] *Manzanar Free Press*, July 7, 1942, 3.

[37] Okubo, *Citizen*, 189–90.   [38] Ibid., 183.

[39] *Manzanar Free Press*, June 2, 1942, p. 1. For an account that emphasized the necessity of making furniture and overlooks the government program to ship furnishings into the centers, see Hirasuna, *The Art of Gaman*, 78–9.

partitions between rooms eventually appeared and there was a "gradual easing of the congestion in the barracks." People upgraded their quarters as others moved out and left vacant space. Linoleum with a choice of three colors – maroon, black, and forest green – replaced the bare wood floors at Manzanar and elsewhere.[40] The Nikkei also found ways to combat the heat. It did not help for the first hot summer at Poston, but by the summer of 1943 many Japanese had ordered air conditioners for their own units, sometimes from Sears Roebuck.[41] At Tule Lake, the worst of the relocation centers, Michi Weglyn has noted that a camp built for 15,000 was made to accommodate 18,000.[42]

Still, that number hardly qualified as serious crowding. In Thereienstadt, the Nazis evicted the inhabitants of the town and turned it into a ghetto. Originally populated by 3,500 Czechs, it soon came to house 50,000 Jewish internees and usually held 40,000.[43] In other European camps conditions varied from bad to worse. Relocation clothing also belied the concentration camp description. In the American deserts, the Nikkei were warmly clad in military garments, left over from World War I. These included the famous Navy pea coats, familiar to anyone from that generation.[44]

[40] Grapes, *Japanese American*, 138.
[41] Hansen and Jesch, *Japanese American*, Part V, Vol. 2, 753; Grapes, *Japanese American*, 154.
[42] Weglyn, *Years of Infamy*, 157.
[43] N. Troller, *Theresienstadt: Hitler's Gift to the Jews*, 25.　　[44] Okubo, *Citizen*, 151.

18

Politics

Probably the most implausible claim of the relocation literature is that relocation was the greatest violation of civil rights in American history. The experience was nowhere near as bad as the discrimination against African Americans in the segregation era and even before.

Relocation deprived Japanese Americans of some of their right to participate in outside politics, but it did not deprive them entirely of their civil rights. Thus, the oft-repeated claim that relocation was the greatest violation of civil liberties in American history, although partially accurate, did not include state and national disfranchisement. In the relocation centers, the residents politicked incessantly and openly, for or against other Nikkei factions, for or against the centers' authorities, or for and against some outside initiative.[1] Despite efforts in California in mid-1942 to disfranchise them, the attempt failed. The issue came up in the US Supreme Court a year later in May, 1943, with the same outcome. In this case, the Native Sons sued to have "the names of Japanese Americans eliminated from the San Francisco list of voters and that all Americans of non-white ancestry, except Negro Americans, be denied the right of franchise." Instead, the Supreme Court affirmed a lower court decision by the US Ninth Circuit Court of Appeals Judge A. F. St. Sure, called the *Regan Case*.[2] The evacuees voted absentee in state and national elections in places as diverse as Minidoka and Manzanar.[3]

---

[1] See, for example, an article by C. Kondo, "Manzanar Metazoa," *Manzanar" Free Press*, July 22, 1942, 2; and Hayashi, *Democratizing*, 76–106.
[2] *Topaz Times*, May 27, 1943, 3.
[3] *Minidoka Irrigator*, November 7, 1942, 5; and November 11, 1944, 2.

In the California gubernatorial election of 1942, the evacuees had a choice only between hostile candidates, Earl Warren and Culbert Olson, both of whom favored relocation. But in the Santa Monica congressional district, they had an opportunity to vote against Congressman Leland Ford, who had led the cry for Japanese removal.[4] As the editor of the *Free Press* noted with some relish, the incumbent "Ford was defeated by a wide margin,"[5] showing wide Caucasian support for the Nikkei.

The evacuees were not disfranchised by relocation, but by apathy. Voter turnout for state and local elections was often abysmal. In Seattle and Kings County elections, Minidokans did best as 84 of 145 eligible citizens voted, yet, in the 1942 general election, Minidoka voters cast 100 votes out of 2,500 eligible to do so. Five of fifteen eligible to vote in Multnomah County [Portland] voted.[6]

Yet center matters of direct interest to the evacuees generated a high turnout. In June, 1942, 73.9 percent of the residents of Minidoka participated in a special election to ratify a proposed Charter for the Community Advocacy Council.[7] Overwhelming majorities also voted on local issues at Topaz. Here, over 3,000 out of 3,167 voters, an astonishing 94.7 percent, elected to amend the center constitution to allow Issei non-citizens to hold office in the Community Council.[8] Of course, voting was a right that the Issei did not enjoy outside the centers.

The evacuees also demonstrated en masse. They conducted labor, political, and hunger strikes, and they generally stood up for their rights within the centers. Historian Arthur Hansen has noted that at one compound at Poston (there were three), the War Relocation Authority actually lost control of the camp to the evacuees.[9] Recent scholarship agrees that Japanese American protest was commonplace.[10] Proponents of the

---

[4] *Manzanar Free Press*, November 5, 1942, 2; November 23, 1942, 1; November 1, 1944, 3.

[5] *Manzanar Free Press*, November 23, 1942, 1.

[6] *Minidoka Irrigator*, November 7, 1942, 5.   [7] *Minidoka Irrigator*, June 19, 1943, 1.

[8] *Topaz Times*, June 10, 1943, 1.

[9] A. Hansen, "Cultural Politics in the Gila River Relocation Center, 1942–1943," *Arizona and the West*, Vol. 27: No. 4 (1985), 327–62.

[10] G. Y. Okihiro, "Tule Lake Under Martial Law: A Study in Japanese Resistance," *Journal of Ethnic Studies*, Vol. 5: No. 3 (1977), 71–85; Okihiro, "Religion and Resistance in America's Concentration Camps," Phylon, Vol. 45: No. 3 (1984), 220–33; A. A. Hansen and D. A. Hacker, "The Manzanar Riot: An Ethnic Perspective," *Amerasia Journal*, Vol. 2: No. 2 (1974), 112–57; S. Davidson, "Aki Kato Kurose: Portrait of an Activist," *Frontiers*, Vol. 7: No. 1, 91–7; H. Ueno, in ed. A. Hansen, et al., "Dissident Harry Ueno Remembers Manzanar," *California History*, Vol. 64; No. 1 (1985), 58–64; E. Bittner, "Loyalty … Is a Covenant: Japanese American Internees and the Selective Service Act," *Prologue*, Vol. 23: No. 3 (1991), 248–52; F. T. Inouye, "Immediate Origins

concentration camp thesis have emphasized refusal, riot, and rebellion to make the point that inmates stood up for their rights and that the authorities were brutal and unscrupulous. There were upheavals at Manzanar in December, 1942, at Tule Lake often,[11] at Topaz in 1943, a threatened doctor and hospital strike at Topaz in 1943, an actual hospital strike at Heart Mountain in 1943, and so forth.[12] Yet, in fairness to the authorities, often hard pressed by the Japanese American resisters from within and by powerful editors, congressmen, pundits, and unions[13] from without, it would seem that the authorities usually tried to be just.

At Topaz, when a sentry killed James Wakasa, who was wandering through the wire, on April 11, 1943, the center went on strike, staged a large public funeral, and demanded redress. They quickly got it. The WRA responded with numerous concessions including the promise that the "day guards inside the camp would be eliminated, and only one soldier would be present at the main gate to check entering people and baggage."[14] The troublemakers were not necessarily innocent in these upheavals. As the pro-Nikkei *Christian Century* explained of the outbreaks of December 1942, the malcontents were a small minority who wanted Japan to win the war.[15]

Evacuees had allies both inside and outside the centers, who looked out for their interests. For example, the July 2, 1942, edition of the *Free Press* reported that the San Francisco and Alameda CIO protested any attempt to disfranchise the internees; the Stockton Methodist Church (district organization) protested the mass evacuation itself; and the American Civil Liberties Union and the Lawyers Guild represented the internees pro bono.[16]

The San Francisco office of the WRA and the California State Bar Association organized a system under which "center residents may choose

---

of the Heart Mountain Draft Resistance Movement," *Peace and Change*, Vol. 23: No. 2 (1998), 148–66; L. Kurishige, "Resistance, Collaboration, and Manzanar Protest," *Pacific Historical Review*, Vol. 70: No. 3 (2001), 387–417.

[11] Weglyn, *Years of Infamy*, 156–89.

[12] L. Fiset, "The Heart Mountain Hospital Strike of June 24, 1943," in M. Mackey, editor and contributor, *Remembering Heart Mountain* (Casper, WY: Mountain States Lithographing, 1998), 101–18.

[13] For notorious charges of coddling, see *Manzanar Free Press*, June 5, 1943, 1. *The Denver Post* "informed" its readers in June 1943 that food was being hoarded at the Heart Mountain camp, that Japanese Americans were not governed by the same rationing rules that governed others, and that many refused to accept well-paid outside job offers. None of these charges was factual.

[14] Taylor, *Jewel* 141. For the Wakasa incident, see 136–43.

[15] *Christian Century*, December 23, 1942, 1580.

[16] *Manzanar Free Press*, July 2, 1942, 2.

a lawyer from a list of 800 California attorneys who have agreed to handle legal matters for evacuees who formerly resided in California." The Bar Association agreed to a standard fee that was lower than the regular one.[17] That 800 lawyers would agree to handle the legal matters of a minority in California during wartime seems significant. Historian Sandra Taylor, in her book about Topaz, put it well when she spoke of the "relatively benevolent jurisdiction of the WRA."[18] The *Manzanar Free Press* agreed that "the relocation centers are far from being concentration camps."[19]

Furthermore, the Nikkei were quite savvy about helping themselves in politics. When the *Topaz Times* reported that Denver area evacuees helped harvest enough sugar beets to feed 748,000 people for a year, they made certain the wartime political implication was understood. "They all thought of their work in terms of the war effort," explained a spokesman, "realizing that by laboring on farms they were making a genuine contribution toward shortening the present conflict."[20]

Although they could not have acquired much surplus property in their desert exile, the Nikkei also participated in "scrap-metal drives, bond sales, Red Cross drives, and blood donations" as Miné Okubo put it, "to keep up with the outside world."[21] The Minidoka Center raised $20,097 toward the war effort in a 1943 bond drive, a remarkable total for a population of 10,000 whose wages ranged from $12 to $19 per month.[22]

When casualties among the 442nd Regimental Combat Team began to mount, the "first mass gathering in Topaz was a memorial service to honor a Japanese-American soldier who died while in service."[23] Dillon Myer spent much of his time shuttling from city to city explaining the WRA and upholding the rights of the Nikkei. Historian Richard Drinnon called Myer the "keeper of [the] concentration camps," but that label is hard to reconcile with either Myer's behavior or his frequent public defense of the Nikkei.[24] In mid-war, Myer told the *Deseret News* in Salt Lake City:

85 per cent of the evacuees are American citizens, and any group who is foolish enough to adopt resolutions that they cannot live in certain areas or engage in certain businesses have [sic] lost sight of our purpose in fighting this war.

[17] *Topaz Times*, October 28, 1943, 3.   [18] Taylor, *Jewel*, 154.
[19] *Manzanar Free Press*, September 11, 1942, 1.   [20] *Topaz Times*, November 4, 1943, 1.
[21] Okubo, *Citizen*, 174.   [22] Story in the *Rohwer Outpost*, March 24, 1943, 4.
[23] Okubo, *Citizen*, 168.
[24] R. Drinnon, *Keeper of Concentration Camps: Dillon Myer and American Racism* (Berkeley, CA: University of California Press, 1987).

Myer insured that Nikkei contributions were known to the media, and they in turn published them appreciatively. In Iowa, said the *Des Moines Register*, "Hardly a business or industry exists in the state which cannot draw from the labor pool which the evacuees in the relocation centers represent."[25]

One of the major failings of the relocation literature has been that it has not appreciated the dicey predicament of the WRA. The Authority was always caught between opposing political forces which greatly complicated its policy. Historians have discussed how malignant the Dies Committee and other anti-Japanese American interest groups were, and they have a point. The hostile part of the media circulated all kinds of hurtful misinformation. From the beginning, the WRA believed that the centers were constitutionally and politically problematical and that the best policy for both the Japanese Americans and the US government was to make the center experience short.[26]

That led to resettlement efforts almost from the outset. Yet powerful political forces outside the wire agitated to keep the evacuees inside it and to deport the Issei after the war. As Tōru Matsumoto perceptively explained: "Until this question [of loyalty] was settled in the minds of the public, the WRA labored under a heavy and most embarrassing handicap." As John Modell later wrote, "This policy [of resettlement] dictated that the Japanese Americans be shown to be the most trustworthy citizens, the truest of the true."[27] That is why the many get togethers at the centers, the religious ceremonies, the demonstrations of the unusual Nikkei agricultural skill, the center festivals, the agricultural fairs, the inter-racial sports, the ice cream socials, the inter-racial Christmas celebrations, the performance of the 442nd Regimental Combat Team, the many barnstorming speeches of Myer, and the many Nikkei letters to the editors of friendly newspapers were so important.

However obvious it is to historians in 2016 that Americans in the 1940s should not have harbored resentments against the Nikkei, many nonetheless did, and resettlement could not proceed until the public mind was put at ease. Matsumoto's opinion was almost certainly borne out by the segregation story of 1943. In July, the announcement of the coming segregation program was followed immediately by "news of the Dies committee's calling off of the Nisei investigation."[28]

---

[25] Quoted in the *Topaz Times*, November 6, 1943, 3.
[26] Matsumoto, *Beyond Prejudice*, 53.   [27] Kikuchi, *Diary*, 35.
[28] *Rohwer Outpost*, July 24, 1943, 6.

19

Culture

Of Judo and the Jive Bombers

The WRA, despite charges of racism against it, or the lesser charge of prejudice, allowed Japanese culture to flourish. They certainly wanted the Nikkei to assimilate, just as the JACL leadership did, but the Nikkei practiced both American and Japanese culture openly.[1] Language is usually considered the fundamental marker of culture, and the Japanese language thrived in the Spartan centers. The WRA allowed center newspapers to publish in both English and Japanese throughout the war.[2] Historian Brian Hayashi thought that Japanese was the lingua franca of the centers. At the very least, because of the ebb and flow of both English and Japanese speakers, they were bilingual. Religious services were conducted in the mother tongue of the Issei, as well as English, and all centers offered Japanese language courses. Rohwer adult education offerings included a course in elementary Japanese. Despite local Caucasian griping, Japanese was spoken openly outside the centers as well, for example, in Twin Falls, Idaho, near Minidoka.[3]

In the very midst of the militant-led potato strike at Tule Lake in the fall of 1943, the WRA had expanded the Japanese adult language classes by

---

[1] For Gila River, see A. A. Hansen, "The Evacuation and Resettlement Study at the Gila River Relocation Center, 1942–1945," *Journal of the West*, Vol. 38: No. 2 (April 1999), 45.

[2] *Manzanar Free Press*, see the issues of June 7, 1942, June 19, June 20,1942, June 25, 1942, July 7, 1942, July 9, 1942, July 20, 1942; and *Manzanar Free Press*, February 3, 1945 through last issue, September 8, 1945; and the *Gila Bulletin*, September 6, 1945, 1, September 12, 1945, 2. See also D. Myer, *Uprooted Americans: The Japanese Americans and the War Relocation Authority during World War II* (Tucson, AZ: University of Arizona Press, 1971), 57.

[3] *Minidoka Irrigator*, June 5, 1943, 1; June 12, 1943, 4.

two, taught by a graduate of Nippon University. Japanese was also offered to elementary school students.[4] So unlike the Germans in World War I, neither the militant activity of the Tule Lake rejectionists nor any underlying cultural or racial bias by the WRA prevented the transmission of a mother tongue whose mother country was at war with the United States. The Japanese language was banned at some assembly centers, but not in the relocation centers.[5]

The arts of both Nisei and Issei cultures, from swing dancing to Kabuki theater, also thrived. For example, the WRA instructions for their community activities program specified that "Adult Activities – including such Issei interests as Goh, Shogi, and Utai –be included."[6] Poetry flourished in particular.[7] At Poston Unit Number One, the Nikkei built a huge "traditional Shibai (Japanese drama) theater." Its dimensions are not available, but in photographs it dwarfs both the actors and the audience.[8] These were fully appreciated by many white observers:

They used to have festivals down there at Poston ... I remember one or two of them. They were quite spectacular. They were taken, I guess from the stage shows that they had in Japan with dancers ... People said that they were really something ... A brother-in-law of ours who was with the Red Cross was there and attended one of them, and he said it was just marvelous. He said in that program they had marvelous entertainers, dancers, and singers who had the most beautiful voices he ever heard.[9]

The Fullerton interviewees often made such statements of appreciation, but one more example by a center worker must suffice, "They made such beautiful stuff out of mesquite wood, [cactus] and things like that."[10]

A perfect example of the bi-cultural nature of the centers occurred during the Manzanar Fourth of July celebration in 1942. One thousand spectators gathered to witness a baseball game between the center National and American league teams and then "a colorful ondo line

[4] *Topaz Times*, November 4, 1943, 2.   [5] Daniels, *Concentration Camps USA*, 106.

[6] War Relocation Authority, "Guidelines on Community Activities" (Washington, DC: US Government Printing Office, 1943), 5. RG 210, Box 2, National Archives. Hereafter WRA, "Guide Lines."

[7] P. T. Suzuki, "Jinji (The Human Condition) in the Wartime Camp Poetry of the Japanese Americans," *Asian Profile* [Hong Kong] Vol. 15: No. 5 (1987), 407–15.

[8] R. S. Nishimoto, *Inside an American Concentration Camp: Japanese American Resistance at Poston, Arizona* (Tucson, AZ: The University of Arizona Press, 1995), 89; see also the artistic "crayon and pencil drawing" entitled "Issei Night" of a Japanese play given to a packed house, Hirasuna, *The Art of Gaman*, 112.

[9] Hansen and Jesch, *Japanese American*, Part V, Vol. 2, 657; Hirasuna, *Gaman*, 17ff.

[10] Hensen and Jesch, *Japanese American*, Part V, Vol. 2, 795.

climaxed the week-end festivities and approximately 300 boys and girls in gay kimonos clicked their bamboo castanets in rhythm with the native music."[11] Young women at beauty pageants, kimono-clad as some were, provide an even more vivid illustration.[12]

Christmas at Minidoka in 1944 featured a Santa Claus and twirling by Myrtle Yamanishi. Side by side a series of Fuki-yoses were performed by little dancers to give "enjoyment and entertainment to the older residents."[13] Speaking of Japanese horticultural art and floral cultivation thriving at Topaz, a *Times* staffer noted: It "makes us proud of our people, who won't permit conflicting conditions to deprive them of their inherent love for beauty and the vigor of color."[14]

Artist Miné Okubo remembered:

Art and hobby shows were of great interest. The residents exhibited vases and desk sets of wood, toys, stuffed animals and dolls, garments and knitted ware, carvings of stone and wood, finger rings of cellophane or fashioned from tooth brush handles, peach seeds or beads, tools made of scrap iron, and beautiful hats made from citrus-fruit wrappings woven with potato-sack strings. Ingenious use was made of everything that could be found in the center.[15]

The numerous festivals and general celebrations upheld both cultures. Outside friends, with both small and capital letters, were forever sending presents to the Nikkei children. At Rohwer, the Japanese celebrated Christmas in 1942 with 3,500 toys from people all over the United States, with Saint Nicholas on hand to deliver them. Group singing of Christmas carols by the "Center chorus" were special features.[16] The center followed that celebration up with a traditional New Year's Japanese Mochigome "traditional custom" and Shibai dramatizations by professionals from Los Angeles and San Francisco. This was topped by a "gala variety show" featuring the usual dramas, dancing, and music.[17]

This plucky unwillingness to suspend their culture has often been seen as another example of Nikkei cultural tenacity. That point is well taken, but the other side of the coin is that the center administrators also accepted and even encouraged this culture. For example, at Poston, the Japanese Americans were trucked out into the desert in center vehicles, as much as twenty-five

---

[11] *Manzanar Free Press*, July 7, 1942, 3.   [12] McAndrew, *Japanese Beauty*, 42–64,191.
[13] *Minidoka Irrigator*, December 23, 1944, 3.   [14] *Topaz Times*, May 27, 1943, 2.
[15] Okubo, *Citizen*, 169. See also Hirasuna, *The Art of Gaman*, throughout.
[16] *Rohwer Outpost*, December 24, 1942, 1, 8.
[17] *Rohwer Outpost*, January 1, 1943, 1. Mochigomi is a sweet rice cake eaten at New Year. Shibai – pron sheebi means dramatization. Conversation with Professor Miles Fletcher, Japanese historian at UNC-CH, May 13, 2009.

miles away from the center, to search for unusual wood or petrified rocks to put into their ornamental gardens or furniture.[18] One father brought his own still to the center with which he brewed sake, which would probably qualify as both an artistic and useful art.[19] One of the most frequently repeated criticisms of the Japanese was that they were non-assimilable. The entire policy of the WRA was based on the opposite hope. The Administrators wanted the Japanese to assimilate, but they also respected those who did not.

FIG. 16. Thanksgiving Day sumo tournament, Gila River Relocation Center, Arizona. The WRA encouraged both American and Japanese sport and culture. Central Photographic File of the War Relocation Authority, 1942–45. Record Group 210: Records of the War Relocation Authority, 1941–89. Courtesy US National Archives and Records Administration.

[18] Hansen and Jesch, *Japanese American*, Part V, Vol. 2, 701.
[19] Grapes, *Japanese American*, 139, 143.

FIG. 17. Woodie Ichihashi Band, Tule Lake Relocation Center, California. The youngsters were dance mad, to put it mildly. Central Photographic File of the War Relocation Authority, 1942–45. Record Group 210: Records of the War Relocation Authority, 1941–89. Courtesy US National Archives and Records Administration.

Despite that, the accommodation was not always comfortable. At Tule Lake the subject of burial triggered a small strike. Buddhist deaths caused no problem because they were handled by a Klamath Falls mortuary, which cremated the bodies supervised by Buddhist priests. However, Christian burial required digging a grave and in Japanese society only special persons, "eta," handled matters of death. Upon a Christian death, the Nikkei assigned to it refused to dig the grave because such people were looked down upon, and thus if they dug one they would be "despised throughout the camp."[20] So Christian burial required the family to excavate the graves.[21]

Yet new ways did thrive, despite this respect for the old. Jeanne Wakatsuki Houston remembered that her "sister Lillian in high school,

[20] For an explanation of the outcast status of the "eta," see Embree, *Japanese Nation*, 23–4, 122–3.
[21] Jacoby, *Tule Lake*, 30.

was singing with a hillbilly band called the Sierra Stars jeans, cowboy hats, two guitars, and a tub bass." "My oldest brother, Bill, led a dance band called the Jive Bombers – brass and rhythm – the cardboard fold-out music stands lettered J. B. Dances were held every weekend in one of the recreation halls." Bill did vocals on Glenn Miller arrangements of "In the Mood," "String of Pearls," and "Don't Fence Me In." She swore that the latter tune was not poking fun at WRA authorities, but one is entitled to wonder. "They would blast it out into recreation barracks filled with bobby-soxed, jitterbugging couples."[22]

The Japanese also took to baseball with a vengeance. They built on a well-established state-wide Nikkei league system in California which developed from the mid-1920s onward. Like the Negro League, this allowed the Nikkei to create a "league of their own" and to attain stardom within their own group.[23] Various other sports, track and field, golf, tennis, basketball, football, and so forth, were embraced as enthusiastically. Historian Nancy J. Gentile noted that "Japanese-American culture was stronger than before [relocation]."[24]

Real concentration camps offered a stark contrast. The Jews in ghettos had little else to do, so underground clubs, libraries, dance, poetry, diary writing, and theater thrived.[25] The Nazis did not encourage culture in the camps or ghettos, and decreed death for anyone "who participated in a Jewish wedding."[26] So marriage, like many of the other camp cultural activities, was practiced secretly, another form of subtle, but determined resistance, like keeping diaries, smuggling food, publishing newspapers, operating libraries, and schooling.

So the Japanese Americans were partially integrated structurally and very integrated behaviorally.[27] Unlike African Americans, who still retained many of their folkways, Nikkei children attended white schools, had Caucasian friends, wore bobby sox, listened to and danced to swing

---

[22] Grapes, *Japanese American*, 143.
[23] *Rohwer Outpost*, January 1, 1943, 11. The phrase derives from the classic movie of the same name.
[24] Gentile, "Survival," 15–32.   [25] Marrus, *Holocaust in History*, 121.
[26] Bennett, *Shadow of the Swastika*, 185.
[27] For the distinction between behavioral or cultural and structural assimilation, see M. Gordon, *Assimilation in American Life: The Role of Race, Religion, and National Origins* (New York, NY: Oxford University Press, 1964), Chapter 3, "The Nature of Assimilation," 60–83 and specifically 67–71, 110–11. To oversimplify, behavioral assimilation means that groups act or behave alike, structural assimilation means they live, marry, associate, educate, and generally interact together. Hayashi uses the terms cultural and structural assimilation to mean essentially the same thing. Hayashi, *For the Sake*, 8.

music, hung out at soda fountains, lusted after cars with white wall tires, had beauty pageants, and generally behaved like Caucasian teens. Even during their stay in the centers, the Nikkei kids' swing dances were practically non-stop and so were their other behavioral customs. Like the second-generation Jews of New York, studied by historian Deborah Dash Moore, Japanese Americans lived mostly together, but lived a solidly mainstream existence.[28] The Chinese were cooped up in Chinatowns and were subjected to much worse prejudice.[29]

The war temporarily overturned this progress, but had the opposite effect on other races and nationalities. World War II benefited African Americans. They secured better jobs in the defense industries; they organized politically; the NAACP grew tenfold; they pressed their struggle in the courts and through the vote, they became a large factor in northern big city politics, like Chicago and New York. So the Second Great Migration to the North and West, like the first, was also an act of enfranchisement.

Their gains on the West Coast were especially noteworthy.[30] In the American South, where genuine racism really did exist, no such timeout occurred. Blacks who fled the South made gains; those who remained still faced the largely intact system of racial segregation, in drinking fountains, restaurants, hotels, railroad cars, neighborhoods, schools, and voting booths. In the West, the Nikkei voted, even in the relocation centers.

As historian Thomas Sugrue has noted, none of these African American gains came without conflict, some of it violent. But when the war ended, African Americans did not flock back to the South. Instead, millions more came north and west, a human stream that did not reverse for many years.[31] The Nikkei made no such regional repudiation. When the war concluded, a majority packed their bags, mostly for California and the West Coast.[32] If the West Coast was an overwhelmingly racist place, similar to the South, why would their culture thrive and a majority of Japanese Americans return and resume their remarkable progress?

---

[28] D. D. Moore, *At Home in America: Second Generation New York Jews* (New York, NY: Columbia University Press, 1981), 3–17ff. Brian Hayashi doubts this assimilation for Nikkei. See his "*For the Sake,*" 149–58.

[29] K. Scott Wong, "War Comes to Chinatown: Social Transformation," Lotchin, *The Way We Really Were,* 164–86; Xiaojian Zhao, *Remaking Chinese America,* 1–77.

[30] Lotchin, *Bad City,* 104–55.

[31] T. Sugrue, *Sweet Land of Liberty: The Forgotten Struggle for Civil Rights in the North* (New York, NY: Random House Trade Paperbacks, 2009), 59–129.

[32] Howard, *Concentration Camps,* 231.

20

Freedom of Religion

Immigration historian Gary Mormino has noted that for wartime Italo-Americans, "Perhaps no single institution played a more important role than the church."[1] Although the relocation centers denied Japanese Americans of some of their rights and property, it did not take away their religious freedom. Until recently, religion hardly entered into the historical discussion of relocation. As historian Anne Michele Blankenship put it:

"The story of the Japanese Americans internment during World War II has been told from a variety of perspectives, but seldom do the religious beliefs and practices of the internees play a role."

Historians Stephen Fugita and Marilyn Fernandez agree.[2] Some of the major works on the centers do not even carry the word "religion" in the index.[3] Nonetheless, as several recent studies indicate, religion was central to the Nikkei. It was vital to their supporters outside of the centers[4] and

---

[1] Lotchin, *The Way We Really Were*, 153.
[2] A. Michele "Blankenship, Sagebrush Trees, Slanty-Eyed Santas and Uncle Sam: Christmas at Minikoda Relocation Center," MA thesis, University of North Carolina at Chapel Hill, Department of Religious Studies, 2008, 1. For a broader perspective that looks at war, religion, American Protestantism, and a developing Asian-American theology, see her "Steps to a New World Order: Ecumenism and Racial Integration during the World War II Japanese Incarceration," PhD thesis, University of North Carolina at Chapel Hill, department of Religious Studies, 2012, Abstract. See also S. S. Fugita and M. Fernandez, "Religion and Japanese Americans' View of Their World War II Incarceration," *Journal of Asian American Studies*, Vol. 5: No. 2 (2002), 115.
[3] See, for example, Daniels, *Concentration Camps USA*, 177–188, *Prisoners*, 135–46.
[4] Kobashigawa, *Okinawans*, 96.

also to the WRA, as Eisenhower learned when John McCloy informed him that "schools, churches and other essential buildings would be erected" at the centers.[5]

According to Fugita and Hernandez, the principal religions of the evacuees were Protestant and Buddhist.[6] Sandra Taylor found 40 percent Buddhists, 40 percent Protestant, 20 percent Catholic and several others like Seventh Day Adventists.[7] The CWRIC put it at 50–50 Buddhist and Christian, and minister Stephen Suzuki thought that Buddhists were more numerous.[8] Historians still debate the percentages of each, but in any case, except for Shinto (which involved Emperor worship) at Topaz, freedom of faith prevailed.[9] The *Manzanar Free Press* reported absolute religious freedom in that center.[10] The presence of the Buddhists in the centers famously illustrates the point. As Roger Daniels pointed out of the prewar period, "if a Japanese American attended a Buddhist temple, the priest was subsidized by the Japanese government."[11]

That a formerly subsidized enemy religious temple system could operate in freedom in a so-called "concentration camp" is quite extraordinary. Buddhists were unable to import their family shrines to the centers,[12] but freely practiced their faith otherwise. At Gila River one Buddhist family had more access to religion than before relocation: "Back home we didn't have a Buddhist Church in town."[13]

The Protestant churches involved themselves with the Nikkei from the very beginning. At the Tolan Hearings at Los Angeles on March 7, 1942, the decision to relocate had already been taken. Dr. E. C. Farnham, Executive Secretary of the Church Federation of Los Angeles, reported that "there have been a great many conferences during the last few weeks while this problem has been before us in most acute form."[14] In every one of the hearings on the West Coast, religious persons appeared to defend the Nikkei. The Protestants admitted the overriding importance of military necessity, but they did not believe that it required mass evacuation.

It is often written that the mayors of every West Coast City, except Harry Cain of Tacoma, favored mass evacuation of all persons of Japanese ancestry. On the other hand, no Christian spokesman or

---

[5] Eisenhower, *The President*, 119. See also the Blankenship, "Steps to a New World Order," 2.
[6] Fugita and Fernandez, "Religion," 113–37.   [7] Taylor, *Jewel*, 155.   [8] CWRIC, 40.
[9] Taylor, *Jewel*, 70.   [10] *Manzanar Free Press*, June 9, 1942, 3.
[11] Daniels, *Prisoners*, 18.   [12] Hirasuna, *Art of Gaman*, 104–05.
[13] Grapes, *Japanese American*, 157.
[14] *Tolan Hearings, Los Angeles and San Francisco*, pt. 31, 11768.

group, whether individual preacher, YMCA or YWCA leader, denominational federation, independent religious figure, or other religious person, spoke at the hearings for mass evacuation. They believed that the overwhelming majority of the Nikkei were loyal and that only the dangerous ones needed to be put in centers.[15] One study concluded that "many mainline Protestant groups first opposed internment [relocation] and then worked to help the imprisoned and resettled Japanese Americans," and so did Catholics and Episcopalians.[16]

They also insisted that if the government was adamant about mass relocation, it make every effort to protect the rights and property of those removed.[17] They tried to monitor the treatment of those initially rounded up. They sent a representative to the Justice Department camp at Missoula and several to the Immigration Stations at Oakland and other places to insure good treatment of the accused.[18] In general, as soon as it was learned that an assembly center was to be established in a locality, the surrounding churches immediately made contact with the Nikkei.

The contiguous Christian organizations, like the Tulare Ministerial Association in the Central Valley, where there was intense bitterness against the AJA, immediately sent preachers into the centers to organize services, just as they had striven to mitigate the impact of relocation at the time the Nikkei were taken from their homes.[19]

How much that act mattered was illustrated at the Tulare Fairgrounds assembly center in the spring of 1942. The Buddhists there approached the Quakers to organize a "union Buddhist-Christian service." The two quickly agreed to do so. When the service began, "the grandstand, holding 2,500 people, was full to the last seat, and the latecomers stood about on the ground below."[20] The Interdenominational Preachers' Meeting of the

[15] *Tolan Hearings, San Francisco*, pt. 29, February 21 and 23, 1942, 11196; *Portland and Seattle*, pt. 30, February 26, 28, 1942, and March 2, 1942, 11572; 11386–87; pt. 31, *Los Angeles and San Francisco*, March 6, 1942, 11628; 11755; 11768.
[16] P. M. Nagano, "United States Concentration Camps," *American Baptist Quarterly*, Vol. 13: No. 1 (1994), 48–78; Nagano, "Reverend Emery E. Andrews: Northwest's 'Man for Others,'" *American Baptist Quarterly*, Vol. 17: No. 3 (1998), 192–202; D. Yoo, "Enlightened Identities: Buddhism and Japanese Americans of California, 1924–1941," *Western Historical Quarterly*, Vol. 27: No. 3 (1996), 280–301; R. Shaffer, "Cracks in the Consensus: Defending the Rights of Japanese Americans during World War II," *Radical History Review*, Vol. 72 (1998), 84–120; L. Popp di Biase, "Neither Harmony Nor Eden: Margaret Peppers and the Exile of the Japanese Americans," *Anglican and Episcopal History*, Vol. 70: No. 1 (2001), 101–117.
[17] *Tolan Hearings, Los Angeles and San Francisco*, pt. 31, 11766–67.
[18] *Tolan Hearings, San Francisco*, pt. 30, February 21 and 23, 1942, 11196.
[19] Matsumoto, *Beyond*, 9–25. [20] Ibid., 28. Thereafter, services were usually separate.

Snake River Valley began working for the Japanese Americans at Minidoka "early in the fall of 1942."[21] This meant a lot to the Nikkei because at this early stage in their experience, they felt almost completely abandoned.

The ability of the Gila River Nikkei to leave the center was sometimes restricted, so two Caucasian ministers "ran a regular 'shopping service' searching Phoenix, Mesa, and other towns for scarce articles, getting up early in the morning to search the want ads for coolers, baby carriages, and other non-buyables, and racing off at seven o'clock in the morning to procure these scarcities for someone in camp."[22] Because of the isolation of many Japanese Americans before the war and the sometime biased reporting of the media, popular ignorance about the AJA was often profound. So the Protestants set out to overcome that misinformation and disinformation by hosting many get-togethers for people of both groups.

They aimed to overcome prejudice against the Japanese Americans by letting the neighbors meet them in person without the brokerage of the hostile part of the press. When the governor of Arizona fronted for the growers hostile to the Nikkei, the ministers requested that he be more tolerant. Whenever possible the churches created young peoples' and other conferences where Nikkei and Caucasians could meet and come to understand one another.[23] When the churches of Idaho held their summer assemblies near Sun Valley, in the stunning Saw Tooth Mountains some 100 miles away, "Minidoka was represented by a good sized delegation" of "young people." The meeting provided the Nikkei youngsters with a much needed respite from center life in addition to the networking.[24]

The churches strove especially to help the Nikkei celebrate Christmas. Christians from all over, Chinese Christians, soldiers, Boy Scouts, Women's Federations, and others poured 17,000 gifts into one celebration, and at another fete 1,000 turned out for the Christmas concerts.[25]

Other ceremonies were less festive, but equally moving. One of the most illustrative came in the wake of FDR's death on April 12, 1945, as "Americans of Japanese ancestry and their loyal parents today mourned the passing of President Franklin D. Roosevelt, commander-in-chief of the nation." They would hardly have done so if they believed, as some historians do, that FDR was a racist. Although the Roosevelt Administration had clapped them into the centers, the Nikkei had enough character not to nurse a grudge. As proof that they shared their nation's

[21] Ibid., 32.   [22] Ibid., 36.   [23] Ibid., 37.   [24] Ibid., 34.   [25] Ibid., 38–48.

grief, "the Community Christian, Maryknoll Catholic, and Buddhist churches" each held special services for the President.[26]

The Buddhist faithful organized as quickly as the others. At Heart Mountain the Buddhists began serving their faithful almost before the tar paper was nailed onto the barracks. By November the group hosted a Sunday school conference which was attended by 1,000 children. In 1943, the group held a five-day hanamatsuri celebration of the birthday of Buddha and a two-day obon later that year. In November, members formed a Young Buddhists Association under the Reverend Gyomei Kubose, the only Nisei priest in the center. Although the organization was based on a Japanese religion, it had a suspiciously American ring to it, with a president, a vice president, women's vice president, a cabinet, research chairman, social welfare chairman, corresponding secretary, recording secretary, forensic chairman, treasurer, public relations chairman, music chairman, and men's and women's athletic managers.[27]

Ordinarily services were separate, but the first at the Topaz Center was also a joint Christian and Buddhist one.[28] Highlighting the religious multiculturalism of the place, the Nikkei created the "Inter-faith Council of the Topaz Relocation Center." It listed Protestant, Catholic, Buddhist, and Seventh Day Adventist groups.

Every group held services in Japanese as well as English. That included regular worship services, Sabbath school, young people's groups, prayer groups, Wednesday evening meetings, usually in both Japanese and English for three groups, Seventh Day Adventists, Protestants, and Buddhists. Catholic services were not listed in this first announcement, but they were members of the interfaith council and maintained some churches in the system.[29] Baptists and Buddhists were especially active. The Butte (Gila River) Young Buddhist Association reported a membership campaign that netted 614 new youths in a single drive in 1943.[30] Miné Okubo sketched an "impressive Buddhist Parade and folk dance to celebrate Hanamatsuri [she called it a Flower Festival] on the anniversary of the birth of Buddha."[31] The Gila River centers featured services at the Butte and Canal Christian churches of Seventh Day Adventists and Buddhists.[32] At Granada/Amache in the fall of 1944, the

---

[26] *Heart Mountain Sentinel*, April 14, 1945, 1.   [27] Ibid., August 12, 1944, 3.
[28] *Topaz Times*, September 17, 1942, 1.   [29] Ibid., September 26, 1942, 4.
[30] *Gila News-Courier*, April 13, 1943, 4.   [31] Okubo, *Citizen*, 187.
[32] *Gila News-Courier*, January 16, 1943, 3.

lineup was Nichiren (one of six Buddhist sects),[33] Catholic, Protestant, Buddhists, and Seicho-Iye.[34]

In addition to mainline denominations, other religious groups served the centers. For example, the YMCA and YWCA, which also provided recreation materials for Americans in foreign prison camps, helped the relocation sites. Manzanar YMCA had its own building in the center.[35] The Salvation Army was also active.[36] As resettlement unfolded, the churches widened their involvement. As Toru Matsumoto explained, "Most of those who first came out [to resettle] were members of the relocation center churches."[37]

That was only the beginning of the Christian churches' involvement. The WRA Administration provided the re-settlers with a ticket to their destinations, three dollars per day for food, and twenty-five dollars per person for adjustment, which was entirely inadequate for their period of transition. So resettlement had to become a joint venture between the churches and the government. The hostel program grew out of this partnership and the work of two Caucasian Manzanar Camp workers. The initial WRA release program was limited to Nikkei who had work permits for jobs on the outside. Thomas Temple of the WRA Community Service section and the Reverend Ralph E. Smeltzer of the Brethren Service Committee at Manzanar found this system unsatisfactory.

Some outside opportunities were not well explained, so the Nikkei did not know what they were getting into. Some jobs proved unsatisfactory; the jobs seldom included housing, and the Japanese Americans did not have time to look for lodgings and hold down employment too. Many drifted back to the centers disillusioned. So Temple and Smeltzer decided that the resettlement effort would have to supply temporary quarters while the Nikkei settled into jobs and then secured more permanent lodgings.[38] That decision led to the hostel program.

After choosing thirteen Manzanar males, the two approached the Bethany Biblical Seminary (Brethren) in Chicago and asked if "a part of the dormitory could be used as a relocation [resettlement] hostel."[39]

---

[33] Embree, *Japanese Nation*, 200–03. For a fuller discussion of Japanese Buddhists see Embree, *Japanese Nation*, 164–220.

[34] *Granada Pioneer*, September 9, 1944, 4. For a brief explanation of these Japanese sects see "Japanese Groups and Associations in the United States," *Community Analysis Report No. 3*, March 1943, 4–6, Griswold Papers, MC 733, Series 3, Box 3, Folder 1, Sp. Coll., U. Ark. Special Collections.

[35] Adams, *Born Free*, 51.   [36] Suzuki, *Ministry*, 17–18.   [37] Matsumoto, *Beyond*, 58.

[38] Ibid., 70–71.   [39] Ibid.

FIG. 18. Entrance, Catholic chapel (V), Manzanar Relocation Center, California. Religion played a key role in the Nikkei experience. Photograph by Ansel Adams. Courtesy Library of Congress Prints and Photographs Division, LC-DIG-ppprs-00334.

Bethany enthusiastically assented and the thirteen boys became the first to leave the centers without having jobs in advance. They arrived at Chicago on January 13, 1943. The Friends Service Committee soon joined the

Brethren to create other hostels in Des Moines, Cincinnati, Cleveland, Washington, Detroit, Philadelphia, Minneapolis, and elsewhere. According to Toru Matsumoto, who was executive director for the Committee on Resettlement of Japanese Americans, the hostels ultimately grew to number many more than 100. He did not provide statistics past November 1945, but at that point over half of the hostels were in California, the supposed center of anti-Japanese sentiment.

All but five of the initial hostels were sponsored by Protestant denominations. In addition, the Buddhists sponsored two in Los Angeles, and Catholics, Protestants, and Jews jointly sponsored the Kansas City hostel, a cooperative. A religiously unspecified group did so for two other hostels.[40] The centers quickly became all-purpose support focal points. Both Protestants and Catholics had considerable experience, stretching back to the original YMCAs in the 1850s, in helping young people adjust to the often bewildering American cities. Jews did too, especially from the era of the settlement houses. Perhaps no cities were more incomprehensible than those sheltering defense workers in World War II.[41]

A male church member would serve as a "house mother" to new evacuees. The house mother met the evacuee at the train station, gave him/her a Cook's Tour of the city, put him/her up in temporary lodgings, and provided leads for both work and permanent housing.[42] Although it was "feared at first that they might become objects of assault as 'Jap houses,' those hostels opened without any serious difficulty," at least until the Boston hostel sought to relocate to Brooklyn. Some of the opponents were neighborhood residents in Brooklyn Heights. Yet some very high-profile people, including conservative governors John W. Bricker of Ohio and Walter Edge of New Jersey, and liberal Mayor Fiorello LaGuardia of New York City, also opposed.[43]

The ensuing struggle claimed national headlines.

It was intensified by an episode in New Jersey in which a group of Nikkei farmers were caught in the middle of a feud between Russian and Polish immigrants over who should cultivate a farm area there. The Nikkei presence was denounced. Governor Edge entered the fray to say that the AJA were not welcome, and various veterans groups backed

[40] Ibid., 142–45.
[41] For the Protestant response to the cities, see P. Boyer, *Urban Masses and Moral Order in America* (Cambridge, MA: Harvard University Press, 1978), 108–61 and for the Catholic response, see J. W. Sanders, *The Education of an Urban Minority: Catholics in Chicago, 1833–1965* (New York, NY: Oxford University Press, 1970).
[42] Matsumoto, *Beyond*, 72.   [43] Daniels, *Concentration Camps USA*, 151.

him up. Unfortunately, the Brooklyn effort came in the wake of this New Jersey flareup.[44] An interfaith group including Catholics, Jews, and Protestants searched unsuccessfully for a house in Brooklyn and finally turned to a fraternity. Hard hit by the draft and thus lacking in rents to support its house, Chi Alpha Rho on 168 Clinton Street in Brooklyn agreed to become a hostel. But before the negotiations were finalized, the *Brooklyn Eagle*, on April 16, 1944, forced the sponsors to reveal the project publicly. That caused a nationwide flurry of articles, for and against. Those of New York City overwhelmingly supported the venture.

A neighborhood petition, circulated in Brooklyn Heights, ostensibly gained 136 signatures which were brought to the attention of Congressman John T. Delaney, who took up the anti-Nikkei torch. The sponsors formed a committee to promote the hostel, headed by an Irish Catholic judge and Brooklyn Heights resident. The choice of the judge was an attempt to demonstrate to multicultural Brooklyn that the hostel was not strictly a Protestant venture. At the meeting held to discuss the matter, Mortimer Brenner, the chair, stressed that the Nikkei had already made unusual sacrifices for the war effort and that they should not be asked to make more. In one of the great speeches of the war, he pointed out that Brooklyn was a city of 3,000,000. The 2,000 Nikkei resettlers would be a drop in that demographic bucket whose presence would hardly be noticed.[45]

However, Mayor La Guardia did notice. He strenuously opposed resettlement of Japanese Americans in New York, or anywhere else on the Atlantic Coast. That brought Harold Ickes, the Secretary of the Interior, a longtime opponent of relocation, who had inherited jurisdiction over the WRA, into the fray. He cited a particularly poignant incident in which 500 girls from Arizona high schools met with girls from the Gila River centers to discuss their "mutual problems" with "tolerance and good will." In an uncharacteristically mild political statement for Ickes, he chided the governors and the mayor for being out of step with the American people: "To me, it [the girls' meeting] is indicative of the way the vast majority of our citizens feel, once they have the facts, toward those of Japanese descent .... 'Little children shall lead them'." That was a taunt that the firebrand, multicultural mayor must have winced at.[46]

[44] Matsumoto, *Beyond*, 73–75.
[45] Matsumoto, quoting the *Brooklyn Eagle* April 25, 1943, *Beyond Prejudice*, 80–81.
[46] Matsumoto, *Beyond*, 82–83. La Guardia's conduct in this situation is treated in two of the important biographies of the mayor. See R. Bayor, *Fiorello La Guardia: Ethnicity and*

Enough other New Yorkers did wince to put the hostels across. The Chi Alpha Rho national in a "fine spirited letter," enthusiastically agreed to the lease, and the neighborhood association agreed to the Nikkei presence. Reverend Smeltzer and his wife settled into the fraternity as sponsors, and the threatened violence did not occur, partly due to the careful guardianship of the New York City Police.[47] That meant victory for the program on the entire East Coast.

Friends, Brethren, Episcopalians, Jews, Congregationalists, and Unitarians had to win another in Colorado. Colorado had stood out from the rest of the Mountain West in refusing to prohibit evacuees' entry to the state before relocation to centers became mandatory. Governor Ralph L. Carr stated that to deny residence to the Nikkei would subvert the principles upon which the country was founded. The Colorado Council of Churches followed up that statement in the summer of 1942 with one upholding the rights of all peoples of color or nationality. They asked Coloradans how they would answer the question: "How do I feel about the Japanese, the Negro, the Spanish-speaking? Am I willing that they should work with me, live in my neighborhood, and go to my church?"[48]

That was an extraordinarily advanced statement for the anxious "Summer of 1942," as the resulting opposition uproar demonstrated. Antagonists soon coalesced around the idea that Japanese migrants to the state were undermining American principles and buying up farm land. Proponents of denying aliens, ineligible for citizenship, the right to own property, tried to put that proposal on the 1944 ballot but could not persuade the legislature to do so. However, they succeeded in getting the issue onto the ballot by a signature petition and that brought a showdown in a statewide referendum.

With both sides claiming to uphold fundamental American principles, they organized for the yes or no vote, with the opponents organizing from a Denver base. The *Denver Post* favored the yes vote, and the *Rocky Mountain News* upheld the no position. Civic, women's, and church groups supported the no position, including two African American churches and the *Intermountain Jewish News*.

Reform (Arlington Heights, IL: Harlan Davidson, Inc., 1993), 172–73; and T. Kessner, *Fiorello H. La Guardia and the Making of Modern New York* (New York, NY: McGraw-Hill Publishing Company, 1998), 536–8. Both treat La Guardia's opposition to the Nikkei as a lapse from his usual liberalism and sympathy for the ethnic underdog, prompted in large part by the war situation.
[47] Matsumoto, *Beyond*, 83–7.   [48] Ibid., 89.

Nor was the issue strictly joined on American versus Japanese American lines. Matsumoto believed that "the original pressure on Governor Vivian by Adams County legislators was seemingly brought at the request of truck farmers, largely of Italian descent."[49] And the referendum bore him out: "In Denver, the Negro and Jewish precincts voted 'no.' Italian and Spanish districts voted 'yes'."[50] Soldiers, who because of their war against the Imperial Japanese, were expected to vote against the Nikkei, upheld them instead, even in Denver where the yes votes carried the civilian population. When all of these identity politics were counted up, the measure had lost.

Historians have traditionally portrayed as racist the California laws prohibiting residents ineligible for citizenship from owning land.[51] Thus the Colorado vote, under extreme wartime conditions, must be taken as the reverse.[52] The Colorado voters delivered a striking indication that racism was much less prevalent than historians have led us to believe.[53]

These religious groups were instrumental in individual cases as well. Helen Murao, who desperately wanted to get her broken family out of Minidoka, was guided by a woman from the Baptist Home Mission Society to the home of a Presbyterian Minister in Madison, Wisconsin, gaining the freedom that she longed for. "They were a terrific family," she recalled. "When I came out of camp, they gave me the support that I really sorely needed, and we have been friends ever since."[54] These stories of help were repeated many times with similar results.

None was more poignant than that told by Bill Hosokawa, eventually one of the most trenchant critics of relocation, of Christmas of 1943. The Nikkei were still settling into their oft yet unfinished center homes, so the Yule celebration of 1942 at Heart Mountain had been spare and drab. The 1943 holiday promised to be comparable to the wintry landscape. Everything seemed dull, gray clouds, gray sagebrush, and gray mountains. Blizzards "whipped snow across the camp" while children and their parents packed the mess halls, hoping to see Santa. The Nikkei leaders labored greatly to stimulate Christmas cheer and finally the crowd, even

[49] Ibid., 94.   [50] Ibid., 95.
[51] For a discussion of "American racism," Daniels, *Concentration Camps USA*, 9, 16–18.
[52] C. Abbott, S. J. Leonard, and D. McComb, *Colorado: A History of a Centennial State* (Niwot, CO: University of Colorado Press, 1984), 304–6.
[53] Matsumoto, *Beyond Prejudice*, 89–96. R. Daniels, one of the founding fathers of the concentration camp thesis, does not mention the role of the churches in the resettlement process.
[54] Grapes, *Japanese American*, 167.

the Zoot Suiters, began to get into the spirit, singing loud and longingly the familiar carols. Suddenly, there came Santa, carried in an olive drab, iconic, Deuce and a Half Army truck, "riding from mess hall to mess hall."

The younger children gasped in pop-eyed amazement ... The gifts were passed out, and there was enough for everyone from the youngest to the oldest grandmother.

There were cards with the gifts. They came from the Joneses, the Smiths and the Browns, and common folk whose names indicated they had come to America with later waves of immigration. The gifts came from Billings and Boston, from a mountain colony in New Mexico and an orphanage where the children had saved pennies to buy gifts for little evacuee children who had no homes either.

The grayness left the camp that night, and never really returned. It wasn't the gifts alone. It was the realization that we no longer were forgotten nor unwanted. They – the American people – remembered us, and had let us know with this outpouring of little gifts from cities and hamlets the country over.[55]

Protestants, Catholics, Jews, and Buddhists, individually and institutionally, played a magnificent role in softening relocation.

---

[55] Hosokawa, *Thirty Five Years*, 32–3. The Christmas story is based on Hosokawa. He was a central observer of both the Heart Mountain center, wartime journalism, and the entire relocation and resettlement process.

21

Education, the Passion of Dillon Myer

"Education was Dillon Myer's passion," wrote historian Robert Harvey. Part of his enthusiasm stemmed from Myer's hope to use education to promote assimilation. Critics have charged that he was destroying Nikkei culture by so doing, but the Nisei assimilation, from a behavioral standpoint, was already a fait accompli. Many of their own leaders like Bill Hosokawa saw assimilation as the best way for the Nikkei to avoid another misfortune like relocation. Closing down the Little Tokyos was the means to open up the promise of American life to the AJA, which Hosokawa believed happened after 1945.[1]

Therefore, the WRA provided an education to 25,000 Japanese American school-age youngsters, including 16,000 secondary students.[2] At a time when pre-primary school education, like kindergarten, was far from universal, the relocation centers provided nursery schools, and Manzanar, Gila River and most others had kindergarten instruction as well.[3] Miné Okubo noted that Topaz alone had three nursery schools.[4] Education for the handicapped and a wide range of extracurricular

---

[1] Hosokawa, *Thirty Five Years*, 44–45.

[2] WRA, *Education Program in War Relocation Centers* (Washington, DC: War Relocation Authority, 1945), 13.

[3] Hansen and Jesch, *Japanese American*, Part V, Vol. 1, 142; B. J. Grapes, *Japanese American*, 157. North Carolina, for example, had only 10.5 percent of its five year olds in kindergartens by the year 1970. R. Murray, *History of the Public School Kindergarten in North Carolina* (New York, NY: MSS Information Corporation, 1974), 8. For the diffusion of kindergartens around the world, see R. Wollons, ed., *Kindergartens and Cultures: The Global Diffusion of an Idea* (New Haven, CT: Yale University Press, 2000), for the United States, 17–42; for Japan, 113–36.

[4] Okubo, *Citizen*, 165.

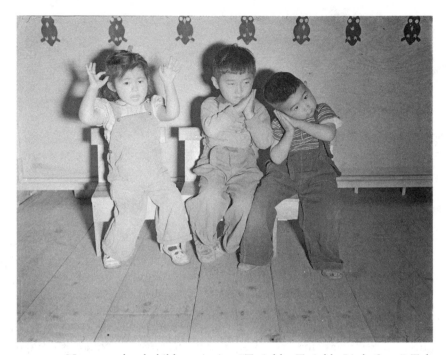

FIG. 19. Nursery school children singing "Twinkle, Twinkle Little Star," Tule Lake Relocation Center, California. Central Photographic File of the War Relocation Authority, 1942–45. Record Group 210: Records of the War Relocation Authority, 1941–89. Courtesy US National Archives and Records Administration.

activities were supplied. Students even operated their own cooperatives and published school newspapers.[5]

High schools followed the tripartite division of college preparatory, general curriculum, and practical arts curriculum.[6] The schools offered the usual educational courses, and English was particularly stressed in nursery and post-secondary levels because youngsters at the bottom and adults at the top of the schools had language deficiencies. The alien character of much of the Japanese American community had singled them out before relocation, and the WRA wanted to escape that problem in the future.[7] The schools were not bountifully supplied with equipment and books, but they were certainly adequately supplied. Schools offered summer programs for those in need of makeup or catch up courses, but

[5] WRA, *Education Program*, 11.   [6] Ibid., 15.   [7] Ibid., 19.

FIG. 20. Grammar school students studying math, Tule Lake Relocation Center, California. The centers provided nursery school, kindergarten, grade and high school, night and vocational schools, and encouraged college education. Central Photographic File of the War Relocation Authority, 1942–45. Record Group 210: Records of the War Relocation Authority, 1941–89. Courtesy US National Archives and Records Administration.

"many students accepted employment in the offices and on the farms during the summer months."[8]

Judgments about these schools have varied.

Charles Wollenberg argues that it was hypocritical to teach democracy to children who were deprived of their homes. But the schools also taught the three Rs and other subjects besides, so the inconsistency did not substantially invalidate center education.[9] And the courses had crucial relevance for the evacuees' post-center life. For example, at Topaz the

---

[8] Ibid.
[9] C. Wollenberg, "Schools behind Barbed Wire," *California Historical Quarterly*, Vol. 55: No. 3 (1976), 210–17; K. L. Riley, "Schools behind Barbed Wire," *Journal of the Midwest History of Education Society*, Vol. 23 (1996), 31–5; At Heart Mountain, the schools pursued the usual curriculum and featured "many extracurricular programs." M. Inouye, "Heart Mountain High School," 56–64.

engineering department spent a year training Nikkei carpenters, electricians, and plumbers. At the time of relocation, most Nikkei worked as farmers, nurserymen, fishermen, and retailers. The new trades were a potential step up into well-paying, union jobs in the urban areas to which they returned. However much we might argue about the quality of these schools, they must have been head and shoulders above those of the towns around the center. Some schools ranged in size up to 2,000, which was often a population greater than the contiguous villages, like Powell, at 1,500.

Perhaps the Topaz and Rohwer high schools were typical. They offered courses in English, social science, mathematics, sciences, foreign languages, commercial, manual arts, physical education, music, and art possibly later.[10] Rohwer High School taught about the same ones. They also offered courses in elementary Japanese language and courses for college credit in algebra, trigonometry, geometry, accounting, and a wide range of courses in the creative arts, especially those which might appeal to people of Japanese ancestry.[11] Some classes seem somewhat problematical in retrospect, like Americanization classes for Issei.[12]

Still, with so many opponents on the outside ready to pounce, these classes doubtless served to help keep the critics at bay, even if they did not benefit the Issei. Yet they probably did. Thus adult education paralleled primary and secondary. And whether the Nikkei baiters like Colorado Senator Ed C. Johnson were aware of it or not, the Japanese language was also taught at Amache and elsewhere after June, 1943. Gila River residents quickly instituted "a large-scale night school" which drew students "in droves" to prepare themselves for the challenges of the postwar world.[13] At Topaz, teacher Toyo Kawakami taught English to both those Kibei and Issei who had little command of it. She remembered the Issei as very respectful students who wanted to master English in order better to understand their own Americanized children and to adapt to the outside English-speaking world after the centers.[14]

Partly because of this desire, night school adult education thrived. At Heart Mountain, the adult education division reported a stunning increase in enrollment from January 1, 1944, to April 1, from 1,202 to 1,720, while at Rohwer the total stood at 1,700 in early 1943.[15] The editors at the *Heart Mountain Sentinel* thought that the rise in

---

[10] *Topaz Times*, October 7, 1942, 2.   [11] *Rohwer Outpost*, January 1, 1943, 12.
[12] Okubo, *Citizen*, 167.   [13] *Gila News-Courier*, January 19, 1943, 2.
[14] Grapes, *Japanese American*, 149.   [15] *Rohwer Outpost*, January 6, 1943, 1.

enrollment stemmed in large part from Issei desire to be able to write to their sons in service and to other Nisei who were now increasingly scattered around the world by resettlement.[16] And at least at Manzanar there existed a junior college, "recognized and accredited by the State of California."[17]

At Manzanar, high school classes began in July, 1942, and Butte High School held its first graduation in February of 1943.[18] At Poston, a new high school, designed by Japanese American architects and built of adobe bricks manufactured on site, commenced construction in January, 1943.[19] Another school, worth $308,000, began construction at the Granada/Amache Center at the same time.[20] Topaz High School graduated 150 students from its first graduating class.[21] Former pupil George Hirano remembered that "school was really a godsend to me." The Topaz schools ultimately claimed 1,000 elementary, nursery school and kindergarten students. The high and junior high pupils eventually totaled 850.[22] At Manzanar, the schools worked closely with the Inyo County schools.[23]

Dorothy C. Cragen, the County Superintendent of Schools, a staunch defender of the Nikkei, noted that all of the Manzanar teachers were Caucasians, who had trained Nikkei assistants. In her opinion, "the teachers who were there [at Manzanar] were very fine, and they all came up and registered their credentials with us just as if they were in our schools, although they didn't have to at all because they were working at a government school."[24] Although one historian believed that the general center personnel "shared the contempt of the general population for 'Japs'," Cragen noted that the school teachers "did everything that they could to promote the idea that they [the Nikkei pupils] were American."[25]

Students from California schools found it hard to adapt, in part, because they had usually come from schools that were integrated. Said one Gila parent, "I also thought at times that it was too bad that my children did not have the Caucasian contacts in the regular school, but

[16] *Heart Mountain Sentinel*, April 1, 1944, 8.   [17] *Rohwer Outpost*, July 31, 1943, 6.
[18] *Manzanar Free Press*, July 2, 1942, 1; *Gila News-Courier*, February 20, 1943, 3.
[19] Estes and Estes, "Letters From Camp," 31.
[20] *Gila News-Courier*, January 9, 1943, 2.   [21] Okubo, *Citizen*, 188.
[22] Ibid., 103–08.   [23] Hansen and Jesch, *Japanese American*, Part V, Vol. 1, 195.
[24] Ibid., Part V, Vol. 1, 194.
[25] Ibid., The Fullerton interviews are full of testimony of people who had no such "contempt" for the Japanese Americans.

I knew that it would not be for all of the time."[26] Often the only Caucasians pupils were the children of the staff. Academic freedom prevailed, at least in some of these settings and probably in all. At Heart Mountain, the WRA instructed teachers to avoid discussing relocation, "but the subject inevitably came up in civics and history classes."[27]

Since the newspaper editors in every center discussed relocation incessantly, it is hard to imagine that students, with Nikkei teachers, would not have. And just as the Nikkei sports teams played outside high schools, those schools involved the evacuees in their educational programs. Right after the Nikkei lads beat Fillmore in football, the center school superintendent announced that "Topaz High School students will participate in Fillmore High School's program . . . honoring National Education Week." The theme was to be "Education for World Understanding."[28] Topaz High drama students presented a play, "The Vane Effort" at the Fillmore High Auditorium.[29]

For several reasons, educators were extremely well qualified. Many of the teachers were adventurous and nurturing, who wanted to make amends to a dispossessed people. In addition, in order "to avoid disrupting neighboring schools," the WRA recruited its teachers nationally. Finally, a nationwide shortage of students at the high school and college levels enabled them to furlough teachers not needed then, but who might be needed later. That created a teaching corps at the relocation centers with 35 percent MA degrees and over 43 percent MA degrees in the high schools. In addition, 55 percent of the teachers had baccalaureate degrees, and only 9 percent had fewer than 120 hours of college. Many evacuees, though not certified to teach, had considerable training and served as teaching assistants. Each teacher had some. Quite a few personnel had advanced degrees. [30]

For example, the head of the adult education program at Topaz, plus Superintendent of Schools, John Carlisle, and acting high school principal, Reese Maughan, were PhDs.[31] Dr. Genevieve Carter, superintendent of the Manzanar High School, was also a PhD, as was Nat A. Griswold, director of adult education at Rohwer and Dr. Lloyd A. Garrison, superintendent of the Amache schools.[32] The schools were generally certified by

---

[26] Grapes, *Japanese American*, 157.   [27] Inouye, "Heart Mountain High School," 59.
[28] *Topaz Times*, November 4, 1943, 2.   [29] Ibid., November 9, 1943, 3.
[30] WRA, *Educational Program*, 3.
[31] *Topaz Times*, October 7, 1942, 2; October 10, 1942, 4; October 21, 1942, 1.
[32] Hansen and Jesch, *Japanese American*, Part V, Vol. 1, 194; *Rohwer Outpost*, January 1, 1943, 12.

the state departments of education where they were located.³³ That was crucial. As the *Granada Pioneer* said, "Graduates from the school [Amache High School] may now be admitted to higher institutions of learning on certificate."³⁴ Dr. Garrison hired a staff "that would be sympathetic to the plight of the Japanese Americans" and most of the teachers were Caucasian, assisted by the evacuees.³⁵ Each of the schools had "advisory school boards of resident evacuees" and Parent Teachers Associations.³⁶

Most schools experienced problems of some sort.

Shortages of books, buildings, furniture, and teachers plagued the first days.³⁷ Again, the subject needs to be placed in context. Primary and secondary education all over the country suffered from chronic shortages of teachers, who were drafted or lured to higher paying defense jobs.³⁸ According to historian Mamoru Inouye, the Nikkei teachers felt the same lure and left Heart Mountain for resettlement or defense jobs more frequently than Caucasian teachers.³⁹

Still, these deficiencies were largely overcome.

The construction was Spartan, but not unforgiving. Classrooms were 32 feet by 21. At a time when many American schools did not have one, Topaz was constructing a 2,000-seat auditorium.⁴⁰ At Amache, the high school received priority and ended up costing $308,000, which included both a gymnasium and an auditorium. Colorado politicians fussed about the expense of teaching "Japs" and got the funding for the elementary schools temporarily stopped. They aired the usual grounds of coddling the Nikkei and wasting money that was not being spent on schools outside the centers, but those schools plowed ahead anyway.

Others did too. Perhaps the ultimate proof of Myer's passion for Nikkei education was the WRA policy that "Education will be furnished

³³ WRA, *Education Programs*, 5.   ³⁴ Quoted in the *Topaz Times*, June 12, 1943, 2.
³⁵ Harvey, *Amache*, 103.   ³⁶ WRA, *Educational Program*, 6.
³⁷ Estes and Estes, "Letters," 30–31.
³⁸ WRA, *Education Program*, 10. For educational problems during the war see I. L. Kandel, *The Impact of the War upon American Education* (Chapel Hill, NC: The University of North Carolina Press, 1948); G. Giordano, Wartime Schools: How World War II Changed American Education (New York, NY: Peter Lang Publishing); and H. M. Bulpett, "The Impact of World War II on American Education: A Nation Looking to Its Schools for Help and Hope," UNC undergraduate seminar paper, Fall 2006; T. James, "'Life Begins with Freedom': The College Nisei, 1942–1945," *History of Education Quarterly*, Vol. 25: Nos. 1–2 (1985), 155–74.
³⁹ Inouye, "Heart Mountain High School," 60.   ⁴⁰ *Topaz Times*, October 26, 1943, 1.

to children of school age" even for the *children of repatriates*, who intended to go to Japan after the war.[41]

Some 2,870–4,500 (the figure varies) AJA students also attended college, mostly in the Midwest and East. Early on, Milton Eisenhower's staff told him that the Nisei college students would have to interrupt their educations if relocation were strictly observed. Even Governor Culbert Olson, one of the supporters of relocation, though a milder version, wanted Eisenhower to prevent that. Several books carry the story of the College Nisei. I have been most influenced by that of Gary Okihiro because it is more consistent with my own research in the primary sources, and that of Robert O'Brien because he was a hands-on expert.[42] Eisenhower, by this time, thought of evacuation as "the tragedy of relocation." So he set out to address the problem by appealing to college presidents all over the country to accept a few of these young people. Every single one turned him down!

Fortunately, several people told him to contact Clarence Pickett, a "prominent Quaker leader." Pickett responded by traveling around the country persuading the administrators to change their minds. He helped establish the National Student Relocation Council, and it proceeded to place the students.[43] However, the Council also had an independent origin in the University of California at Berkeley, where some sixty representatives of YWCAs and YMCAs met in March, 1942, and launched their own council.[44]

The two merged and these strands came together to form the Japanese American Student Relocation Council.[45] It had the blessing of President Roosevelt and Assistant Secretary of War John J. McCloy among others.[46] Many college and religious denominations, including Jews and Catholics, but mostly Protestants, did too. Christian bodies, YMCAs, YWCAS,

[41] WRA, "Comprehensive Statement in Response to Senate Resolution 166," 34, RG 210, Box 2, NA.
[42] Okihiro, *Storied*, 49–117; O'Brien, *College Nisei*; see also K. L. Riley, *Schools behind Barbed Wire: The Untold Story of Wartime Internment and the Children of Arrested Enemy Aliens* (Lanham, MD: Rowan and Littlefield Publishers Inc., 2002) deals with children in Justice Department camps, not relocation centers. See also A. W. Austin, *From Concentration Camp to Campus: Japanese American Students and World War II* (Urbana, IL: University of Illinois Press, 2004).
[43] M. Eisenhower, *The President*, 120–21. I have used both names to avoid mistaking Milton Eisenhower for Dwight.
[44] Jacoby, *Tule Lake*, 61.   [45] O'Brien, *College Nisei*, 60–72.
[46] For another, but consistent version of the College Nisei, see G. Y. Okihiro, *Storied*, 28–48.

missionaries, Friends, denominations, seminaries, Bible Institutes, Salvation Armies, and Wesleyans – Connecticut, Ohio, Illinois, Dakota – are written all over the story.[47] By the 1945–46 school year, 2,870 students enrolled in 448 universities, 45 percent in the Midwest.[48]

Before Pearl Harbor destroyed their foothold, some 3,259 AJA attended college on the West Coast, including 2,567, or 79 percent, in allegedly racist California. The University of California at Berkeley, still the flagship school of the system in 1941, led at 485. More than 100 enrolled at Los Angeles City College (265), UCLA (244), Pasadena Junior College (123), Sacramento Junior College (224), San Francisco Junior College (145), San Jose State (111), and the University of Southern California (113).[49]

The figures for the University of California and Sacramento Junior College were especially revealing for both the argument about race and Nikkei advance into the mainstream. The Berkeley numbers represented a substantial Japanese American presence at the school with the highest prestige in the state. Because of the McClatchy newspaper chain, Sacramento was a center of opposition to the Nikkei. Yet their presence at Sacramento Junior College was almost equal to their numbers at UCLA. The Nikkei youth had a solid foothold (fourteen to eighty) in the less prominent schools in the interior at Modesto, Bakersfield, Fresno, Riverside, Salinas, San Bernardino, Stockton, Redlands, and Yuba City. In Oregon, the Nikkei had forty-one representatives at Oregon State and twenty-seven at the University of Oregon and a substantial 458 at neighboring University of Washington.[50] In June, 1940, Stanford alone graduated fourteen Nisei.[51] Given the fact that in 1941 the average age of the Nisei was only nineteen, these statistics imply a creditable record for both schools and students.

Moreover, the presence of Nikkei in college meant that they were accepted educationally all over the country. These figures are especially revealing of the pre-Pearl Harbor Nikkei position. To make an accurate comparison, no African American attended any predominantly white college in the American South in 1941. Nor were there any all-Nikkei colleges on the West Coast comparable to the many segregated universities in the historic South, such as Howard, Tuskegee, Atlanta University (5) and circa 100 others. Real racism prevailed in that section, compared to which the animus against AJA on the West Coast was minimal and did

---

[47] Ibid., 111, 113, 131.   [48] O'Brien, *College Nisei*, 60–91, 112–13, 116.
[49] Ibid., 132–3.   [50] Ibid., 135–6.   [51] *Rafu Shimpo*, June 14, 1940, 1.

not preclude minority admission to the best colleges all over the West.[52] The Nisei themselves understood the difference and said so unequivocally: "The Nisei have nothing to complain about racial prejudice in this country if they would but consider the plight of the Negroes," wrote columnist Tad Ueno, in mid-1940.[53]

That disparity was true even though African Americans had been in the British colonies and the United States since 1619. It is often argued by members of the race school that the Nisei went to college because they could not obtain jobs in the mainstream economy.[54] That argument is oblivious to the nature of Japanese American culture. Nikkei respect for education stemmed from "Confucian ideology and Buddhist schools during the Tokugawa period (1600–1868)" but they were also a very shrewd, heady, business people, and it is not likely that they would have invested in a college education if their children were going to end up working in family flower shops anyway. Their college specialties[55] certainly did not correspond with the Nikkei parochial economy. For example, in June, 1940, CIT first awarded a PhD to a Nikkei, Dr. Kenichi Watanabe, who majored in physics and "will continue his research studies atop Mount Palomar," the world-renowned Southern California observatory. At the same time, Cal-Berkeley awarded William J. Furuta, a graduate student in pathology working under "the supervision of Dr. Hermann Becks of the George Williams Hooper Foundation for Medical Research, a $1,000 fellowship."[56] And since the average age of the Nisei was only nineteen, most of the College Nisei would not have been college graduates when the war broke out. So it is not possible that a large number could have been turned away by mainstream American businesses.

In addition, some 23,000 Nikkei lived outside the West, the supposed home of anti-Japanese sentiment.

At the very least, their college training would have prepared the Nisei for the many jobs they could hold working for Japanese firms in the United States and the Pacific economy. Facility with the Imperial tongue was actually an advantage in applying to American firms dealing with the Orient. As one JACL spokesmen explained of his experience after college,

[52] This list does not even include all African American schools like Lincoln in Pennsylvania and Wilberforce in Ohio, nor Pembroke University in North Carolina, a predominantly American Indian school.
[53] *Rafu Shimpo*, June 14, 1940, 1.   [54] Daniels, *Concentration Camps, USA*, 111.
[55] For these, see also Okihiro, *Storied*, 46ff.   [56] *Rafu Shimpo*, June 14, 1940, 1.

"I made application to some of the larger companies on the coast, and the first thing they asked me was 'Can you speak and write Japanese?'"[57]

As experience proved, the Nikkei who resettled outside the West were in high demand. The center newspapers carried countless want ads for Japanese Americans in many different positions all over the country. Outside the West they were not restricted to Japanese firms. For example, the *Heart Mountain Sentinel* carried notices that Nikkei had left to work for the Northwestern Railroad at Emory and Marshall, Washington; another departed for Chicago to employment by Sears Roebuck; another, to Kansas City headed for Ace Radio and Refrigerator Service; and yet another for the C. Hausermann Company in Melrose Park, Illinois.[58] According to historian John Stephan, some 23,000 AJA already lived outside the West Coast when the war began. Migrating from one's difficult home market was the traditional way that immigrants/in migrants improved their lot.[59] Apparently, quite a few Nikkei understood that it was possible to get jobs elsewhere.

Historian Valerie Matsumoto argues that for young Japanese women, college liberated them from their patriarchal families.[60] Historians have sometimes considered the Nikkei college experience problematical, but the Nikkei themselves would have disagreed. May Yoshino wrote to the *Topaz Times*, "There are sixty-five Nisei students at the University [of Utah] . . . Having attended the University of California my first impression naturally was that things here were on a smaller scale, but the attitude of the students and faculty is a friendly one." She went on that "there are plenty of school girl jobs here for those who want to study at the university."[61] Cromwell Mukai wrote from the University of Nebraska that "it was rather a strange feeling to be among all Caucasians again," but that "the people here are very nice and friendly to us."[62] Others understood the complexity of the situation. A student from Huron College wrote from South Dakota that

[57] *Tolan Hearings, San Francisco*, pt. 29, 11355. It would be interesting to learn how many Caucasians the Imperial Japanese firms employed. It would certainly have been to their advantage to do so.

[58] *Heart Mountain Sentinel*, April 8, 1944, 6.

[59] J. Bodnar, The Transplanted: A History of Immigrants in Urban America (Bloomington, IN: Indiana University Press, 1985), 43–5, 57–71.

[60] V. Matsumoto, loc cit, 447. See also L. A. Ito, "Japanese American Women and the Student Relocation Movement, 1942–1945," *Frontiers*, Vol. 21: No. 3 (2000), 1–24.

[61] *Topaz Times*, October 24, 1942, 3.   [62] *Topaz Times*, October 28, 1942, 3.

most of the young college men of this city are going off to war, and I wonder how the parents feel as to our coming ... The going is rather awkward at first, and at times, embarrassing. Some of these people have never seen a Japanese, according to my guess. Naturally they wonder what we're like and whether we can be trusted.

In some places they were trusted a lot. Paul Tani, a member of the first graduating class of Topaz High School, was elected freshman class president at Heidelberg College in Ohio.[63] A student wrote from Huron College that "I found the real meaning of campus life here. I have lost my racial consciousness and students treat me like 'one of them,' showing neither favoritism nor intolerance."[64] Still, the Arkansas authorities opposed higher education for the internees of their centers.[65] In a few places the College Nisei encountered hostility to their presence,[66] but overall they faced "remarkably little opposition."[67] The students received a good education and enjoyed access to an extraordinary range of extra-curricular activities.[68]

Given these oft repeated pro-Nikkei sentiments, it is clear that lots of westerners were not racist. Except for *Storied Lives*, I am not aware of any book that sets out to document the friendly side of western or American culture that the letters in the center newspapers of college Nisei repeatedly reveal. Professor Okihiro found the same predominance of friendly feeling in archival sources as are found in letters to the oft-maligned center newspapers.

In contrast, in European camps, education was simply outlawed because the Nazis wanted the record of Jewish existence "expunged from the collective memory of European history."[69] The Nazis did not put children into schools; they put those over ten years of age into slave labor camps and "selected" those younger for death camps. As these pages indicate elsewhere, Japanese American children did not live in Eden, but they enjoyed many advantages over those living in concentration camps. They went to school, had student government, played sports and were cheerleaders, participated in honor society and student council, hiked and camped in the mountains, and above all, they lived with their families. Most historians of the relocation center experience stress the strain put on

---

[63] *Topaz Times*, October 19, 1943, 1.   [64] O'Brien, *College Nisei*, 85.
[65] For other accounts, M. A. Robertson, "Wanda Robertson: A Teacher for Topaz," *Utah Historical Quarterly*, Vol. 69: No. 2 (2001), 120–38.
[66] Okihiro, *Storied*, 69, 75–76, 80–81, 98ff.
[67] *Christian Century*, November 4, 1942, 1294.   [68] Okihiro, *Storied*, 76, 79, 89–97.
[69] Bennett, *Shadow of the Swastika*, 182.

Japanese American families. They also stress that the institution of the family endured.[70]

The difficulty of evaluating the outcomes of education is enormous and that of the centers has often been questioned. Nonetheless, the Nikkei kids who had some part of their education in the relocation centers did extraordinarily well in later years, usually placing in the top cohort of standardized tests.

The College Nisei leadership experience puts the American and European contrast in high definition. When the Russians marched into Poland and the Baltic states in 1939, they sought to exterminate the leadership classes of those four countries. Between 1939 and 1941, the Russians rounded up the Polish, Estonian, Latvian, and Lithuanian elites – lawyers, priests, businessmen, scientists, teachers, government servants, soldiers, and politicians. The Soviets deported some to the wastes of Siberia, some to their own concentration camps, the gulags, and some to the forests to be shot. The infamous Katyn Massacre of Polish officers was only the most astounding example of this policy. In their place the Russians put their own followers. In turn, when the Nazis reversed those conquests with their own, they also reversed the attacks, rounding up the allies of the Soviets, marking them for slave labor, extermination in the forests, or genocide in the death camps. The point of both approaches was to rid Poland and the Baltic nations of leadership groups who might oppose Soviet or Nazi rule, with the added Nazi motive of genocide against Jews and Slavs. It should probably be called by the modern term "ethnic cleansing" from the top down.

Playing off one ethnic, racial, or nationality group against another is as old as history and is just as nefarious. But the American approach was markedly different. The Nisei were just emerging before the war to assume leadership in their own community. The aging Issei did not always yield gracefully, but they must have seen the writing on the wall, and they were giving way. Yet instead of destroying a leadership cadre, the WRA sought to preserve and nurture it through education and thus access to the mainstream. They did not send the Nisei young people, their future leaders, to slave labor; they sent them to college.

---

[70] M. Mackey posits the "destruction of the family unit," but some other studies do not go beyond noting strains on the family.

22

The Right to Know

Information and the Free Flow of Ideas

In the American centers, inmates had access to myriad sources of information. From the outset, Milton Eisenhower intended that the Nikkei should have their own newspapers. These were established everywhere, sometimes using the equipment from the prewar Japanese ethnic press which had ceased publication after May 1942, largely because their readers were now in the centers instead of San Francisco and Los Angeles.[1] On other occasions, the local town newspapers printed the center sheets on their own equipment, as did the Cody *Enterprise* for the *Heart Mountain Sentinel*.[2]

In either case, AJA published these newspapers, with, depending on the historian one cites, more or less government oversight. For example, the *Denson Tribune*, edited by Paul Yokota in the Arkansas relocation centers, was noted for its editorial independence, especially that concerning constitutional and human rights.[3] Elsewhere historians found less freedom.[4] Yet center newspapers disputed this claim and argued instead

---

[1] Mizuno, "Self-Censorship by Coercion," 50.   [2] Hosokawa, *Frying Pan*, 52–5.

[3] J. Friedlander, "Journalism behind Barbed Wire, 1942–44; An Arkansas Relocation Center Newspaper," *Journalism Quarterly*, Vol. 62: No. 2 (1985), 243–6, 271.

[4] L. Kessler, "Fettered Freedoms: the Journalism of World War II Japanese Internment Camps," *Journalism History*, Vol. 15: Nos. 2–3 (1988), 70–9; B. Hosokawa, "The Sentinel Story," *Peace and Change*, Vol. 23: No. 2 (1998), 135–47; T. Mizuno, "Journalism under Military Guards and Searchlights: Newspaper Censorship at Japanese American Assembly Camps during World War II," *Journalism History*, Vol. 29: No. 3 (2003), 98–106 and Mizuno, "Government Suppression of the Japanese Language in World War II Assembly Camps," *Journalism and Mass Communication Quarterly*, Vol. 80: No. 4 (2003), 849–65; C. A. Luther, "Reflections of Cultural Identities in Conflict: Japanese American Internment Camp Newspapers during World War II," *Journalism*

that they had absolute freedom.[5] Harold Jacoby, who knew the Tule Lake administrators personally, said that he knew of no instance in which a newspaper edition was submitted to the center authorities before publication, nor an instance when an editorial or article was "planned for publication." He thought it possible that the close working relationship between the center press corps and the WRA administrators might have inhibited them somewhat. But outside of that there was no official influence over the press.[6]

Nobody in the press ever has absolute freedom, but this view was closer to the reality of center papers. Luckily, we have a record of the *Heart Mountain Sentinel* from Bill Hosokawa's autobiography to guide the historian. He was recruited by the staff to start the paper and was able to draw on the paper supply of the *Cody Enterprise* and the talents of San Francisco and Los Angeles veterans of the *Nichi Bei* and *Rafu Shimpo*. Eventually circulation climbed to 6,000 within the center and outside to supporters in the West.[7]

The center newspapers discussed a wide variety of issues and pulled few punches. The *Heart Mountain Sentinel* editorial policy called for reporting the center news and any outside domestic news that affected the interests of the Nikkei.[8] It was typical. For example, when the San Francisco government and development interests began an attack on health conditions in "Japtown" in that city, calling it a "Japanese slum," *Topaz Times* editor Tomoye Takahashi took them to task. When the district was a Nikkei neighborhood, it was both neat and clean, he reported. Wartime overcrowding led to the present rundown condition, where "Negroes have been forced to pile in because they cannot find other housing."[9]

Bill Hosokawa, in an editorial reprinted in the *Topaz Times*, vigorously attacked the Martin Dies Committee for "witch hunting" the Nikkei.[10] Harumi Kawahara sounded a similarly critical, if mournful note when he described the irony of the first anniversary of the Topaz relocation:

May, always a beautiful month, but for us a raw reminder of another May when we were expelled from our homes and lives of tranquility to contend against the unknown. Wonder where we'll be, May 1944.[11]

History, Vol. 29: No. 2 (2003), 69–81. Kessler and Mizuno found more censorship; Hosokawa, Luther, Jacoby, and Friedlander found less.
[5] *Manzanar Free Press*, editorial, June 9, 1942, 2.   [6] Jacoby, *Tule Lake*, 49.
[7] Hosokawa, *Frying Pan*, 52.   [8] Ibid., 51.   [9] *Topaz Times*, June, 19, 1942, 5.
[10] Ibid., June 19, 1943, 2.   [11] Ibid., May 27, 1943, 2.

Barry Saiki, editor of the *Rohwer Outpost*, "greeted" the new year of 1943 by reminding the government that it had divested the Nikkei of both their property and civil rights.[12]

In short, the center newspapers criticized anything that they thought needed it, the US government, their political opponents, each other, the WRA, the San Francisco government, the Dies Committee, California racists, politicians like Earl Warren, and constitutional and political decisions affecting the Nikkei. The only two issues that passed largely unreported were town, state, and national politics and the war itself. The English language sections of the press did not report on military developments except to cover the exploits of the 100th Battalion and 442nd Regimental Combat Team.

Unlike the pre-war *Rafu Shimpo*, the *Japanese American News* (*Nichi Bei*), and the *New World Sun*, each of which often if, politely, championed Imperial Japanese over American foreign policy,[13] the center papers stayed away from the subject of foreign affairs.[14] Otherwise, it is hard to imagine what the supposed government censorship actually censored. What was left unsaid? Which Nikkei rights went unsupported?

In any case, the point of censorship is problematical because of the existence of the *Pacific Citizen*, the organ of the JACL, published in Salt Lake City, which was outside the jurisdiction of the Western Defense Command and the WRA and thus not subject to their editorial restraint. The *Citizen* published on a wide range of subjects, denouncing censorship of letters at the Tule Lake camp, the alleged "fascism" of the opponents of the Nikkei. Likewise, it denounced the transgressions of Nikkei enemies like Representative Leland Ford or Assistant LA County District Attorney Clyde Shoemaker's touting the great American naval win at Midway and the lesser one at the Coral Sea.

The scathing article by JACL president Saburo Kido denouncing conditions at Poston in its early days was as hard hitting as it gets.[15] To prove the power of the Nikkei press, when the *Pacific Citizen* revealed that outgoing letters from the Tule Lake center were being censored (which was not authorized by the WRA), the practice soon ceased.[16] The anti-

[12] *Rohwer Outpost*, January 1, 1943, 4.
[13] Nishimoto, *Inside*, 116. Nishimoto found earlier examples going back to 1931.
[14] See almost any issue of these papers, January 1, 1940–December 7, 1941: for example *Rafu Shimpo*, February 18, 1940, 2 or *Japanese American News: Nichi Bei*, January 9, 1940, 1; January 12, 1; January 14, 1; January 18, 1. Hereafter *Nichi Bei*.
[15] *Pacific Citizen*, July 30, 1942, 2–3.   [16] Ibid., July 16, 1942, 4; July 23, 1942, 4.

WRA *Rocky Shimpo* published in Denver provided another check on censorship. The Nikkei had numerous media outlets.

The mechanics of center newspaper publication make it equally unlikely that the newspapers were collaborationist, that is, taking the WRA side and not mirroring majority center attitudes. The reason is simple enough. The center newspapers were owned by the center cooperatives, to which nearly every family belonged and, as Hosokawa noted, were very widely read. It is not likely that the Nikkei majority would subsidize newspapers to publish opinions and news that would outrage their own. And the evacuees also had access to outside newspapers, so that they knew as much from that source as Americans outside the centers did. The Topaz Center was typical. Since so many of its residents were from the San Francisco Bay Area, the center library regularly received both the SF *Chronicle* and the *Oakland Tribune*.[17] The major magazines of the era, *Life, Time, Popular Mechanics*, and others circulated freely in the deserts as well.[18]

So whatever degree of oversight/censorship the government exercised over the center papers, these actions did not materially disrupt the flow of information into or out of the centers. For example, the papers followed avidly news like the hearings of the Martin Dies congressional committee, the reception of Japanese American servicemen in various communities like Seattle, the adaptation of former residents who had resettled, the activities of friends on the outside, the US Court decisions on the legality of relocation, and so forth.[19] They also exchanged mail with people from the outside. The residents of the Poston, Arizona, center not only sent letters, but complained in them of their conditions as well.[20] So did the Portland detainees at the YWCA-run assembly center.[21]

This flow of information was reinforced by a continual stream of visitors shuttling in and out. Many of these were soldiers, so they brought news from all over the United States and, if wounded, from the Italian and Pacific fighting fronts as well. As Bill Hosokawa noted, the war made the Nikkei a much more cosmopolitan group.

[17] Grapes, *Japanese American*, 150.   [18] *Rohwer Outpost*, January 23, 1943, 3.
[19] *Minidoka Irrigator*, June 19, 1943, 1; Hosokawa, *Frying Pan*, 53.
[20] Estes and Estes, "Letters," 22–33.
[21] M. K. Gayne, "Japanese Americans and the Portland YWCA," *Journal of Women's History*, Vol. 15: No. 3 (2003), 197–203; B. Tong, "Race, Culture, and Citizenship Among Japanese American Children and Adolescents during the Internment Era," *Journal of American Ethnic History*, Vol. 23: No. 3 (2004), 3–40.

The same was true of other Americans, whether they stayed at home, moved, commuted to war work, or did some of each. Numerous civilian visits supplemented the flow of information from the military men.[22] One of the great services to historians of the center newspapers was to publish lists of residents and military personnel shuttling in and out of the centers.[23] These give a very informative account of mobility through the barbed wire. *The Heart Mountain Sentinel* on three days in 1944 was typical and reported on February 26, 1944, visiting servicemen from Camp Hale, Colorado; Camp Grant, Illinois; Fort Des Moines, Iowa; Camp Shelby, Mississippi; Fort Warren, Wyoming, and civilians from Boulder; Chicago; Minneapolis; Stevensville, Montana; Salt Lake City; and Powell. On April 22, 1944, servicemen flowed in from Minneapolis and Berkeley, Texas, and civilians from Denver, Granada, and Fort Lupton, Colorado; Chicago; Minneapolis; St. Louis; Richfield, Utah; Spokane, and Thermopolis. Another stream eddied through the wire on July 8, 1944, from Camp Maxey, Texas; Chicago; Idaho Falls; Des Moines; Philadelphia; Spokane; and Casper, Cowley, Powell, and Worland, Wyoming.[24] And throughout the months after January, 1943, other people drifted out of the centers and wrote back from literally hundreds of American cities, towns, and farms.

Print supplemented word of mouth. Poston had one school library and one created by the evacuees.[25] The Topaz camp library began with 5,000 volumes donated by "California schools, colleges, and public libraries." The library eventually obtained inter library loan privileges from "college libraries of Utah" and the University of California at Berkeley.

The Nikkei possessed the newer information technology and some of the older as well. Inventors and entrepreneurs created the first American radio stations in 1920, and by World War II radio ownership was practically universal. A radio repairman in the centers remembered that the machines were ubiquitous there as well. He recalled:

there were many of the evacuees who brought their radios to my apartment to get fixed ... "Some of the Issei wanted me to put in shortwave systems for them, but I refused to do this. I know that there were a few short waves in camp, but I never located them myself.[26]

[22] M. Inouye and G. Schaub, *The Heart Mountain Story: Photographs by Hansel Mieth and Otto Hagel of the World War II Internment of Japanese Americans* (Cummings Printing Co. 1997), 76–7.

[23] Grapes, *Japanese American*, 149–50.

[24] *Heart Mountain Sentinel*, February 26, 1944, 3; April 22, 1944, 1; July 8, 1944, 6.

[25] Estes and Estes, "Letters," 30.   [26] Grapes, *Japanese American*, 156.

Possession of radios in the Japanese POW camps in the Pacific Theater brought a severe beating if discovered. But most Americans had no short wave sets, so that some Japanese Americans were free to listen to information that most Americans could not. Telephones supplemented the newer gadgets. As early as January, 1943, Rohwer boasted of telephone service, one for "every four-block area."[27] The phones were communal, but they still enhanced the considerable flow of information.

The United States Post Office delivered letters to and from the centers. Some of these may have been censored, but it is doubtful if the government cared about the personal business and family concerns of the evacuees. Astonishingly, by late 1942, it was "now possible for residents of this Center [Minidoka] to send messages to their relatives in Japan through the International Red Cross."[28] The length of the messages was limited and had to be personal, but still represented the WRA's good faith efforts to make center life humane for a population greatly concerned with family. The barbed wire was completely permeable to outside information.

In Europe, "as the ghettos were usually cut off from the outside, the Jewish inmates received relatively little information." Neither did Russian prisoners of war, who were not covered by the Geneva Convention. As a result, uncontrollable and cruel rumors raged through both ghettos and camps. Reports spread like wildfire that they were all to be shipped off immediately, that the coup against Hitler had succeeded, or that the Allies had won the war and all were to be liberated. These rumors triggered jubilant celebrations, which were soon crushed by a pitiless reality.[29]

---

[27] *Rohwer Outpost*, January 6, 1943, 2.
[28] *Minidoka Irrigator*, November 25, 1942, 11.
[29] Bennett, *Shadow*, 175; Marrus, *Holocaust in History*, 119.

23

Administrators and Administration

The contrasting reality of the centers' government stood out in bold relief in their administration and staffing. Urban political historians, political scientists, and sociologists have long pondered the question of "who governs" cities and the nation, and that question should further illuminate the contrast of European camps and American centers.[1] In the latter, center staff were usually drawn from the idealistic or humane professions. Administrators and staff came from the ranks of New Deal bureaucrats in general, the Department of Agriculture, the Interior Department in particular, the Indian Bureau, then under the reformer John Collier, from the Settlement House Movement, from the ranks of the Baptist, Quaker, and Brethren religious denominations, from theological seminaries, from the YMCA and YWCA, and from former school administrators, recreationists, school teachers, and nurses. The first two directors of the WRA, Milton Eisenhower and Dillon Myer, were both 1940s liberals, and the center guards were carefully screened to ensure that no Nikkei haters became one.

It is interesting to imagine where else the centers might have drawn their personnel if not from the service professions, since, they have also been called prisons. Yet no administrator came from such famous American penal institutions as Sing Sing, Alcatraz, San Quentin, or Joliet Maximum Security Prison. If these centers were comparable institutions, one would have expected some crossover.

[1] The question has brought forth dozens of books, but was initiated by C. Wright Mills, Floyd Hunter, and Robert Dahl. F. Hunter, *Community Power Structure* (Chapel Hill, NC: the University of North Carolina Press, 1953); R. A. Dahl, *Who Governs?* (New Haven, CT: Yale University Press, 1966).

In the real concentration camps, Nazi authority was both absolute and always dictatorial. In contrast to the philanthropic staff of the WRA, that of the concentration camps was misanthropic. Since the SS (Schutzstaffeln) ran the concentration camps, its staffing was appalling enough to begin with. Yet the Nazis could always find ways to make it more so.

The SS stood at the top of the command structure and under them were layer upon layer of riff raff.

Criminals often ended up in the camps, and the SS soon realized that these men made perfect foremen or kapos, who would drive the workers remorselessly. To these the Nazis added Eastern European gentile POWs who hated each other and sometimes Jews as well, and they willingly collaborated in the grim business of slave driving.

Finally, there was often an underground among the camp prisoners. Since the communists were already organized in underground activity before they came into the camps, they often won out in the struggles to dominate the barracks underground. This control gave them some bargaining power with the SS, who incorporated them into the camp government, a sort of Hitler-Stalin Pact redivivus, writ small. These then functioned as a subset of de facto Nazis who made work assignments, doled out whatever miserable privileges there were, allotted food, and excused prisoners for sick leave. Of course, the communists used this authority to favor their own people. They were the real collaborators, as opposed to fanciful ones in American relocation centers.

Although she accepts the Concentration Camp Paradigm, Professor Sandra Taylor has nonetheless summed up the administrative and power relationships of the relocation centers about as ably as they can be. In *Jewel of the Desert* she wrote:

The community forged by the Japanese Americans at Topaz was a peculiar blend of self-government and individual initiative coupled with submission to a Caucasian authority that was, if ultimately absolute, rarely dictatorial or coercive.[2]

[2] Taylor, *Jewel*, 105, 154.

PART III

THE DEMISE OF RELOCATION

24

The Politics of Equilibrium

Friends and Enemies on the Outside

In late summer, 1943, an unusual scene occurred at the Fremont Street Cemetery in Portland, Oregon. As the *Minidoka Irrigator* described it:

Under the direction of the Portland Fellowship of Reconciliation, Negroes, whites, Jews, Catholics, Protestants and Americans of Chinese descent gave the afternoon toward reconditioning and beautifying the grounds [of the Nikkei cemetery].

On Sunday August 15, 1943, a Bon Matsuri service was held on behalf of the Portland Japanese Americans who were evacuated to the Minidoka Center. The speaker, E. Odgers, [Rodgers?] said, "It is felt this gesture of friendship to members of a group unable to be present will not be amiss in a world too often characterized by hatred and bloodshed."[1] The Multnomah County Sheriff at first prohibited the weed eradication, but then relented.

As we have seen, Christians, ministers and congregants alike, were among the most redoubtable friends of the AJA before and during relocation. As historian Robert Shaffer has adroitly shown, Protestants, especially the Federal Council of Churches and the *Christian Century*, led the way. They were joined by many secular liberals, some socialists, pacifists, students, some authors, teachers, social work schools and associations, universities, and editorial writers.[2] Peoria, Illinois, the frequent standard of the mainstream, is a case in point. As reported in the Pekin, Illinois,

---

[1] *Minidoka Irrigator*, August 15, 1943, 1.
[2] R. Shaffer, "Opposition to Internment: Defending Japanese American Rights during World War II," *The Radical History Review* (1998), *85–104*; and "Cracks in the Consensus: Defending the Rights of Japanese Americans during World War II," *Historian*, Vol. 61: No. 3, 597–620.

Daily Times (Pekin is across the Illinois River from Peoria), two young Japanese Americans got jobs in a Peoria chain of groceries, but were discharged because three disgruntled women complained. The Peoria Ministerial Association promptly wrote to the St. Louis headquarters of the grocery chain protesting the firing. The two Nikkei were swiftly reinstated.[3]

At about the same time, a Kalamazoo bakery hired two Nikkei after firing two other men for incompetence. The latter were spreading rumors that the bakery was replacing Americans with Japanese. The bakery came under pressure, but backed by the ministerial and teachers associations, the YMCA, and a Red Cross worker, the bakery "stood its ground" and the Nikkei kept their jobs.[4]

The evacuees also faced considerable other opposition from the outside. Both the American Legion and the Elks Lodge opposed the Portland beautification and the Japanese rite on grounds that the ceremony would be an outrage during a war against Japan and that the ceremony would be "boosting Buddhism."[5]

The powerful anti-Nikkei political bloc opposed any concessions to them. Because of this stiff antagonism, the loyalty questionnaire was, in part, the WRA's attempt to neutralize the Dies Committee, Senator Reynolds, Dave Beck of the northwest Teamsters, the Sons of the Golden West, and the other anti-Japanese.

Even before the war unleashed the passions of nationalism onto the West Coast, the Nikkei had several potent enemies. The opponents included the California Joint Immigration Committee, led by Valentine S. McClatchy and its constituent California State Federation of Labor, California Grange, California American Legion (sometimes), and the Native Sons. Several powerful newspaper chains like the Hearst Press (the LA *Examiner* and *San Francisco Examiner*) and the McClatchy Chain opposed the Nikkei. Sometimes the LA *Times* joined them and sometimes it did not.

The Native Sons and the California Joint Immigration Committee are the best known of these entities which had fought since the Progressive Era to limit or deport the Japanese.[6] On western waters, the West Coast Congressional Committee and the Committee of California legislator Jack Tenney (often called the "Little Dies Committee") provided further heft to an already formidable set of interest groups. Powerful political

---

[3] *Heart Mountain Sentinel*, April 15, 1944, 5.   [4] Ibid.
[5] *Minidoka Irrigator*, August 21, 1943, 3.
[6] For this battle see Daniels, *Politics of Prejudice*, 79–106.

commentators Walter Lippmann, Robert Hughes, and Westbrook Pegler also condemned the Japanese Americans. Certainly these men were anti-Nikkei, but the direct evidence of their influence on the political decision-making process is less certain.

Finally, as we have seen, some California growers wanted to limit or destroy Japanese American competition, and some California produce dealers and florists did too. Less well known were senators Robert Reynolds, Ed Johnston of Colorado, and the US Senate Committee of A. B. "Happy" Chandler of Kentucky.

According to historian Ellen Eisenberg, there were Jewish groups working against the Nikkei. She demonstrated that most Jews opposed relocation, but feared to speak up because of their own problematic position created by Hitler's anti-Semitism.

It is surprising that the Jewish Americans were assumed by Eisenberg to be in the wrong. As we have seen, there was plenty of evidence that the prewar Imperial Japanese were spying on the West Coast and that many Nikkei were cheering for their Fascist government before and after Pearl Harbor. However natural this might have been in the context of the 1940s, it could not have been disregarded by either the government or other minorities. Ethnic groups like the Jews were heavily involved in anti-Fascist activities, and their fight against Fascism took priority.[7]

Potent though they were, by the fall of 1944 these opposition groups were fighting an uphill battle. Nonetheless, they continued to wage it. The anti-Japanese Americans charged that the WRA coddled the Nikkei in the centers and that they were allowed to buy goods not available to the general population. They charged that the policy of resettlement would loose saboteurs on the unsuspecting communities where Nikkei resettled. Supposedly, once released, they were disappearing into the social wood-work. The resettled Japanese Americans should be rounded back up and returned to the centers; the Army should assume control of the centers, and the militants in the centers should be segregated from those who were not.[8] The more extreme critics continued to demand the deportation of all Nikkei, citizen and non-citizen alike, or at the very least, as Earl Warren demanded, prevent their return to the West Coast.[9] Thus, the return of the Nikkei was often painful.

---

[7] Eisenberg, *The First to Cry Down Injustice?* throughout, but especially, 71–146.
[8] L. A. McClatchy, "Host to the Japs," *American Legion Magazine*, Vol. 35: No. 4 (October 1943), 20, 49–50.
[9] Ibid.

The story of how public opinion shifted to pro-Nikkei needs telling. We know much about the swing of West Coast public opinion[10] *against* the Nikkei in late January, 1942. We also know of the desertion of the Nikkei by public figures. Also important were some California growers, the behind-the-scenes machinations of military bureaucrats Karl Bendetsen and Allen Gullion,[11] the vacillation of General John DeWitt, and the sometime anti-Nikkei leadership of the Los Angeles Chamber of Commerce. Yet, with the exception of studies of the court cases that freed the Nikkei, we have no comparably dense literature of good works to balance this record of woe.

Surely the Japanese would not have been accepted by the West Coast and America if it was rife with racism. Certainly the Nikkei would have repatriated to Japan if America as a whole was as biased as some historians have contended. Unless racism was like a light fixture which could be switched on and off, there must be more to the story.

In fact, there was. Public sentiment was shifting to a pro-Japanese American stance long before the Endo decision. This swing was proof that attitudes about the Japanese Americans were not set in stone; they were not unchanging and immutable, as racism is thought to be. In truth, as the early chapters indicate, racial attitudes were beginning to shift dramatically even before the war.[12] The outbreak of the conflict temporarily halted this movement, but by 1943 it had re-emerged. The growing movement came from different sources, at least as early as mid-1943, and gained increasing momentum in 1944. First and foremost, the military threat to the West Coast had vanished, and the media and politicians could no longer conjure it up.

Then as information of the evacuation began to surface in the hitherto uninformed East, people there began to ask questions about both the continued military necessity and constitutionality of relocation. Without

---

[10] At this stage we do not have a careful study of whether other parts of the country supported relocation, or accepted it in a fit of absent mindedness.
[11] I have not emphasized the roles of Allen Gullion and Karl Bendetsen because I do not think that historians' hostility to them is well grounded. For example, both have been considered racist by historians, yet Gullion as Provost Marshall General of the Army, although he was eventually overruled, opposed the idea of an all-Nikkei segregated combat team on grounds that it would create the same problems as the Army was then facing with African American segregated units. He also favored the right of Issei aliens to serve in the Army. Allen W. Gullion, to Assistant Chief of Staff, et al., November 2, 1943, 2, Arthur C. Braun Papers, MC 946, Series 2, Box 1, File 2, Special Collections, University of Arkansas. Hereafter Sp. Coll., U. Ark.
[12] *Rafu Shimpo*, February 11, 1940, 1.

the spur of a national defense emergency to influence their judgment, many easterners concluded that continued Japanese evacuation was no longer needed. Simultaneously, as more Nikkei resettled at places as diverse as Salt Lake City, Des Moines, Chicago, and Cleveland, Americans got to know the Nikkei personally for the first time. As missionary to Japan, Reverend Galen Fisher noted, most Americans had never seen any Japanese in 1943. When they actually did, the barriers crumbled.

Elites in the fields of broadcasting, newspapers, higher education, employment, magazine journalism, Christian and Jewish religions, and others helped smash them. They quickly grasped that most AJA were not only not dangerous, but very good workers and neighbors. With the widespread resettlement program which scattered workers from Utah to New York State, ordinary Americans began to comprehend what elites did. Dispersal had been a part of the JACL strategy all along: scatter the Nikkei about the country so they could get acquainted and so they would not appear to be an unassimilable lump concentrated in "Little Tokyos." The rest would take care of itself, as the Nisei leaders reckoned on the good sense of the American people to recognize the merits of this obviously model minority. The model minority characterization has come under fire recently, but the more I study the term, the more appropriate it seems to me, whether as nurserymen, as artists, in agriculture, or as American soldiers in combat.

The JACL (and Army) counted on the courage of the 100th Infantry Battalion and the 442nd Regimental Combat Team. The JACL knew that their generation of young men would fight. That strategy paid ever bigger dividends, as praise for the valor and fighting skill of the Nisei began to pour into American communities in soldier and sailor letters and then inevitably into print. As a part of this reappraisal, people on the West Coast were no longer intimidated by the hue and cry of the anti-Nikkei.

One of the more powerful pro-Nikkei forces developed in the national media as high-profile figures began to call for redress. One of the first to do so was Elsa Maxwell, columnist for the *New York Post* and "famed" hostess for the elite. "Most of the Japanese in the centers [except for the Kibei] are loyal to America, and in industry, business, and professions, would have much to offer," she wrote.[13] The widely syndicated radio broadcaster, H. V. Kaltenborn, agreed. Upon returning from a trip to the Pacific Theater, he wondered (somewhat simplistically) why there was

[13] *Heart Mountain Sentinel*, January 29, 1944, 3.

a "Japanese problem" on the West Coast when there was none in Hawaii.[14] The famous poet Carl Sandberg pointed out that missionaries to Japan thought that the Kibei sent there for education ended up 120 percent American instead of the reverse. From a rather different part of the political spectrum J. Edgar Hoover pointed out the military record of the Nisei, their low crime rate, and their lack of involvement in sabotage or espionage.[15] Hoover was a high-profile friend and much better informed on security matters than almost anyone, so his adherence to the Nikkei cause from mid-August, 1944, counted for a lot.[16]

Important politicians were coming to the same conclusion. Luckily, Secretary of the Interior Ickes' department had just assumed control of the WRA. The fiery liberal Republican held that it was intolerable to exclude the Nikkei from American life and that the majority of Americans who believed in "fair play and decency, Christianity,[17] in the principles of America, in the Constitution" would no longer be dominated by the anti-Nikkei minority who did not. "As a part of the Department of the Interior [the WRA] is directly represented in the President's cabinet ... and it can no longer be kicked around as an orphan agency."[18]

The Protestant churches had tried to stem the growth of "hysteria," post-Pearl Harbor, testified at the Tolan Hearings against evacuation, supported religious services in the assembly centers, and carried them over into the relocation centers. They sponsored meetings that got the Nikkei temporarily out of the centers, and led the resettlement effort to get them out permanently.

As 1944 unfolded, ever more Protestant churches, even in allegedly rabid California, called for the end of relocation. At first, it was a minister here and one there, like Fred R. Morrow of Saratoga or Aaron Heist of the First Methodist Church in Santa Maria.[19] In a supposedly muzzled center newspaper, Heist characterized "the evacuation order as probably the most un-American official act in the history of the country," and continued that "this nation should be vigorously engaged in restoring the rights of American citizens of Japanese ancestry."[20] He continued that there was

---

[14] Ibid., February 26, 1944, 5. As noted, there were good reasons for this.
[15] Ibid., August 12, 1944, 1. Nishimoto found a high crime rate at Poston 1 and even police violence. See Nishimoto, *Inside*, 134, 141, 146.
[16] Ibid., August 12, 1944, 1.
[17] Obviously, others besides Christians believed in fair play too.
[18] *Heart Mountain Sentinel*, April 22, 1944, 4.
[19] Ibid., February 26, 1944, 5; March 4, 1944, 4.   [20] Ibid., February 26, 1944, 5.

no longer any military necessity and that Nikkei young men were making magnificent contributions to this victory.[21]

By July 15, 1944, general resolutions, representing entire denominations or larger branches of Christianity, came on like a flood. Many churches held their national gatherings at about the same time, and the 41st International Conference of the Methodist Church, representing 8,000,000 members, was not the least of them.[22] The biennial General Assembly of the Congregational Christian Churches, the General Assembly of the Presbyterians, the *annual* Conference of the Methodist Church, the Northern Baptist Convention, and the General Synod of the Reformed Church in America all raised their voices for the restoration of Japanese American rights.[23] The Canadian Episcopalians chimed in from afar.[24] By 1944, the Catholic churches stood shoulder to shoulder with them. As the *Sentinel* put it, "The good churches, both Protestant and Catholic, have been powerful in their aid toward us."[25] As the Los Angeles Catholic Interracial Council report of December, 1944, said of their fellow Christians:

Supporting these evacuees was a magnificent group of fearless, hard fighting Protestant ministers. They saw the issue early and began to fight tooth and nail and were extremely effective. They preached, they wrote, they opened up their meager purses, they bought space in newspapers to tell of the evils of racism. Under their ecclesiastical system, their deeds are even more praiseworthy. They have been giants.[26]

The same report admitted that heretofore Catholics had been timid "and seemed to be afraid of the issue," that speaking up for the Nikkei would brand them as unpatriotic or too close to the Protestants and Communists, who were speaking up. Perhaps, but once the Catholics decided to get into the game, they stepped up to the plate and started swinging for the fences.

They battled the anti-Nikkei press in LA, stood up for the pro-Nikkei *Los Angeles Daily News*, threatened the politicians, sassed the generals, belittled the unions, exposed the economic rascals, scolded their flocks, nurtured the weak, and bludgeoned the strong. Their heroic statement of December, 1945, was a fine chronological summary of the struggle from start to finish.[27]

Just as the anti-Nikkei had their own organizations like the Native Sons, organizations sprang up on the other side to oppose them. The most

[21] Ibid.   [22] Ibid., May 20, 1944, 1.   [23] Ibid., July 15, 1944, 5.
[24] *Rocky Shimpo*, July 5, 1944, 1.   [25] *Heart Mountain Sentinel*, loc cit, July 15, 1944, 4.
[26] Catholic Interracial Council, *Report of December 16, 1945*, 434–40.   [27] Ibid.

high-profile one grew up in San Francisco Bay, where "a group of prominent citizens recently organized the Committee on American Principles
and Fair Play," explained the *Outpost*.²⁸ Actually, the Fair Play
Committee had begun in the fall of 1941, one of the earliest. The group
included Robert Gordon Sproul, president of the University of California
at Berkeley, businessman Maurice E. Harrison, Rabbi Irving E. Reichert,
scholar and activist for the poor Paul Taylor, missionary Galen Fisher,
legendary columnist Chester Rowell, and others. They reminded the
legislature that "similar groups of citizens opposed to discriminatory
legislation against Americans of Japanese ancestry are forming in many
communities in Central and Southern California, as well as in Oregon and
Washington."²⁹ Pro-Nikkei opinion was forming all over the country.

National magazines offered their own. *Fortune Magazine* devoted
its April, 1944, issue to the Japanese American and stated emphatically
that the Army should allow the Nikkei to return to the Coast.³⁰ Both
Colliers Magazine and *Time Magazine* published testimonials to the stead-
fastness of the Nikkei in battle.³¹ *Time* followed this with another article on
the entire 442nd Regimental Combat Team.³² By mid-1944 the *Sentinel*
thought that "the majority of newspapers and the leading magazines have
been shocked" by the discrimination against one racial group.³³

Testimonials also came in a steady stream from the fighting fronts.
The words of soldier after soldier commended the bravery of the 100th
Battalion or the 442nd Regimental Combat Team. As in most of their
narrative, the Nikkei also helped themselves. Most Americans did not
know the story of relocation, and as Gary Okihiro points out, Nikkei
speakers set out all over the country to change that.³⁴

Newspapers everywhere also began to stand up for AJA rights.
The Kansas City *Sunday World Herald*, while admitting military necessity
might have justified relocation in the first place, vehemently opposed any
plan to deny the Nisei their postwar citizenship on supposed dual loyalty
grounds.³⁵

²⁸ *Rohwer Outpost*, March 24, 1943, 4.
²⁹ C. Wollenberg, "'Dear Earl': The Fair Play Committee, Earl Warren, and Japanese
   Internment," *California History*, Vol. 89: No. 4 (2012), 24–55.
³⁰ No author, "Issei, Nisei, and Kibei," *Fortune Magazine*, April 1944, 1–20. Republished
   by the American Council on Public Affairs, Washington, DC in *Heart Mountain Sentinel*,
   April 22, 1944, 4.
³¹ As noted, the center papers reprinted many of these articles from major media. *Heart
   Mountain Sentinel*, March 4, 1944, 5.
³² Ibid., August, 2, 1944, 2.   ³³ Ibid., August 12, 1944, 4.
³⁴ Okihiro, *Storied*, 106, 115–16.   ³⁵ *Manzanar Free Press*, November 11, 1944, 2.

Just as journalists Walter Lippmann, Robert Hughes, and Westbrook Pegler had tried to put the Nikkei away, now radio journalist H. V. Kaltenborn helped to spring them.[36] Kaltenborn reached a much broader audience than did Walter Lippmann. The radio commentator pointed out that the Nikkei servicemen were helping to win in both the Pacific and European theaters and like Reverend Heist, found no Japanese problem in Hawaii. "Why in the world we had to create one here I don't know," he argued.[37]

The chorus continued to gain fresh voices. Aaron Heist reminded Roosevelt that he had promised "to restore evacuees the right to return to the evacuated areas as soon as the military situation will make such restoration feasible."[38] A couple of high-profile incidents further illustrated the shift, long after the military necessity had faded. One was reported in the influential *Christian Century*. Missionary author Galen Fisher reported that "evidence of a saner public sentiment is at hand from that anti-Japanese hotbed, Southern California." There the Japanese Exclusion Association circulated a legislative initiative petition that was a tougher version of the earlier land laws. However, the petition failed to gain the 100,000 signatures required.

In one city, the Native Sons circulating the petition were routed by nine ministers who protested against the petition in the newspapers. Then when Esther Takei received permission from the Army to register at Pasadena Junior College, the anti-Japanese lobby tried to stop her. They met a wall of pro-Japanese American sentiment. The editor of the student newspaper, himself a veteran, argued that 90 percent of the student body sided with Miss Takei. So did the Board of Education, whose letters "on the issue" ran over ten to one for the young Nisei. When Dillon Myer spoke at a meeting supporting Miss Takei, he, Dr. Robert Millikan, "head" of the California Institute of Technology, and Mrs. Maynard Thayer, a leader of the Fair Play Committee, spoke so strongly in favor of the young woman that George Kelley, who was leading the other side, was persuaded to drop his opposition. He actually relented and joined the Fair Play Committee himself![39]

Other attempts to discriminate against the Nikkei triggered support for fair play all over the country. When the Missouri House of Representatives debated a bill that would have prevented a Nikkei doctor from ministering to the sick in a state tuberculosis hospital, Representative

[36] *Heart Mountain Sentinel*, February 26, 1944, 5.   [37] Ibid.   [38] Ibid.
[39] *Minidoka Irrigator*, November 11, 1944, 2; November 18, 1944, 2.

O. K. Armstrong rose to denounce the proposal. As a white man, he called for fair play to peoples of other colors as well as the right of Missouri tubercular patients to receive treatment from qualified personnel.[40]

In late November, when K. Osada, of the Topaz Center, became the first Nikkei to return to Sacramento, he found overwhelming acceptance. Despite western miscegenation laws, Osada was already married to a Caucasian woman who had continued to operate their real estate business in his absence. Although Sacramento was the home base of the McClatchy newspaper chain, famous for its opposition to the Nikkei presence in the state, he received a warm welcome home.

we have received a continuous stream of old friends and well-wishers expressing satisfaction and every felicitation upon the turn of events which has brought me home. From all my own observations I should say that the reaction of the public in general is all that I could possibly wish.[41]

One of the center editorials recognized this spirit at Christmas, 1944.

Thanks to the many people on the 'outside' who so generously contributed to the center children, Christmas was spent happily among the Children when Santa in his rented suit handed out the gifts to the respective blocks.[42]

Perhaps surprisingly in view of all the writing about California racism, the returnees to the West Coast found that "with the exception of a few, most returned evacuees have discovered that the majority of west coast residents are friendly and cooperative."[43]

By mid-1945, things had turned a corner as one observer summed up. One newspaper put a railroad union action against the Nikkei in Chicago and another hostile incident in Laramie, Wyoming, into the proper context. "With only a few scattered 'incidents' we can be sure that nearly all of the 25,000 former evacuees are striding forward" wrote the *Sentinel*.[44]

Nonetheless, the scattered hostile incidents could be painful and demeaning. The WRA counted some twelve attacks by unions, state

---

[40] *Heart Mountain Sentinel*, April 29, 1944, 5.   [41] Ibid., November 25, 1944, 2.

[42] Ibid., December 23, 1944, 2. The celebration of Christmas at Minidoka is also sensitively treated by A. Blankenship in "Sagebrush Trees, 'Slant-Eyed Santas' and Uncle Sam: Christmas at Minidoka Relocation Center," MA Thesis, Department of Religious Studies, University of North Carolina at Chapel Hill, 80–2. Nonetheless, she found "subtle" acts of resistance in the outward conformity to Christian and patriotic celebrations.

[43] *Heart Mountain Sentinel*, December 23, 1944, 2.

[44] Ibid., August 2, 1944, 4. The oft-derided center newspapers are nonetheless a priceless source for following the growing pro-Nikkei feeling.

governments, or vigilantes in the first half of 1945.[45] Army Air Corps Sergeant Ben Kuroki, the hero of Heart Mountain, was one of the victims of this shameless treatment, which went on even after the war was over. To treat a man who had more than fulfilled his duty in combat in such a way was egregious. Still, according to John Howard, some 50 percent of the Japanese Americans were able to return to the Coast when the war concluded. The trend line was clearly in the direction of toleration.[46]

That vindication was expressed in the outcome of the various attacks on the Nikkei. By early 1945, the pro-Nikkei forces clearly outnumbered their opponents. Prominent figures like Secretary Ickes, the national media, ad hoc local committees, politicians like Earl Warren, and others joined the barnstorming director of the WRA, Dillon Myer, to rout the Nikkei's enemies. The reputation of the 442nd Regimental Combat Team made attacks on their parents and siblings extremely unpopular. Even the well organized and tactically sophisticated Hood River, Oregon, movement against the Japanese Americans was forced to relent.

If the government was really as bigoted as the race paradigm holds, it would not have dealt with the Japanese Americans as tolerantly and humanely as it did, and there would not have been so many testimonials to this fact. In the American South where African Americans suffered from genuine racism, the powers that be did not provide good health conditions, lots of food, widespread recreation programs, cultural enhancement, good schools down to the nursery school level and up to adult education, encouragements to attend college, cultural respect, freedom of the press, sound lodgings, and so forth to the victim group. So little did white Southerners respect black culture that the renowned Duke Ellington and other great African American swing bands of the 1940s often had to stay in black private homes because they could not find a hotel to spend the night.

It has often been thought by historians and contemporaries that the Japanese American narrative made a mockery of American democracy, that it was hypocritical to teach the evacuees about democracy and citizenship. Yet that argument ignores the political dimension of the Nikkei experience.

As I have argued, military necessity rather than political pressure brought about General DeWitt's decision to remove the Nikkei from the West Coast. If public opinion and political pressure played a role, it was to give the military cover for what they had to do anyway. As acute observers

[45] WRA, "Semi-Annual Report, January 1 to June 31, 1945," 9–15, Sp. Coll. U. Ark.
[46] Ibid.

at the time stated, there was never a public majority that favored putting the AJA into centers. There was no such thing as "West Coast racism," to quote one historian.

There certainly was widespread anger at the Nikkei, which the war created and fanned out of control. It was only after that point, after voluntary evacuation had failed, that the centers became inevitable. I know of no historical study of the Japanese narrative that presents *systematic evidence* that the general public favored putting the Nikkei into centers, much less that they did so on racist grounds. Universal or even majority bias is merely an unproven assumption by historians, which might be considered the next great task of the burgeoning historiography of this one-tenth of one percent of the population. Writers should be able to prove or disprove the existence of majority racism and its decisive influence on General DeWitt and FDR. Assumptions do not amount to evidence. Poll taking was not so omnipresent then as now, but the two most professional polls do not uphold the canon. The Gallup polls of the forties found no discriminatory bias against the Nikkei.[47] The Roper polls found that no majority favored relocating them to centers in the first place.[48]

In any case, if democracy helped force the Japanese Americans into the centers, democracy also helped spring them. In the end, the widespread questioning of the continued operation of the centers gave cover to the Supreme Court, the Army, and the Roosevelt Administration to close them. Minority rights won out in the end. Military necessity got the Nikkei off the Coast; widespread resentment of various kinds got them into the centers. But unlike the camps of the Soviet Union or Nazi Germany, democracy got them out again. Democracy has never been a simple matter. As historian Robert Shaffer has reminded us, the Nikkei had lots of friends on the outside. [49]

[47] Lotchin, "A Research Report," 399–417.
[48] Lotchin, "Race, Class, and Nationality: The 1940s National Opinion Research Center Polls, American Japanese and the Reach of American Racism," unpublished manuscript, 1–58.
[49] I have not included the subject of government in this study because it did not bear as directly on the subject of racism or concentration camps as my other topics did.

25

Endgame

Termination of the Centers

To end with a final gruesome contrast, how were the two kinds of organizations – concentration camps and relocation centers – terminated? As the Allied armies approached the localities of the Polish and German camps, it was no longer possible to transport prisoners to the death and concentration camps. So Hitler commanded that all inmates be killed.[1] That prompted a series of death marches where thousands of sick and emaciated prisoners stumbled to the West.[2]

In the United States, relocation was ended legally. In 1944, various Nisei and ACLU parties brought suit to test the constitutionality of relocation. In the last of these cases, the *Endo Case*, the Supreme Court refused to rule on the constitutionality of relocation. Instead it destroyed the legality of relocation by ruling that "the government could no longer continue to detain citizens whose loyalty had been established."[3] Before the decision was made public, the Roosevelt Administration decided to beat the Court to the punch by declaring an end to the system.[4] It took more than another year for the remaining residents to leave, but when they did, they were in good physical health. A majority of the evacuees returned to California and the West, by bus or train, not on foot.

---

[1] See P. Berben, *Dachau, 1933–1945: The Official History* (London: The Norfolk Press, 1968), 179–87, for the confusion and anxiety surrounding the death orders in one camp.
[2] E. Le Chene, *Mauthausen: The History of a Death Camp* (London: Methuen and Co. Ltd., 1971), 139–59, for a full discussion of the death marches from the East, see; Marrus, *Holocaust in History*, 196.
[3] L. K. Bannai, *Enduring Conviction: Fred Korematsu and His Quest for Justice* (Seattle, WA: University of Washington Press, 2015), 104–5.
[4] P. Irons, *Justice at War* (New York, NY: Oxford University Press, 1983), 341–2.

Perhaps because of a shortness of funds, the WRA sought to close the centers quickly. It allotted the evacuees enough money for transportation and a pittance for settling in. Although the Japanese Americans faced complex problems when returning home, the government did not do much to resolve them before the Nikkei arrived. Toshi Ito correctly summed up this failure when she said: "The government should not have released the internees while the war was not over."

That was the final blunder of the Roosevelt Administration. As she said: "The worst part of the whole experience of being incarcerated was our return home to a hostile environment: we were the enemy!"[5] Her own experience indicates that this was an exaggeration, but real problems did exist.[6] As usual, Miné Okubo captured the poignancy of the moment especially well when she left Topaz. "My God! How do they expect those poor people to leave the only place they can call home."[7]

The Japanese Americans overcame this reluctance in their traditional cooperative manner. Ito explained that the evacuees, like millions of immigrants before them, usually sent out one or two family members to test the waters. Many remained in the centers waiting for conditions in California to improve. If they had, the scouts wrote home and the families followed them.[8] So when they did leave, a majority went right back to their former homes.

Either the Californians were not as hopelessly biased as they have been portrayed, or the Nikkei had no choice. As we have seen, Californians were not hopelessly biased, and in fact, the Nikkei had considerable choice. Testimonials had been rolling in from myriad American places that were ready to have Nikkei neighbors, workers, or students. The places ranged from small settlements like Hardin, Montana, and Granger and Cedar Rapids, Iowa, to large ones like Des Moines, Chicago, Omaha, Cincinnati, and Milwaukee.[9] Two indicators provide some measure of how welcome the Nikkei were. The center newspapers carried advertisements of businesses in localities needing workers as well as re-settler destinations.

For 1943, as the war effort reached a crescendo, a total of 259 localities in thirty-seven states and British Columbia welcomed Japanese from the

[5] Ito, *Memoirs*, 62.
[6] The postwar adjustment of the Nikkei goes beyond the World War II scope of this book.
[7] Okubo, *Citizen*, 209; Nishimoto, *Inside*, 164.   [8] Ito, *Memoirs*, 60–5.
[9] *Heart Mountain Sentinel*, March 4, 1944, 5; February 26, 1944, 4; February 5, 1944, 3; February 12, 1944, 1; March 18, 1944, 4.

Minidoka Center alone.[10] Idaho led all states, with fifty-two, with Illinois and Utah virtually tied for second.[11] We need more studies like this to determine exactly how many places welcomed the Nikkei, but John Howard's breakdown of resettlement gives us a further reliable estimate. He found that 50 percent of the Nikkei left the centers for places other than the West Coast,[12] so that would have meant that 56,000 (of the original 112,000) were welcome somewhere else. The Japanese Americans had considerable choice.

Both their leaders, like Bill Hosakawa and the Washington, DC, correspondent of the *Heart Mountain Sentinel*, had spent considerable effort persuading the American Japanese, long before the war ended, to sally forth into the wider world. So how does one explain this seeming disconnect of a displaced people turning down asylum where thousands of their sons and daughters had already found it?[13] Why return to neighborhoods supposedly suffused with racism and teeming with violent racists?

The answer has always been out there, but has been ignored. Morton Grodzins, in one of the earliest studies of relocation, pointed out several times that an organized pressure group movement was responsible for relocation and not the majority of West Coast residents.[14] That theme was repeated often in 1944 and 1945 by those Californians and others who wanted the Nikkei to return.[15] Quaker Floyd Schmoe of Seattle spoke for them when he said in early 1944, "I have frequently said and I believe it is true, that the Japanese Americans still have more friends on the West coast – yea, even in California – than they have enemies."[16]

A WRA analysis of LA and San Joaquin Valley farmers in 1945 reached the same conclusion. "Both groups of farmers had good Caucasian-Japanese relations in their immediate neighborhoods before the war and neither suffered virulent antagonism after war was

[10] *Minidoka Irrigator*, January 1, 1943–December 31, 1943.
[11] These numbers were compiled from the *Minnidoka Irrigator*, for 1943. I assumed toleration for the Nikkei if businesses from a locality advertised for workers in the *Irrigator* or if *Minidoka* residents resettled in a given locality.
[12] Howard, *Concentration Camps*, 231–2.
[13] There was considerable reluctance to leave the security of the centers, especially among the Issei, because they feared the outside opposition to them. There were a number of anti-Nikkei incidents, well publicized by the LA *Times*, but these were exaggerated by the media. See Nishimoto, *Inside an American*, 163–233.
[14] Grodzins, *Americans Betrayed*, 209, 221.
[15] *Heart Mountain Sentinel*, January 29, 1944, 4;   [16] Ibid.

declared."[17] They admitted that the majority had been intimidated and outmaneuvered by a vocal and self-interested minority. That explains the apparent disconnect in Nikkei behavior. The West Coast was not such a bad place after all, which the heady Nikkei eventually recognized even if we historians have not.

[17] WRA, Community Analysis Section, "Project Analysis Series No. 21: Relocation at Rohwer Center," Griswold Papers, MC733, Series 2, Box 3, Folder 15, Sp. Coll., U. Ark.

26

Conclusion

The Place of Race

This book has proposed one principal thesis and several sub-theses that derive from it. The primary hypothesis is that racism and anti-Japanese bias have been greatly *exaggerated* and that they were much more complex and nuanced than has usually been assumed. It is not too much to say that historians of the Japanese American experience are infatuated with race and prejudice.[1] They are part of an even larger historiographical school about "whiteness."[2]

One would hope that the foregoing discussion has made the point that great numbers of Americans were not racist, nor anti-Japanese American. They were striving to come to terms with race and nationality in a war-torn world. In the modern world, ethno-cultural conflict is both brutal and complex and can lead to intra-racial, intertribal, religious, cultural, and nationalist atrocities. Yet, by 2016 historians of the Nikkei have elevated racism into a crime against humanity, a negative pedestal. In the 1940s, race was only one issue among many awful trends.

Perhaps the most stark statement of this negative pedestalization came from Scott Kurashige. As he put it: "millions of Americans viewed the war against Japan as a crusade to exterminate the Japanese race."[3] Of course,

---

[1] For this obsession with race, see the extended studies of "immigration" by P. Spickard, *Almost All Aliens*, and E. Robert Barkan, *From All Points* and lots of other works as well.
[2] For a brief discussion of the "whiteness" school of thought, see E. M. Eisenberg, *The First to Cry Down Injustice?* chapter 1 entitled "Western Jews, Whiteness, and the Asian 'Other'," 1–40, and N. Ignatiev, *How the Irish Became White* (New York, NY: Routledge, 1995), 1–5, 34–61ff. For contemporary race obsession see the *Christian Century*, throughout.
[3] S. Kurashige, *The Shifting Grounds*, 117. How Kurashige arrived at the estimates beyond the cited books by Roger Daniels and Peter Irons is not explained.

there was no "Japanese race," and even if there were, there is no *systematic evidence* that millions of Americans wished to "exterminate it." The Roper and Gallup polls provide no such evidence.[4] Historians who take these immoderate positions have come perilously close to accepting the interpretation of the Imperial Japanese Fascists who famously claimed that the war in the Pacific was a race war, and they are also close to inserting the doctrine of collective responsibility back into American history.

The WRA records show that its policy was consistently anti-racist, literally suffused with toleration, cultural sensitivity, political complexity, cultural curiosity, religious ecumenicalism, interest in the Japanese mindset, and transnational understanding, even of the Tule Lake militants and their openly pro-Japanese Fascist behavior.[5]

The political context of America's largest cities in the twentieth century may help us to further understand the place of race. As Ronald Bayor and Thomas Kessner have famously written about New York City in the Depression and World War II, ethnic groups fought tooth and nail for position and pelf and played the nationality card continuously. Mayor Fiorello La Guardia of New York City was both famous for, and expert at, the instigation of identity animosities among groups.

If anything, as the works of John Allswang and Alex Gottfried show, Chicago was even more of a cultural cauldron. The N word along with the M, K, H, and W words of contempt echoed around Chicago politics from 110th Street to Howard Avenue.

At this time, racism was not considered a crime against humanity, but just another bias in an urban political realm full of them. African Americans were not even key players in LaGuardia'a New York, nor in contemporary Boston. Nationality was vastly more important.[6]

---

4 For a more systematic analysis of the extermination charge, based on public opinion polls, as well as many other wartime canards, see, Lotchin, "A Research Report," 399–407.

5 See, for example, see the WRA position paper discussing the Japanese festival of "Boys Day." WRA: Community Analysis Section, "Community Analysis Notes No. 10, Boys Day," March 13, 1945, Griswold Papers, no file or box, Sp. Coll., U. Ark. See also 1351 the quarterly and semi-annual reports of the WRA. For instance, see WRA, *First Quarterly Report, March 18 to June 30, 1942* (Washington, DC: US Government Printing Office, 1942); WRA, *Semi-Annual Report, January 1 to June 30, 1943* (Washington: WRA, 1943); WRA, *Semi-Annual Report, January 1 to June 30, 1944* (Washington: WRA, 1944); or *Myths and Facts about Japanese Americans: Answering Common Misconceptions Regarding Americans of Japanese Ancestry* (Washington: WRA, April 1945). Throughout in each case. See also Muller, *Free to Die*, 192, 198.

6 R. H. Bayor, *Neighbors in Conflict: The Irish, Germans, Jews, and Italians of New York City, 1929–1941* (Baltimore, MD: The Johns Hopkins University Press, 1978); J. F. Stack, Jr., *International Conflict in an American City: Boston's Irish, Italians, and Jews, 1935–*

From the exaggeration of race, several sub-theses derived. One is that the American centers were not comparable to any kind of concentration camp *known to history in the 1940s*, not Nazi, South African, Cuban, nor Philippine ones, nor American Indian reservations. Nonetheless, since most of the historians who employ the term "concentration camp" will not refrain from using it, we should at least remind ourselves what kind of existence prevailed in the centers.

Thus, they were settlements with a fully elaborated and fully accredited education system; recreational opportunities galore; freedom of the press, information, and religion; opportunities to attend college; freedom to go and come through the useless barbed wire enclosures; plenty to eat; adequate housing and clothing allotments; consumer privileges that would have made an Okie or an Arkie envious; work opportunities enough to support themselves; free and more than adequate health care; a degree of self-government; the right to vote; lots of friends on the outside; and a normal adult death rate and rate of infant mortality.

Crucially, they enjoyed the right to leave definitively beginning in early 1943, sometimes less than six months after the centers opened. Perish the thought that we should mention Boy and Girl Scout jamborees in Yellowstone National Park or children's summer camp in the House Mountains! Almost none of these rights existed in any real world concentration camps. Hard time camps were specifically and categorically rejected at the Tolan Hearings.

Novelist James Michener, who believed that relocation was a farce, said in his "Introduction" to Michi Weglyn's *Years of Infamy*, "Two remarkable facts must be pointed out. Our internment camps were not allowed to become hell holes of starvation or death .... The majesty of character they [Nikkei] displayed then and the freedom from malice they exhibit now should make us all humble."[7]

A third sub-thesis is that the Roosevelt Administration stumbled into the relocation centers. It had a wartime plan for coping with the dangerous Nikkei minority, but not for dealing with the vast majority of non-dangerous ones. It had not foreseen how its diplomacy, nor its unsettling

---

1944 (Westport, CT: Greenwood Press, 1979); A. Gottfried, *Boss Cermak of Chicago: A Study of Political Leadership* (Seattle, WA: University of Washington Press, 1962); J. M. Allswang, *A House for all Peoples: Ethnic Politics in Chicago, 1890–1936* (Lexington, KY: The University Press of Kentucky, 1971); C. H. Trout, *Boston, the Great Depression and the New Deal* (New York, NY: Oxford University Press, 1977). Throughout in each case.
[7] Weglyn, *Years of Infamy*, 31.

FIG. 21. Amache Summer Carnival Parade, Amache Granada Relocation Center, Amache Granada, Colorado. The Boy Scouts upheld the flag. Central Photographic File of the War Relocation Authority, 1942–45. Record Group 210: Records of the War Relocation Authority, 1941–89. Courtesy US National Archives and Records Administration.

of public opinion might affect the Nikkei society and economy. In fairness to the President, he was overwhelmed by political, economic, and military problems in the first half of 1942, but his underlings could have done this policy better.

Relocation occurred because two nation states collided in Southeast Asia and their collision triggered unavoidable and unpredictable reactions on the American West Coast. In sum, World War II [8] was not a race war in the American West, nor anything close to one. It was an anomaly for American history, not likely to occur again.

---

[8] *Heart Mountain Sentinel*, January 16, 1943, 1.

APPENDIX

Historians and the Racism and Concentration Center Puzzles: A Compact with Comity by Zane L. Miller

Gary Okihiro opened his 1999 study by asking why we need yet another book on Japanese American relocation. He answered that the field should move beyond its preoccupation with racism to pay more attention to those Americans who were more friendly toward the Japanese Americans – in his words, those who were "anti-racist." Professor Lotchin has tried to do that in this book and in the process provide a critique of the racism/concentration camp interpretation of the relocation sites. Yet it remains puzzling why these interpretations have so dominated the immense and extremely one-sided relocation literature.

Succinctly put, this view holds that Japanese Americans always suffered from an especially egregious form of racism, and after Pearl Harbor anti-Japanese leaders in the West, motivated by hysteria, greed, and racism, took advantage of the ensuing war to dispossess Japanese Americans by "interning" them in concentration camps. Allegedly, the anti-Japanese assault stemmed from both economic and racial factors. Purportedly some of the relocation advocates wanted Japanese American agricultural lands, or at least the termination of Japanese agricultural competition on leased agricultural territory. Others supposedly sought to defend the ancestry base of California and the West. But whatever the case, these accounts for the most part ignore or discount other more nuanced explanations for relocation. Hysteria, greed, and racism dominate the argument, and both hysteria and greed derive from the latter. Racism is the key.

At the highest estimate, relocation affected 130,000 Japanese Americans.[1] That figure represents one-tenth of one percent of the total 1940 American population. This has more World War II homefront literature than for any other American group, several of which number in the millions. In fact, most American groups have almost no home-front history, if indeed they have any at all.[2] Japanese Americans, women who entered the workforce, Hispanics, and African Americans do, but most everyone else has hardly any. It can be argued that the experience of each of these groups, Japanese Americans, blacks, women, Jews and Hispanics, was quite extraordinary, perhaps decisive enough in their histories to warrant disproportionate coverage. But still, the tremendous treatment of this extraordinarily small minority of a minority group seems excessive.

To give one example, there are at least four books about the education of Japanese Americans in the relocation centers and internment centers or outside them in the colleges during the war – a child cohort of 130,000 people. That is about as many books as there are about the wartime education of everyone else in the entire country – a child cohort of 130,000,000 people. Was the experience of Japanese American children so unusual as to justify this imbalance? Hardly, yet one can understand it and empathize with this overproduction of orthodoxy, even if not agree with it.

However, it goes without saying that such orthodoxies need to be challenged and that is the purpose of this book. There are hundreds of studies that defend the orthodox position. There need to be some publications which doubt it. Building on the insights of professors Okihiro and John Stephan, one sees clearly that this orthodoxy exaggerates the importance of racism, both as a general phenomenon in 1940s America and as a specific motivation for relocation actions.

I am not at all certain why historians have become obsessed with the racial and concentration camp interpretations of Japanese relocation. That people who were smart, reasonable, and well intentioned could have first embraced this interpretation and then elevated it into an orthodoxy remains a puzzle to me. Perhaps such an explanation of the racism

---

[1] The figures cited by historians vary from 107,000 to 130,000. I have accepted the WRA figure of 112,000 since they ran the relocation program. See WRA, *Wartime Exile: The Exclusion of the Japanese Americans from the West Coast* (Washington, DC: US Government Printing Office, no date) 22.

[2] Poles, Greeks, Jews, and a few others have claimed some attention, but most of that literature is about the experience of their nationality groups in Europe rather than on the American home front.

obsession might explain it as a mid-twentieth century phenomenon. The impulse for this behavior seems to come largely, or at least in part, as a response to the barbaric treatment of minorities in the 1930s and 1940s by several regimes, most notably those in Germany, Japan, and the Soviet Union, and the corresponding fear that such evil behavior might come to be regarded as banal, as a characteristic of human nature, and an attitude that any group, part of a group, or government anywhere, including the United States, might adopt, and hence as something that deserved identification and denunciation wherever and whenever it manifested itself.

In the United States, this phenomenon led to a new respect for the legitimacy of all socio-cultural groups and their rights, including the rights as members of a democratic polity. This phenomenon also has led us to focus on white racism in American history, since in the United States some whites held the upper hand for centuries and over the years treated callously and often cruelly several racial minority groups, including native Americans, Africans, Chinese, and Japanese, and some other ethnic groups.

The focus on this kind of white racism and its potentially virulent consequences if unchecked has led to some admirable scholarship and public policy initiatives, especially in the latter case as a consequence of the civil rights movement in the last half of the twentieth and the first part of the twenty-first centuries.

But it also yielded some well intentioned but misleading handling of certain events, including a mono-causal racist interpretation of the origins and nature of Japanese relocation during World War II, and of that interpretation's by-products, repeated reference to the relocation centers as concentration camps. That rhetorical flourish which, in the post-World War II context, evoked visions of Nazi concentration camps and was a way of warning readers about the "banality of evil," the frailties of human nature in America as well as elsewhere.

Over the years this view of Japanese American relocation became something of an orthodoxy, and as such, something taken for granted, something adhered to unreflectively and therefore uncritically and uncontextually, as the rehabilitation of Germany and Japan and the collapse of the Soviet Union encouraged their view that racism triumphed there and tenaciously so. But here the crisis of racism led instead to the successes of our civil rights movement, including an apology to and compensation of Japanese relocatees by the federal government and eventually to the widespread acceptance of African Americans at all levels of society.

With the waning of the moralistic zeal which both undergirded the racist/concentration camp approach and ignited the civil rights movement, it seems appropriate to revisit the Japanese relocation episode. That should also lead us to reevaluate the racist/concentration camp approach to this regrettable experience. As it turns out, the pinpointing of some of the shortcomings of the orthodox view renders relocation no less regrettable while at the same time presenting a more encouraging view of the strength, promise, and possibilities of the human capacity for intergroup tolerance. We may not all sign up for multi-culturalism, but this review of the relocation experience supports the view that Americans can, when they try, keep alive their compact with comity, even in a dark time seventy years ago when racist totalitarianism seemed virtually irresistible.

Bibliography

BOOKS, ARTICLES, AND BOOK CHAPTERS

Abbott, Carl, Leonard, Stephen J., and McComb, David. *Colorado: A History of a Centennial State*. Niwot, CO: University of Colorado Press, 1984.

Abend, Hallett. *Japan Unmasked*. New York, NY: I. Washburn, Inc., 1941.

Adams, Ansel. *Born Free and Equal: The Story of Loyal Japanese Americans, Manzanar Relocation Center, Inyo County, California*. Bishop, CA: Spotted Dog Press, 1944.

Adelman, Melvin L. *A Sporting Time: New York City and the Rise of Modern Athletics, 1820–1870*. Urbana, IL: University of Illinois Press, 1990.

Ahr, Johan. "On Primo Levi, Richard Serra, and the Concept of History." *Journal of the Historical Society*, Vol. 9: No. 2 (2009), 161–89.

Allswang, John M. *Bosses, Machines, and Urban Voters*. Baltimore, MD: The Johns Hopkins University Press, 1986.

A House for all Peoples: Ethnic Politics in Chicago, 1890–1936. Lexington, KY: The University Press of Kentucky, 1971.

American Council on Public Affairs. *Fortune Magazine*, April 1944, 1–20.

Arendt, Hannah. *The Origins of Totalitarianism*. Cleveland, OH: The World Publishing Company, 1958.

Austin, Allan W. *From Concentration Camp to Campus: Japanese American Students and World War II*. Urbana, IL: University of Illinois Press, 2004.

Bailey, Beth and Farber, David. *The First Strange Place: Race and Sex in World War II Hawaii*. Baltimore, MD: Johns Hopkins University Press, 1992.

Baker, William J. *Sports in the Western World*. Urbana, IL: University of Illinois Press, 1988.

Baldwin, Davarian L. *Chicago's New Negroes: Modernity, Migration & Black Urban Life*. Chapel Hill, NC: The University of North Carolina Press, 2007.

Barkan, Elliott Robert. *From All Points: America's Immigrant West, 1870s–1952*. Bloomington, IN: Indiana University Press, 2007.

Barth, Gunther. *City People: The Rise of Modern City Culture in Nineteenth-Century America*. New York, NY: Oxford University Press, 1980.

Baumler, Ellen. "Justice as an Afterthought: Women and the Montana Prison System." *Montana: The Magazine of Western History* Vol. 58 (2008).

Bayor, Ronald H. *Neighbors in Conflict: The Irish, Germans, Jews, and Italians of New York City, 1929–1941*. Baltimore, MD: The Johns Hopkins University Press, 1978.

Bearden, Russell. "Life Inside Arkansas's Japanese-American Relocation Centers." *Arkansas Historical Quarterly*, Vol. 48: No. 2 (1989), 169–96.

Bennett, Rab. *Under the Shadow of the Swastika: The Moral Dilemmas of Resistance and Collaboration in Hitler's Germany*. New York, NY: New York University Press, 1999.

Berben, Paul. *Dachau, 1933–1945: The Official History*. London: The Norfolk Press, 1975.

Bergerud, Eric M. *Fire in the Sky: The Air War in the South Pacific*. Boulder, CO: Westview Press, 2000.

Bernard, Richard M. and. Rice, Bradley R, eds. *Sunbelt Cities: Politics and Growth since World War. II*. Austin, TX: University of Texas Press, 1983.

Biase, Linda Popp, di. "Neither Harmony nor Eden: Margaret Peppers and the Exile of the Japanese Americans." *Anglican and Episcopal History*, Vol. 70: No. 1 (2001), 101–17.

Biddle, Francis. *In Brief Authority*. New York, NY: Doubleday and Company, Inc., 1962.

Bittner, Eric. "Loyalty … Is a Covenant: Japanese American Internees and the Selective Service Act." *Prologue*, Vol. 23: No. 3 (1991), 248–52.

Blackbourn, David. *The Long 19th Century: History of Germany 1780–1920*. New York, NY: Oxford University Press, 1998.

Blankenship, Anne. *Christianity, Social Justice, and Japanese Incarceration during World War II*. Chapel Hill, NC: University of North Carolina Press, 2016.

  "Sagebrush Trees, [sic] 'Slant-Eyed Santas' and Uncle Sam: Christmas at Minidoka Relocation Center." Unpublished MA Thesis, Department of Religious Studies, University of North Carolina at Chapel, Hill, 2008.

Bodnar, John. *The Transplanted: A History of Immigrants in Urban America*. Bloomington, IN: Indiana University Press, 1985.

Bosworth, Allan R. *America's Concentration Camps*. New York, NY: Bantam Books, 1967.

Boyer, Paul. *Urban Masses and Moral Order in America*. Cambridge, MA: Harvard University Press, 1978.

Brands, H. W. *Bound to Empire: The United States and the Philippines*. New York, NY: Oxford University Press, 1992.

  "The Coils of Empire." *Diplomatic History*, Vol. 33: No. 1 (January 2009).

  Traitor to His Class: The Privileged Life and Radical Presidency of Franklin Delano Roosevelt. New York, NY: Anchor Books, 2009.

Brighton, Terry. *Patton, Montgomery, Rommel: Masters of War*. New York, NY: Three Rivers Press, 2008.

Brooks, Charlotte. *Alien Neighbors, Foreign Friends: Asian Americans, Housing, and the Transformation of Urban California.* Chicago, IL: The University of Chicago Press, 2004.

"In the Twilight Zone between Black and White: Japanese American Resettlement and Community in Chicago, 1942–1945." *Journal of American History*, Vol. 86: No. 4 (March, 2000).

Brothers, Thomas. *Louis Armstrong's New Orleans.* New York, NY: W. W. Norton, 2006.

Buck, Pearl S. *Dragon Seed.* New York, NY: Beaufort Books, 2010.

Bulpett, Heather Marie. "The Impact of World War II on American Education: A Nation Looking to Its Schools for Help and Hope." UNC undergraduate seminar paper, Fall 2006.

Caughy, John and La Ree. *Los Angeles: Biography of a City.* Berkeley, CA: University of California Press, 1976.

Cayton, Horace and Drake, St. Clair. *Black Metropolis.* New York, NY: Harper and Row, 1945.

Chang, Iris. *The Rape of Nanking: The Forgotten Holocaust of World War II.* New York, NY: Basic Books, 1997.

Chuman, Frank. *Bamboo People: The Law and Japanese Americans.* Del Mar, California: Publisher's Inc., 1976.

Churchill, Winston S. *The Island Race.* New York, NY: Dodd, Mead and Company, 1964.

Cogan, Frances B. *Captured: The Internment of American Civilians in the Philippines, 1941–1944.* Athens, GA: The University of Georgia Press, 2000.

Cohen, Lizabeth. "Is There an Urban History of Consumerism?" *Journal of Urban History*, Vol. 29: No. 2 (January 2003), 87–106.

Collingham, Lizzie. *The Taste of War: World War II and the Battle for Food.* New York, NY: Penguin Books, 2011.

Corbett, F. Scott. *Quiet Passages: The Exchange of Civilians between the United States and Japan during the Second World War.* Kent, OH: The Kent State University Press, 1987.

Dahl, Robert A. *Who Governs?* New Haven, CT: Yale University Press, 1966.

Japanese Exclusion. Berkeley, CA: University of California Press, 1962.

Daniels, Roger. *Asian America.* Seattle: University of Washington Press, 1988.

Concentration Camps USA: Japanese Americans and World War II. New York, NY: Holt, Rinehart and Winston, Inc., 1972.

The Politics of Prejudice: The Anti-Japanese Movement in California and the Struggle for Japanese Exclusion. Berkeley, CA: University of California Press, 1962.

Prisoners without Trial: Japanese Americans in World War II. New York, NY: Hill and Wang, 1993.

Davidson, Sue. "Aki Kato Kurose: Portrait of an Activist." *Frontiers*, Vol. 7: No. 1 (1983).

Davis, Margaret Leslie. *Rivers in the Desert: William Mulholland the Inventing of Los Angeles.* New York, NY: Harper Perennial, 1994.

Dick, Bernard F. *The Star-Spangled Screen: The American World War II Film.* Lexington: University of Kentucky Press, 1985; 1995 paperback edition.

Doherty, Thomas. *Hollywood, American Culture, and World War II.* New York, NY: Columbia University Press, 1993.

Dower, John W. *War without Mercy: Race and Power in the Pacific War.* New York, NY: Pantheon Books, 1986.

Drinnon, Richard, *Keeper of the Concentration Camps: Dillon S. Myer and American Racism.* Berkeley, CA: University of California Press, 1987.

Dubofsky, Melvyn, *We Shall Be All: A History of the Industrial Workers of the World.* Chicago, IL: Quadrangle Books, 1969.

Egmi, Hatsuye, *Wartime Diary* reprinted in *Topaz Times*, December 12 and 14, 1943.

Eisenberg, Ellen M. *The First to Cry Down Injustice: Western Jews and Japanese Removal during WWII.* Lanham, MD: Lexington Books, 2008.

Eisenhower, Milton. *The President Is Calling.* Garden City, NY: Doubleday and Company, Inc., 1974.

Embree, John F. *The Japanese Nation: A Social Survey.* New York, NY: Farrar and Rinehart, Inc., 1945.

Estes, Donald H. and Matthew T. "Letters from Camp Poston, The First Year," in Mackey, Mike, ed., "Japanese Relocation in the American West" (Special edition). *Journal of the West*, Vol. 38: No. 2 (April, 1999).

Fairbanks, Robert B. *Making Better Citizens: Housing Reform and the Community Development Strategy in Cincinnati, 1890–1960.* Urbana, IL: University of Illinois Press, 1988.

Feeley, Francis McCollum. *America's Concentration Camps during World War II: Social Science and Japanese Internment.* New Orleans, LA: University Press of the Old South, 1999.

Feifer, George. *The Battle of Okinawa: The Blood and the Bomb.* Guilford, CT: The Lyons Press, 2001.

Ferguson, Niall. *The House of Rothschild: Money's Profits, 1798–1848.* New York, NY: Penguin Books, 1998.

Fiset, Louis, "Health Care at the Central Utah (Topaz) Relocation Center." *Journal of the West*, Vol. 38: No. 2 (1999).

"The Heart Mountain Hospital Strike of June 24, 1943," in Mackey, Mike, ed. and contributor, *Remembering Heart Mountain.* Casper, WY: Mountain States Lithographing, 1998, 101–18.

"Public Health in World War II Assembly Centers for Japanese Americans." *Bulletin of the History of Medicine*, 73 (1999).

Fiset Louis, and Nomura, Gail M., eds. *Nikkei in the Pacific Northwest: Japanese Americans and Japanese Canadians in the Twentieth Century.* Seattle, WA: University of Washington Press, 2009.

Franklin, Ruth. *A Thousand Darknesses: Lies and Truth in Holocaust Fiction.* New York, NY: Oxford University Press, 2011.

Frielander, Jay. "Journalism behind Barbed Wire; An Arkansas Relocation Center Newspaper." *Journalism Quarterly*, Vol. 62: No. 2 (1985).

Fryer, Heather. *Perimeters of Democracy: Inverse Utopias and the Wartime Social Landscape in the American West.* Lincoln: University of Nebraska Press, 2012.

Fugita, Stephen S. and Fernandez, Marilyn. "Religion and Japanese Americans' View of Their World War II Incarceration." *Journal of Asian American Studies,* Vol. 5: No. 2 (2002), 113–37.

Fugitana, Takashi. *Race for Empire: Koreans as Japanese and Japanese as Americans.* Berkeley, CA: University of California Press, 2001.

Gane, Mary K. "Japanese Americans and the Portland YWCA." *Journal of Women's History,* Vol. 15: No. 3 (2003), 197–203.

Gentile, Nancy. "Survival behind Barbed Wire: The Impact of Imprisonment on Japanese American Culture during World War II." *Maryland Historian,* Vol. 19: No. 2 (1988), 15–32.

Gilje, Paul. *Rioting in America.* Bloomington, IN: University of Indiana Press, 1996.

Giordano, G. *Wartime Schools: How World War II Changed American Education.* New York, NY: Peter Lang Publishing.

Glenny, Misha, *The Balkans: Nationalism, War, and the Great Powers, 1804–1999.* New York, NY: Oxford University Press, 1964.

Gordon, Milton. *Assimilation in American Life: The Role of Race, Religion, and National Origins.* New York, NY: Viking, 2000.

Goren, Dina. "Communications Intelligence and the Freedom of the Press: The *Chicago Tribune's* Battle of the Midway Dispatch and the Breaking of the Japanese Naval Code." *Journal of Contemporary History,* Vol. 16: No. 4 (October 1981).

Gottfried, Alex. *Boss Cermak of Chicago: A Study of Political Leadership.* Seattle, WA: University of Washington Press, 1962.

Grapes, Brian. *Japanese American Internment Camps.* San Diego, CA: Greenhaven Press, Inc., 2001.

Greenburg, Cheryl. "Black and Jewish Responses to Japanese Internment." *Journal of American Ethnic History,* Vol. 14: No. 2 (Winter 1995).

Gregory, James. *American Exodus: The Dust Bowl Migration and Okie Culture in California.* Oxford: Oxford University Press, 1989.

Grodzins, Morton. *Americans Betrayed: Politics and the Japanese Evacuation.* Chicago, IL: University of Chicago Press, 1949.

Grossman, James R. *Land of Hope: Chicago, Black Southerners, and the Great Migration.* Chicago, IL: The University of Chicago Press, 1989.

Guilfoyle, Timothy J. *A Pickpocket's Tale: The Underworld of Nineteenth Century New York.* New York, NY: W. W. Norton and Company, 2006.

Guterl, Matthew Pratt. *The Color of Race in America.* Cambridge, MA: Harvard University Press, 2001.

Hajimu, Masuda. "Dissident Harry Ueno Remembers Manzanar." *California History,* Vol. 64: No. 1 (1985), 58–64.

"Rumors of War: Immigration Disputes and the Social Construction of American Japanese Relations, 1905-1913." *Diplomatic History,* Vol. 33: No. 2 (January 2009).

Hansen, Arthur A. and David A, Hacker. "Cultural Politics and the Gila River Relocation Center, 1942–1943." *Arizona and the West*, Vol. 27: No. 4 (1985), 327–62.

"Dissident Harry Ueno Remembers Manzanar." *California History*, Vol. 64: No. 1 (1985), 58–64.

"Evacuation and Resettlement Study at the Gila River Relocation Center, 1942–1945." *Journal of the West*, Vol. 38: No. 2 (April 1999).

"The Manzanar Riot: An Ethnic Perspective." *Amerasia Journal*, Vol. 2: No. 2 (1974).

Harvey, Robert. *Amache: The Story of Japanese Internment in Colorado during World War II*. Dallas, TX: Taylor Trade Publishing, 2004.

Hayashi, Brian Masaru. *Democratizing the Enemy: The Japanese American Internment*. Princeton, NJ: Princeton University Press, 2004.

For the Sake of Our Japanese Brethren: Assimilation, Nationalism, and Protestantism among the Japanese of Los Angeles, 1895–1992. Stanford, CA: Stanford University Press, 1995.

Hayawshi, Yuka. "Anti-Korean Voices Grow in Japan." *Wall Street Journal*. May 15, 2013.

Herman, Arthur. *Freedom's Forge: How American Business Produced Victory in World War II*. New York, NY: Random House, 2012.

Higgs, Robert. *Depression, War, and Cold War: Challenging the Myths of Conflict and Prosperity*. Oakland, CA: The Independent Institute, 2006.

Hirasuna, Delphine. *The Art of Gaman: Arts and Crafts from the Japanese Internment Camps, 1942–1946*. Berkeley, CA: Ten Speed Press, 2010.

Hitler, Adolf. *Mein Kampf*. New York, NY: Reynal and Hitchcock, 1939.

Hosokawa, Bill. *Nisei: The Quiet Americans*. New York, NY: William Morrow and Company, 1969.

Out of the Frying Pan: Reflections of a Japanese American. Boulder, CO: University of Colorado Press, 1998.

"The Sentinel Story." *Peace and Change*, Vol. 23: No. 2 (1989), 135–47.

Thirty Five Years in the Frying Pan. New York, NY: McGraw-Hill Book Company, 1978.

Houston, Jeanne Wakatsuki and Houston, James D. *Farewell to Manzanar*. San Francisco, CA: San Francisco Book Company, 1973.

Howard, John. *Concentration Camps on the Home Front: Japanese Americans in the House of Jim Crow*. Chicago, IL: The University of Chicago Press, 2008.

Hoyt, Robert S. *Europe in the Middle Ages*. New York, NY: Harcourt, Brace and Company, 1957.

Hughes, Rupert. "After the Nips Surrender." *American Legion Magazine*, Vol. 38: No. 5 (May, 1945), 16, 33–34.

Hunter, Floyd. *Community Power Structure: A Study of Decision Makers*. Chapel Hill, NC: University of North Carolina Press, 1953.

Huthmacher, J. Joseph. *Senator Robert F. Wagner and the Rise of Urban Liberalism*. New York, NY: Atheneum, 1971.

Ichioka, Yuji. *Before Internment: Essays in Prewar Japanese History*. Stanford, CA: Stanford University Press, 2006.

Ienaga, Saburō. *The Pacific War, 1931–1945: A Critical Perspective on Japan's Role in World War II*. New York, NY: Pantheon Books, 1978.

Ignatiev, Noel. *How the Irish Became White*. New York, NY: Routledge, 1995.

Inouye, Frank T. "Immediate Origins of the Heart Mountain Draft Resistance Movement." *Peace and Change*, 23 (1998).

Inouye, Mamoru. "Heart Mountain High School, 1942–1945." *Journal of the West*, 38 (1999), 56–64.

Inouye, Mamoru and Schaub, Grace. *The Heart Mountain Story: Photographs by Hansel Mieth and Otto Hagel of the World War II Internment of Japanese Americans*. Hookset, NH: Cummings Printing Co., 1997.

Inouye, Miyako. "Japanese-Americans in St. Louis: From Internees to Professionals." *City and Society*, 3 (1989).

Irons, Peter. *Justice at War*. New York, NY: Oxford University Press, 1983.

"Issei, Nisei, and Kibei," *Fortune Magazine*. April 1942, 1–20. Republished by the American Council on Public Affairs, Washington, DC in *Heart Mountain Sentinel*, April 22, 1944, 4. As noted, the camp papers reprinted many of these articles from major media. *Heart Mountain Sentinel*, March 4, 1944, 5.

Ito, Leslie. "Japanese American Women and the Student Relocation Movement, 1942–1945." *Frontiers*, Vol. 21: No. 3 (2000), 1–24.

Ito, Toshi Nagamori. *Memoirs of Toshi Ito: USA Concentration Camp Inmate, War Bride, Mother of Chrisie and Judge Lance Ito*. Bloomington, IN: Anchor Books, 2009.

Jackson, Kenneth T. *The Ku Klux Klan in the City, 1915–1930*. New York, NY: Oxford University Press, 1967.

Jacoby, Harold Stanley. *Tule Lake*. Grass Valley, California: Comstock Bonanza Press, 1996.

James, Thomas. "'*Life Begins With Freedom.*' The College Nisei, 1942–1945." *History of Education Quarterly*, Vol. 25: Nos. 1–2 (1985), 155–74.

Jeffreys, Diarrmuid. *Hell's Cartel: IG Farben and the Making of Hitler's War Machine*. New York, NY: Metropolitan Books, 2008.

Judd, Denis & Surridge, Keith. *The Boer War*. London: John Murray, 2002.

Kaiser, Charles. *The Cost of Courage*. New York, NY: Other Press, 2015.

Kandel, I. L. *The Impact of the War upon American Education*. Chapel Hill, NC: The University of North Carolina Press, 1948.

Kashima, Tetsuden. *Judgment without Trial: Japanese American Imprisonment during World War II*. Seattle: University of Washington Press, 1993.

Kennedy, David M. *The American People in World War II: Part II Freedom from Fear*. New York, NY: Oxford University Press, 1999.

Kessler, Loren. "Fettered Freedoms: The Journalism of World War II Japanese Internment Camps." *Journalism History*, Vol. 15: Nos. 2–3 (1988), 70–79.

Kessner, Thomas. *Ethnicity and Reform*. Arlington Heights, Illinois: Harland Davidson, Inc., 1993.

   Fiorello H. La Guardia and the Making of Modern New York. New York, NY: McGraw-Hill Publishing Company, 1998.

Kobashigawa, Ben. *History of the Okinawans in North America*. Berkeley, CA: University of California Press and the Okinawin Club of America, 1988.

Kramer, Paul A. *Race, Empire, the United States, and the Philippines*. Chapel Hill, NC: The University of North Carolina Press, 2006.

Kurashige, Lon. "Resistance, Collaboration, and Manzanar Protest." *Pacific Historical Review*, Vol. 70: No. 3 (August 2001).

Two Faces of Exclusion: The Untold Story of Anti-Racism in the United States. Chapel Hill, NC: The University of North Carolina Press, 2016.

Kurashige, Scott. *The Shifting Grounds of Race: Blacks and Japanese Americans in the Making of Multiethnic Los Angeles*. Princeton, NJ: Princeton University Press, 2008.

Lane, Roger. *Murder in America*. Columbus, OH: Ohio State University, 1997.

Lange, Dorothea, Woods, John, and Wright, Peter. *Manzanar*. New York, NY: New York Times Books, 1988.

Le Chene, Evelyn. *Mauthausen: The History of a Death Camp*. London: Methuen and Co. Ltd., 1971.

Leonard, Kevin Allen. *The Battle for Los Angeles: Racial Ideology and World War II*. Albuquerque: University of New Mexico Press, 2006.

Levi, Primo. *If This Is a Man & the Truce*. London: Everyman's Library, 2000.

Linehan, Thomas M. "Japanese American Resettlement in Cleveland during and After World War II." *Journal of Urban History*, Vol. 20: No. 1 (1993).

Longerich, Peter. *Heinrich Himmler*. New York, NY: Oxford University Press, 2012.

Lotchin, Roger W. *The Bad City in the Good War: San Francisco, Los Angeles, Oakland, and San Diego*. Bloomington, IN: Indiana University Press, 2003.

Fortress California, 1910–1961: From Warfare to Welfare. New York, NY: Oxford University Press, 1992.

"Research Report: The 1940s Gallup Polls, Imperial Japanese, Japanese Americans, and the Reach of American Racism." *Southern California Quarterly*, Vol. 97: No. 4 (Winter), 399–417.

San Francisco: From Hamlet to City. New York, NY: Oxford University Press, 1974.

ed. *The Way We Really Were*. Urbana, IL, University of Illinois Press, 2000.

Lowe, Keith. *Savage Continent: Europe in the Aftermath of World War II*. New York, NY: St. Martin's Press/Picador, 2012.

Lowman, David D. *Magic: The Untold Story of US Intelligence and the Evacuation of Japanese Residents from the West Coast during WWII*. Stanford, CA: Athena Press, Inc., 2000.

Luckingham, Bradford. "Phoenix: The Desert Metropolis." Bernard, Richard M. and Rice, Bradley R., eds., *Sunbelt Cities: Politics and Growth since World War II*. Austin, TX: University of Texas Press (1983), 309–27.

Luther, Catherine A. "Reflection of Cultural Identities in Conflict: Japanese American Internment Camp Newspapers during World War II." *Journalism History*, Vol. 29: No. 2 (2003), 69–81.

Lyons, Michael J. *World War II: A Short History*. Boston, MA: Prentice Hall, 2010.

Macintyre, Ben. *Agent Zig Zag*. London: Bloomsbury, 2007.

Double Cross: The True Story of the D-Day Spies. New York, NY: Crown Publishers, 2012.

Mackey, Mike. *Heart Mountain: Life in Wyoming's Concentration Camp.* Powell, WY: Western History Publications, 2000.

Mack Smith, Denis. *Mussolini.* London: Weidenfeld and Nicolson, 1981.

McClatchy, Leo A. "Host to the Japs." *American Legion Magazine* 35 (October 1943).

McKay, Susan. *The Courage Our Stories Tell: The Daily Lives and Maternal Child Health Care of Japanese American Women at Heart Mountain.* Casper, WY: Mountain States Lithographing, 2002.

McKibben, Carol Lynn. *Racial Beachhead: Diversity and Democracy in a Military Town, Seaside, California.* Stanford, California : Stanford University Press, 2012.

Democratizing. Urbana, IL: University of Illinois Press, 2006.

McWilliams, Carey. *Prejudice: Japanese-Americans: Symbol of Racial Intolerance.* New York, NY: Archon Books, 1971 (reprint of 1944 original).

Manvell, Roger and Fraenkel, Heinrich. *Goering: The Rise and Fall of the Notorious Nazi Leader.* London: Frontline Books, 2011, paperback edition of 1962 Simon and Schuster original.

Maolo, Joseph. *Cry Havoc: How the Arms Race Drove the World to War, 1931–1941.* New York, NY: Basic Books, 2010.

Marrus, Michael R. *The Holocaust in History.* New York, NY: Penguin Books, 1987.

Matsumoto, Tōru. *Beyond Prejudice.* New York, NY: Arno Press, 1978 [1946].

Matsumoto, Valerie. "Japanese American Women during World War II." *Frontiers* 8 (1984).

Mizuno, Takeya. "Government Suppression of the Japanese Language in World War II Assembly Camps." *Journalism and Mass Communication Quarterly,* Vol. 80: No. 4 (2003), 849–65.

"Journalism Under Military Guards and Searchlights: Newspaper Censorship at Japanese American Assembly Camps during World War II." *Journalism History,* Vol. 29: No. 3 (2003), 98–106.

"Self-Censorship by Coercion: The Federal Government and the California Japanese Language Newspapers from Pearl Harbor to Internment." *American Journalism* (Summer 2000).

Modell, John. *The Economics and Politics of Racial Accommodation: The Japanese of Los Angeles, 1900–1942.* Urbana, IL: University of Illinois Press, 1977.

Kikuchi Diary: Chronicle from an American Concentration Camp. Urbana, IL: University of Illinois Press, 1973.

Monkkonen, Eric. *Murder in New York City.* Berkeley, CA: University of California Press, 2001.

Moore, Deborah Dash. *At Home in America: Second Generation New York Jews.* New York, NY: Columbia University Press, 1981.

Mormino, Gary Ross. *Immigrants on the Hill: Italian-Americans in St. Louis, 1882–1982.* Urbana, IL: University of Illinois Press, 1986.

Mormino, Gary Ross and Pozzetta, George. "Ethnics at War: Italian Americans in California during World War II." Lotchin, ed., *The Way We Really Were.* Urbana, IL: University of Illinois Press, 2000.

Mullan, Michael. "Sport, Ethnicity, and the Reconstruction of the Self: Baseball in America's Internment Camps." *International Journal of the History of Sport*, Vol. 16: No. 1 (1999), 1–21.

Muller, Eric L. *American Inquisition: The Hunt for Japanese American Disloyalty in World War II*. Chapel Hill, NC: The University of North Carolina Press, 2007.

   Free to Die for Their Country: The Story of the Japanese American Draft Resisters in World War II. Chicago, IL: The University of Chicago Press, 2001.

Murata, Kiyoaki. *An Enemy among Friends*. Tokyo: Kodansha International, 1991.

Murray, Rebecca. *History of the Public School Kindergarten in North Carolina*. New York, NY: MSS Information Corporation, 1974.

Myer, Dillon. *Uprooted Americans: the Japanese Americans and the War Relocation Authority during World War II*. Tucson, AZ: University of Arizona Press, 1971.

Nagano, Paul M. "United States Concentration Camps." *American Baptist Quarterly*, Vol. 13: No. 1 (1994), 48–78.

   "Reverend Emery E. Andrews: Northwest's Man for Others." *American Baptist Quarterly*, Vol. 17: No. 3 (1998), 192–202.

Nash, Gerald D. *A. P. Giannini and the Bank of America*. Norman, OK: University of Oklahoma Press, 1992. Bloomington, IN: Indiana University Press, 2003.

Nelson, Douglas W. *Heart Mountain: the Story of an American Concentration Camp*. Madison: State Historical Society of Wisconsin, 1976.

Neufeld, Michael. *The Rocket and the Reich: Peenemunde and the Coming of the Ballistic Missile Era*. Cambridge, MA: Harvard University Press, 1995.

Nishimoto, Richard S. *Inside an American Concentration Camp: Japanese American Resistance at Poston, Arizona, edited by Lane Ryo Hirabayashi*. Amazon, 1995.

Noble, Antoinette Chambers. "Heart Mountain: Remembering the Camp." *Wyoming History Journal*, 68 (1996).

O'Brien, Robert. *College Nisei*. Palo Alto, CA: Pacific Books, 1949; 1978 Arno Press reprint.

Okamura, Raymond Y. "The American Concentration Camps: A Coverup through Euphemistic Terminology." *Journal of Ethnic Studies*, 10 (1982).

Okihiro, Gary Y. *'For the Sake of Our Japanese Brethren': Assimilation, Nationalism, and Protestantism among the Japanese of Los Angeles, 1895–1942*. Stanford, California: Stanford University Press, 1995.

   "Religion and Resistance in America's Concentration Camps." *Phylon*, 45 (1984).

   Storied Lives: Japanese American Students in World War II. Seattle, WA: University of Washington Press, 1999.

   "Tule Lake under Martial Law: A Study in Japanese Resistance." *Journal of Ethnic Studies*, Vol. 5: No. 3 (1977), 71–85.

Okubo, Miné. *Citizen 13660*. Seattle, WA: University of Washington Press, 1983.

Packenham, Thomas. *The Boer War*. New York, NY: Random House, 1979.

Reeves, Richard. *Infamy: The Shocking Story of the Japanese Internment in World War II.* New York, NY: Henry Holt and Company, 2015.

Regalado, Samuel. "Incarcerated Sport: Nisei Women's Softball and Athletics during Japanese American Internment." *Journal of Sport History*, Vol. 27: No. 3 (2000), 431–44.

"Sport and Community in California's Japanese American 'Yamato Colony,' 1930–1945." *Journal of Sport History*, Vol. 19: No. 2 (1992), 130–43.

Riess, Steven A. *City Games: The Evolution of American Urban Society and the Rise of Sports.* Urbana, IL: University of Illinois Press, 1991.

Riley, Karen L. "Schools behind Barbed Wire." *Journal of the Midwest History of Education Society*, Vol. 23 (1996), 31–5.

Schools behind Barbed Wire: The Untold Story of Wartime Internment and the Children of Arrested Enemy Aliens. Lanham, MD: Rowan and Littlefield Publishers, Inc., 2002.

Robertson, Marion Anderson. "Wanda Robertson: A Teacher for Topaz." *Utah Historical Quarterly*, 69 (2001).

Robinson, Gerald. *Elusive Truth: Four Photographers at Manzanar.* Nevada City, CA: Carl Mautz Publishing, 2002.

Robinson, Greg. *By Order of the President.* Cambridge, MA: Harvard University Press, 2001.

Tragedy of Democracy: Japanese Confinement in North America. New York, NY: Columbia University Press, 2009.

Roosevelt, Franklin D. "Shall We Trust Japan?" *Journal of the American Asiatic Association*, Vol. 23 (July 1923).

Rudwick, Elliott. *Race Riot at East St. Louis, July 2, 1917.* New York, NY: Atheneum, 1972.

Sanders, James W. *The Education of an Urban Minority: Catholics in Chicago, 1833–1965.* New York, NY: Oxford University Press, 1970.

Senkiewicz, S. J., *Vigilantes in Gold Rush San Francisco.* Stanford, CA: Stanford University Press, 1985.

Shaffer, Robert. "Cracks in the Consensus: Defending the Rights of Japanese Americans during World War II." *Radical History Review*, Vol. 72 (1998), 84–120.

Sies, Mary Corbin and Silver, Christopher, eds. *Planning the Twentieth-Century American City.* Baltimore, MD: Johns Hopkins University Press, 1996.

Silber, Kate. "Wood Blocks and Water Colors." *National Parks Magazine* (Summer 2013).

Sinclair, John A. "California on the Alert." *American Legion Magazine*, Vol. 32: No. 4 April 1942.

Smith, Harold F. "The Battle of Parkville: Resistance to Japanese American Students at Park College (Missouri)." *Journal of Presbyterian History*, Vol. 82: No. 1.

Smith, Jack. "The Great Los Angeles Air Raid," in Caughey, John and Laree, eds, *Los Angeles: Biography of a City.* Berkeley, CA: University of California Press, 1976; Paperback ed., 1977.

Smith, Page. *Democracy on Trial: Japanese American Evacuation and Relocation in World War II.* New York, NY: Simon and Schuster, 1995.

Snyder, Timothy. *Bloodlands: Europe between Hitler and Stalin*. New York, NY: Basic Books, 2012.

Spickard, Paul R. *Almost All Aliens, Immigration, Race, and Colonialism in American History*. New York, NY: Routledge, 2007.

Stack, John F. *International Conflict in an American City: Boston's Irish, Italians, and Jews, 1935–1944*. Westport, CT: Greenwood Press, 1979.

Stavrianos, L. S. *The Balkans Since 1453*. New York, NY: Holt, Rinehart and Winston, 1958.

Stephan, John J. *Hawaii under the Rising Sun: Japan's Plans for Conquest after Pearl Harbor*. Honolulu: University of Hawaii Press, 1984.

  "Review of Nikkei Amerikajin No Taiheiyo senso." *Journal of American History*, (December 1998).

Stimson, H. L. *Diaries*. UNC microform copy, Vol. 37, January 1, 1942, February 28th, 1942.

Sugrue, Thomas. *Sweet Land of Liberty: The Forgotten Struggle for Civil Rights in the North*. New York, NY: Random House Trade Paperbacks, 2009.

Sullivan, Neil J. *The Dodgers Move West*. New York, NY: Oxford University Press, 1987.

Suzuki, Lester. *Ministry in the Assembly and Relocation Centers of World War II*. Berkeley, CA: Yardbird Publishing Company, 1979.

Suzuki, Peter T. "Jinji (the Human Condition) in the Wartime Camp Poetry of the Japanese Americans." *Asian Profile (Hong Kong)*, Vol. 15: No. 5 (1987), 407–15.

Tajiri, Ron. "Relocation." *Topaz Times, Supplement*, May 12 and 14, 1943.

Tarr, Joel Arthur. *A Study in Boss Politics: William Lorimer of Chicago*. Urbana, IL: University of Illinois Press, 1971.

Taylor, Sandra C. "Japanese Americans and Keetley Farms: Utah's Relocation Colony." *Utah Historical Quarterly*, Vol. 54: No. 4 (1986).

  Jewel of the Desert: Japanese American Internment at Topaz. Berkeley, CA: University of California Press, 1993.

  "Leaving the Concentration Camps: Japanese American Resettlement in Utah and the Intermountain West." *Pacific Historical Review*, Vol. 60: No. 2 (1991).

Teaford, Jon. *The Unheralded Triumph: City Government, 1870–1900*. Baltimore, MD: Johns Hopkins University Press, 1984.

tenBroek, Jacobus, Barnhart, Edward N. et al. *Prejudice, War and the Constitution*. Berkeley, CA: University of California Press, 1968 edition.

Tone, John Lawrence. *War and Genocide in Cuba, 1895–1898*. Chapel Hill, NC: University of North Carolina Press, 2006.

Tong, Benson. "Race, Culture, and Citizenship among Japanese American Children and Adolescents during the Internment Era." *Journal of American Ethnic History*, Vol. 23: No. 3 (2004), 3–40.

Trentmann, Frank. *The Empire of Things: How We Became a World of Consumers. From the Fifteenth Century to the Twenty First*. New York, NY: Harper Collins Publisher, 2016.

Troller, Norbert. *Theresienstadt: Hitler's Gift to the Jews*. Chapel Hill, NC: University of North Carolina Press, 1991.

Trout, Charles H. *Boston, the Great Depression, and the New Deal*. New York, NY: Oxford University Press, 1977.

Tuttle, Wm. M., Jr. *Race Riot: Chicago in the Red Summer of 1919*. New York, NY: Atheneum, 1972.

Ueno, Harry, Hansen, Arthur, et al., "Dissident Harry Ueno Remembers Manzanar." *California History*, 64 (1985).

Van Hartesveldt, Fred R. *The Boer War*. Phoenix Mill, UK: Sutton Publishing Company, 2000.

Verge, Arthur C. *Paradise Transformed: Los Angeles during the Second World War*. Dubuque: Kendall/Hunt Publishing Company, 1993.

Voights, David. *American Baseball: From Gentlemen's Sport to the Commissioner System*. Norman: University of Oklahoma Press, 1966.

Walker, R. Todd. "Utah Schools and the Japanese American Student Relocation Program." *Utah Historical Quarterly*, Vol. 70: No. 1 (2002).

Warren, Earl. *Conversations with Earl Warren*. Berkeley, CA: Regional Oral History Project, 1971–72.

The Memoirs of Earl Warren. Garden City, NY: Doubleday & Company, Inc., 1977.

Waseda, Minako. "Extraordinary Circumstances: Music in Japanese American Concentration Camps." Densho Encyclopedia (September 2013), 171–209.

Weare, Walter. *Black Business in the New South: A Social History of the North Carolina Mutual Insurance Company*. Durham, NC: Duke University Press, 1993.

Weglyn, Michi Nishiura. *Years of Infamy: The Untold Story of America's Concentration Camps: An Updated Version*. Seattle, WA: University of Washington Press, 1996.

Weinberg, Gerhard. *A World at Arms: A Global History of World War II*. Cambridge: Cambridge University Press, 1994.

Hitler's Foreign Policy: The Road to War, 1933–1939. New York, NY: Enigma Books, 2005.

Wollenberg, Charles. "'Dear Earl.' The Fair Play Committee, Earl Warren, and Japanese Internment." *California History*, Vol. 89: No. 4 (2012), 24–55.

"Schools behind Barbed Wire." *California Historical Quarterly*, Vol. 55: No. 3 (1976), 210–17.

Wollons, Roberta, ed. *Kindergartens and Cultures: The Global Diffusion of an Idea*. New Haven, CT: Yale University Press, 2000.

Wong, K. Scott. "War Comes to Chinatown: Social Transformation." Lotchin, ed., *The Way We Really Were, The Golden State in the Second Great War*. Champaign, IL: University of Illinois Press, 2000. 164–86.

Yamada, David T. and Oral History Committee, MP/JACL, *The Japanese of the Monterey Peninsula: Their History and Legacy, 1895–1995*. Monterey, CA: Monterey Japanese American Citizens League, 1995.

Yang, Daquing. "'Convergence or Divergence': Recent Historical Writings on the Rape of Nanking." *American Historical Review*, Vol. 104: No. 3 (June 1999).

Yoo, David. "Enlightened Identities: Buddhism and Japanese Americans of California, 1924–1941." *Western Historical Quarterly*, Vol. 27: No. 3 (1996), 280–301.

Yoshiko, Uchida. "Topaz, City of Dust." *Utah Historical Quarterly*, Vol. 48: No. 3 (1980).

Zhao, Xiaojian. *Remaking Chinese America: Immigration, Family and Community, 1940–1965*. New Brunswick, NJ: Rutgers University Press, 2002.

ARCHIVES

US National Archives, Record Group 210.
Special Collections, University of Arkansas Colorado State Archives.
WRA, "Education Program in War Relocation Centers, February 1, 1945."
John F. Embree, "Dealing With Japanese-Americans."
McConnell, Reverend John P. "Understanding of Japanese-American Brothers." December 1943, 1–6.

PRIVATE REPORTS

Catholic Interracial Council, *Report of December 16, 1945*, 434–440.
McWilliams, Carey. *Japanese Evacuation: Interim Report*, American Council Paper, No. 4. New York, NY: American Council and the Institute of Pacific Relations 1942.

PERIODICALS (ARTICLES)

American Legion Magazine, 1940–1945.
Christian Century, 1940–1945.

GOVERNMENT REPORTS AND DOCUMENTS

United States Army, *Monograph on [the] History of [the] Military Clearance Program* (Screening of Alien Japanese and Japanese American Citizens for Military Service).

US Congress, *Congressioinal Record*.

US Congress (77th), 2nd Sess., House, Select Committee Investigating National Defense Migration, Pursuant to H. Res. 113, *Hearings, Seattle & Portland, pt. 30*, Washington: United States Government Printing Office (GPO), 1942. (*Tolan Hearings*).

US Congress (77th), 1st Sess. House, Special Committee on Un-American Activities of the House of Representatives, *Investigation of Un-American*

Propaganda Activities in the United States: Hearings on H. Res. 282 Washington: US GPO, 1942 (Dies Committee).

US Congress (77th), 1st, House, Special Committee on Un-American Activities, 2d Session (75th), and H. Res 26 (76th Cong.), *Special Report on Subversive Activities Aimed at Destroying Our Representative Form of Government*, Report 2277, Pursuant to H. Res. 282 (Washington, DC: US GPO, 1942).

US Congress (78th), 1st Sess., House, *Hearings before a Subcommittee of the Committee on Naval Affairs, Persuant to H. Res. 30*: Part 3, San Francisco, Calif., Area, April 12, 13, 14, 15, 16 and 17, 1943. Washington: GPO.

US Congress (78th), 1st sess., House: Committee on Un-American Activities, *Investigation of Un-American Propaganda Activities in the United States: Hearings before a Special Committee on Un-American Activities* on H. Res. 282, June and July, 1943, Washington: GPO, 1943.

US Congress (78th) 1st Sess., Senate, Subcommittee of the Committee on Military Affairs, *Hearings on S. Res. 444, Part 4, Nov. 24, 1943* (Washington, DC: GPO, 1944).

US Congress (79th), 1st Sess. House, *Hearings before the Subcommittee of the Committee on Immigration and Naturalization, Pursuant to H. Res. 52*, Part 5, Aug. 31, 1945. Washington: GPO.

US Congress, Commission on Wartime Relocation and Internment of Civilians. *Personal Justice Denied. Report of the Commission on Wartime Relocation and Internment of Civilians.* Washington, DC: United States Government Printing Office, 1982, Report 39.

US Congress, 98th 2nd Sess. House, Subcommittee on Administration, Law, and Governmental Relations, Committee of the Judiciary, Hearings on *Japanese American and Aleutian Relocation*. Washington: GPO, 1984.

US National Archives, Record Group 210.

United States Army, *Monograph on [the] History of [the] Military Clearance Program* (Screening of Alien Japanese and Japanese American Citizens for Military Service).

US Commission on Wartime Relocation and Internment of Civilians. *Personal Justice Denied: Report of the Commission on Wartime Relocation and Internment of Civilians.* Washington: US Government Printing Office, 1982. *Report, 39*.

US Congress. *Congressioinal Record, 1940–1945.*

Roberts, Justice Owen J. *The Roberts Report. The Roberts Report* was published in full in both the *San Francisco Chronicle* and the *Los Angeles Times*. See the *Los Angeles Times*, January 25, 1942, I, 1.

US Congress, House, 77th Sess. Select Committee Investigating National Defense Migration, "National Defense Migration: Hearings before the Select Committee Investigating National Defense Migration, House of Representatives Pursuant to H. Res. 113, a Resolution to Inquire further into the Interstate Migration of Citizens, Emphasizing the Present and Potential Consequences of the migration caused by National Defense Migration," 10697–11945. [*Tolan Hearings*] Washington, DC: United States Government Printing Office, 1942.

US Congress, 78th: 1st sess. *Report and Minority Views of the Special Committee on Un-American Activities in Japanese War Relocation Centers.* Washington: US GPO, Sept. 30, 1942, 1–16.

Lieutenant General DeWitt, John. L. Commanding General. Headquarters Western Defense Command and Fourth Army. *Final Report: Japanese Evacuation from the West Coast, 1942.* Washington, DC: United States Printing Office, GPO, 1943.

Eisenhower, Milton S. "Memorandum for Members of Congress," April 20, 1942. *Statistical Abstract of the United States* GPO, 1943.

US Congress, 78th: 1st sess., House, Subcommittee on Naval Affairs. *"Hearings before a Subcommittee of the Committee on Naval Affairs, Persuant to H. Res. 30"* Part 3, San Francisco, Calif. Area, April 12, 13, 14, 15, 16 and 17, 1943.

US Congress, 77th, House, "Investigation of Un-American Propaganda Activities in the United States," *Hearings on H. Res. 282 Before a Special Committee on Un-American Activities,* Washington, DC: United States Government Printing Office, 1942.

US Congress, 79th, 1st sess., House, *Hearings before the Subcommittee of the Committee on Immigration and Naturalization,* Pursuant to H. Res. 52, Part 5, Aug. 31, 1945, [*Dickstein Committee.*] November–December 1943.

US Congress, 78th, 1st sess. Senate, Subcommittee of the Committee on Military Affairs, *Hearings on S. 444, Part 4, Nov. 24, 1943* (Washington, DC: United States GPO. 1944).

US Congress, 98th Congress: 2nd session, Subcommittee on Administration, Law, and Governmental Relations, Committee of the Judiciary, *House, Japanese American and Aleutian Relocation.* Washington, DC: Government Printing Office, 1984.

US Congress, Senate, 78th 1st session, Subcommittee of the Committee on Military Affairs, United States Senate, *Hearings on S. 444, Part 4, Nov. 24, 1943.* Washington, DC: United States Government Printing Office, 1944, 235–6.

US Congress, 77th, 1st, House, 2d Sess., Special Committee on Un-American Activities (75th Cong.) and H. Res 26 (76th Cong.), *Special Report on Subversive Activities Aimed at Destroying Our Representative Form of Government,* Report 2277, Pursuant to H. Res. 282 Washington, DC: US GPO, 1942).

US Congress, 78th: 1st, House, Special Committee on Un-American Activities. *Reports of the Majority and Minority.* Washington, DC: US GPO, June–August, 1943, 19–28.

US Congress, 78th: 1st, House, Special Committee on un American Activities on [sic] Japanese War Relocation Centers, *Report Number 717 and Minority Views.* Washington, DC: US GPO, September 30, 1943.

US Congress, 78th: 2nd sess., House, Subcommittee of the Special Committee on Un-America Activities, Hearings on H. Res. 282 To Investigate the Extent, Character and Objects of Un-American Propaganda Activities in the United States ..., *Committee Report on the Tule Lake Riot of Nov. 1, 1943.* Washington, DC: US GPO No date of publication.

US Congress, 78th: 2nd sess., Subcommittee of the Special committee on Un-American Activities [Costello Committee] *Committee Report on Tule Lake*

Riot of November 1, 1943. Washington, DC: US GPO, 1944. WRA [Wade Head & Harold Townsend]. "Conversation between W. Wade Head, Project Director, and H. H. Townsend, Supply and Transportation Officer," On December 1, 1942.

[D. S. Myer]. "A Statement of Guiding Principles of the War Relocation Authority."

[Harold Townsend]. "Statement of Testimony of Harold H. Townsend. Before the House of Representatives Sub-Committee of the Special Committee on Un-American Activities, Los Angeles, California, May 26, 1943."

[Herman P. Eberhalter]. "Remarks of Representative Herman P. Eberhalter to the Costello Sub-Committee, August 26, 1943."

[Dillon Myer] "Supplementary Statement by Mr. D. Myer before the Senate Sub-Committee of the Military Affairs Committee, January 20, 1943."

"Administrative Notice No. 54: Summary of Leave Clearance Procedures."

Community Analysis Section. "Boys Day" Community Analysis Notes No. 10, [position paper discussing the Japanese festival of Boys Day] March 13, 1945.

"A Comprehensive Statement in Response to Senate Resolution No. 166."

"Guide Lines on Community Activities." Washington, US GPO, 1943.

Analysis Section. "Project Analysis Series No. 19, Part I "Community government in the relocation centers, One Year of Community Government at the Gila River Relocation Center."

First Quarterly Report, March 18 to June 30, 1942; Semi-Annual Report, January 1, to June 30, 1943; Semi-Annual Report, January 1 to June 30, 1944, Semi-Annual Report, January 1 to June 30, 1944; Semi-Annual Report, January 1 to June 30, 1945; Semi-Annual Report, January 1 to June 31, 1945; Semi-Annual Report, July 31–December 31, 1945. Washington, DC: US GPO.

"Administrative Notice No. 54: Summary of Leave Clearance Procedures."

"Summary Notes on [the] Segregation Conference of W.R.A. Officials," Denver, Colorado, July 26–27, 1943.

"Comprehensive Statement in Response to Senate Resolution 166."

Community Analysis Section, "Project Analysis Series No. 29, November 6, 1944," 13–14.

"Semi-Annual Report, July 31–December 31, 1945," Ark. Western Defense Command and the War Relocation Authority, "Employment of Japanese Evacuees in Agriculture Outside of Assembly Centers: Summary of Assurances Required by the Western Defense Command and the War Relocation Authority," no specific date, RG 210, Box 2, NA.

Myths and Facts about Japanese Americans: Answering Common Misconceptions Regarding Americans of Japanese Ancestry. Washington, DC: War Relocation Authority, April 1945.

Wartime Exile: The Exclusion of the Japanese Americans from the West Coast. Washington, DC: US GPO.

"Comments by the War Relocation Authority on Remarks of Representative John. M. Costello Made in the Library of Congress, Legislative Reference Service." "Summaries of Committee Hearings Costello Subcommittee of the Special committee to Investigate Un-American Activities [Dies committee] Hearings of July 1 and July 2, 1943."

House, June 28, 1943, reprinted in the *Congressional Record*, Vol. 89: No. 121.

[Dillon Myer]. "Evidences of Americanism among Japanese Americans." WRA, July 7, 1943.

"Comments by the War Relocation Authority on Statements reported in the Press," Allegedly Made by Witnesses before the Committee on Un-American Activities during Hearings in Los Angeles between June 8 and June 17, [1943].

"Comments by the War Relocation Authority on Statements Reported in the Press Allegedly Made by Witnesses before the Subcommittee [Costello Committee] of the House Special Committee on Un-American Activities Committee [Dies Committee] between June and July 1943."

"Comments by the WRA on Newspaper Statements Attributed to Representatives of the House Committee on Un-American Activities, July 19, 1943."

Baker, John C. [Chief, Office of Reports.] *Newspaper Attacks on Japanese Americans by Marjorie Young*. Washington, US GPO, November 13, 1942.

New Neighbors among Us. Washington, DC: US GPO, April 1944.

Introducing English to Adults, Washington, DC: US GPO.

[Myer, Dillon,] Director, WRA. *The Relocation Program: A Guidebook for the Residents of Relocation Centers*. Washington, DC: US GPO, May 1, 1942.

[Myer, Dillon]. *The Relocation Program: A Guidebook for the Residents of Relocation Centers*." Washington, DC: US GPO, May, 1943 [an update of previous guidebook]. 1943.

[Embree, John F.] "Dealing with Japanese-Americans."

Community Analysis Section, "Japanese Groups and Associations in the United States," *Community Analysis Report No. 3*, March 1943.

[Adams, Lucy]. "Looking Ahead." Library of Congress, Legislative reference Service, Summary of committee Hearings, Costello Subcommittee of the Special. Subcommittee to Investigate Un-American Activities. Washington, DC: US GPO, July 8, 1943.

Statement by the WRA in Response to testimony of Toki Slocum to HUAC, July 1, 1943.

Legislative Reference Service. "Newspaper Comments to HUAC." *Los Angeles Examiner*, June 8 to June 17, 1943. Subcommittee to Investigate Un-American Activities, Hearings, July 8, 1943."

Legislative Reference Service, Summaries of Committee Hearings of Costello Sub-Committee, July 2–3, Western Defense Command [DeWitt, General John and Rowe, James, Department of Justice]. "Transcript of a conference, January 4, 1942."

United States Army. *Monograph on [the] History of [the] Military Clearance Program* [Screening of Alien Japanese and Japanese American Citizens for Military Service].

PHOTOGRAPHIC ARCHIVES

Library of Congress

US NATIONAL ARCHIVES

Manzanar Relocation Center
Amache Relocation Center
Tule Lake Relocation Center
Minidoka Relocation Center
Topaz Relocation Center
Poston Relocation Center
Heart Mountain Relocation Center
Rohwer Relocation Center
Gila River Relocation Center

JAPANESE AND JAPANESE AMERICAN NEWSPAPERS

Daily Tulean Dispatch
Gila News-Courier
Granada Pioneer
Heart Mountain Sentinel
Manzanar Free Press
Minidoka Irrigator
Pacific Citizen
Rafu Shimpo
Rocky Shimpo
Rohwer Outpost
New World Sun
Nichi Bei,
Tokyo Times and Advertiser
Topaz Times

ENGLISH LANGUAGE NEWSPAPERS

Los Angeles Daily News
Los Angeles Examiner
Los Angeles Times
Sacramento Bee
San Diego Union
San Francisco Chronicle
San Francisco Examiner

ORAL HISTORY

Hansen, Arthur A. and Jesch, Nora, eds. *The Japanese American World War II Evacuation Project*, 4 Vols. Munich: K. G. Saur: Munich, New Providence, and London, Paris, 1993–1995.
Ibid., 2 Vols. London: Meckler, 1993.

Index